COUNSELING AND DEVELOPMENT SERIES

ALLEN IVEY, Editor

THE AFRICAN UNCONSCIOUS
Roots of Ancient Mysticism and Modern Psychology

Edward Bruce Bynum

GILI'S BOOK
A Journey into Bereavement for Parents and Counselors

Henya Kagan (Klein)

CONSTRUCTIVIST THINKING IN
COUNSELING PRACTICE, RESEARCH, AND TRAINING

Thomas L. Sexton & Barbara L. Griffin, Editors

RESEARCH AS PRAXIS
*Lessons from Programmatic
Research in Therapeutic Psychology*

Lisa Tsoi Hoshmand & Jack Martin, Editors

THE CONSTRUCTION
AND UNDERSTANDING OF
PSYCHOTHERAPEUTIC CHANGE
Conversations, Memories, and Theories

Jack Martin

The African Unconscious

Roots of Ancient Mysticism and Modern Psychology

EDWARD BRUCE BYNUM

Foreword by
LINDA JAMES MYERS

TEACHERS COLLEGE PRESS

Teachers College, Columbia University
New York and London

Published by Teachers College Press, 1234 Amsterdam Avenue, New York, NY 10027

Library of Congress Cataloging-in-Publication Data

Bynum, Edward Bruce, 1948–
    The African unconscious : roots of ancient mysticism and modern
psychology / Edward Bruce Bynum ; foreword by Linda James Myers,
        p.   cm. — (Counseling and development series)
    Includes bibliographical references and index.
    ISBN 0-8077-3775-5 (hardcover : alk. paper), — ISBN 0-8077-3774-7
(pbk. : alk. paper)
        1. Subconsciousness.   2. Africa—Civilization—History.
    3. Civilization, Ancient—History.   4. Human beings—Origin.
    I. Title.   II. Series.
    BF315.B95   1999
    155.7—dc21   98-51477

ISBN 0-8077-3774-7 (paper)
ISBN 0-8077-3775-5 (cloth)

Printed on acid-free paper

Manufactured in the United States of America
06 05 04 03 02 01 00 99   8 7 6 5 4 3 2

Dedication

To my Father, my fathers and the memory of my father,
To my sons, their sons and their daughters,
To the spiritual destiny of the Human Race.

CONTENTS

FIGURES

NOTE FROM
THE SERIES EDITOR

Scholars agree that humanity originated in Africa. However, Western society tends to believe that civilization "really" began with the Greeks, with small footnotes granted to Egypt and other Mediterranean cultures. The idea of civilization beginning in Africa is a challenging one for the Western mind indoctrinated by centuries of Eurocentric thought and education.

Bruce Bynum's book will be controversial. I am well aware that many disagree with the validity of the Afrocentric paradigm. This book extends the framework to a new level. Our "shared sea of consciousness" is not an easy construct to accept in an empirically driven logical positivist world. Intergenerational transmission of thoughts and ideas and the collective unconscious are not central to pragmatic ideology. Bynum provides a challenging and formidable narrative.

What do I gain from this book as a psychologist and theoretician? First, I find the idea that we are One in our origins important and comforting. As a person-environment psychologist, committed to the place of history in our lives, Afrocentric concepts have always made intellectual sense to me. Nonetheless, some will fear Bynum's constructions and believe that the connectedness of Afrocentric thought somehow denigrates our differences and uniqueness. In no way does this book deny the importance of the Greeks. In no way does this book deny the vitality of Western civilization.

Yet, the distinctiveness of Bynum's narrative is something that I hope we will all consider thoughtfully. The Oldawan—Ancient Soul—could be said to be in us all. Chapter 2 provides us with an important summary of two key (and challenging) constructs, both important to the generation of a more holistic psychology.

First, the nonlocality of the unconscious. Bynum reminds us that we do not "own" our unconscious experience, but rather we have the whole of history within us. Jacques Lacan, the French psychoanalyst, drawing from

Hegel, makes a parallel point when he speaks of the "discourse of the Other." Lacan suggests that we do not speak, but are spoken. Consciousness and the ego are at best feeble. Bynum argues that Afrocentric unconscious remains vitally influential in human experience. Acknowledging this connection will not be easy.

Second, personalism. Bynum presents a holistic version of reality in which persons, objects, situations, and forces become One. This holistic view is very different from the Cartesian frame. However, in modern terms, we note that any change in a part of the system changes the total system. We are constantly transforming and being transformed. There is no fixed and final point. Truth constantly evolves. For those who seek finality and "end points," this moving view of truth is most difficult. It does not deny temporary truces that are "true," but as in Hegel's philosophy we are constantly moving to new syntheses.

This is not an easy book. I do not agree with everything that Bruce Bynum writes, but I do believe that his major thesis of an African unconscious existing within us is something that we all need to consider carefully. If we were to accept Bynum's thesis, I rather think we shall have made a large step toward a more inclusive and interdependent world. Linda James Myers' foreword places Bynum's argument within a larger context of Afrocentric thought. Whether or not we agree with all the specifics, the Afrocentric idea is here to stay.

Allen E. Ivey, Ed.D., A.B.P.P.
Distinguished University Professor (Emeritus)
University of Massachusetts, Amherst

FOREWORD

When Bruce honored me with his request to write the foreword to his magnum opus, my immediate question was how do I help place this work for the reader in a meaningful context in light of its extraordinarily vast scope and depth, and given that the holistic and integrative mindset of its emergence is not common. Having spent most of my career as a psychology professor at a large university in the heart of America, I understand all too well the volatile and complex nature of the reactions to studies seeking to push the boundaries of consciousness beyond the hegemonous limitations of a mindset fragmented and bound to assumptions and principles no longer supported by the prevailing wisdom.

Just last month I read a newspaper article reporting the resistance to anomalies research being done at an Ivy League university; some critics suggested that such research questions should not be raised, nor such investigations undertaken. When you compound the type of resistance in that closed mindset with the probable controversy that issues of race and African culture would add to the mix, you then have a challenge. Not to worry, I determined. We have come to the stage in the evolution of humanity when a transformation of consciousness is needed—a substantive change in our understanding of the nature of reality and our relationship to it. The prevailing quality of mind in the West, and now throughout the world, has been masterful at creating technological wonders, but at the expense of overwhelming social and ecological crises. The type of thinking that has created the dilemma is extremely limited in its capacity to solve it. In the face of this mindset—one fostering the intellectual hegemony of white supremacy (among other things) and fear regarding that which is not understood—the challenge put forth by *The African Unconscious: Roots of Ancient Mysticism and Modern Psychology*, is a monumental and loving one, assuredly invaluable to those who would seek to meet it.

Our scientific knowledge across cultures now requires the explicit inclusion of consciousness as an active agent in the establishment of physical reality. Even within Western models of science, a generously expanded model of reality—one allowing consciousness a proactive role in the establishment of its experience of the physical world—has been found necessary. Such a comprehensive model of reality, a model whose origins can be traced to the beginnings of human culture and civilization in the tradition of African people, is put forward in *The African Unconscious*. Incorporating modern evidence of the active role of consciousness in the establishment of reality, this model of reality holds sweeping implications for our view of ourselves, our relationship to others, the cosmos in which we exist, and also to that which exists as a part of consciousness, but of which we are unaware: the unconscious.

Some may have difficulty accepting the African cultural and historical roots of human consciousness. This resistance can be understood to reflect internalization of negative images, stereotypes, misinterpretations and misrepresentations of a very different way of being in the world. We have been reluctant to acknowledge a worldview different than that with which we are familiar, particularly in the Western academy; even some of us acknowledging African descent are fearful of suggesting that such a difference in worldview exists, particularly if its cultural or racial origins are identified.

In the new paradigm, our African rootedness has the cultural and historical capacity to unite all humanity in "our common connection to the earth, the non-local intelligences, and the stars," so that we are truly one people, interconnected. The potential of all being in everything is acknowledged, preventing any human attribute from being the exclusive property of any grouping by human diversity marker, although trends and predispositions are also acknowledged. Whether born and raised on the continent, or elsewhere, in contemporary times or ancient, the contingencies around the awareness of a way of being in the world in which we are one with the source of life itself are multi-fold.

Having been transplanted and socialized in the West, I have had the opportunity to scrutinize and explore first-hand the realities of both worldviews. One major strength of *The African Unconscious: Roots of Ancient Mysticism and Modern Psychology* is that it provides entry to a similar opportunity for everyone, if they choose to take advantage of it. Bynum's thorough treatment of the subject allows us to bring so many aspects of our humanity to conscious awareness, to explore and interrogate any sense of alienation from our African past; his book provides the rationale for embracing the whole. Bynum makes a major contribution to the investigation and understanding of the heritage from which humanity emerges.

People often fear that which they do not understand; they may also in their ignorance fail to respect the misunderstood. In *The African Uncon-*

scious, Bynum goes a long way toward weaving together in one volume strands of the human experience that have heretofore remained unconnected. Starting with the basic essentials of life itself, carbon and light, Bynum shows the potential interrelatedness and interdependence of life forces within a model of reality that embraces the transformed consciousness of modern psychology and ancient mysticism. From its African beginnings, we can see variations of this model of reality, its essential tenets intact, as it has proliferated among all human cultural groups.

Despite its essential universality, this worldview, which acknowledges the primary role of consciousness in human experience, is only now beginning to gain preeminence in modern times, having continued over the ages to meet with resistance from those who would seek to legislate undue power and control over others. Aspects of conceptual incarceration and intellectual imperialism have created barriers so that the transfer of knowledge across various human diversity markers (i.e., races, cultures, disciplines, educational settings, and so on) has been limited. As a consequence there has not been the kind of collaboration across groups that we will need in the future to maximize our possibilities as a humanity. We have here the opportunity to push toward new levels of moral and spiritual development.

The African Unconscious speaks to a cultural tradition in which wisdom has unified, contained, and transcended the aspects of human experience that we think of as polar oppositions, for example positive and negative. It is a tradition of deep thought characteristic of those who, from the most ancient of days to the present day, have shared a consciousness informed by a logic that productively unites the seeming oppositions of the subjective and the objective, the scientific and the spiritual, the analytical and the aesthetic, the intellectual and the intuitive.

The wisdom tradition of which I speak, and see reflected in Bynum's work, focuses on the height of a cohesive consciousness functioning across humanity and cultures. It could be described as transpersonal. For many without experiential knowledge or education, this tradition does not exist as a part of their conscious awareness, but rather becomes for them a part of that of which they are unconscious, possibly taking on the stature of impossibility, myth or mystery. The model leaves room for multiple realities—conceding that whatever you are believing *is* true, *is* your reality while you are believing it—but the favored reality is that which sustains the greatest harmony, balance, compassion, propriety, reciprocity, order, and justice the longest.

It would be easy to argue that we live in a world in crisis. There are social crises: family structures are deteriorating; steady diets of illicit sexual behavior and violence continuously bombard our senses and sensibilities in popular culture; children are arming themselves, killing parents and schoolmates. There are ecological crises: the air and water are polluted; there are holes in the protective ozone layer; natural resources are being depleted. There are political-economic crises: blatant graft and corruption pervade our political structures to the extent that people have lost faith in the system; while a small economic elite grows wealthier, the masses are exposed to increased poverty; instability created by ethnic divisions perpetuate the threat of war. There are moral crises: moral leadership is lacking; absence of an agreed-upon ethical standard lends itself to a might-makes-right immoral order; our ability to accomplish things technologically has outstripped our ability to reason effectively the costs and benefits of our endeavors. In these days when chaos and confusion seem to reign supreme in the inner lives and outer world of so many, voices that would help us make sense of it all are sorely needed.

The African Unconscious: Roots of Ancient Mysticism and Modern Psychology will be a significant work to bring us into the 21st century, with the holistic insight and depth of understanding needed to uplift our humanity and improve the human condition. With *The African Unconscious* we have the opportunity to delve into a clearer spiritual/material reality that takes us out of the realm of the disconnected non-human and places us back into the fullness of what it is to be human, embracing the entire human experience culturally, historically, psychologically, and socially. Taking us back to the beginnings of humankind, the interdisciplinary treatment of humanity presented here lays the groundwork for the wisdom of the unconscious to be united with the wisdom of consciousness. As always, when such a sweeping change or shift in the prevailing paradigm occurs, there may be resistance to the knowledge, even when the new knowledge provides much-needed solutions to problems. For those who have been seeking a cohesive, integrated means to explore consciousness, *The African Unconscious* is an invaluable resource.

The way is open for a new height of consciousness, unifying that which is as ancient as humankind itself with that which is now being made conscious and confirmed in modern times. *The African Unconscious* leaves us with hope for greater light and love for all of humanity, as we grow in knowledge, wisdom, and understanding. It has been said that perfect love casteth out all fear, and in the wisdom tradition of African deep thought, many will find a stronger, non-contradictory, more sound basis for faith in our humanity, which transcends us.

Linda James Myers
Department of African American and African Studies
Ohio State University

ACKNOWLEDGMENTS

The author wishes to make special mention of his debt to the following people for their work, support, and inspiration in the creation of this book:

My editors at Teachers College Press who believed in this book from the first, for their meticulous attention to detail and for keeping me on track;

Sandra Martin of Paraview, for her steady patience, humor, and support;

Professor Allen Ivey, Ph.D., scholar, gifted teacher, and explorer throughout all his work, who brought me to the attention of the publisher;

Professors Rowland Abiodun, Olasupo Olasoebikan, and Wande Abimbola, who helped me both in intimate and intellectual ways, here and in Africa, to see the world of Ifa;

Professor Linda James Myers, Ph.D., for her scholarship and vision of an Optimal world for the human spirit; Runoko Rashidi, who looked deeply where few others would; and Richard D. King, M.D., who opened the door for me with his scholarship and insight, that to this day still holds me in awe and wonder;

Harry Rockland-Miller, Ph.D., a clinician and administrator who supported and respected me in this work when others turned away; Brother Bill Jones and Sister Kefa Nephthys of First World Alliance, who gave me a warm audience and house to speak in;

My oldest friends and fellow writers, William Boylin, Ph.D., and Ernest Stableford, M.F.A., who keep me afloat and steady in this work; Natercia Teixeira LICSW and Kent Poey, Ph.D., who keep my counsel, and shepherd and sustain me in my day-to-day work;

and my wife, Alyse Carol Bynum, who, after more than two decades and two children with me, remains still the most beautiful.

INTRODUCTION

"Le monde demain appartiendra à ceux qui lui ont apporté le plus grand espoir." [*The world tomorrow will belong to those who bring it the greatest hope.*]

—Found on the bulletin board of Notre Dame cathedral by Teilhard de Chardin

There is a new wind flowing across the landscape of Africa and across the inner landscape of African diasporic peoples. It is a wind that sweeps before it the idols of a civilization shaken to its roots by a technology that pollutes the seas while extending some lives; is adrift amidst the appalling moral contradictions of extravagant wealth and extreme poverty; and watches helplessly over the decay of cities, the rising grip of multinational corporations, and the final painful death spasm of outmoded political and economic paradigms. Communism as a force in the world is dead. Its cousin, the welfare state, is a sick child. In the United States, the greatest market of this empire, the vast majority of people feel its citadel is in moral and spiritual decline, its vision of itself sinking in sensationalism and ashes.

You need not be a devotee of Nostradamus, or the myths and prophecies of ancient peoples, to know that our current world order is in a severe crisis and that monumental changes are afoot that will alter our sense of self, origin, and identity. Whether this comes peacefully or in some prophesied war or series of global economic depressions, such cataclysms tend to stimulate a search for our deeper origins in order to have a fuller union. That deeper union—body, genes, and psychic profusion—is the Africoid element of everybody. With a new view of mind, this has scientific and spiritual implications. The eye of civilization is beginning to turn, and it will embrace what it has most feared in recent centuries, its African genesis.

A new wind is emerging in human history, and the winds of this sirocco will sweep before it the ashes of the old empire and usher in a new age of beauty and spiritual genius. Europe, Asia, and the Americas are inextricably connected with the destiny of Africa. For Africa is where our species first arose and contemplated the stars. This book is but a wave on the shore of this ocean, a small study in the abyss of what we can know.

An intellectual imperialism has haunted African studies and indeed the modern study of human knowledge itself. We have bisected, carved, disemboweled the human consciousness into departments and specialties, abstracted the spirit from the body, and by a reductionist science pronounced it dead. And like Osiris, it has risen again. We have no problem with method, no argument with analysis, no adolescent rebellion against discipline and replication. But we do argue that feeling is first in human experience, that spirit is primary, that matter, energy, and the intellect itself are epiphenomena of consciousness and Being in a creative evolution of intelligence and bliss.

In this book, our methodology will embrace a comparative study of psychology and mysticism, using science and ethnology to focus our lens. The analytical approach will unfold a transpersonal emphasis. This in turn will lead to a synthesis of forces that incorporate historical, anthropological, developmental, and evolutionary neurobiological trends in the unfoldment of our subject. The "facts" of science are often in transition, and what is ultimate today becomes a limiting case tomorrow. So we will borrow from science to flesh out a vision. The world is getting wider and more incorporative, not smaller. Reductionism, in many of its forms like logical positivism, is a treasured relic of 20th-century thought. The "classical" scientific ideal of an exact one-to-one correspondence between physical reality and physical theory has been replaced by closer and greater probabilities in measurement, especially in quantum mechanics. Consciousness, our human consciousness, at the very least is *causal* and *embedded* in the world. A new vision is naturally arising from the fall of the classical ideal. What this new ideal will be is as yet unknown. We turn our gaze here with great expectation to the third millennium and what may unfold beyond it.

Any worthwhile theory in science must be both a tool and a goal in itself. As a tool, it must be able to orient and at times direct empirical investigation, while simultaneously organizing and ordering the vast array of empirical knowledge in order to suggest certain predictions and also to understand natural phenomena. Its body contains not only observations, but constructs and hypotheses that can be tested under certain conditions. This makes it a functional theory where the theory and its data are developed interdependently, each feeding off the other, each pulling the other along with it. Our form of explanation here in this comparative method will be a constructive one in which phenomena will be described in terms of more abstract and higher-order constructs of enfoldment. Our goal is to demonstrate, not by manipulation but by a self-consistent and coherent vision, that the diverse "facts" of the situation will fit together from that perspective and observation. Darwin did not invent the facts of evolution; he observed them. Archeology does not create bone and skull fragments; it reconstructs them in history and geology. Astronomy and cosmology do not manipulate the stars. As in all theory, however, there cannot be an ultimate stand in the empirical world, only increasing empirical probability and neatness of aesthetic fit. In this sense, we must always embrace informed intuition and again realize that today's liberating insight is tomorrow's limiting case.

For the present time, we accept and *extend* the tenets of the so-called cognitive revolution in psychology and science that overthrew the mechanistic-behavioral and physicalistic-reductionist explanatory modes. The new vision suggests that emergent mental forces are actually causal and supervenient over lower-order brain and physical states. We *extend* it here to suggest that higher-order enfolded consciousness is prior to, all-pervasive within, and causal over even emergent mental states and, indeed, reaches into the generative order of creativity and consciousness itself. This higher-order enfoldment embraces the very root stock of our species and its primordial mental states with powerful implications for phenomena that emerge in the context of certain psychospiritual disciplines. Evolution is not merely random serendipity reinforced by survival dynamics, but seems to respond to all these emergent forces, thereby causing selective choices in this process of evolutionary unfoldment. It all suggests intelligence and an even deeper origin to our sinewy drama.

In this volume we will suggest that our species evolved from the same root and the same place, and that this African origin has a relevance to human psychology largely ignored—and not only in the West. In support of this we will cite many new and sometimes overlooked sources in our trek across this landscape. Some of these themes will bear repeating throughout the text. There are historical, genetic, and embryological reasons for our assertions, and it will carry us to places we have not yet been. The collective unconscious is immediate and African in its psychobiological roots and origins. For human identity in much of the so-called civilized world, the genetic and psychic aspects of this African root consciousness are the "threatened return of the repressed." And yet these roots may enfold the destiny of the human race. We must unfold its secrets. We must embrace it in order for the collective unconscious to turn back upon itself and in the process expand and reach the Omega point. Wherever our species travels in the future, beyond the local stars and beneath the seas, we will take this inheritance within us. The world process is an energetic phenomenon suffused with personhood, consciousness, and levels of coupling strength. Kundalini, an authentic evolutionary phenomenon, is a biogenetic and consciousness-transforming force that animates the spiritual trajectory of our species and has been with us, consciously, for nearly 6,000 years. The dreaming species must awaken.

In this text, we put ourselves on the line in many places, recognizing that many, Black, White, and other, will find fault or even be offended by the very idea that there is a distinct worldview or zeitgeist embedded in an African-rooted sensibility. After all, they will reasonably argue, there are many kinds of people of African lineage and a diversity of experiences within that. Others will be upset, or even embarrassed, that so many seemingly unscientific ideas and intuitions are being associated with an African apprehension of the world process. Some may be disturbed by an apparent willingness to seemingly embrace mere speculation in areas of both ancient and emerging earth sciences into this paradigm. It would be so much safer to leave these controversial ideas out and stay within the margins of conventional discourse and avoid the confrontation with a technologically dominant worldview and culture. Our response is that this very technological and spiritual culture is at root an unfoldment of this ancient worldview. In the future this apprehension of the world process will open to new sciences of the body and spirit, just as it has in the past.

The ancient texts agree that a spiritual force animates human existence and evolution itself. Evolution is more than random selection and capricious adaptation. There is a luminous unfoldment from more subtle realms of order. The perennial testimony is that there is a path and a multiplicity of paths on the One Path to self-discovery and illumination. It has signs, roadblocks, detours, and predictable experiences available to the disciplined seeker, just as do the other paths of knowledge in the fields of human endeavor. I have addressed this before in *Transcending Psychoneurotic Disturbances* (Bynum, 1994) and *The Family Unconscious* (Taub-Bynum, 1984). The path of mystical or spiritual unfoldment is rooted in the physical body and can be directly experienced, through the human mind, body, and nervous system. It corresponds to what we know and hints at things that we can only dream about.

At present, the dynamics and phenomena that surround melanin and neuromelanin in embryology, neurobiology, and anthropology make it the *leading candidate* to explain certain internal luminous phenomena observed in spiritual practices across the Earth from ancient times. These are shared phenomena, a deep-structure process common to all branches of the human family. It is merely the neurobiological unfoldment of our kind. This neuromelanin hypothesis may later be disconfirmed or incorporated into more inclusive schemas of development. This is fine and a part of the scientific tradition. For now, this leading candidate shows a certain "neatness of fit" and perhaps, like all knowledge of the material world, is but a "spiraling approximation" of the truth. This leading candidate, however, allows us to travel, and travel we will.

The African unconscious, then, is paradoxically both the dark and the luminous deep structure that lives in each of us, regardless of surface racial and ethnic diversification. This will be echoed throughout each chapter. The book has four interrelated goals on which the themes, facts, and ideas are based:

1. To explain how the genetic, psychic, spiritual, and cultural origins of our species, *Homo sapiens sapiens*, are traceable to a collective and common African origin in spite of apparent differences between peoples based on "race," language, cultural style, spirituality, geographic location, and even era in history
2. To reveal the innumerable ways in which all human beings are interwoven on the loom of a primordial collective African unconscious
3. To demonstrate how the many pathways to our literally felt and experienced psychospiritual awakening and unification with the energy of the universe are inextricably connected to the genetic, psychic, spiritual, and cultural processes that are rooted in the African origin of our species
4. Finally, to openly and nonapologetically encourage human beings, regardless of race and ethnicity, to individually and collectively strive for enlightenment and unification with themselves, other living beings, and the wider ecological and planetary energy that binds the whole of the universe together

At some point our analysis will lead us like seafaring voyagers across the oceans to India and the Americas, where the conflicts and struggles of our species around race and ethnicity still provide an explosive mix for society and real politics. This confrontation is not only in the streets and the boardrooms and neighborhoods of the cities, but also in the academy, in the churches, in the images of the media, indeed implicit in even the shared social contract and mind itself.

Our peering into both remote history and later antiquity will reveal waves and waves of humans moving up and out of Africa, not only anthropologically, but culturally and beyond. In recent millennia, this African wavefront has beached itself and gone through endless transformations yet can still be discerned in the mysterious seafaring Celts of the North, in the astronomical language and hieroglyphs of the Algonquins of the West, and in the Yoga roots of the Dravidians of India, in the Melanesians, in the Australian Aboriginals, in the Kundalini phenomena of the San or Bushmen of the forbidding Kalahari in the South. This great undercurrent, this deep structure is oddly unstudied in the academies of modern times. This, however, is in the process of change and these ideas will find a home in the consciousness of many others.

For many years I had been preoccupied with the collective unconscious and the racial memory in connection with my research on *The Family Unconscious* and *Families and the Interpretation of Dreams*. The idea had been implicit and then partially articulated in *Transcending Psychoneurotic Disturbances*. Then by a serendipitous event, a Washington, D.C., scholar and eminent clinical researcher, Dr. John Johnson, picked up a copy of my *Family Unconscious* and shared it with some of his colleagues when he traveled to the Szondi Institute in Zurich, Switzerland. They contacted me and a long correspondence ensued. Several years later, I happened to see the phrase "African unconscious" in connection with Dr. Johnson. I then added the phrase to the text I had already written on this idea called *Oldawan*, which was the logical extension of my book on the family unconscious. I do not know the exact content of his meaning of the phrase, but the idea is implicit in Freud, Jung, their forms of the racial memory and the findings of modern science, especially in anthropology, paleontology, genetics, and history.

The African unconscious, you see, is simply implicit in the vast, emergent parallels and synchronicities of data. Anyone looking in this direction could have written this book. In that sense, its ideas and interlocking field connections are like the forms in the marble that Michelangelo would feel call out for expression as he stood in front of them in the rock quarries outside of Rome. As with every other artist who uses sciences and techniques to flesh out a vision, the limits of the artist will be everywhere manifest. The great voices in the stones, however, still call out. Science in this sense, even the most abstract of sciences, shares this essential creativity with art.

And so for us the more our science separates matter and energy, biology and genetics, the more our essential Oneness emerges on the scene. Yes, there are differences among us in skin tone, in language, in many other ways long since known. But there are *no known significant differences* in the central nervous system, in embryology, or in the neuromelanin activity of the brain. We all belong to the same species, *Homo sapiens sapiens*; we are all of the same genetic mother, the mitochondrial DNA mother of humanity, "Eve." Yes, we are of the same family, the same world, the same great Alajobi.

A great cycle is drawing to a close half a millennium after Columbus: The phoenix from its ashes rises again. We live out these dynamics in the postmodern era. The first 40 years of postcolonial rule have brought mixed results in Africa. Their first new leaders came as poets and socialist revolutionaries, many left as martyrs or bloated kleptomaniacs. Forty years of civil rights activism in the United States have brought a bigger Black middle class, political power, and the evil gravity of the welfare state. A new wind is blowing across the inner landscape of African diasporic peoples, and in its wake it brings a lush new rain and life-enhancing force to the peoples of Africa, the Americas, and all those who recognize in this movement a shared destiny and a friend.

Ecological spirituality is the great beacon of the 21st century, and the primordial spirit is the new missionary to the West. Each of us is a force who couples with every other force in the known universe. Let us personalize this to our best. Generations ago, when faced by a similar situation, James Joyce, a sage, writer, and distant cousin from one of the northernmost branches of this spiraling African race, replied:

> So be it. Welcome, O life! I go to encounter for the millionth time the reality of experience and to forge in the smithy of my soul the uncreated conscience of my race. (1916/1964, pp. 275–276)

Edward Bruce Bynum, Ph.D.
Ile-Ife, Nigeria, West Africa/Amherst, Massachusetts

All truth passes through three stages . . .
First it is ridiculed.
Second it is violently opposed.
Third it is accepted as being self-evident.

—Arthur Schopenhauer

1

KIASPORA, OR THE GREAT DISPERSION

One can therefore grasp the impossibility of the polycentric thesis. The appearance of Homo sapiens sapiens *in the various hypothetical centers ought to be even older than those of Africa if they are to explain the independence of this polycentric genesis in relation to Africa. On the contrary, all of the so-called centers of the appearance of modern man are more recent than those of Africa and can therefore be explained with Africa as the starting point.*
— Cheikh Anta Diop, *Civilization or Barbarism*

It is somewhat more than probable that our early progenitors lived on the African continent than elsewhere.
— Charles Darwin, *The Descent of Man*

PROLOGUE: THE AFRICAN ORIGIN
OF HUMAN CONSCIOUSNESS

S WEPT up as we are by the great currents of history and science, today we know unmistakably that ancient humanity began in Africa. On this issue modern science has no doubt. The most recent specialization of the primates stretches back to perhaps some 12 million years ago to the middle of the Miocene age. There on the African savannas and in the forests, small ape-like creatures arose whose remains we have not yet found, despite all the evidence pointing in this direction. This common ancestor lived for millions of years. Then came a cataclysmic event of Biblical proportions. Vast tectonic forces in the Earth emerged some 8 million years ago in East Africa, creating the Rift Valley. A great furrow arose and cut perpendicularly from north to south across the equator. Vegetation and climate shifted. Wetlands to one side became dryer as humidity decreased. Hominids began to emerge and gradually evolved with this arid change (Coppens, 1994). The link with the ape line had been broken.

Perhaps some 4.4 million years ago, a recently unearthed hominid-like creature, *Ardipithecus ramidis*, roamed the north-central landscape of Ethiopia. However, it is not absolutely certain whether this creature walked on two legs or developed a gait going between two legs and four. A cousin, *Australopithecus anamensis*, unearthed by Meave Leakey and Alan Walker in the Turkana region of East Africa, lived about the same time and probably did move about on two feet. Its thick tibia bones supported the extra weight of the upright body, and the fact that the top of the tibia is concave rather than convex, as in the apes, thereby creating more balance and stability in the knee joint, supports the view that it may have walked upright.

The first clearly established true hominid, however, was *Australopithecus afarensis*, the small, dark, bipedal or two-legged creature who, though upright, still held close to the trees. She could stand over 4 feet tall and arose on the scene some 4 million years ago. From her came the other Australopithecines and their other Homo descendants and variations—*Australopithecus africanus*, *A. boisei*, *A. robustus*, *A. aethiopicus*, and maybe others as yet undiscovered. Some 2.5 million years ago even more sophisticated hominids broke away from their close cousins on the Australopithecus family line and began the march toward modern humanity called *Homo sapiens sapiens*. The other offshoots and diversifications of humanity, such as *Homo rudolfensis*, headed for extinction for as yet unknown reasons. This may have been connected to the global cooling cycle that began around 2.7 million years ago and dried out some of the African forests and increased the size of the great savannas; we don't know.

Tools have been found with hominid remains from at least 2.3 million years ago. *Homo habilis*, the tool maker, arose with others, perhaps 2 or 2.5 million years ago, thrived, then vanished about 1.5 million years ago, leaving primarily *Homo erectus* on the scene. *Homo habilis* may have had some primitive speech as we know it, since casts of his skull show the faint presence of Broca's area, the left frontal region of the brain associated with language and intricate muscle control needed for using fine tools and manual dexterity. Despite this, he died out anyway.

Eventually the whole lineage flowed into only *Homo erectus*, the first to travel from Africa, the mother continent. Eventually from the split of this one branch—the hominids—our lineage (including our indirect ancestor the gentle Neanderthals) continued on through subtle variations until we arrived at modern humanity today. All the while, like elemental background music, ecology and climate changed imperceptibly. This is the studied opinion of modern science and also among the earliest speculations of Charles Darwin (Darwin, 1859/1964; Johanson and Edey, 1981; Leakey & Lewin, 1977). It was a traveling race out of Africa, and it was Black. (See Figure 1.)

The anthropological and ethnographic studies of humanity's 4-million-year history in Africa, prior to leaving Africa, is well documented (Diop, 1991; Putman, 1988). After their cradle period and development in East Africa, the tribes of hominids spread to other continents. This occurred over an immense span of time from our human perspective but was just a flash of time from an evolutionary perspective. As the young race evolved and stood upright toward the sun, greater and greater stress was placed on the body, especially on the female's hips and thighs and birth canal, leading to a slower brain maturation outside the womb for the infant, more dependence on the mother, and thus a longer childhood development and family life. This stimulated more intimate social and behavioral responses, behaviors that are still with us. Undoubtedly, this is the womb of human culture. The significance here is that the template of humankind—the psychic and genetic roots of all present-day humanity—was nestled in East Africa for at least 2.5 million years before leaving the continent. This includes the deep-structure archetypes of the species that germinated as our social and behavioral patterns, all of which evolved over the eons in these tight family units.

There are no modern bones or *Homo sapiens* human remains found outside Africa that date prior to the last half million years. We do find the remains of the Australopithecines in other places in Africa, for example, in the south and central areas, but all are found in Africa. The overwhelming preponderance of ancient hominid skulls and bones are unearthed in Africa.

FIGURE 1. The Hominid Family Tree: A Probable Lineage.

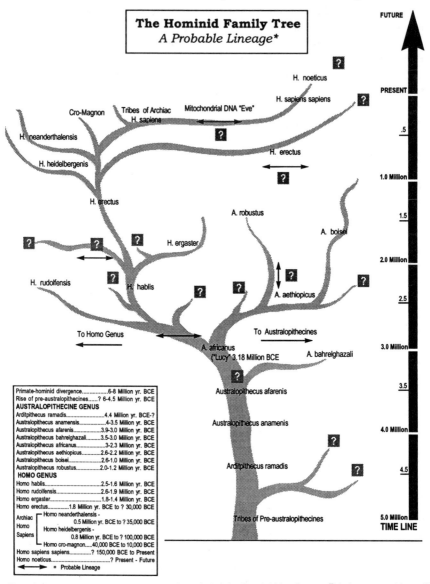

New discoveries every year are constantly updating the hominid family tree. This is a general but still controversial consensus currently of the lineage "unearthed" and here culled from the findings of the famed Leaky family, D. Johanson, R. J. Blumenschine, J. Ebert, D. Pilbeam, A. Mann, A. Kershaw, L. Aiello, A. Walker, B. Wood, and C. Swisher. (Copyright © 1999 Teachers College, Columbia University)

All the variations and diversifications from the earliest of all to *Homo sapiens sapiens* arose in Africa.

Then *Homo sapiens sapiens* left to travel the world as *Homo erectus* had millennia earlier. In fact, there is every indication that there were several waves of migration of the hominid family out of Africa in the four directions, particularly up the east coast of Africa out over into Asia and eventually into the Americas, while the other branch moved up over into Europe. There are incomplete branchings of the hominid line scattered throughout Europe and Asia. The *entire* sequence, however, is found in Africa and in abundance as compared to the other continents. In other words, again, only in Africa can we find the complete record and genetic blueprints of our species. This template, this basic genetic stock of humanity, is the source stock of all other unfolding branches of the human family. From this last family of travelers civilization was born.

This story of stories is the archetype of all human stories. For as the spirit that is now humanity rose through the apes and early hominids, it also rose from all fours to stand upright. This rise upward toward light, toward higher consciousness, toward a "reunion" with the light above it, will be repeated throughout this story. It is a root motif in the evolutionary music.

The Scope of the Journey

H. G. Wells, the great historian of early civilizations, speculated on the origins of humanity, but in particular on the origin of African-related peoples in the southern parts of India, the people once known as Dravidians. The pan-Dravidian race was considered to be a race of Negroids out of Africa into southern India. Wells and others believed that this group of humans at one time lived in a common culture that spanned from the east coast of India to the west coast of Africa. Today we know that there are not only physical or phenotypical near identities, but also blood or serological and genetic parallels between these groups, which is what the ancient Greeks believed (Finch, 1990). Today we suggest an even deeper interconnectedness than this, that literally all the tribes are woven on a common loom.

It is from this vista that the goals and directions of this book's journey can be seen. We hope to outline the saga and the deeper implications of our traveling race's rise from obscurity among the mammals and herds of the Earth to eventual dominance—the rise of civilization and our unmet destiny among the stars and planets that we will travel to someday. In this book we will gather the scattered bits of data emerging from our vast interconnectedness as a species. Indeed, we are all implicated in each other historically, anthropologically, embryologically, and, yes, genetically in the very fabric and structure of our shared DNA.

At some unknown point, speech itself arose among our lineage and further separated us from the other higher primates and perhaps hominids. Chimpanzees do not talk, and no doubt there is a complex feedback among speech, syntax, and neural processes that reached an evolutionary flashpoint in the explosion of language. How this happened we do not know, although many believe it is rooted deeply in biology in the development of the brain's capacity to control rapid airflow and articulation (Lieberman, 1991). Interestingly enough, deep-structure syntax is something we all share and, therefore, this again suggests our common genetic pool. We will return to this when we look at the idea of an original tongue in early human speech.

This book will unfold a radical interconnected thesis. Radical, that is, only in our own day, but we believe one that will be street knowledge in ages to come. Here we will suggest and support that the parents or origin of modern humanity is Black and African. All variations and ethnic groups are but interesting and creative multicultural and ethnic diversifications *within* a common species. They are not speciations, but merely "surface-structure" modifications. In support of this, subsequent chapters will look at "deep-structure" unifying commonalities such as embryonic development and morphogenesis. We will see a dark melaninated line that intelligently guides our fetal development from the first hours of life and echoes back to an earlier African genesis, a genesis we each recapitulate regardless of surface racial and ethnic characteristics. It is the deep-structure genetic language of our species and it enfolds the fountainhead of our shared psychic and spiritual unfoldment.

This interconnectedness of our common embryogenesis is also reflected in the embryogenesis of civilization itself. For we shall posit that civilization, like the human embryo, first emerged out of a rich, dark, creative synthesis of life forces along the Nile, then spread and unfolded across the Earth, evolving specializations in seemingly separate areas of the globe, but always secretly interconnected by consciousness and genetic roots, like the different organs of the human fetus unfolding out of the elongated neural crest and developing into the seemingly separate organs and areas of the body. Each chapter will zoom in on a separate area of development. Because human history and civilizations are mammoth areas of study filling volumes and libraries, we cannot possibly cover everything. What we will offer is a possible library code and index, a way of seeing how the library developed and where it may be going. We will briefly trace the movements of civilization, as well as the travels of *Homo erectus* and later *Homo sapiens sapiens*, out of Africa into Europe, the Middle East, Asia, and over into the Americas. We will show the cross-fertilization and mutual enrichments of the tribes and nations. This is the case not only genetically and historically, but also in the realm of consciousness itself. We even believe there is a Mother

Tongue hidden in the towering Babel of contemporary languages that reflects and echoes back to an original language our species spoke prior to all the permutations and diversifications.

In following the steps of early man across the globe, it will become quickly apparent that it was and is no linear journey, but rather a journey punctuated by nonlinear movements and unpredictable influences. The many branchings or bifurcations of the tribes and species and their encounter with unusual situations, from climatic changes to shifting food resources, led to extinctions, more bifurcations, and creative tensions. Just when apparent chaos would seem to reign, a new higher order would emerge on the scene. The environment, in concert with an evolutionary impulse to manifest higher and more subtle realms of order, served to prune the hominid tree and either covertly direct or reinforce the flower of this tree to bloom richer and richer flowers and fruit. We believe this new, more integrated situation is the reflection of a deeper, more implicate order unfolding from nature, not only a Darwinian selection. As we will suggest later, it is not only organic life that is involved with the drama of evolution; nonorganic matter seems to exhibit sentient or consciousness-like behavior and reaches for greater expressions of order over time.

When it comes to the emergence of civilization in many areas of the Earth, we will observe how the presence at critical times of Kemetic influence along the Nile profoundly affected an emerging civilization. This "butterfly effect" or "sensitive dependence on initial conditions" is seen in early Olmec and Dravidian civilization. Also, this influence in concert with the natural tendency of systems to re-create themselves from a common mold will be seen to reinforce this belief and perception. This is the so-called self-similarity of structures, or the "infinite nesting" effect. This can operate because again there is a common root, a shared stock of genetic, anthropological, morphological, embryological, and blood or serological reality to work with. These all point through the depths of history and blood to the African origin of human consciousness. On this root and living organism is a common sea of psychic and psychological reality that gives rise to a common deep-structure religious and spiritual consciousness.

This final area of a shared sea of consciousness may at first appear to be a radical thesis, but only for the moment. We believe that egoic consciousness, as well as religious and spiritual consciousness, is the shared inheritance of all humanity and that individual consciousness is an interesting but transient wave upon a great, deep ocean of consciousness, to which the present human species has access by way of disciplined insight and psychospiritual technology. This shared sea of consciousness has not only social, political, and spiritual implications, but also clear medical reverberations. Each chapter will seek to unfold this notion in a useful way.

Last but not least, the shared brotherhood of humanity has, it seems, immense implications for our notions of identity, psychic processes, and future evolutionary development in the solar environment of the stars. Since the very dawn of her thinking, this risen ape has dreamed of the angels. So let us travel now with the ancient ones and hint at what our progeny may find.

WAVES OF HOMINIDS AND THEIR STOCK

After *Homo habilis*, the tool user, *Homo erectus*, upright standing man, began the first great wave out of Africa. *Homo erectus* arose perhaps 1.7 million years ago in East Africa. She moved into Asia through the Middle East and into Europe over the link between Africa and Spain. She left signs in many places. Her million-year-old remains were found in Israel; in China at Lantian she is dated at 700,000 years; at Narmada in India she is half a million years. Earlier hominid remains are known in Africa, of course. At Makapansgat in South Africa, 3 million years; at Laetoli in Tanzania, 3.7 million years; at Lake Turkana in Kenya, 1.6 million years; and at ancient Lake Baringo in Kenya, 5 million years. So by the time *Homo erectus* unfolds in the evolutionary drama in Tighenit, Algeria, 700,000 years ago and Isernia, Italy, at about the same time, the hominid model and lineage out of which she came and the major genetic experiments were well under way. Although most agree that she died out over 250,000 years ago, there is the controversial suggestion that she may have survived in such isolated areas as Java as late as 53,000 or even 27,000 years ago. She gave rise not only to the *Homo sapiens* of Neanderthal and Cro-Magnon, but also to us—the *Homo sapiens sapiens*. (See Figure 2.)

It is nearly impossible to discern exactly when our own species, *Homo sapiens sapiens*, arose: The range is anywhere between 150,000 and 200,000 years ago, but perhaps earlier, around 270,000 years ago. But her oldest markings, as we said earlier, are all in Africa. She is cited in many places in East Africa and the south. Her ancestors were smaller but had more robust bones and a more limited brain case. She, too, was a traveler. She traveled out of Africa along many of the same routes as the first wave of *Homo erectus* into all of Europe and Asia. Her remains were found in eastern Europe at Mladeč. At Liujiang in China she is dated at 67,000 years, and further north in Siberia, perhaps 30,000 years. This proliferation in Europe's Upper Paleolithic period lasted approximately 35,000 to 11,000 years ago. Small bands of families lived peacefully and in general *cooperation* with each other because of the survival value, if nothing else. In the Middle East her remains are found at Qafzeh cave from 92,000 years ago. As in Europe, bands of small families lived together in a cooperative culture complete with

FIGURE 2. Hominid Dispersion from East Africa to the World.

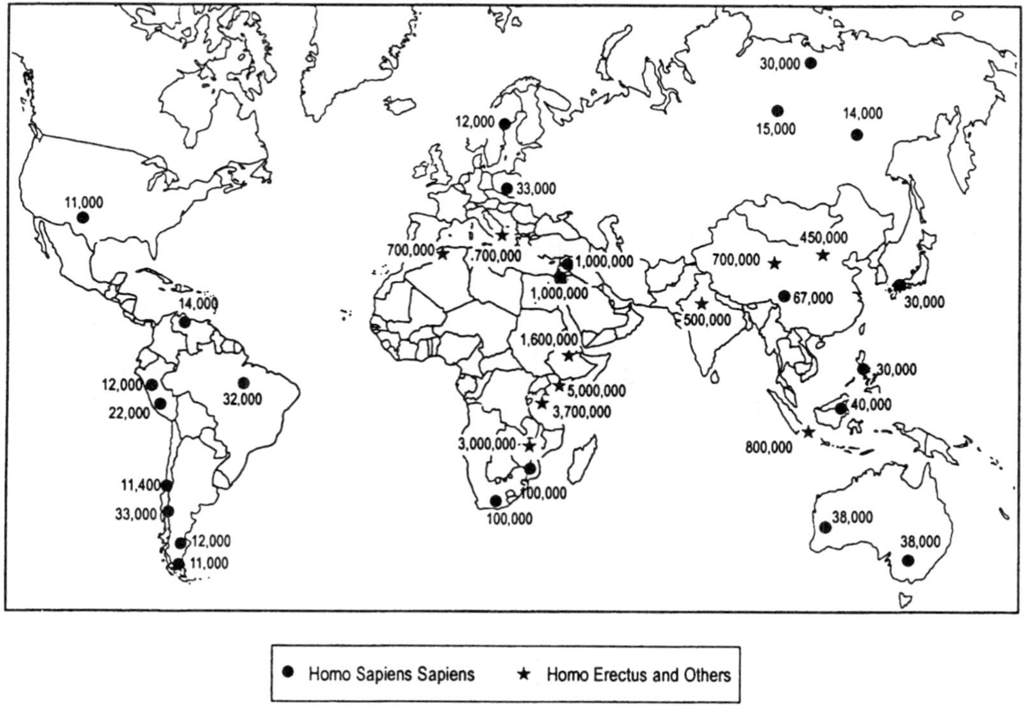

Current data suggest that the hominid line arose in the East African region and moved outward in a slow migration. There is some support for a south African origin, but the preponderance of bone deposits and other evidence pinpoints the eastern region. This is true for both *Homo erectus* and *Homo sapiens sapiens*. (Copyright © 1999 Teachers College, Columbia University)

ritual, technology, and a close, necessary affinity with the environment. Despite this stability, she continued to travel.

From the Middle East and Asia, she went south and east to the Philippines. Tabon Cove has figures from 30,000 years ago. In Australia the first *Homo sapiens sapiens* arrived approximately 50,000 years ago. As the climate changed, the great glaciers of the Earth periodically absorbed enough water to dry up certain seas and open land bridges. This is how many tribes moved into Australia from Asia and, as we shall see, up from Asia to the Americas over the Bering Strait, and perhaps also by island hopping over the shallow ocean of the south Pacific to the tip of South America. The sunken east Pacific rise and submerged Chile rise are only 600 feet deep in some places along these mountainous ridges. With Ice Age absorption of water in the North and Beringia between Siberia and Alaska, a string of islands no doubt arose and suggested a travel route with friendly wind and sea currents. This route combined with the northern migration took the Americas over time in a pincer movement and established the eastern branch of *Homo sapiens sapiens* in the New World. Bone remains in the Americas suggest this. For now let's just note that her remains have been dated in Upper Swan and Lake Miengo in Australia from 38,000 years ago; from the Huon peninsula in New Guinea some 40,000 years ago; and even from Japan perhaps 30,000 years ago.

Thus some 40,000 years ago our ancient ancestor was well established in Africa, in Europe, in Asia, and in Australia. Civilization as we have come to know it did not yet exist, but human culture and diversity were in great abundance. Neanderthal was heading for evolutionary oblivion after a saga from at least 300,000 to 35,000 years ago. She too was a traveler, a tool maker, and seems at times to have buried her dead; she was also a spiritual seeker. She failed the great test of adaptation, however, and over a few thousand years ceased to exist. She did not intermarry with *Homo sapiens sapiens* in the north to create the European branch of our species. Eventually, *Homo sapiens sapiens* alone was the only hominid to walk the earth. She studied the stars and the seasons, and, like her forebears, traveled the planet in search of food, community, and the gods. As these waves and waves of hominids became implicate in her genes and dreams, over time she came to carry our common story.

Her Genetic Anlage

Beyond historical, anthropological, and ethnological data on our interconnectedness, there is also the evidence of modern science concerning the very structured and intimate corridors of the human cell that reflect this common story and truth. The notion of the DNA "mother of humanity" has gained more and more acceptance in modern scientific and intellectual circles.

It would seem that this Eve has even reached the popular press and news media. She lived approximately 150,000 to 200,000 years ago and echoes in our blood today. (See Figure 3.) The meaning of this is that all the diverse races with their colors and variations are all unfolded from a common human or parent stock, who in all likelihood was a small, dark-skinned African. This is the personal lineage of every human being—an ancient dark mother. Y chromosome agent studies of people throughout the Earth also show little variation, strongly suggesting that ancient humanity formed a small concentrated population as recently as 270,000 years ago. According to computer analysis, this mitochondrial "Adam" lived some 188,000 years ago. There is no polygenesis! In all probability he too roamed the changing savannas of Africa on his evolutionary trek to your era. It seems that the first human families were also dark, or "moro" and "negrito," a psychic reality buried deep in the human psyche and held there by strong repressive forces.

Racial diversity as we think of it today only began approximately 25,000 years ago (Diop, 1991). Racial diversification within the *Homo sapiens sapiens* species began at that time in Europe, Asia, Africa, and the Americas. Before that, all humankind was dark-skinned and Africoid. Humankind is essentially a traveling species. Out of Africa into Europe came the Grimaldi Negroids, who, many believe, through climate and diversification, became the foundations of the various European "races." There are some speculations that Cro-Magnon man mutated out of this early Grimaldi Negroid. Perhaps. Even today, the Basque people of France and Spain show enough genetically unusual Rh-negative blood types and language traces distinct enough from other European groups to suggest their connection to this early European type. Future research should tell us more about this. However, most of modern science is in agreement that the Neanderthal, who also lived at the same time, was an evolutionary dead end for humanity.

The interaction of neurobiological forces and the increasing receptivity to light and intelligence in the human species remain one of the great mysteries of evolution. For instance, thick lips and tight curly hair, along with large broad nostrils, help the body—especially the head, where 85% of the body's heat is lost—increase moisture loss in a hot climate and thus be adaptive to the requirements of respiration. However, to adapt to a cold climate, a longer, more narrow nose would help retain body heat, as would a thicker build, more body hair, and longer hair on the head. Increasing distance from the equator, by Golger's Law, also leads to a lightening of the surface skin and vice versa. Recent computer mappings of a host of genetic markers suggest that the Asian branch first diverged from the original *Homo sapiens sapiens* African stock. The African and Asian lines then mixed to create the

FIGURE 3. Paleolithic Age.

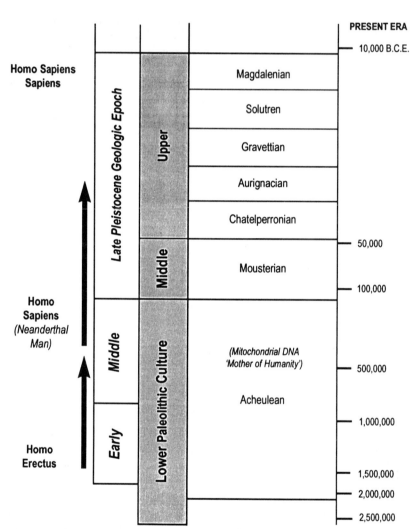

The Paleolithic Age, often called the "Stone Age" due to the use of stone tools before the use of metal and the cultivation of crops, has several levels. Each level represents an "advance" in some degree toward the present age. The mitochondrial DNA "mother of humanity" Eve is thought to have lived perhaps 150,000 years ago. (Copyright © 1999 Teachers College, Columbia University)

hybrid European branch with 65% Asian and 35% African genes (Cavalli-Sforza, Menozzi, & Piazza, 1994). It is generally held that the White or European branch of *Homo sapiens sapiens* evolved around 25,000 to 30,000 years ago in the regions of southern France or more likely in the Eurasian steppes and Caucasus Mountains, areas deeply inundated by the ice sheet glaciers of the Cold Wurm II stadial period.

During the Upper Paleolithic period, from 10,000 to 79,000 years ago, an enormous amount of Europe's water was locked up in glaciers that created fog and mists. The sea level was some 300 feet lower in some areas than today. This is how caves like Cosquer in southern France could be reached and painted by the peoples, but one needs scuba gear to reach the cave today. The often overcast skies meant reduced sunlight and the necessity of covering the body to retain heat, thus further decreasing sunlight on the skin. Both led to biochemical changes in the skin with melanin. There arose an initial vitamin D deficiency before a natural compensation and eventually an adaptive white skin, which has a greater resistance to cold temperatures than black skin (Finch, 1990). Blue or light eyes may also be more perceptive in foggy and misty climates. Such is the probable ingenuity of nature inherent in *Homo sapiens sapiens*.

Even so, some pockets of the original African line survived into historical European time, usually where fish oil and other mineral-rich sources were located, such as on the coast. This is why Erik the Red found Blacks in Greenland. Also, smaller migrations of Africans moved into Europe, for example in 1079 B.C.E., into Spain after the great drought. Hundreds of years later, the Carthaginians of North Africa during the Punic Wars at times invaded the Iberian peninsula as did many scattered others (Van Sertima, 1992). All we know for sure is that the humankind that emerged out of Africa had to be mobile and adaptive to local conditions and that because of Golger's Law, it was originally dark-skinned and Africoid in appearance. This dynamic and creative process led to the diversification of the basic stock of humanity that now covers every area of the globe. The unique capacity of the human species to absorb light quanta and also to protect itself from light by the use of melanin has become a scientific study of the most serious kind. For not only was melanin in the early species of mankind absolutely necessary as an exterior covering, but the genetic roots of this can be found in the structure of the nervous system and even in the neuromelanin-guided embryogenesis of every human life (Bynum, 1994; King, 1990). Thus from the earliest of times we see the roots of the African parent stock in humanity, from its melanin-informed neurobiological embryogenesis to the present biological unfoldment of humankind. Melanin, as we shall see later, *absorbs light*; it literally arches up toward light, a fact with immense evolutionary, neurological, and psychospiritual implications.

Humankind indeed did spread and proliferate out of Africa to the other continents of the world. From the eastern shores of the great lake humanity moved toward the center of Africa. From the center of the great lake of eastern Africa the Negroid species moved up through northern Africa into Europe and, as mentioned earlier, perhaps by way of the Grimaldi Negroids to become the basis of the Aryan, Alpine, and Slavic races of Europe (Diop, 1991). Out of the same eastern lakes area up through the Near East, the traveling African became the foundation of the various so-called Mongol and other Asian races. Many suggest that a branch of the early Khoisan or south African "Bushman" type—with yellow-brown skin, slight body hair, epicanthal folds around the eyes, and short stature—migrated from Africa to the steppes of Siberia 20,000 to 30,000 years ago and thereafter underwent adaptive changes to evolve into the Asiatic expression of *Homo sapiens sapiens* (Finch, 1991).

Genetic data from recent studies (Cavalli-Sforza, Menozzi, & Piazza, 1994) of blood antigens, antibodies, and other proteins in the population also suggest that this Khoisan type may be an ancient mixture of Black Africans and west Asians in the Middle East or further east. This early human being used her high intelligence and adapted to the changing environment. Her short descendants today can be seen in the pygmoid or pygmy types of southeast Asia, India, and in the south Pacific. And, yes, some have been unearthed in South America and the tip of Tierra del Fuego! It is known that they mined the earth for ochre and iron.

KIASPORA INTO THE ANCIENT AMERICAS

The Ice Ages of the Pleistocene epoch, which dawned 1.6 million years ago and ended only around 10,000 B.C.E., sucked up seas and flooded valleys for millennia while bands of modern humans migrated and developed. We have bones from Siberia over 30,000 years old, the same in Japan, and from seafaring Papua New Guinea, even earlier, perhaps 40,000 years. The great glaciers came in waves and on several occasions for many centuries nearly dried up the oceans of the North and revealed the continent of Beringia that connected eastern Siberia, Alaska, and the Yukon in North America. We have relics from Maiorych in Siberia from 18,000 years ago and Bluefish Cave in Alaska from 13,000 years ago. This is because some 18,000 years ago Beringia was again a great passage way into the Americas. This was during the late Wisconsin glaciation of 18,000 years ago when great ice-sheets covered large parts of North America, the so-called Laurentide and Cordilleran glaciers. Most of this is no longer controversial. Yet recent evidence points to an even earlier crossing by this traveling species, and her face and lineage still bore the unmistakable stamp of an African.

The earliest Americans came out of Asia and were Asians, but the first Asians were Black (Rashidi, 1985). Indeed, as we have mentioned several times in reference to racial diversification within the *Homo sapiens sapiens* species, this did not occur until some 25,000 years ago or so. Prior to 25,000 to 30,000 years ago, all *Homo sapiens sapiens* were Black and Africoid (Diop, 1991). The first Americans appear now to have entered North America around 36,000 years ago. In other words, the very first Kiaspora into the Americas was Black.

Continuing the early work of the American Harold Sterling Gladwin in his book *Men out of Asia* (1947), Rinoco Rashidi (1985) and others outline that there was not one, but at least four separate waves of movement into the Americas from Asia. The first to arrive were the Australoids approximately 50,000 to 60,000 years ago. They must have brought with them the seeds of the dreamtime religion and worldview, a paradigm of dream consciousness as a real state—that dreaming is an entry into an objective condition where contact with ancestors, with forces of animate nature, and where wider biospiritual interactions with the environment are dynamic and possible. Survival technologies emerged from this, such as the so-called "dream travel" and effective medicinal remedies of a practical kind. Fanciful writers have capitalized on this for literary purposes, but the core reality is true (Morgon, 1991). This intuitive embrace, this dreaming physionomic apprehension of the world process has implicit within it curves and vectors in space–time that keep alive a tradition of humankind that one day may yet revolutionize the collective thrust of human consciousness.

By following herds of animals, especially great bison, horses, and wooly mammoths, these Australoids appear to have traveled up from Australia into Siberia, over the Bering Strait and Beringia's steppe-tundra of grass and herb-rich vegetation, down the coastal regions, perhaps all the way down to the tip of South America. Again, this took thousands of years, but their remains have been found in Tierra del Fuego. The remains are those of small, Africoid peoples. The Bering Strait was available for travel by foot and watercraft during at least four separate extended periods. They appear to be the first migration of *Homo sapiens sapiens*, but certainly not the last. They moved into Central and South America during the great mid-Wisconsin glacial period of 40,000 years ago in a slow and gradual way along the coastal ranges. Even during the great late Wisconsin Cordilleran glaciation, the ice-sheets were mostly confined to the mountains and foothill valleys, which would have left passages open periodically through the upland and alpine areas along the eastern side of the continental divide (Fladmark, 1986). Also, the milder weathered coastal areas, rich with fish, bird eggs, and other sea-food and shellfish, would have been open to navigation by watercraft and mixed-age population groups. Below the glacial ice-sheet, perhaps between 55 to 60 degrees north latitude, they spread eastward and further south. One of their skulls, the so-called Punin skull, was found in 1923 high in the Andes and is dated between 15,000 and 20,000 years ago. There are crude flake tools at Pikimachay, Peru, 22,000 years ago and sophisticated obsidian blades from Tlapacoya, Mexico, from 24,000 years ago.

While the Ice Ages dried up the northern seas and opened a land bridge across Siberia, they may also have dropped the southern oceans enough for this traveling race to cross it in small boats. During the late Wisconsin glaciation, the sea level fell nearly 300 feet! There is little reason to believe that peoples, over the millennia, after traveling out in boats from the continent of Australia and large islands of the south Pacific, would stop here. Bands conceivably sailed eastward, stopping at various islands, some of which are presently submerged, until they reached South America. There are winds and sea currents that move from Australia and the south Pacific to the shores of South America, the so-called Peru current, a veritable transpacific water road, just as there are three currents from the coasts of Africa to South America and the Caribbean. (See Figure 4.)

This route to colonization is equally plausible. We must remember that we have found their rock art carvings and remnants of culture from 34,000 years ago! There are pebble tools at Monte Verde in Chile and rock paintings at Pedra Furada in Brazil also from 34,000 years ago. From this view they are a branch of that unfolding dark line, expanding and elongating out of the original body of humankind, an expression of its cultural embryogenesis, creating a seemingly new organ in a site distant from where it began. On this new shore it would take root, grow, and await its new contact in a crisis that would give rise to more complexity in a new synthesis—a synthesis sometimes purchased at a high price.

The next great wave, as discovered by Gladwin (1947) and elaborated by Rashidi (1985), consisted of the so-called "Asiatic Negroids." They came in larger waves and resembled the more Melanesian-looking peoples of the south Pacific. We should remember that over 100 million Blacks live in Asia today. The nostrils, hair, lips, skin color, and other surface or phenotypical characteristics are Africoid in *obvious* appearance, and there are striking genetic and serological connections. The sickle cell hemoglobin, or HgS, is one of the most consistent indicators of the African racial type and where it has traveled. It is found in over two-thirds of Africa. The only other place that comes close to this percentage is in southern and central India, especially among the Dravidian peoples, the original authors of Indian civilization and the earliest practitioners of Yoga. These people are scattered throughout

FIGURE 4. Transpacific Ocean Currents.

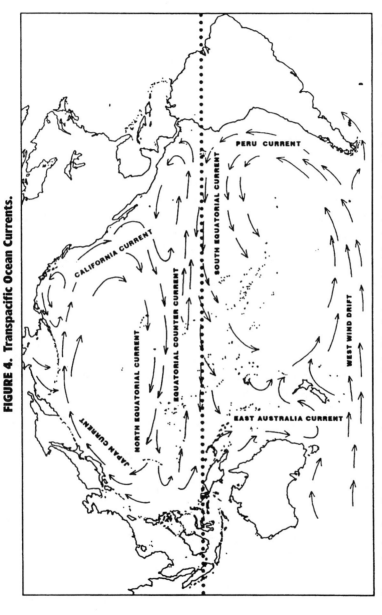

During the Ice Ages large amounts of water were locked in glaciers and ice-sheets, lowering sea levels in many areas and allowing submerged areas to become land passes to the Americas. Also, there are natural currents from the south Pacific area, the so-called Peru current, that could ferry travelers by a southern route to the Americas. (Copyright © 1999 Teachers College, Columbia University)

southern Asia and the Pacific islands and constitute much of the population of India, Melanesia, Australia in ancient times, Sumatra, and even early Arabia (Van Sertima & Rashidi, 1990).

These Asiatic Negroids, like the earlier Australoids who resembled the Australian Aborigines, had their own distinctive culture and signs. They encountered the earlier Australoids and fought, collaborated, traded, inter-married, and all the usual things humans of the same species have done for eons. These Asiatic Negroids came in even larger waves beginning perhaps 15,000 years ago and gradually absorbed the Australoid population. They established and advanced a more technological hunting culture with spear making with which they hunted Ice Age mammoths, bison, and other ani-mals some 12,000 years ago. Their fluted-pointed spears were quite large and sharp, and hence more accurate than earlier spears. This represented a significant technological advance over the earlier wave of Australoid peoples and allowed the population to expand as their hunting skills increased in proficiency among the huge herds of bison and other animals roaming the plains and fields below the ice-sheets that covered large sections of America.

They have been found from British Columbia to northern Mexico to Nova Scotia and even to the far east in Florida (Mehringe, 1988). These "Paleo-Indians," like the so-called "Proto-Egyptians" of Dravidian India and the "Habashi" of the Bible and the "Hamuritic" of Africa, are all vari-ous vague ways to describe what to the naked eye of today would be a person of clear African descent. These people, whose major relics we have from 10,000 to 12,000 years ago, established the Clovis and Fulsom Point cultures, taken from the name of the sites in New Mexico. Rashidi and the data suggest that instead of referring to them as "Paleo-Indians," we call them the Clovis-Fulsom Point Blacks.

It is worth mentioning that although the pre-Clovis cultural artifacts are present from 20,000 years before the Clovis were in North America, there are fewer such data in South America. When the Clovis suddenly ap-peared around 11,500 B.C.E., they were mostly in North America and highly evolved. This suggests that the early settling of the South American sites may not have come from the northern Beringia passageways, but, as we suggested earlier, from a southern route—the South Sea island route.

The third wave into the Americas from Asia began very slowly over the centuries, perhaps 32,000 years ago, but would eventually come to be the primary branching of the Native American population. These were the so-called "Algonquins." Again, their culture and technology were sufficiently different from those of the Australoids and Asiatic Negroids/Paleo-Indian/Clovis-Fulsom Point Blacks that they are seen as a distinct culture. These Algonquins eventually came in large numbers and spread to all parts of North America and Canada. They, too, diversified into the nations of the

Delaware, Cree, Shawnee, Black Foot, and others. Their descendants, especially the Micmac and Wabanaki, later had contacts with other Africans who navigated the Atlantic Ocean in large ships to the Americas long before Columbus (Van Sertima, 1976).

The last wave of Asiatics to move into the Americas were not Africoid at all, but Mongol. These were the Eskimo or Inuits. This began perhaps 2000 B.C.E. and seems to have occurred over four separate migrations. They also came in large, steady numbers for a long time and absorbed much of the earlier diminishing Australoid and Asiatic Negroid population and intermingled with the larger Algonquin population. The earlier Blacks were absorbed and faded away into myths and legends of the early founders of the nations. This seems to have also occurred with the Blacks of early Europe. The Vikings report "little Blacks" living in northern Europe as late as 1000 C.E., in small groups near the sea. The European unconscious is full of tales of elves, leprechauns, and little people who are dark in color and associated with mysterious rites (Clegg, 1975; Van Sertima & Rashidi, 1990). Yet we know that they truly existed before they were supplanted and absorbed by later groups in the cultural embryogenesis of the human organism unfolding across the globe. We have human artifacts from Brazil from 34,000 years ago and from New Mexico from 36,000 years ago that suggest this scenario. As we shall see with the rise of civilization itself, these ancient peoples, including the Algonquins, were again to meet and flourish with African peoples who came in ships from the East long before Columbus and the Europeans arrived.

Genetic and blood antigen differences tend to support this multiwave view of the peopling of ancient America. The three primary groups, classified by language family, are also genetically different. The Amerind group, which predominates in most of North and South America, are of primarily type O blood. The Na-dene group, which is centered in Canada, Alaska, and the southwest United States, has type O primarily, but also a healthy admixture of type A blood. However, in the Inuit or Eskimo groups of Canada and Alaska, we find types A, B, AB, and O blood groups, which reflects that of the rest of Earth. This suggests a series of waves of migration genetically and in language groups. We will return to this later when we look more closely at language, genetics, and the search for the mother tongue.

THE RISE OF CIVILIZATION: THE EGYPTO-NUBIAN LEGACY

After thousands and thousands of years of experimentation, cross-fertilization, branching, dead ends, and sporadic successes, humankind emerged upward toward the life and light of civilization. It seems that all the great early civilizations—the Egypto-Nubian, the Mesopotamian, Chinese, Olmec and Andean, Cretan, and Harappa-Dravidian of the Indus Valley—arose in river valleys. Many believe that the primary civilizations originated as a direct consequence of the climatic changes that occurred after the last great Ice Age in the Pleistocene era. Over the centuries, after the ice-sheets began to retreat, there was a growing drying of the Earth that led eventually to the emigration of diverse peoples into plains and river valleys where they could make use of and even partially control the supply of water (Coulborn, 1959). These were the last pages of the Stone Age or the so-called Paleolithic age.

The earliest signs we have of movement toward human civilization are again in the upper Nile Valley and the lakes region of eastern Africa. Our species first began to cultivate and harvest grain in the Nile Valley from 17,000 to 18,300 years ago, which profoundly affected population size, religious beliefs, and social life (Wendorf & Schild, 1981). This was the real dawn of the Neolithic age. With crop cultivation comes an increased awareness of the cycles of birth, growth, death, and seasonal-symbolic rebirth. Millennia earlier in this general region but farther south, the hominids had arched upward from all fours to stand upright. We have information and relics from early peoples and cultures in the Neolithic age to reflect this common understanding. Indeed, from the earliest known civilization of Upper Egypt and Nubia we have their classical writings that reflect their own version and story of their origins. They, too, tell the story of the inescapable movement of culture and civilization from the lakes region of the upper Nile, down the Nile Valley, and then eventually into the delta region.

Between 6000 and 4000 B.C.E. the river people emerged along the Nile and also along the Niger and Congo. The Amratean and Badarians populated the Nile Valley along the great Fayum Lake with its numerous serpents! The Ishango people over in west central Africa in Zaire introduced a form of the mathematical abacus. It spread on the trade routes. Van Sertima (1976) and others, on the basis of linguistic evidence and ancient written records, showed that the early peoples migrated to the delta as the rivers of the once lush Sahara and other areas dried up, creating a catastrophe of Biblical proportions. Satellites have confirmed the existence of these rivers below the Sahara, which once reached all the way over to huge Lake Chad. The base of the mysterious sphinx, which was built in the pre-dynastic era, reveals marks of water erosion, not wind and sand erosion, another indication that the vast desert was once lush and fertile. The whole area was crisscrossed with trade routes that allowed trade even by sea with the earliest Harappan and then eventually Dravidian peoples of ancient India.

The Dravidians and Nubians of 6000 B.C.E. were nearly identical phenotypically (Van Sertima & Rashidi, 1990), and the historian H. G. Wells (1940) and others believed that the two groups comprised a common "pan-

Dravidian" culture and civilization that stretched from the shores of India to the coast of West and North Africa. Their trade was in goods and ideas. However, the vast majority of this trade in goods, religious ideas, and technology occurred in the then-fertile Sahara and in the lands to the south (Davidson, 1969). The Greek traveler and historian Herodotus confirms this and even speculates on the ancient myths and legends of vanished high civilizations (Rawlinson, 1858). These legends chronicle the migration of their peoples in historical, mythological, and religious terms. We see that the cultivation of cattle, crops, plants, and so forth were first mastered in this region of the world around 18,000 B.C.E. Archeological evidence abounds in support of this. Fire was first cultivated in this general area 1.4 million years ago. From what we know today, the Nubian is the oldest known civilization. It is the origin of writing, approximately 4000 B.C.E. (Diop, 1974).

Herodotus also confirmed that there were *two* Black or "burnt-faced" Ethiopian nations in the lands to the South—the land of the Kemets and also that of the Indus Valley. The latter was undoubtedly the remains of the earliest Harappan sites that were later absorbed into the eventual Dravidian complex. It was, however, the younger sister of the Nubian genesis.

This Nubian civilization, a civilization now known to have arisen in the Sudan, is currently accepted as the origin of the later Egyptian civilization (Davidson, 1967; Fairservis, 1962). By "origin" we mean the Nubian evolved first and the Egyptian came next through a rich cross-fertilization and differentiation, like a new organ from a developing embryo. Egyptians called lands south of the Nile valley Ta-Kenset or "placenta-land." These were "ethnic" differences within the same indigenous Africoid population. The Ta-seti, Egyptian for "land of the bow," referring to its fierce Nubian archers, lived in the Sudan and were a crossing site of early civilization in 3300 B.C.E. Their civilization extended far beyond the Nubian lands and, at times, encompassed peoples of diverse backgrounds and regions. At its zenith it stretched over a thousand miles along the Nile, from the South of contemporary Egypt to the middle of the Sudan. (See Figure 5.) Recent excavations have unearthed other large burial grounds and a written language at least four generations older than Ta-seti, yet only 100 miles away. It is the oldest known site of early civilization so far. Twelve Nubian kings ruled in the Middle East *before* the first Egyptian dynasty (Van Sertima & Rashidi, 1990)! We know this from the excavation of the royal Nubian tombs and the matrilineal lineage written in their script. Many religious ideas came from here, including the divine feminine image. Would this be the collective unconscious origin of archetypes and motifs of the Black Madonna that abound through Africa and Europe and the Near East? Or perhaps it is a deep unconscious memory of the mitochondrial DNA mother, the "she-who-has-no-name" (Bynum, 1993). She is certainly the origin of the Black Madonna and the Black virgin cults of Isis in later Egypt.

FIGURE 5. Ancient Nubia.

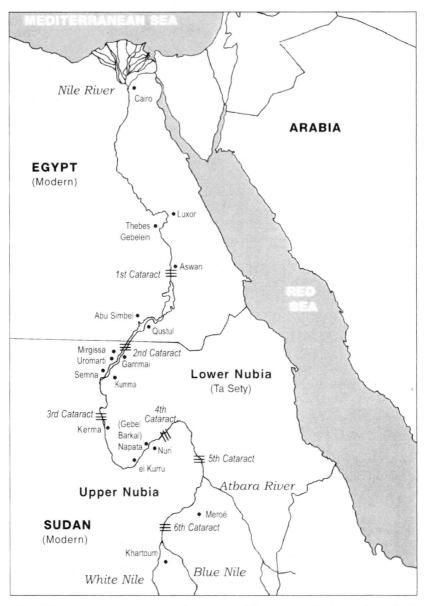

Ancient Nubia was the passageway culturally and ethnically between the interior kingdoms of Africa and those of pre-dynastic and later dynastic Egypt. At times ruler and ally, at other times vassal and enemy of Egypt, the two were the cultural dynamic that gave rise to the first human civilization. Nubia stretched from around the first cataract of the Nile near Aswan in present-day Egypt in the north, to below the sixth cataract near Khartoum in the Sudan in the south. Its southern boundary engulfed the white and blue Nile. At times Nubia was divided into upper and lower Nubia. (Copyright © 1999 Teachers College, Columbia University)

Ancient Nubia overlaps with present Sudan. *Sudan* is the Arabic word for "land of the Blacks." *Abyssinia* is the Arabic name for ancient Kush, and *Ethiopia* is the Greek word for the same peoples and land. *Alkebu-Lan* is the name these Ethiopians/Abyssinians and the later Moors gave to the continent of Africa itself (Ben-Jochannan, 1970). We know from the 1906 excavations of Riesner in Nubia, near where the Aswan Dam was to be, that since 6000 B.C.E. ancient Nubia was the site of a thriving culture and the crossroads from the African interior to the Mediterranean. The Nubians traded with Egypt and later Persia, Syria, Greece, and Rome, and they were often at war with the Egyptians. Although the Egyptians differentiated themselves from the European and Semetic "racial" phenotypes in their numerous paintings and reliefs, their differentiation from the Nubian was based on clothing, dress, subtle skin colorings, and religion. In other words, *the Egyptians and Nubians looked very much alike and saw themselves within the same racial type.* This observation seems to be overlooked by most Egyptologists. (See Figures 6 to 15.)

Excavations in Nubia reveal six major and distinct cultures. Khartoum was a Mesolithic site of the earliest recorded era, from perhaps 8000 to 6000 B.C.E. Some of the earliest ceramics and funerary objects in Africa and in the world were found here. They predate Egypt by an awesome 3,000 years! The earliest Egyptians, again, resembled these Nubians. When you look at it closely, without bias, the profile of the sphinx is really a Nubian visage with all that that implies. Nubia's geographical position made it an ideal area for the synthesis of Mediterranean currents and the older cultural flows from the African interior. Their art in these and later periods reflected both Egyptian motifs and African wildlife from farther south. The spread of influence here was from South to North. This culture existed from then until 3000 B.C.E., when the people mysteriously left, not to return until 2000 B.C.E.! It was from this soil that the flower of Egyptian civilization took root farther down the Nile. From this time on, back and forth, the two would war with and cross-fertilize each other in waves of influence. Waves of people, like consciousness itself, can unfold, then retreat and eclipse itself, only to reemerge ages later.

The second culture or unfoldment, called the "A Group Kings," emerged and thrived from 3100 to 2800 B.C.E. They were a wealthy group. There is some suggestion that the idea of royal kingship arose and became systematized here. This era saw extensive trade with the Near East, especially with Yemen and Egypt. In time, they too faded, only to be replaced by a new wave. The "C Group," as they are called, arose in northern Nubia like the "A Group Kings" and were established between 2000 and 1700 B.C.E. They lived peacefully with the Egyptians and excelled in ceramics. Another group, the so-called "Pan Grave People," also existed then and overlapped in time.

**FIGURE 6. Pharaoh Zoser of the
Third Dynasty.**

The Third Dynasty is noted for its massive new
architectural works. Here Zoser is depicted wearing the crown of the north. His "old kingdom" dynastic era was highlighted by the step pyramid and
tomb at Saqqara. Others followed in his early foot-
steps. (The Metropolitan Museum of Art, Rogers
Fund, 1911)

FIGURE 7. Man Hunting Geese and Ducks.

This wall painting of a charioteer hunting is from the tomb of a royal scribe, User-het, in Thebes,
the 18th Dynasty circa 1430 B.C.E. (The Metropolitan Museum of Art)

FIGURE 8. Shawabtis Figures of Pharaoh Taharka.

These figures were buried with the pharaoh to serve him in the new life after death (690–664 B.C.E.). There were over 1,000 such figures, each unique and with a written script on them. (Museum Expedition. Courtesy Museum of Fine Arts, Boston)

FIGURE 9. Pharaoh Taharka (Bronze Statuette).

At different times Nubia ruled Egypt and Egypt ruled Nubia. Taharka's army was defeated by the Assyrian invasion in 667 B.C.E. Afterwards he lost control of Egypt and returned to Nubia and ruled until his death. Here he is depicted wearing the classic necklace of three ram-headed pendants, the formal sign of Kushite authority. (Museum Expedition. Courtesy, Museum of Fine Arts, Boston)

FIGURE 10. Sandstone Statue of a Queen Between Two Goddesses.

Gebel Barkal, First Century B.C.E. (Museum Expedition. Courtesy, Museum of Fine Arts, Boston)

FIGURE 11. King Aspelta.

This is a colossal Nubian stone figure in black granite of King Aspelta, who ruled
(600–580 B.C.E.) along with his brother King Anlamani (620–600 B.C.E.). Gebel
Barkal, Sudan. (Museum Expedition. Courtesy, Museum of Fine Arts, Boston)

FIGURE 12. King Senkamenisken, Napatan Period.

(Museum Expedition. Courtesy, Museum of Fine Arts, Boston)

FIGURE 13. Statue of Sehetep-ib-senna-ib.

Statue of a high official from upper Egypt that was probably imported into Nubia as an export in goods. It belonged to a king at Kerma (Sudan) near the third cataract, circa 13th Dynasty, 1786–1668 B.C.E. (Museum Expedition. Courtesy, Museum of Fine Arts, Boston)

FIGURE 14. Pharaoh Mycerinus and Queen Kha-merer-nebty II.

This 4th Dynasty king ruled from 2548–2530 B.C.E. in the "old kingdom." This was unearthed in Giza. The Nubian and Egyptian dynamic was quite active during the old kingdom. (Harvard–Museum Expedition, Courtesy, Museum of Fine Arts, Boston)

FIGURE 15. Avenue of the Sphinxes and Nile Valley at Karnak.

In the distance is the Nile and the stone platform for the docking of ships. Built by Amenhotep III, it shows the epic scale of design. Under his rule, temples, tombs, forts, canals, the Fayum dam, and other monuments were constructed or completed. A beautiful literature developed. Trade with Asia and the African interior flourished. He ruled from 1850 to 1800 B.C.E. in the 12th Dynasty of the Middle Kingdom. (Neg./Transparency no. 254922. Courtesy Dept. of Library Services, American Museum of Natural History)

Their reign arched around 2200 to 1700 B.C.E. They excelled as bowmen and archers in southern Egypt and Nubia and were often hired as soldiers by the Egyptians. They are famous for their bows and beaded belts. Great stele or grave stones were used by them, a practice later expanded by the Kemetic Egyptians.

At Kerma, on the third cataract of the Nile, a culture arose between 2000 and 1500 B.C.E. that rivaled Egypt. From Kerma they ruled southern Egypt and northern Sudan. It was a major trade center and apparently a huge city culture. It is about this time that the Egyptians begin to refer to the Nubians as "Kushite" and the area as the kingdom of Kush. Its roots stretched from early in the third millennium B.C.E. to influences in culture, politics, and style more than four centuries after Christ (Bonnet, 1983). A vast cemetery complex evolved at Kerma for the royal internments, and there is evidence that the burials were sacrificial. It is also significant that they had extensive contact with the Black ruling dynasties of southern Arabia, particularly in what is today Yemen. Prior to 1500 B.C.E., although the details of its history are shadowy, Yemen was also an extensive trading center under the aristocratic monarchies that claimed descent from the mysterious dark Khatan and "Himyar the Dusky." From 1500 to 700 B.C.E. it was ruled by Mineans, from 700 to 75 B.C.E. by the famous Biblical Sabeans, and then from 75 B.C.E. to 525 C.E. by Himyarites (Chandler, 1985). Some of these elements later rode with the prophet Muhammad.

By 1500 B.C.E., Egypt had gained control of Kush. Abu Simbel is erected near the second cataract. Gebel Barkal, at the fourth cataract, became the southern boundary of Egypt's domination over Nubia, which lasted some 400 years until Egypt itself went into decline. When this occurred, then Napata arose as the dominant city-state in the region. The Nubians expanded again, cross-fertilizing with the Egyptians again to the North. These "Kushites" ruled Egypt from Thebes. This is the famous 25th Dynasty, which will be mentioned again in a subsequent context for its extensive contacts with areas beyond Africa. We see in the civilization an exuberant flowering in the arts and literature, and its 60-year rule in the 8th century B.C.E. cast a great shadow across the profile of Africa and early civilization. Although these "Kushites" honored Egyptian values and expanded beyond them, they still brought their dead back to Nubia for burial. Their smaller stone pyramids were in the Egyptian style. However they did not use mummification and they stopped the practice of human sacrifice in the royal internment although their funerary beds were the same. The 25th Dynasty saw the pharaoh Taharqa, who came to the rescue of the Jews on the battlefields of the Middle East, a piece of history mentioned in the Bible.

At Gebel Berkal another sacred center was constructed, probably to the god Amon. Indeed Napata, in two different sites, and other urban areas were the focus of religious practice, trade, and government. The two cultures obviously cross-fertilized each other to the point that we can really refer to them, including the six cultures of Nubia, as one extensive flowering of culture and civilization. The Nubians had two cobras on the royal crown; the Egyptians had one. There are many other parallels between them.

The Nubians left Egypt in 660 B.C.E. and reestablished themselves to the south, near the fifth and sixth cataracts, at Meroe, another great city-state and funeral city. Meroe flowered between 270 B.C.E. and 370 C.E. Meroe, as we shall mention in other contexts, was really the seat of the empire south of Khartoum. They, too, built pyramids and traded with the African interior and the Mediterranean states of Greece, Rome, Syria, Persia, and even distant India. Actually there are more pyramids in this region than there are in Egypt. They revived the art of mummification and coffin burials. Their Meroirtic script consisted of 24 symbols, and as of this date, it has yet to be deciphered. We can only imagine what present and future excavations will reveal that now lies sleeping beneath the sands.

From this early civilization and the peoples of the Nile Valley, civilization it seems climbed and moved eastward. Radiocarbon (carbon-14) methods date early peoples, often called Badarians, around the Fayum Lake settlements in the vicinity of 6400 B.C.E. (Libby, 1955). Radiocarbon dating places Ta-seti at 3300 B.C.E., Egypt at 3100 B.C.E., and Mesopotamia at 2800 B.C.E. along the Tigris and Euphrates Rivers. Many of the kings and royal rulers of Sumer and Elam in Mesopotamia were Black from what we have unearthed in the royal tombs and reliefs (Van Sertima & Rashidi, 1990). The Dravidians of south India and other dark-skinned peoples of Southeast Asia are direct lineages of this earliest of migration of peoples and civilization. The "proto" blacks of H. G. Wells and the pan-Dravidians of Will Durant are of the same stock. The skulls found in their cities of Harappa and Mohenjo-Daro in southern India are the same as those found in Nubia from 4000 B.C.E. We also see from the writings of scholars (Fairservis, 1962; Jackson, 1970; C. Williams, 1987) that early Nubian civilization became, in many ways, the foundation of later Egyptian and other civilizations. The civilization of the southeast Indians, the Dravidians, also was highly evolved and had spread outward at least 1,000 years before the Aryan invasions of the North that destroyed these cities and urban cultures. This civilization, which had contact with the Egypto-Nubian parent civilization, arose in southern India and may have come from the small, dark-skinned peoples we have spoken of before, the same branch that migrated eventually over the Bering Strait and perhaps across the low Ice Age oceans to first colonize the Americas (Van Sertima & Rashidi, 1990).

Religious Transcendence and the Rise of Civilization

A word in passing about great religions and the concomitant rise of civilization. Like the winds, the oceans, electromagnetism, and gravity, spirit is discovered by man, not created. The first truly new and radically transcendent notion to arise in human consciousness since the burial of the dead and the mysteries of the priesthood was the notion of resurrection and reincarnation. These ideas were formulated long before the dynastic era of early Egypt and no doubt were in germination for millennia among the people of the great lake and upper Nile, where crops were first cultivated. Nowhere is this better observed than by the most well-known English translator of the *Egyptian Book of the Dead*, or Papyrus of Ani, E. A. Wallis Budge, the late Keeper of the Egyptian and Assyrian Antiquities in the British Museum:

> All the essential texts comprised in the *Book of the Dead* are in one form or another, far older than the period of Menes, the first historical King of Egypt. Certain sections, indeed, appear to belong to the Predynastic Period . . . older than three thousand years before Christ. We are in any case justified in estimating the earliest form of the work to be contemporaneous with the foundation of the civilization which we call Egyptian in the valley of the Nile. (Budge, 1960, pp. 6–7)

Furthermore, Budge goes on to say that

> The great change which took place in the religious views of the Egyptians a little before the beginning of dynastic history was, I believe, due entirely to the rise and spread of the cult of Osiris throughout Egypt. Whether it was introduced into Egypt by a people coming from the shores of the Mediterranean, or by a Libyan tribe, or by "proto-Semites" from the east or southeast, or whether it was of purely native growth, need not concern us here. What is all-important to note is that the teachers of the cult of Osiris preached that the dead body of a man was a sacred thing, and that is was not to be devoured by men or beasts, or burnt or mutilated. . . . The Osiris taught that from it would spring the translucent, transparent, immaterial, refulgent, and glorious envelope in which the Spirit-soul of the deceased would take up its abode with all his mental and spiritual attributes. (1960, p. 5)

However, according to Budge, despite the fact that the religious texts which dealt with the dead and their new life as spirit in the realm beyond material embodiment existed at least from "4000 B.C.E. to the early centuries of the Christian era," an era that saw its dawn long before the appearance of these so-called "proto-Semites," Indo-European Greeks, obscure Libyans, or unnamed Mediterraneans (i.e., "White people"), Budge assumes that these mysterious non-Africans must have created this new doctrine because the indigenous Africans could not have compiled the text. Why? Simply because "the work presupposes the existence of ideas which the aborigines did not possess" (p. 4). In reference to other indigenous ideas such as the "neters," which we will return to later, Budge suggests that "such views about the meaning of *neter* may well have been held by the cultured and philosophical Greek, but their abstract character puts them out of the range of the mind of the native Egyptian, which was incapable naturally of formulating ideas of this kind" (1960, p. 99).

The earliest spiritual intuitions of eternal life in some psychoenergetic permutation lived in the heart of this religion that inspired human civilization and over the eons went through many transformations from its seed idea brought down the Nile. The presence of "advanced and abstract" intellectual and spiritual ideas in the core of this African creation was both an annoyance and perceived anomaly to most European scholars of the era. Again Budge:

> The essential beliefs of the Egyptian religion remained unchanged from the earliest dynasties down to the period when the Egyptians embraced Christianity, after the preaching of St. Mark the Evangelist in Alexandria, A.D. 69, so firmly had the early beliefs taken possession of the Egyptian mind. And the Christians in Egypt, or Copts as they are commonly called, the racial descendants of the ancient Egyptians, seem never to have succeeded in divesting themselves of the superstitious and weird mythological conceptions which they inherited from their heathen ancestors. (1960, p. 52)

As we shall see when we turn to the rise, spread, and implications of the Osirian saga, these "heathen" beliefs and formulations had a profound effect on the actual development of Christianity, Islam, and Judaism. They are echoed in certain doctrines of the Bardo Throtol, or *Tibetan Book of the Dead*, compiled millennia later but taken by Eurocentric scholars to be an "advanced" spiritual text and system of related disciplines.

We point this out here not to detract from a great scholar but to demonstrate how subtly and deeply racist notions are woven into the texture of science. It seems from the work of Budge and many other early Egyptologists that even back then Africans labored under the bell-shaped curve! Hopefully, in this book we can try to look at the process in a different way.

Embryogenesis and the Unfoldment of Civilization

The situation from ancient Nubia, then Kemetic Egypt, Dravidian India, and other places now begins to appear more and more like a series of non-linear, seemingly unpredictable occurrences, but one that is also unfolding some deeper order and organization among the human tribes. From the rich, dark, creative synthesis of life currents in Nubia, from the branchings and bifurcating tribes, a certain cross-fertilization arises. Just as an embryo's dark neural crest flows along a line in an intelligent fashion, unfolding and differentiating into more discrete, articulate organs and functions, cultural embryogenesis works along a rich dark line, sensitive to light and unfolding more subtle realms of order along a kind of neural crest or pathway—the same pathway and routes the earlier hominids took on their Kiaspora out of

Africa. It is a creative synthesis that keeps looping back upon itself with diversity and a form of nonlinear creative intelligence. This is possible because on some intimate level—psychically, genetically, and perhaps even spiritually—it is still one organism through all its branchings and cross-fertilizations. The separate wave and wavefront of every human life is intimately implicated in the wavefront and inner landscape of each other human life. This is more than a metaphor, and its genetic, morphological, embryological, and archeological cross-currenting opens all of us, on some level, to the same creative ocean of shared consciousness.

The mitochondrial DNA mother of humanity reflected this same creative synthesis in her gene pool as did this area of early civilization. Novel situations that confronted these diversifications, such as the drying of the great Sahara, gave rise to a creative synthesis that matured into the first civilization known to us. Perhaps a form of "morphic resonance," or a deeper evolutionary order in matter and human organizations, unfolded here in early civilization itself and flowed in the four directions. These processes would repeat themselves many times over, as we shall see, giving rise to more and more similarities and interconnections.

In addition to this, we see great similarities in religion and in other early practices between the peoples of the African east coast and those of southeast India. This is no surprise, since many trade routes were in effect at this time, which would help to communicate both religious ideas and technology of various kinds.

It is significant that the earliest calendars were developed in this area. The day was divided into 24 hours beginning at midnight, and had 12 30-day months and five festival days; instead of 365¼ days a year with a leap day every four years, these early calendars had a leap year every 1,460 years. We also know that Africans were the first to smelt iron (Van Sertima & Rashidi, 1990). We even have evidence of a Kemetic Egyptian sphinx found in southeast Russia dating from the earliest periods of Egypt (Diop, 1974).

THE EMERGENCE OF KEMETIC EGYPT AND ITS CONTACT WITH OTHER PEOPLES: ASIA, MESOPOTAMIA, "OLDE EUROPE," AND WEST AFRICA

The first sustained civilization we know of for sure is the Egypto-Nubian civilization of the Nile Valley. This is why it is our reference point, our orienting position. It is the classical civilization of Africa and one of the parents of Greco-Roman antiquity. The earliest Egyptians, the dark-skinned migrating inhabitants of the upper Nile Valley, called themselves "Kemits," from the "Land of the Blacks." It does not translate as "Black Land" (Diop,

1974; Williams, 1987). Today's archeologists, historians, and researchers of early civilization pretty much agree—despite the discomfort it causes to the older cultural historians—that Egyptian civilization was founded by the indigenous population of Black Africans moving up from the south and migrating from the drying west (Davidson, 1969; Fairservis, 1962; Jackson, 1970; Williams, 1987). (See Figures 1–7.) The modern scholars who have seen "mixed" racial origins of the early Egyptians say so because the modern idea of race was unknown at that time (Bard, 1992). They seem unwilling to acknowledge that people who arose in the Sudan and sub-Saharan Africa, with dark skin, full lips, wooly hair, and related features as in the visage of the sphinx, would be seen today as something other than African in lineage. No, early and dynamic middle Egypt was an indigenous African creation (Van Sertima, 1993). There were and are ethnic differentiations within the indigenous populations, but clearly the overwhelming preponderance of the population was Africoid. *This is being repeated here not out of the "uplift school" but in the service of breaking through repression!* Our repressions and fears of Africa go deep.

Many different words that are still in use today are drawn from the word "Kemetic." The phrase "al-Kemit" refers to the science and religion of the earliest Kemetic Egyptians before they were transformed later by the Arabs who, in their jihads, attempted to sweep it out of existence when they came through northern Africa. This later became the word "alchemy." This ancient religion was suppressed by the Arabian migration. However, it spread through other areas of Africa, particularly through the interior and the west coast of Africa. Some feel that the interior of Africa gave rise to Egypt and Nubia, not vice versa. This is certainly possible in terms of peoples. However, there simply is no real evidence to suggest that the germ of civilization began there. They no doubt cross-fertilized each other innumerable times and the last truth was buried long ago in the lost and forgotten cities of Africa (Davidson, 1959). It is the ancient indigenous hermetic tradition of the science of transformation which we will explore in future chapters. This hermetic tradition is actually a distortion of the original ancient sun worship and light theology of the indigenous peoples of this area. These are the people who discovered the earliest science and also the functioning of the still-mysterious processes of the subtle nervous system known as Kundalini.

India and West Africa

From Kemetic Egypt and Nubia, the warm dark thread of human civilization moved eastward and north, unfolding like organs from the embryonic neural crest. It also moved south and west. Great familial systems were involved in this spreading. To the East in India it stimulated and cross-fertilized with the civilization of the Dravidians, with the earliest great cities being Mohenjo-Daro and Harappa. Actually the Harappan episode came first, with its greatest flowering between 3000 and 2500 B.C.E. Its earliest towns and villages reach back to 7000 and 6000 B.C.E. When the Indo-Aryans descended into the Indus Valley, the Harappan episode had already been absorbed by other Black populations, who in time became known to us as the Dravidians. The Aryan text of the Rig-Veda tells us of the horrific war that occurred when they encountered the dark Dravidians. The Harappan-Dravidians were described as "dark and ill favored, bull-lipped, snub nosed worshipers of the phallus . . . they are rich in cattle and dwell in fortified places called Pur" (Basham, 1959, p. 32). When they arrived, the Aryans found peoples already practicing a religion that went back millennia, which today is called Jainism. Jainism's lineage included Mahavira, Parsava, and the whole religious Tirthankara line, all rooted in a pre-Aryan antiquity (Zimmer, 1969).

In Harappan artwork we see, as Basham (1959, p. 22) and others point out, numerous images of "nude men with coiled hair; their posture, rigidly upright, with the legs slightly apart, and with the arms held parallel to the sides of the body but not touching it." This interestingly enough is the origin of the first references we have to the science of Yoga. In southern India, most scholars now believe that small Australoid peoples had moved back up into India from Australia. And later larger African Blacks entered southern India from Africa (Van Sertima & Rashidi, 1990). The gradual merging of these peoples created first the Harappan and then the Dravidian civilization and their cities.

The cities themselves—Mohenjo-Daro, Harappa, Chanhu-Daro, Quetta, Lothal, and Kalibangan—were marvels of sophisticated city planning. Many of these unearthed city streets were set in a modern grid-like pattern with 30-foot wide streets, two- and three-story buildings, and courtyards with running water and trash shoots. There were sophisticated sluice gates for dockyard shipping. They had a highly evolved written script. When the Aryans came down out of the snowy Caucasian steppes and perhaps over a 200-year period destroyed this civilization, they established the caste system and absorbed the Yogic religion of the indigenous population. The indigenous population was reduced to the lowest caste. Mass graves show that there were bloody, savage battles for racial and cultural dominance in the Indus Valley. The prize was the mastery of a whole subcontinent, cultivated lands, and a mysterious psychoreligious technology of the most sophisticated kind that elevated the mind to the regions of a sublime consciousness through discipline and study. The great Vedas are the Aryan translations of that ancient religion, a religion that had disciples in the sacred "houses of life" in Egypt, over a continent away, who practiced a similar psychospiritual

technology. Here again we seem to be looking at nonlinear but interconnected processes of influence. The internal religious and philosophical structures show a certain self-similarity and may be a reflection of what has
come to be thought of as "infinite nesting."

From Kemetic Egypt and Nubia, human civilizations went westward to
the West African societies in levels of successive migrations. Many peoples
of West African extraction have origin myths and chronologies for thousands
of years that trace their lineage to ancient Egypt and Nubia, for example,
the Dogon of Mali, the Fon of Dahomey, the Bambara of eastern Guinea,
the Yoruba of Nigeria, and peoples of other areas of the coast. This led even
further in later years, along with indigenous currents, to the rise of the state
and to the civilizations of West Africa, whose influence in consciousness
was then in a perverted sort of way carried on by the slave trade to the
Americas. However, interestingly enough, prior to the slave trade migration
to the Western Hemisphere, there is ample evidence of the presence and
influence of Africans in the New World, especially the early Olmec culture
and civilization of Mexico (Van Sertima, 1976). The presence in the Americas of African people was later augmented radically by the slave trade. The
African presence in the New World came in three major waves. The earliest
wave was as seafarers, explorers, and traders from ancient Egypt, probably
in the 25th Dynasty. The second wave was during the medieval period of
West Africa seafarers, and the third wave as indentured servants and slaves
and to a minor extent as freedmen with the conquistadors of Spain and
Portugal.

Greeks and Celts

It is also significant that out of Kemetic Egypt the evolving embryo of
civilization moved toward Europe by way of the "Greek miracle." This transformation of the indigenous Kemetic science and religion of Egypt into the
civilization of Europe was done by way of the adventurous and expansive
mind of the Greeks. It is a modern historical error to assume that the Greeks
were the exclusive originators of Western civilization. This is manifestally
not true (Bernal, 1987; Davidson, 1969; Diop, 1974; Fairservis, 1962; Jackson, 1970; Williams, 1987). What we see is a magnificent transformation by
the Greeks of certain aspects of an older Egyptian civilization, a civilization
dating back to 5000 B.C.E. The Greeks invaded Egypt in two successive waves,
and learned greatly. They in turn, as part of the shared body, differentiated
and contributed new and striking trends. The Greek alphabet was derived
from the Phoenicians and their mathematics and astronomy from the Egyptians. They then advanced on these in a rich cross-fertilization which is the
process of civilization's interconnected unfoldment. Greek civilization, it

seems, given a "sensitive dependence on initial conditions" with Kemetic influence, began to expand, replicating a certain variation of the self-similarity of systems or "infinite nesting," which we see so often with similar systems of order. We will be discussing the contribution and the observation of the Greeks in later chapters.

By 1000 B.C.E. the civilized world in the West was focused in Africa. The year 1000 B.C.E. saw Europe shrouded in either quiet agricultural cultures or plunged into barbarism. Rome was a future dream; England an undeveloped land; and early shoots of the Ostrogoths and Visigoths roamed through the Germanic lands. The Celts and the Druids of England did not arrive on the scene until approximately 500 to 700 C.E. The Celts, who by the way did so much to bring written records, or Ogam, to Britain and Ireland, and yes, to the shores of New England before Columbus, were for a while inhabitants of North Africa and the Iberian peninsula and were a great seafaring people (Fell, 1989). Their monuments are dated here from at least 500 C.E., as Christian missionaries. However, there are scattered references to an earlier year, perhaps 500 B.C.E., from the Celtic names found on certain temple ruins in New England. We shall see later in Chapter 7 how these same Celts will meet in the Caribbean centuries later with slaves and captured warriors of the West African Diaspora and leave their mark on the syncretic fusion of earth religions and psychology that later became known as Voudoun.

China

During the first millennium B.C.E., and even before, there were emergent and then submergent civilizations in the Middle East, China, and India, several of which were prior to the Aryans. An African presence is found in these early centers. Black Mongolian horsemen can be discerned in some of the sculptures and reliefs of the East. Some skeletal remains appear Africoid. While the African type has mostly faded away in China, it is significant to note that in the Chinese legends of divine dynasties the first king of China, Fuhsi (or Fu-Hsi/Fu-hi), was described as Black with woolly hair. He and his family are believed to have ruled from 2953 to 2838 B.C.E. (Rogers, 1967). An entire dynasty, the Shang dynasty, was described as ruled by Blacks from 1766 to 1100 B.C.E. The Chou, who conquered them, described them as having "Black skin," and the Moso, with whom the Shang fought, described them as "Black men" (Van Sertima & Rashidi, 1990).

One of the roots of this Africoid extension into China is associated with the group of people and language family known as the Bak families. The language and people of the Bak immigrated into China around 2282 B.C.E. to the banks of the Loh River in Shensi. Their leader was the legendary Yu Nai Hwang-Ti, a primary figure in Taoist philosophy. However, he was really a leader and represents a family of peoples. These peoples were racially and ethnically descended from the Black populations of the Elamites and Akkadians of Mesopotamia. This is based on archeological and philological data and has been quietly known for over a century (Lacouperie, 1892). What is rather interesting is that these elements of Meso-Sumerian west Asian civilization who brought a well-defined sociopolitical structure, writing, philosophy, and economic processes to China also brought a system of moral and ethical and spiritual philosophy that is at the root of diverse mystical systems.

By 2000 B.C.E. the Xia dynasty had texts in which aspects of the *I Ching*, or *Book of Changes*, could be found! Elements of the pre-cuneiform writing style of the Meso-Sumerians of Mesopotamia can be discerned. The *I Ching* shows a striking similarity to certain fragments of texts from the library of Ashurbanipal, where it is identified with the ancient king of Sippar in Mesopotamia (Chandler, 1995a). This Text of the antediluvian king Enmeduranki, or so-called Tablet of Destiny, was found around the present-day area of Iraq and is believed by many to be the root of or even identical to the great *I Ching*. The original text of the Tablet of Destiny is thought to have been composed in 2800 B.C.E. When we discuss the African mystical and religious systems, we will see how this *I Ching* with its binary system of 64 permutations or hexegrams is intimately associated with the system of the Mesopotamian Essene sects and the West African system of Ifa. Needless to say, the *I Ching* has profoundly influenced Chinese thought and civilization. But this influence is also echoed in the other spiritual traditions of China.

If one looks at the tight curly hair and many of the facial features of the early Buddha, they are quite Africoid, as are the figures and early representatives of the south Indian Krishna and Mahaviera of the Jains. Indeed, the martial arts first appear in China around 1500 B.C.E. but do not become well known until they are taught to the Shaolin monks in southern China by the monk Bodhidharma, a.k.a. Talmo, an Indian of Dravidian ancestry. He, like Tieguai, was a great teacher. (See Figure 16.) Talmo was the founder and first patriarch of Ch'an (Zen) Buddhism, who introduced the foundations of the martial arts to the Shaolin monks of southern China's Songshan province. Born in 440 C.E. in the southern Indian kingdom of Pallava, he lived in one of the oldest cities, Kanchi. His integration of martial techniques, breathing exercises, and philosophy of "Chi energy" helped establish Shaolin ch'üan fa, or "temple boxing." These and innumerable other facts and artifacts document a distinct African presence in ancient Asia that had a profound influence on the development of that civilization (Van Sertima & Rashidi, 1990). It is not that China was a Black civilization, not at all. Only that it

FIGURE 16. Tieguai, One of the Nine Immortals of Taoism.

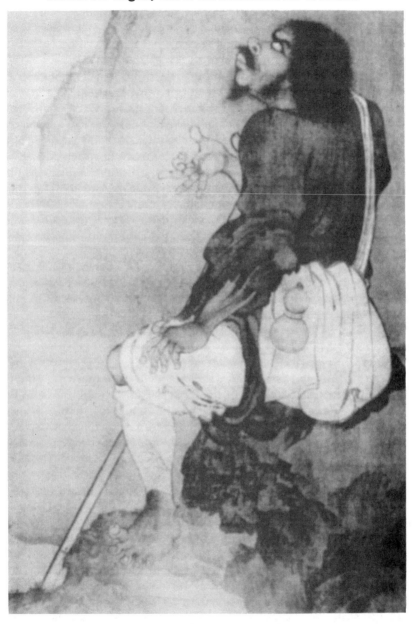

Tieguai was an accomplished martial artist. Known as the "Iron-Staff Immortal," he lived during China's "Golden Age." Hand-printed on silk, early Yuan Dynasty, 13th century C.E. (Photo by Wayne B. Chandler, permission of Editor Runoko Rashidi, *African Presence in Early Asia*, Transaction Publishers, 1995)

had elements of an African presence at the foundation, genetic and psychic, just as did the civilizations of Mesopotamia.

Mesopotamia

Mesopotamia had mixed elements of African, Asian, and European in it from the earliest times. Unlike Egypt, it was never federated and so its powerful city-states rose and fell over the millennia while Egypt had an unbroken civilization from the time of the Nubians and the later First Dynasty of Menes. However, as mentioned earlier, 12 Nubian kings ruled in the Middle East *prior* to the Egyptian First Dynasty. In ancient Sumer, excavation has unearthed the dynasty of those who called themselves "the Black-heads." The anthropologist Dieulatoy, excavating in Elam in Mesopotamia, found African skulls, bones, and actual terracotta sculpture decorating the royal tombs of the rulers. At the start of this royal line was King Gudea, governor of Sumer and clearly an African from the southern migrations of earlier times.

For most of its history Sumer was largely composed of independent and powerful city-states. From time to time, they would indeed integrate into kingdoms led by one powerful ruler or another. In the pivotal third millennium B.C.E. Sumer flourished and set the tone for all the other city-states to follow. Sumer's greatest and most famous city-state was Ur and its greatest dynasty was the third. The third dynasty reigned from 2112–2015 B.C.E. and elevated Ur to the status of a great empire ruled by five successive kings. It was during this time that Gudea rose from a governor to a king. He subjugated ancient Susa and much of the Biblical Elam. It was this period that saw the rise of the great ziggurats, the pyramids of Mesopotamia. However, the end came with increasing Semitic and Indo-Aryan nomads who had domesticated the horse early on in their culture. At first they were vassels of Sumer until they eventually grew strong enough to wage war on her. By 1700 B.C.E. the Sumerian Black-heads were in steep decline and after a thousand years of creating the foundation of Mesopotamian civilization, they passed into the dust of history.

Elam, another Black culture whose people were the Biblical Elamites, was located in the present-day area of Iran. They were goddess worshipers and a short, brown, robust people of a Negritic race whose ethnic stock pervaded much of this region of Asia at the time. While contemporaneous with Sumer for centuries, Elam outlasted Sumer and left branches of itself through the Bak peoples who spread into China. But its days would also come to violent end. By the dawn of the seventh century B.C.E., the wars with the Assyrians began. They had gobbled up the Sumerian Black-heads and turned their attention to the Elamites. From their capital of Nineveh, the Assyrians spread out in legions of skilled soldiers eviscerating whole towns and populations. In the reign of Ashurbanipal (669–626 B.C.E.), their power was supreme. Between 667 and 663 B.C.E. they twice invaded Egypt. The great temples and libraries at Thebes were burned and looted. Assyrian armies sent panic through the Phoenicians at Tyre and soon were also at war with the Elamites. With his forces now spread thin, Ashurbanipal had to give up Egypt in 655 B.C.E. in order to subdue the Elamites. By 639 B.C.E. the Elamite conquest was secure and they became a minor people in the area.

In what is today far eastern Iran, western Pakistan, and southern Baluchistan there was a land known as Gedrosia, which means "the country of the dark folk." They had contact with another group of Blacks in the general area who had arrived much earlier. These were the Colchians, who described themselves as a colony of Egyptians who had come there with the army of Sesostris III in the nineteenth century B.C.E. Other data suggest the army of Sesostris I or Ramses III. In any event, the Colchians attested to their Kemetic Egyptian lineage openly, and Herodotus described them as "black-skinned with woolly hair." In either case, Africoid elements continued to exert an influence in the affairs of Mesopotamia during this age. This of course includes the land to the south known as Arabia.

The Arabian Peninsula

Historically, there is a dynamic African presence in the Arabian peninsula from the earliest days. The first racial type in Arabia is recorded by cave drawings and paintings which are presently housed in the Riyadh Museum in Saudi Arabia. They are clearly the Africoid type that inhabited the area in Neolithic times (Diop, 1991). These people intermixed with Caucasoid types and produced the Semitic type, which became the stable dominant type at around 1000 B.C.E. This dominance was in the northern areas, however, and not in the southern regions until relatively recently in historical terms. The southern tip of the peninsula is also where most of the germs of Arabian civilization were cultivated.

Indeed, Yemen, Oman, and Hadramant were teeming with African civilizations long before 1500 B.C.E. This area was a natural gateway to the Far East trade routes and as such became a pivotal area for commerce and the exchange of ideas. Gold, frankincense, and myrrh, which were used in medicines, embalming, and other practices, were the blood of the trade routes from the remotest of times. This area was the *Arabia felix*, or "happy Arabia," of Roman literature. Prior to 1500 B.C.E. it was ruled by the legendary Black Adites, whence comes the name of the Gulf of Aden. By 1500 B.C.E. the Black Mineans took over and increased commerce with the Black populations of southern India and the larger islands of Southeast Asia, Indonesia, and East Africa. Ship building and maritime traffic made the area wealthy.

By 700 B.C.E., however, a new age was coming that saw the rise of new powers. The Black Sabeans reached out from Ethiopia and conquered the Adites and soon established a line of powerful queens who ruled with an iron fist. The Biblical queen of Sheba, known as Makeda to the Ethiopians and as Bilquis in the Koran, was only the most famous in a long line of queens. Her confluence with King Solomon of Israel led to the lineage from Melelik down to the modern reign of Haile Selassie of Ethiopia, "the conquering Lion of Judea." But this was a turbulent era, for by 75 B.C.E., after nearly six centuries of rule, the Sabeans themselves were overcome by another African empire, the Himyarites. The Himyarites ruled over 300 years down into Roman times. Even the Roman legions under the command of Aelius Gallus were unable to subdue them in 24 B.C.E. Eventually, they too entered the dust of history under the heels of the Christian Abyssinians in 525 C.E.; before they left they created the initial script of Arabia, the Himyaritic script.

During this period of intense activity in the southern regions of the peninsula, the Arabic and Semitic peoples lived primarily in the more northern and arid regions. From time to time they intermarried with the darker more Africoid elements of the southern populations and were often involved in raids on the caravans. Over time their numbers and influence grew greater. By the time of the prophet there was considerable political as well as spiritual unrest. The Black element of the population had decreased and the Semitic and mixed elements swelled. Caravan raids, commerce, and business practices began producing wealthy clans, which eventually elevated the tribe of Koreysh to a powerful position that was to last for several generations. From this prosperous line came the light of the prophet Muhammad, whose family lineage was infused with many dynamic elements from the Blacks, the Semites, and the region's deep psychospiritual forces. The vision of the prophet galvanized both the political and religious elements of the southern region, and after his death the face of North Africa, southern Europe, Mesopotamia, and parts of Asia was changed forever.

Blacks were an integral part of the military and religious movement of the prophet. Bilail, a Black, was a close aid of the prophet and "the third pillar of the faith." Over time there were three caliphs who were Black. When the Islamic jihads, or holy wars, swept across Egypt, they suppressed the older Kemetic faiths and carried the message by passion and sword to Morocco, Mauritania, and Spain by way of the Moors, a predominately Africoid population. The Moors ruled Spain and Portugal for 700 years until the days just before the voyages of Columbus. During their reign they established more than sixteen universities, as compared to

Europe's two. The Islamic empire, of which the Moors were its Western expression, stretched from Spain to India. They brought in a new mathematical language—the zero from India—new foods, arts, sciences, and agriculture and in the process laid the foundations of the Renaissance, or the second rise of Europe.

When they were expelled in 1492, they left behind a new civilization. Also, the Jews were no longer protected by the Moors of Islam and were quickly persecuted, killed, or driven out of Spain. Arabic, the language of science and medicine for 700 years, had been banned behind the Christian curtain. Public baths were outlawed. Soon large numbers of slaves began to be sucked out of the northwest and coastal regions of West Africa and sent to the New World. World history arched in a new direction. One can only speculate on the history of the world if the Moors had not been turned back at a little battle in the small west-central French town of Tours in 732 C.E. by Charles Martel and the army of the Franks. In essence, civilization did not move from north to south, but from south to north.

The Far East

Further east than the Arabian/Yemen states or the older Mesopotamian city-states, and even further south than the Dravidians and Indo-Aryans of India, Africoid elements can be seen in the early populations. For untold eons the Melanesian peoples have inhabited the islands and land masses of Southeast Asia. Over the centuries, while they were the primary group, they interbred with other peoples, giving rise to many states and genotypical variations. In early Southeast Asia, Angkor (802–1431) arose and earlier than that the legendary Funanese, whom the Chinese chroniclers described as "ugly and black . . . their hair is curly." (See Figures 17, 18, and 19.) The Funanese, in fact, have a close connection to the Khmer peoples in phenotype. These peoples of an earlier African migration had been there for millennia of course. Their "contact" with civilization, while in sporadic touch with ancient Egypt, came mostly from southern Dravidian India and to some extent China. The Indo-Aryans never penetrated that far.

Over the centuries, several powerful kingdoms arose from these peoples, kingdoms that warred with China, especially the upper and lower kingdoms of Chenla. Huge unearthed figures and heads in stone plus thousands of figurines with distinctive Africoid features testify to their presence all the way down to present-day Vietnam, Campuchea (Champa), Malaya, and Sumatra. Over time, the Sino or Chinese-Asiatic phenotype became more prominent through interbreeding, but not before numerous kingdoms and empires rose and fell, weaving a strong latticework of the Africoid presence into the foundational elements of the population (Rashidi, 1985).

FIGURE 17. Stone Figure of Lord Shiva.

Note Afro-Asiatic features of this depiction of Lord Shiva, the Lord of Yoga. From Vietnam (Champa). (Photo by Wayne B. Chandler, permission of Editor Runoko Rashidi)

FIGURE 18. Africoid Figure, Early Vietnam.

Note Afro–Asiatic features. (Photo by Wayne B. Chandler, permission of Editor Runoko Rashidi)

FIGURE 19. Colossal Africoid Figure, Southeast Asia.

(Photo by Wayne B. Chandler, permission of Editor Runoko Rashidi)

By 1000 B.C.E. the Africoid type in the Far East was almost completely assimilated into the emergent Sino-Asiatic genotype. Yet even in legend, folklore, and written history its presence was known. In distant Japan anthropologists noted that "the earliest population of Japan was in the main a blend of Proto-Australoid and Proto-Negroid types and thus similar in the ancient underlying stratum of the population, southward along the whole coast and throughout Indo-China and beyond to India itself" (Dixon, 1923). This influence extended into the period of the first shoguns in the early Heian royal court (794–1185 C.E.). The anthropologist and historian Alexander Francis Chamberlain noted that "when in far-off Japan the ancestors of the modern Japanese were making their way northward against the Ainu, the aborigines of that country, the leader of their armies was Sakanouye Tamuramaro, a famous general and a Negro" (1911, pp. 484–485). The Sakanouye family, reportedly an immigrant family line from Korea to Japan, were well known for archery, martial leadership, scholarship, and the arts from the 7th to 14th centuries C.E. Sakanouye no Tamuramaro, whose career began in the Nara period (710–794 C.E.), was to become the archetype of the noble warrior, or samurai, which flowered in the Japanese imagination and culture for centuries. James Murdoch in *A History of Japan* (1925) goes on to say that Tamuramaro "was not only the first to bear the title of sei-i-tai-Shogun, but he was also the first of the warrior statesmen of Japan." The scholar Jagi Atsura's encyclopedia of Japan (1983) indicates that this first in the line of great shoguns "was buried at the village of Kurisu, near Kyoto, and it is believed that it is his tomb which is known under the name of Shogun-Zuka. Tamuramaro is the founder of the famous temple Kiyomizu-dera. He is the ancestor of the Tamura daimyo of Mutsu." He seems to be the source of the old Japanese proverb "For a samurai to be brave he must have a bit of Black blood." Here again, the subtle theme of the African presence is deeply rooted in a nation's unconscious, largely outside of their awareness yet exhibiting an influence that is strong and enduring.

In Mesopotamia and China, and also southern India and Southeast Asia, African-ruled dynasties held sway over these civilizations at different times for extended periods (Van Sertima & Rashidi, 1990). However, the Kemetic civilization of the Nubian Egyptian is the earliest, longest, and most sustained civilization known to humankind. It was the prototype for the others. Again, it is not that Chinese, Mesoamerican, Mesopotamian, or European civilization is African civilization. That is absurd. However, the evidence suggests that there are profound elements of African influence in them, for example, through the Akkado-Sumerians who entered ancient China at the Loh River in Shensi and by way of Egyptian lineage that we find in early Greece. Egypto-Nubian civilization was also an indigenous African civilization. No one here argues that China, Meso-America, or England were exclusively founded by

Blacks. Yet how often in the study of high African civilizations is there the idea that is was "created" by non-African peoples simply because they were present in small numbers! Such is the case in "Olde Europe."

"Olde Europe"

In the England of the Megalithic period we see the impact of an African-Kemetic influence in the presence of the Egyptian-Phoenician contact. The Phoenician and Sidonian navigators of the Bronze Age are contemporaneous with the 18th Dynasty of Egypt. We know this because tin was mined and taken from the Sorliguan Islands by the Phoenicians and sold to the Egyptians. By this time, the Black type had largely died out in European civilization, although there are numerous reports of Africoid groups and individuals among the populations of Britain, Greenland, Scotland, Ireland (Celt origin), and the Iberian peninsula. The Roman Pliny reports fighting African troops in England, as did the Roman general and emperor Theodosius in Europe (?346–395 C.E.), who described the "nimble blackamores" as looking as dark as the Ethiopians.

This doesn't mean these blackamores created or sustained or were the central element of British civilization. Yet whenever the evidence shows even one drop of European blood in the veins of the African Egyptians of ancient times, the academic question immediately focuses on whether the Egyptians were "really African Negroids" or not! The same applies to the Chinese Shang dynasty when African elements are found. No, they were not the central element, but they were present, and perhaps at crucial times. Obviously Chinese civilization is not an African creation. However, in the last two centuries society has tried endlessly to de-Africanize Egypt and any place in Africa where civilization has flowered. We must set the record straight for the racially painful present and hopefully better, more peaceful future. This is not impossible (Van Sertima, 1991).

Marija Gimbutas (1982, 1992) has shown ample evidence of an earlier, peaceful European culture from approximately 7000 to 3500 B.C.E., which is known to have emerged from the Upper Paleolithic and Mesolithic periods. As an emergent Neolithic culture, it was characterized by agriculture, a sedentary life, and the cult of the earth mother goddess of fertility—a matrilineal, peaceful, egalitarian society similar to those of Africa. The Neolithic period in Europe arose around 6000 B.C.E., in the Middle East a little before 8000 B.C.E., and in Africa by the Nile and later by Fayum Lake around 18,300 to 17,000 B.C.E. (Wendorf & Schild, 1981). This culture of "Olde Europe" lasted approximately 3,000 years and in many ways gave birth to the cultures of central and southeast Europe from the Balkans along the Danube to other fertile valley areas.

This gentle and cooperative culture was violently overthrown and absorbed by the rise and spread of Indo-European tribes between 3000 and 2000 B.C.E. The new domestication of the horse gave the Indo-Aryans a great range of motion over the land and a powerful new weapon. They came out of the eastern steppes of Russia and the Caucasus Mountains in a fierce storm moving into western Europe and gradually down into northern India. The feminine came under brutal attack—physically, socioculturally, and symbolically. The old matriarchy, including its goddesses and cultural and religious symbols and practices, was subdued and replaced by a more hierarchically organized system. The pre-Osirian goddesses were largely repressed and the new, angry patriarchal gods of Olympus and the north were ascendant (Gimbutas, 1992). Only a few isolated areas of Europe escaped this historical process. For example, the Basques of Spain are certainly European, but not Indo-Aryan, in language and custom.

Eventually the two cultures merged, but the male–female dynamic tension gave each region in the European landscape its own psychocultural tonality. Well-known cultural cycles of civilization arose in Bulgaria, Hungary, Greece, Romania, and in the provinces of northern Macedonia. However, in terms of written language, the arts, and the sciences, none of these societies reached the level of sophistication that we find in the older more articulated human civilizations of Egypt.

As we have said before, even the Celts or red-haired, freckled Irish are part of this story. The Irish of today were known as the Milesian race of the past, due to the Celtic people supposedly being descended primarily from Milesius of Spain, whose sons are said to have invaded Ireland around 1000 B.C.E. Before this branch of the Celts came, there were two other peoples already in place. The Firbolg or Firbourages, who escaped from slavery in Greece, were attached by an African sea people, the Formorians, landed in Ireland, and then encountered another people, the Tuatha De Danann. These Formorians it seems extended their reach up the Atlantic to Ireland and established a strong beachhead on Torrey Island. From this northwestern coastal region they raided and then traded with the Firbolg and the mysterious Tuatha De Danann. All these elements are believed to have blended into the great Gaelic stream.

There are some indications that other strong elements of the Formorians later joined with these Celts in their journey to the north. A De Danann warrior champion, Breas, was probably the son of a Formorian noblemen and for a time ruled the land. However, he was disliked and eventually overthrown. With help from his Formorian father, Elatha, he made war on the De Danann but lost and was driven from the land. These Formorians may be the ancient origin of the now-pejorative phrase "the Black Irish."

These Celts of Europe, principally the Milesians, had ruled for centuries over the German tribes of Europe; then the Celtic tribes, after being defeated, scattered in waves and some went westward over the Pyrenees into Spain and across the seas into England, Scotland, and Ireland (MacManus, 1977). The largest waves of these Milesians came to Ireland through Egypt, Crete, and later Spain. They were called the Gaedhal (Gael) because legend has it that their remote ancestor in the days of Moses was Gaodhal Glas. Glas's grandson, Niul, married the pharaoh's daughter, Scota, from which the name Scotia is derived. Eventually, they too were driven from pharaonic Egypt, reached Spain, stayed, then journeyed to Ireland, where they blended with the earlier tribes of Celts from the continent. When this last wave reached Ireland, their leader was Miled or Milesius. Their written script, although deeply steeped in myth and lore, no doubt has a germ of truth at its core. The Celts, however, were not the only ones to create a written script to record the national soul.

The Europeans gradually developed several scripts to write their sounds and language. They were the Greeks, the Russians, and the Romans. After their conquest of England, the Romans provided the preliterate Anglo-Saxons with a script. The Celts and Phoenicians developed scripts and both had close associations with the Africans. The Africans developed several scripts: the hieroglyphic of Egypt with its earliest expression in Nubia, the Akan, Afafa, Mande, Himyaritic, Meroitic, and other variations. The Egyptians, through Greece, appear to have had contact with the peoples of the fertile European valleys also, and it was mostly peaceful.

We can see the influence of central African civilizations around the Mediterranean from the existence of archetypes and images unearthed by archeologists, in particular, the Hellenic Black virgins and goddesses such as the Black Demeter Phigalia in Arcadia, the Black Aphrodite of Arcadia and Corinth, the Black version of St. Victor in Marseilles, and the black virgin of Chartres. In contemporary times, for Christians who are open to it, this Black Madonna is manifesting to them in their visionary and religious experiences. These epiphanies interestingly enough are occurring on a worldwide scale primarily to Whites! Numerous shrines throughout this century have been erected to her, most notably the Black Madonnas of Montserrat in Catalan Spain, Czestochowa in Poland, and Guadalupe in Mexico. These Black mother figures are spiritually embedded in the deeper regions of the shared unconscious. They are all derived from the cult of Isis of ancient Egypt, and were taken from that migration of civilization up into Europe and Greece. The city of Paris is named for her, that is, the *par*, or temple, of Isis. This influence of course had a unique expression in Africa itself, especially in traditions and languages.

West Africa

The influence of Kemetic Egypt on the civilizations of West Africa has been continuous, with its intensity waxing and waning over the centuries. Van Sertima and Rashidi (1990) and others have documented a vanished system of rivers and trade routes from the upper Nile that interconnected much of the ancient African world. Trade routes by river and caravan cut across the upper Nile, around the tropical forests to the western kingdoms of Gao, Ghana, and legendary Timbuktu. From these centers of commerce the lines spread through the denser forests to the coastal regions of Benin. The trans-Sahara trade would ebb and flow with the rise and fall of the rivers and sands, but it was continuous throughout a long period (Davidson, 1959; Jackson, 1970; Lugard, 1964). There are objects and customs found by ethnologists that increase each year on the Zambezi River area and elsewhere in the interior of the continent that echo rituals, customs, and beliefs found in the ancient papyri of Egypt. (Homburger, 1941; Van Sertima & Rashidi, 1990) These extend to linguistic connections:

> The differences of structure and of morphological character between the later forms of Egyptian and the modern Negro languages are very small and represent the continuation of an evolution whose beginning is found in the history of Egypt itself. . . . Certain groups underwent the influence of Egyptians speaking Coptic dialects, such as the Ewe and the Mande . . . other groups are connected with the populations of the oases who already spoke a debased Egyptian in the time of Herodotus; finally, others adopted Nubian forms representing an ancient state of Egyptian which evolved in contact with the mother language, such as the Bantu. (Homburger, 1941, pp. 306–307)

There are several major language families in Africa, and the way they interact with each other is very complex. Perhaps they cross-fertilize in ways we shall never completely understand, but clearly they are all interconnected with each other as are the great language families of Europe and Asia. In a later section, we will take up the story of the Mother Tongue, which is believed to be the original language that our species spoke prior to the great dispersion and which is hinted to exist in some permutation beneath all the modern tongues of humankind. Africa, Europe, and Asia share a deep structure of syntax and genes—the trade routes and migrations over the millennia would ensure this. The Benue River of West Africa that nurses the great Niger River has a deep valley that has been navigated by large trading ships for at least a thousand miles from the sea to the interior. At one time, around 500 B.C.E., Lake Chad was as large as the Caspian Sea, with numerous cities around its shore. Over the centuries this great waterway would swell and contract, engulfing cities now lost to history and the deep, encroaching forests.

C. G. Seligman, in *Egypt and Negro Africa* (1934), explicates striking parallels between the burial rites and customs of ancient Egypt and those in Nigeria and the Congo. This similarity extends to royal offices, rituals, and other beliefs, including cosmological ones. There are other such findings and objects located in the great lakes and Congo region (Diop, 1974). This cross-fertilization reached a high point in the old kingdom in the days of the pyramids. Seligman, however, like many other scholars of his time, was trapped by the myth of white supremacy. Finding such parallels to Egypt, a civilization he greatly admired, he was perplexed as to exactly how they got to the interior and west of Africa. He had originally held that cattle-rearing and indeed the rise of civilization itself was brought *into* Africa by a race he called Hamites, who were a quick-witted, handsome type of dark paleo-Mediterranean white race who, though pastoral, gave rise to Egyptian civilization. The idea of African self-germination or that Egypt was indigenously African or that Egypt gained anything from other parts of Africa was simply beyond him.

Many ethnic groups, especially in West Africa, have origin legends that point to the East, Nubia–Egypt in particular. The Ashanti, especially the ruling classes, refer to an eastern origin. The Akan of the western coastal regions believe they descended from a Black people from ancient Mesopotamia. Diop (1974), Jackson (1970), and others point out that Black pharaohs did rule large parts of Mesopotamia during the days of Kemetic expansion. The Yoruba suggest an Egyptian migration origin (Lucas, 1948). The Dogon assert unequivocally a pre-dynastic origin in ancient Kemet. Such assertions find some support in linguistic analysis (Diop, 1991). However, even more striking are parallel religions and cosmological beliefs.

The religious conceptions of pre-dynastic Egypt and Nubia were the fertile soil for later dynastic visions of the soul, the cosmos, and the divine unfoldment of the world process. This was indigenous to Africa and later spread out, not an Asian or European import. With the rise of a stable fusion of Egypto-Nubian civilization in the First Dynasty of Menes arose almost simultaneously the Osirian cult. Here we find, as Budge (1960) points out, all the seminal ideas enfolded that later give rise to the genius of ancient Kemet. They include not merely life after death, which we find in all human cultures, but also something quite new—the intuition of an immortal soul, resurrection of the spiritual body, the continuation in some subtle psychospiritual sense of the dynamics of the heart, the soul, the shadow, and the double. Here was formulated the metaphysics behind the spiritual transmutation of offerings, the sacrifices, and the power of the name, of words, of writing, and of magic. Here also was the germinal belief of moral judgment after death that was to exercise such a profound influence on the later Semitic conceptions of Islam, Christianity, and Judaism. These ideas, unfolded fully at the dawn of civilization in the Osirian conception, existed in some form even prior to that.

The existence of parallels and interconnections between ancient Kemetic Egypt and Nubia in terms of language, burial practices, cosmological speculations, and even origin legends does not necessarily mean that Kemet *created* these other civilizations. To be sure, there was extensive contact and exchange of ideas over the rivers and trade routes for thousands of years, including trade and conceptual exchange between East African and southern Harappan and Dravidian India. This connection is even detectable in the distribution of sickle cell hemoglobin, HgS, which arose as a mutation in Africa and is distributed densely among most of her population. Southern and central India are the only regions of the earth where the HgS gene is as prevalent as in Africa (Finch, 1991). But there were also local spreads and pressures, including climatic and ecological changes in the deserts, lakes, and forests, that contributed to developments which interacted with eastern influences to unfold what occurred. The cycles of the Sahara and the tides of the Niger and Lake Chad are only a few. The influx of peoples responding to these along with indigenous peoples led to conflicts, cooperations, and, in places, the rise of the state in West Africa. Much the same can be said of southeast Africa above the Nile. Numerous similarities can be seen in these diverse peoples and the creative mix of ideas in the *Egyptian Book of the Dead*. However, there is even another, more intriguing possibility.

The numerous parallels, some of which will be explored in more detail later, are often characteristic of pre-dynastic Egypt, Nubia, and other parts of the continent, especially West Africa (Perry, 1923, 1924). This suggests that perhaps it is not so much a matter of Kemet spreading out to others, as Seligman and a host of early Egyptologists believed, but rather that there was a great common source from which all these emanated out to the rest of Africa as some Horus iron smithing traditions suggest. This may better organize the origin legends of many people of a great pulsating migration from the East. It should be remembered that the sphinx was ancient even in Egyptian–Nubian times, no one knowing who built it or when! From the water erosion markings at its base, the limestone figure was carved when the Sahara was lush with rivers, lakes, and rainfall, at least 10,000 to 8000 B.C.E., long before the first known dynasties. It was dug from the sand and partially repaired by rulers who were mystified by its appearance even back then. Diop has intimated an ancient civilization; so has Schwaller de Lubicz (1961). *Serpent in the Sky* (West, 1970) boldly suggests the existence of a high civilization prior to Kemet as we know it. Since there were no Greeks or Romans of this time and Abraham of the Jews and Muslims lived millennia later, the only possible people this could have emerged from were the indigenous Africans. H. G. Wells and others have suggested a pan-Dravidian or pan-African culture of interconnected ideas, trade, and commerce that stretched from the south of India, across Egypt and Nubia to the west coast of Africa. Beyond these we have only the myths of Lemuria, Atlantis, and Mu. Who knows. My own bias here is that these beliefs, in a great, pulsating origin from the eastern regions of Africa, are the collective unconscious or genetic racial memory of our origins as *Homo sapiens sapiens*, echoing back perhaps 200,000 years ago to the area around the great lakes and valleys of the mother continent. They are the deepest memories of Oldawan, the African unconscious. This is the stuff of future research.

THE KIASPORA INTO THE AMERICAS DURING EARLY CIVILIZATION

Several times now we have mentioned contacts between African peoples and those in the Americas prior to the coming of Columbus. We have already cited the early migrations of the Australoids and the Clovis-Fulsome Point Blacks. They came in successive waves of migration across the Bering Strait, and perhaps by island hopping across the south Pacific when the Ice Ages drew up the seas in the North. These were from the earliest of times, prior to civilization, prior to scripts, prior to metallurgy, chemistry, and the pyramids. Recent unearthings, however, show unmistakably an African presence in the Americas at about the same time as the indigenous population was arching its way up to civilization. The Atlantic Ocean currents and a long history of large watercraft navigation in both the Mediterranean and Africa's Lake Chad made this technologically possible. While this is certainly no linear cause-effect scenario, there is, it seems, a nonlinear kind of influence, one where a branching comes together again with an earlier branching in a novel situation. This seems to be that "sensitive dependence on initial conditions" that leads or increases the tendency toward higher-order systems at times. In this case it would be Kemetic influence in the Olmec Americas prior to Columbus. We believe this is possible because these events occurred in the shared life of the same hominid organism, an organism with a shared primordial genetic, embryological, and morphological structure, an organism immersed in the same sea of memory, ideation, and spiritual unfoldment.

Columbus himself actually documented in the journal of his second voyage the stories Native Americans told him of tall Black men from the South who traded with them in gold, copper, and silver. They gave him some of these gold-tipped spears and he sent them back to Spain, where the metallurgists of Ferdinand and Isabella's land, newly liberated from the African

Moors, found that they were identical in composition to those from Guinea and further south in Africa. The Portuguese had already documented that the Africans were sailing somewhere in the Atlantic to trade, but they did not know where. The chronicles of the Arab scholar from Damascus al-Umari in his *Masalik-al-Abasar and al Qalqashandi* recorded that seafarers from medieval Mali, probably the Mandinkas, traveled by sea to the Americas in 1311–1312. Great ships had already been used to traverse huge inland Lake Chad. Also certain strains of cotton from the Caribbean had been introduced to Africa prior to the Columbian voyages. Clearly something had occurred between the Americans of the New World and the Africans of the Old (Van Sertima, 1976). Other Europeans of the era also reported seeing Africans in the Americas. Vasco Nuñez de Balboa witnessed this in 1513. Lopes de Gomara, Father Ramón Pane, and Fra Gregorio García reported the same. These reported citings stretched from Mexico to the Caribbean to Colombia.

Upon closer inspection, it appears that contact between the African and American worlds goes back even to ancient Egyptian times. In La Venta in the Gulf of Mexico, we find four huge Negroid stone heads in Egyptian-type helmets and a Mediterranean figure, possibly a Phoenician-Libyan, along with them carved on a stele. There are also Negroid dancers side-by-side with reliefs in Assyrian style, a representation of the Egyptian god Ra in its bird aspect, and a sculpture of the Egyptian sphinx. They are at the site of Monte Alban, the place where the Olmec civilization of ancient Mexico, the mother civilization of Meso-America, arose. This Olmec civilization rose then fell and in its wake gave birth to the Toltec, the Aztec, and the curious Mayans and Inca to the south. These date to the time of Taharqa, the Nubian pharaoh of the 25th Dynasty, who, along with others in succession, ruled from 751 to 654 B.C.E. Their empire stretched from the borders of Ethiopia to the Mediterranean, across a quarter of Africa, and apparently had contact with the dawn of civilization in Olmec Mexico.

We mentioned earlier that the ancient Celts in their origin legends pointed to North Africa and the Iberian peninsula as their source. Diop (1991) has stressed how the Grimaldi Negroids were the first *Homo sapiens sapiens* to go into Europe and Spain from Africa, but we need not go back that far. We have extensive records and monuments of a Celtic presence in New England as far back as 2000 B.C.E. (Fell, 1989)! At that time they worshiped the sun god Bel, sported an Afro hairstyle, and wrote in an Ogam script. There is a strong affinity between the Celtic script and two African scripts. It is similar to the semicursive version of the late Numidian script in its transitional phase to becoming the Tifinag alphabet of the African Berbers, and also to a formerly African script later used by Phoenicians in Spain in the first millennium B.C.E. These are noted by an Irish scribe around 1370 to 1390 C.E. in the Book of Ballymote in which an Ogam alphabet is recorded along with several other alphabets known by the author of the Ogam tract (Fell, 1989). This African presence is seen in part in the original Celts of Spain and Portugal of the Iberian peninsula *prior* to their presence in the Americas, and also after their Christian conversion and voyages to America from Ireland.

Actually the Egyptians and Phoenicians (Libyans) have left traces and monuments of their presence in the Americas scattered from the Gulf of Mexico to Iowa, the Dakotas, and west to the Cimarron River. While the Celts are confined mostly to New England, the Kemetic Egyptian presence is in full view in Mexico, parts of the Caribbean, and South America. Although more controversial, certain Africoid-Nubian relics have been found in the Hopewell Mounds of Ohio. Kemetic inscriptions from 700 B.C.E. have been reportedly located in Iowa—the so-called Davenport Stele calendar of Osiris, and the new year Djed festival, and the engravings of animals indigenous not to America, but to Africa. Research historians believe the Egyptians and their Libyan colleagues, in their trading with the Native Americans of New England of the ninth century B.C.E., left inscriptions similar to the Micmac hieroglyphics which translate into "A ship's crew from upper Egypt made this stele with respect to their expedition" (Fell, 1989). In the face of this written evidence in stone and other relics, the natural question arises as to how these early travelers got to the Americas.

There are three natural currents flowing from Africa to the Americas and an ocean span of only 1,500 miles. (See Figure 20.) From Europe the span is 3,000 miles. Huge ships were not only on the seas but also on Lake Chad in West Africa some 3,000 years ago. These ships were seaworthy. Indeed such huge ships, in pieces, have been found in the ancient pyramid tombs of Egypt. But beyond this, in 1513, a Turkish admiral, Piri Reis, found intact in a library in Alexandria, Egypt, a portion of a larger precise map, authored centuries earlier, that correctly linked latitude and longitude long before it was discovered in Europe. The map even plotted South America, including miles of the Amazon River, something not done in Europe until a century later. From 1000 B.C.E. there is evidence of contact, trade, and interconnectedness between American and African peoples and their civilizations. Africans did not *create* Olmec civilization any more than "aliens" from outer space "created" Kemetic Egyptian civilization. Rather, as Olmec civilization, the civilization that later gave rise to the Aztec and Mayan flowering, arose, it met and exchanged knowledge, technology, and metaphysical ideas with an *older* African civilization.

How continual these contacts were is at present unknown. But we do know they occurred and that the contact enriched both. There are terracotta skulls of Africans found in great abundance among the Olmec. There are also skull and skeletal remains. But more than this is in evidence and

FIGURE 20. Transatlantic Winds and Currents.

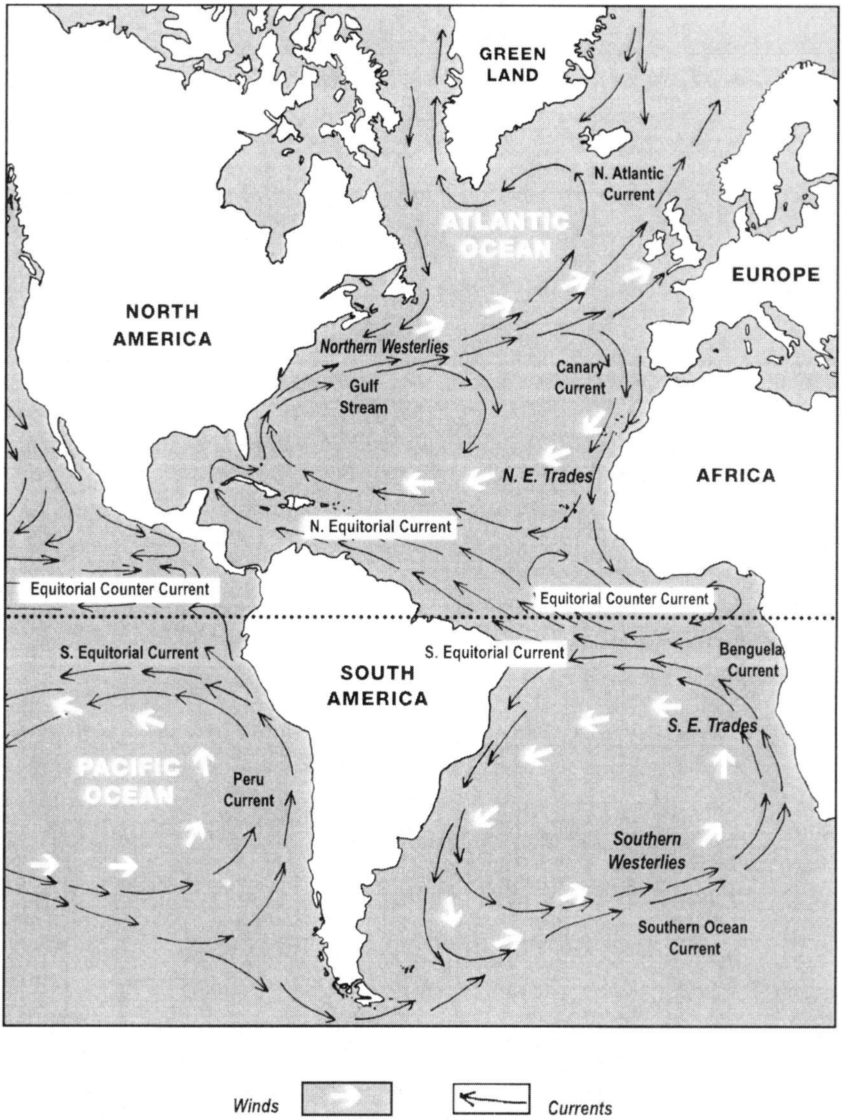

There are no less than three natural ocean currents flowing from Africa to the Americas over a span of 1,500 miles. Huge ships that navigated Lake Chad were seaworthy to make this voyage. Egyptians and West Africans probably reached the Americas before Columbus using these currents. (Copyright © 1999 Teachers College, Columbia University)

suggests a diffusion of certain elements of Kemetic science, technology, and metaphysics throughout the Americas. As pointed out earlier, an Egyptian hieroglyphic-type script was found in use among the Micmac Indians (Fell, 1989; Maillard, 1921). The style is very similar to that in Egypt around 1400 B.C.E. Some 80% of the Wabanaki Indian vocabulary for astronomy is reportedly Egyptian. Further south in Mexico, both the stepped and conical pyramids suddenly appear in the Americas about the time of the dated Egyptian contact, but there is no prior history of their development in this region of the world. All at once they appear and in full development! In Egypt and Nubia, it took centuries of experimentation to perfect the pyramid, and the earlier attempts are scattered across their landscape. The first such stepped pyramid appears in La Venta where the huge Negroid heads are found and when and where Olmec civilization first flourished. (See Figure 21.) Another appears at Cholula, dedicated to Quetzalcoatl in 150 B.C.E., and another at Teotihuacan near Mexico City. The latter, like the Egyptian, has a movable capstone and is almost the exact same size of the Great Pyramid of Egypt. They served as both tomb and astronomical observatory for both groups. The Egyptians had stopped their own such pyramid building by 1600 B.C.E., but the Nubians had continued on a minor scale during this period and even partially revived the art.

Aside from the pyramids, astronomy, and other technological interchange that occurred in these remote times, so did religious ideas. There is an uncanny self-similarity of structures here beyond those just cited. The Olmec kings, like the pharaohs, wore a duel crown, a symbol of Menes' great union of the North and South of Kemet. Both had the royal flail; the plumed serpent suddenly replaces the royal jaguar; purple is the royal color. The Olmec books, most of which were burned deliberately by the Europeans, had black and red kings in royal purple. Artificial beards appear on both, as they did on the African pharaohs. There is even the exact same royal pattern of three concentric circles and three colors to the feathered sunshade. There is the same loom style in Mexico and Peru as in Egypt. The complex lost wax technique, used in Egypt and ancient Nubia and then spread to West Africa's Yoruba and Bini peoples of Nigeria in the medieval period after the collapse of Kemetic civilization, appears suddenly in the Americas with no gradual technological history (Van Sertima, 1976). The Egypto-Nubian surgical technique of trephination, where a surgical hole is drilled in the skull to relieve pressure on the brain, is suddenly performed in both ancient Mexico and Peru by the hundreds in the *identical fashion*, with circular and square hole techniques. And the gods? The Egypto-Nubian god Aton with no face and two ropes emerging from his mouth suddenly appears in ancient Mexico.

FIGURE 21. Olmec Heartland and the Gulf of Mexico.

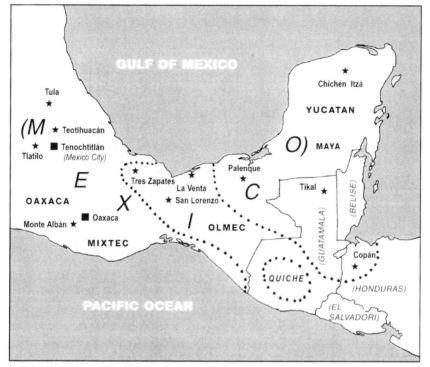

The Olmec was the "mother civilization" of ancient Mexico, seeding many later empires. It had crucial contact with seafaring African civilizations. In the areas of San Lorenzo, La Venta, Tres Zapotes, and others, huge Africoid stone heads and smaller terra-cotta heads have been unearthed by Alexander von Wuthenau and others from these pre-Colombian sites.

From the collapse of ancient Egypt, through the Roman interlude, up to the sweeping tide of Islam we hear little of this earlier contact across the seas. By the dawn of medieval West Africa, however, new contacts were made. From the coastal areas, ships that had sailed great Lake Chad again crossed the three natural currents from Africa to South America. There are hundreds and hundreds of African terra-cotta skulls and many large faces unearthed and photographed in Mexico (Van Wuthenau, 1975). They appear to be from around 1300 C.E. The African contacts with Olmec and other later Meso-American civilizations from what we can see were primarily through trade and cooperation. There was no invasion and colonization, no cataclysmic encounter or conflict, no conquistador tradition of

Columbus, Cortez, DeSoto, the Pizarro brothers (Francisco, Gonzalo, Juan, and Hernando), no Pedro de Mendoza and thousands of others who brought death, disease, degradation, and slavery! The peoples involved in the early African contacts, in all likelihood, were from the kingdoms of Mali. Mali at that time was a rich and powerful empire with contacts not only in the interior of Africa, but across Lake Chad to Egypt, Nubia, and Ethiopia, and also apparently across the seas to the Americas. This influence spread to Mexico and to a lesser extent the North America peoples. We have records and relics of these contacts in the cross-fertilization of technology, science, and religion.

THE DARK AGES AND MEDIEVAL EUROPE

During this medieval period, there was a continuation in the northern part of Africa that had begun centuries earlier. The Black presence was in Yemen and the Arabian peninsula prior to 1500 B.C.E. Then through the time of the legendary Adites (Gulf of Aden), the Black Sabeans, the Himyarites, and the Christian Abyssinians this part of the world was active and wealthy. Through the tribes Koreysh, which were primarily Semitic with strong African elements in their lineage, came the prophet Muhammad who transformed the area after years of struggle. In the early years after the death of the prophet, Islam swept across the northern expanse of Africa and under Jebel-al-Tarik in 711 C.E. crossed into the Iberian peninsula of Spain and Portugal defeating the armies of the Visigoth King Roderick. The first of these Islamic invaders were dark-skinned Moorish Africans from Morocco, with a small mix of Arabs. Later came the blackamoors and tawny Moors of the medieval period. Centuries earlier they had served with the Black Carthaginian, Hannibal. They are largely responsible for setting the Renaissance foundation for the second rise of Europe after the Roman fall and ensuing Dark Ages. Many inventions usually credited to the Renaissance, including a more sophisticated science of mapmaking for navigation, higher mathematics, architectural revival, new machines, new foods and agricultural methods, the nearly forgotten works of the classical scholars Aristotle, Plato, and others, plus much more were introduced. This had a tremendous influence on Europe's university system as it reawakened to the grandeur of antiquity and the birth of the newer medieval sciences (Van Sertima, 1992). The Christian Church had banned many of these areas of study from Europe's two universities, but they flourished in the 14 Moorish universities. The only other areas of light during the European "Dark Ages" were to the north in Ireland, "the isle of saints and scholars." From the fall of Rome to the rise of Charlemagne, the monks and scribes of Ireland maintained and transmitted the record of Western civilization (Cahill, 1995). If not for them, over the centuries even more would have been lost.

Interestingly enough, in the world of antiquity, the Greeks had looked very much to ancient Egypt in both science and religion. Much of Egyptian science and philosophy was beautifully "transmitted" to Europe by the Greeks and later the Romans, who admired them both. After the fall of Rome, the light of learning was kept alive in the West by African and Arab scholars and a few isolated sanctuaries of Irish monks, the great Celtic spiritual tradition. When Europe rose again in its Renaissance, it initially, again, looked to its brother and sister of African antiquity, Egypt, for inspiration. By the 16th and 17th centuries, Egypt was again the ancient model. Hermeticism and Rosicrusianism were strong again, as was the imitation of ancient architecture. There were expeditions to Egypt, a great revival of the rites of antiquity. This stopped, however, under the "psychological" pressure of the slave trade. The financial success of African slavery in the Americas fueled an emerging racial imagery crisis for Europeans. The Europeans could not enslave a race that they also felt was one of the primary sources of the rise of their own civilization. A psychological shift occurred. Soon Blacks were psychologically *erased* from Egyptian history as anything other than slaves. Blacks were "scientifically" lowered to the level of simpleton, sensuous, inferior, brutish, bodily, etc., etc. etc., and therefore "naturally" suited to slavery. Civilization was soon understood to have been imported *into* Africa by advanced others, be they Greeks, Semites, Brown Mediterraneans, or vague Asiatics. The fascination among European intellectuals turned now to India. Blacks were psychologically erased from all but "primitive," "brutish," "dark and backward" Africa. Suddenly, Sanskrit became "recognized" as a variation of the language of the ancient Indo-Europeans, the noble Aryans. Even though the majority of Indians were dark-skinned, and a very significant portion of Dravidian southern India had the features of Africans—e.g., woolly hair, dark to black skin, broad nose, full lips, etc.—they were seen "psychologically" to be Whites, albeit devalued Whites. This rise of India and fall of Egyptian Africa occurred between 1740 and 1880 (Bernal, 1987). The Indians of Asia were not quite suited for slavery, but they were perfectly suited to be servants for the British Empire. The Africans, in larger and larger numbers, became associated with manual labor as slaves to the Europeans. This included the skilled Africans stolen from the decaying empires of West Africa, many if not most of whom were sold into slavery by other Africans as the spoils of war between warring groups. The Arabs greatly contributed to this exodus of human lives also, as slave traders in concert with Europeans and warring, greedy Africans.

During the period after the fall of the western Roman empire, the African and Egyptian cults and sciences that had thrived in Rome—e.g., cults of

Isis, Osiris, astronomy, medicine, mathematics, etc.—either receded and went underground to the small libraries of monks or were forgotten. The only places in the West where they thrived were the Islamic/Moorish Iberian peninsula, scattered European monasteries, and the Celtic sanctuaries. Europe forgot that there had been an African presence on the Mediterranean islands and Greece of antiquity, that Africans had populated the religious hierarchy of early Europe with saints and Madonnas, and that African spiritual lineages had flourished in imperial Rome at the apex of its power. It even gave Jesus the Christ a psychological reworking. Yes, even though Jesus the Christ was thought to have been of lowly Jewish birth, never having gone farther north than Israel, who lived for at least 12 years in Africa (Egypt), and was explicitly described in the Bible as having skin the color of bronze and hair like sheep's wool, despite all this, Jesus the Christ is depicted as a tall, blond, blue-eyed, thin man with fair skin and Nordic features! The reawakening of Egyptian models led to an exploration of Egypt's past. When that past, beyond the Arab and Greek influences of the later centuries, was seen to be Black and Africoid and similar to the population it was increasingly enslaving, a great revulsion occurred, a recoil from the threatened return of the repressed. By a cultural shift, the African was erased out of European history except as a slave. Scholars can often be sophisticated prostitutes who follow the money, and the money at that time was in capitalism, slavery, and the expansion of Europe into Africa and the Americas.

Eventually, it became almost inconceivable in the West that Africans could have accomplished or created anything, let alone a great science, art, and civilization. The Egyptians, therefore, had to be either White or at least mixed with some White from the very beginning. How else could anything in Africa have arisen! These are not sterile academic debates because they are about the deep images we all have about our fellow beings and dynamically influence our behavior, perceptions, and politics. Even today, despite accumulating data and archeological evidence, there remain those for whom these notions are counterintuitive. They argue that African "civilization" is really only a self-esteem-enhancing myth in response to present-day revisionist politics and that the real Africa is much, much less than this (Alpern, 1992); that Greece, pretty much like Topsy, just suddenly grew up by itself and borrowed very little from Egypt or anywhere else (Coleman, 1992); and that the ancient Egyptians were neither Europeans nor migrating sub-Saharan Blacks, but rather simply people in Africa "whose skin was adapted for life in the subtropical desert environment" (Bard, 1992). These scholars are rightly appalled at some of the flaky myth-making about African history currently floating around in the debates in this area—e.g., ancient Africans created an airplane. Ideas such as these are always held up as the root or essence of an "Afrocentric" view, then attacked publicly in an attempt to discredit all scholarship in this area. Then a more "conservative and responsible voice" or scholar in the field is offered up as representing a more reasonable position. It is an old story. It is apparent that they are defending, on a more subtle level, the academic and political status quo. It is very, very difficult, after centuries of indoctrination, a dynamic cultural milieu of racial images, both conscious and unconscious, and a psychological predisposition to diminish most of what is associated with "Black" and "Africoid" to adopt anything else. This is overtly the case with people who identify themselves as cultural "conservatives," White and Black. It is particularly so for those who like to think of themselves as "liberals."

For the medieval Europeans awakening in the years after the Renaissance, it is understandable, especially those of the Iberian peninsula. After all, they had been forcibly invaded and subdued for 700 years by an alien race and religion who no doubt lorded this financial and political superiority over them in every way. It was only in 1492 that the dark-skinned African Moors were finally expelled from Spain. Without their Islamic protection, the Jews were soon persecuted, killed, "Christianized" or expelled. The Jews went into a new exodus that eventually led them to their great mystical flowering in the Kabbalistic period and their eventual political, increasingly financial and strong cultural influence in parts of middle and eastern Europe. The last great west African ruler died that year, and the African himself was also about to take a great exodus, a vast migration out of the motherland.

By the time the last wave of Africans came to the Americas, they came not as traders and seafarers or even , except for a few, as voluntary explorers as in earlier times. They came in chains and as conquered labor. But they, like their distant relatives, the Jews, held a secret consciousness and a story that is still new and weaves us together in startling and luminous ways. Indeed, a great dark, unknown current interconnects all our lives, historically, anthropologically, embryologically and genetically. It is our belief here that it also implicates us all spiritually and in consciousness itself.

DISPERSION, GENETICS, AND THE MOTHER TONGUE

Before we leave this area about the historic, genetic, and anthropological dispersion and cross-fertilization of the ideas and memories of our traveling race, we need to look more closely at another possession this species has carried with it perhaps from the earliest times—a common instinct for language. Hints have already been given in this story about a Mother Tongue. It has been demonstrated beyond doubt that *Homo sapiens sapiens* are descended from a common genetic stock. Within an African template there is great diversity in phenotype and surface structure. Deep structure arrows towards a fundamental unity. All the hominids we know of dispersed from east Africa in waves over time and in the four directions to populate the world. Many, like Diop (1991), suggest that until some 25,000 years ago the only phenotype was an African one, and then the present variations on the theme began. There is no polygenesis, no speciation, merely surface mutations of a deep structure unity. Perhaps this is also the case with language.

As our species traveled across the continents and oceans, relocating ourselves in new environments of all kinds and creating branches of humanity and civilization itself, subtle changes occurred on the surface. Along with phenotypic genetic modulations and adaptations to environmental demands as our ancestors moved about, changes would also occur in the speech and language of these early groups. "Genetic drift" in phenotypical or surface structures is well known and has been touched on earlier. Living in East Africa for millennia as *Homo sapiens sapiens*, then moving out, our progenitors no doubt spoke a language that also experienced some "phonological drift." This is inherent in all mutation and permutation. Language acquisition is innate. A Swede born in China can learn to speak Swahili under the right conditions because of a deep-structure similarity rooted in the structure of our speech organs, ears, facial gestures, and connotative intuitive tones common to all children. It is rooted in our genetics and no doubt in our common nervous systems and brain structures. The discipline of linguistics is still young. While estimates vary, there are roughly some 6,700 languages currently spoken in the world; only 50 or so have been studied in depth and perhaps only 20 or so examined in microscopic depth. Yet like the unconscious world of emotions, images, and motivations, the netherworld of the deep linguistic structures suggests that it too possesses ideas and archetypal apprehensions of reality. The question here is whether there are signs of a primary language of which all the other approximately 6,700 are permutations, just as there is a common parent stock of the human race in terms of gene pool and point of origin. If so, did it exist in East Africa as our ancestors did prior to the great dispersion? Did all the languages cross in a common language millennia ago as our mitochondrial DNA gene pools did in a common ancestor, the so-called "mother of humanity," Eve, some 150,000 to 200,000 years ago? Are there correlations between the waves of *Homo sapiens sapiens* and the different structure of language groups?

This is a most controversial area, and for this reason has been held back here until now, so that we could establish a foundation for this intuitive leap based on some syntactic data, a good deal of genetics, strong archeological and anthropological support, and a wealth of paleological and historical information that points in this direction. After all, unlike these other areas, there are no archeological remains of historical records as we know it to be unearthed. There is no written history of speech earlier than 5000 B.C.E. There are no genetic remains, and so we need to look elsewhere for "data."

The study of linguistics in the light of migration and racial dispersion may be useful. Complex verbal language really is unique to human beings on this planet. Even though other mammals, such as whales and dolphins, use modulated sounds to communicate new thoughts, it, so far anyway, appears less complex than human speech. Other higher primates, such as chimpanzees, are capable of simple reasoning, have basic sounds, and can create tools; they cannot, however, talk. Language and the capacity to speak any language appears to be an inherent ability that comes with a normal human life.

Since the time of Charles Darwin's (1809–1882) *The Descent of Man* (1871/1936) we have believed that language is at least partially instinctive. Language appears in every human society without exception. Within society everyone with a normal neurological web generates very complex language skills whether or not they have any sort of formal schooling. Societies may be thought of as "primitive" at times, with all the negative connotations that come with the term, but there are no primitive languages! Written language itself is a relatively new invention and has occurred only in a few societies. Many of the greatest figures in human history did not read or write, e.g., Charlemagne, Chaka Zulu, etc. The language you are reading now, English, was only *written* down in the 800 to 900 C.E. era, inspired by Alfred the Great (? 849–899), Overking of England. This is barely over a thousand years ago. This was in "old" English, not present English, and in a Latin script. There is no English script. Before this, England was a preliterate society!

Human languages appear to be variations of a single design rooted in two fundamental principles (Pinker, 1994). First the word, the pairing between a sound and a meaning. Sometimes the sound can appear overly related to the meaning, but usually not. A thought is represented by a sound, or more accurately, a vibration. Being immersed in a shared community of sound, vibration and meaning leads to language acquisition. The second principle is grammar, the rules for the meaningful use of these sounds. These are quite complex in all human societies. The "surface" sounds may be different and the rules of association may vary, but the primary rules, the "deep-structure" syntax or grammar, is similar for all human languages (Chomsky, 1965). This intricate similarity interwoven through the diversity of human languages reflects a subtle design of the mental and neurological processes every normal child inherits.

Language and "intelligence" of course are not identical. You can have damage done to specific areas in the left hemisphere of your brain and not

be able to speak clearly or understand the subtlety of sentences, yet be in charge of your other intellectual abilities. You can also have a so-called learning disability and yet be able to speak and reason normally. You can be highly intelligent, gifted, and articulate and yet emotionally unstable and even dangerous. There are other examples we could list, but you get the point. Language itself is a rather specific function associated with certain neurological processes of the brain common to all *Homo sapiens sapiens*.

Just when this capacity arose is another question. Chimps don't talk. The chimpanzee and hominid lines separated 6 or 8 million years ago after our descent from a common ancestor. Between that common ancestor and us, through all the pre-Australopithecines, Australopithecines, varied hominid cousins, and so forth, this capacity no doubt evolved. That is perhaps 350,000 generations ago. Then in East Africa *Homo sapiens sapiens* arose, existed as a small group until at least as far back as 270,000 years ago, then began to spread out and diversify. A diversification from a common tongue in all probability also began at this time and spread in great waves across the continents and oceans in families, tribes, and clans. Then suddenly 50,000 years ago an explosion of human symbolism and cultures scattered across Africa, Asia, and Europe. The greatest experiment since the discovery of fire had begun.

Linguistic analysis puts all these different languages into families based on relationships with each other. Many linguists believe that in language today, despite phonological drift, chance correlations, and other shifts and permutations over time, there exist remnants of an original language, a Mother Tongue of early humankind. Some nouns, pronouns, words for body parts and for common objects in the environment tend to have sounds associated with them that remain stable over long periods of time. Enormous methodological problems of analysis still confront them. Problems of drift in phonation, borrowing from other groups, etc.—all these put aside, there is still a strong pull in this direction from the genetic, paleological, and other data we have given.

Linguistic analysis (Wright, 1991) does suggest a group of primary languages with a deep-structure unity or at least striking similarity. The languages of Europe are related to each other, the languages of Asia reveal intimate correlations, and the languages of Africa reveal a complex and ancient intermarriage. But beyond this, these great regions show a spiraling interrelationship to each other on a deeper level. There are currently thought to be four to seven groups of primary language roots, superfamilies of languages, if you will. These may be descendants of some original language, some Mother Tongue dispersed through the Babel of modern speech and echoing back to primordial days. Just as there is no polygenesis of races, they are suggesting, then perhaps there is no polygenesis of languages either.

When the tribes and branches left East Africa, they went in the four directions, leading eventually over the eons to the four to seven superfamilies of languages. Joseph Greenberg, the noted linguist, sees a deep commonality in modern African languages and believes they belong to four basic groups, or phyla. Greenberg (1973) replaces the outdated classifications of "Semitic" and "Hamitic" with the more integrative "Afro-Asiatic." The four basic language groups, through migrations and integrations of peoples over time, created many branchings, but the four great roots have remained. A deep unity underlies the surface diversity. Thereby Arabic, Hebrew, Aramaic, Phoenician, and Amharic are united with early Egyptian, Chadic, Kushitic, and Hausa. The Mother Tongue in this scheme would have arisen in the highlands of Ethiopia, just as did our species itself.

Vitaly Shevoroshkin, the Russian linguist, sees the Indo-European language family as only one of six branches of an even more extended language family (Wright, 1991). This superfamily, the so-called Nostratic family, stretches from the South, subsuming the languages of northern Africa, the Middle East, and the non-Aryan languages of India, all the way to the North and East, incorporating the languages of Finland, Siberia, Japan, and Korea. The comparative analysis is based on syntactic structure, rules of grammar, and common phonological root words and sounds. The notion here is that all these tongues are variations and "offshoots" of a proto-Nostratic tongue common to the peoples who lived in these regions long before 10,000 years ago, and perhaps even as much as 50,000 or even 150,000 years ago, the time of the mitochondrial DNA mother of humanity! Most linguists, however, feel that scientific methods only let us reconstruct languages as far back as 10,000 to 15,000 years. But the *idea* of a common genetic and linguist root is still an acceptable hypothesis. The Nostratic notion is currently the most well-funded and researched. This Nostratic family, defined by Illich-Svitych in the 1960s, enfolds half the world's peoples, including the Semitic, Afro-Asiatic, Indo-European, and Uralic-Yukaghir languages, the last of which includes the northern Finnish language, Estonian, and Hungarian. It also embraces language groups of northeastern Asia, the Turkish tongues, and others (Wright, 1991).

Greenberg (1973), who saw African tongues as permutations of four basic groups, also saw how Native American tongues may be derived from three primary languages. In his 1987 book, *Language in the Americas*, he organized the 1,000 known Native American languages into Na-dene in Canada mostly, Eskimo-Aleut in the North, and the great Amerind, which arches from the tip of Tierra del Fuego in South America up to southern Canada. This correlates well with the migrations of *Homo sapiens sapiens* into the Americas beginning long before 10,000 B.C.E. The first were the Amerind, the last the Aleut-Eskimo.

There are many legitimate criticisms for the belief in an original language of early *Homo sapiens sapiens*, in a Mother Tongue, and the development of our thesis in this book is not at all dependent upon this controversial hypothesis. However, in the context of our genetic, paleological, anthropological, and historical knowledge of humankind's travels, dispersions, and deep-structure commonality, the idea of a Mother Tongue has the intuitive pull of a great harmonic chord of sound toward which the whole music is flowing. There are even public television programs on this commonsense faith, which testifies to its popularity and wide appeal. But it is really an ancient fascination not limited to our own day (Wallace, 1992). We need only look at the fascination our species has had throughout its cultural and spiritual history with secret and symbolic languages with hidden meaning and powers pulling us toward embracing it. The Kemets of the earliest Egypto-Nubian times, who began writing itself, had hidden written and spoken languages. The temples were the repositories of these secret languages. They used word play, secret symbols, and special sounds to unfold the mysteries from what they believed were the higher, more subtle realms of reality. The later Kabbalistic Jews, who had more than a passing affinity with these ancient Kemets, as we have suggested, elaborated a system of word play with language and the mystical recombinations of letters in specialized conditioned states of consciousness as part of their seeking to discern the hidden truth of God's secret language, the original divine speech of the cosmos. Look at free association in psychoanalysis today. So for eons up until even our own day, our species has suspected a hidden mystery wrapped in the symbols and sounds of language. Much in the traditions was directed to revealing this profundity and, thereby, liberating consciousness and the human soul. This, it seems to us, like seeking the depths of the unconscious itself, is another way of striving intuitively to touch our origins, to embrace our most remote beginnings in ideation, in form, and yes, in the word and vibration itself. This secret ambition has been with us through all our travels.

SUMMARY

We suggest that essentially humanity's earliest roots spiral back to Africa approximately 13 million years ago to the middle of the Miocene age, the age of the great apes. Millions of years later, it further specialized and split off from the ape line that had included the chimpanzees and others, then evolved down through the Australopithecus, moved through *Homo habilis*, arched up in *Homo erectus*, and began to travel. Dynamic interactions with climatic, geological, and ecological forces quickened the pace of development. Neanderthal flourished, then faded, but *Homo sapi-*

ens refined even further to *Homo sapiens sapiens* and kept on walking. This was a race of African origin, dark and primordial, and out of her all others began.

There is little debate that Africa is the birthplace of both *Homo erectus* and *Homo sapiens sapiens*. The first race of humans "born" near the great lakes of East Africa had to be black in skin tone due to Golger's Law, which says that the skin of warm-blooded mammals for reasons of survival must be pigmented in a hot and humid climate. All permutations of the human race are descendant from the African race of *Homo sapiens sapiens* that began its present great expansion at least 100,000 years ago, but there are suggestions of an even earlier dawn. We have abundant anthropological, ethnological, and morphological studies to support this belief. Some 150,000 to 200,000 years ago, our gene pools were interconnected by a common ancestor, a "primordial Eve" as recent mitochondrial DNA studies show, and in all likelihood she lived in Africa.

As the African stock moved out of Africa, it spread to different parts of the world. Out of East Africa through northern Africa into Europe came the Grimaldi Negroids. The Grimaldi Negroids are believed by some to be the root or parent stock of the European racial diversifications. A variation of *Homo sapiens sapiens*, perhaps the short, yellow/brown-skinned San or Bushman type, with its slight body hair and epicanthal folds around the eyes, migrated from the mother continent to the Siberian steppes and there, like the Negroids of Ice Age Europe, underwent adaptive phenotypical changes to emerge into the Asian-Mongol branch of the family. These branches in various combinations along with climatic influences produced the various faces of humanity. However, underneath these surface phenotypical structures, there is a deep structure that is genetically rooted, a shared racial and collective unconscious that lives even within the European peoples who also are of this African stock. The same is true of Asia, the Middle East and the Americas.

The impact of this is to be seen in our collective and shared unconscious. Even in our dreams. This same genetic root and collective unconscious gave rise to civilization in Africa and spread up through Europe and also over through Asia. Like the human embryo itself unfolding from the neural crest, civilization in its earliest hours unfolded from a dark and creative synthesis of life forces along the umbilical Nile River, then moved along a dark line that over time evolved into discrete organs, trading centers and functional cities, and eventually became interconnected over great distances. This early civilization is the origin of our first sciences of consciousness and also of a material technology. From East Africa, humankind had moved eastward by way of India and Asia Minor to form the Dravidians of India and Australoid populations of Australia. Descendants of these peoples migrated up the continent and eventually over the Bering Strait, and also perhaps across the islands of the south Pacific, to the Americas in several great waves over millennia. Other human tribes moved westward to form the peoples of West Africa and southward to form the peoples of southern Africa. Civilization in many ways followed the same pathways from upper East Africa to the lower Nile Valley through Asia Minor, North Africa, and into Europe. The "Greek miracle" was largely a brilliant learning from and adding to a significantly older civilization, a civilization at least 3,500 years older. Untold millions of people presently categorized as "White" have images and memories in their dreams of their African origin. A smaller number, perhaps only in the thousands, actually remember or have visions in their dreamlife of their connection to an ancient Egyptian or other African existence. In contemporary times for sociopolitical and cultural reasons these recollections can sometimes produce complex identity issues for these individuals. This is why we say that the awareness of the African element in the deep psyche of many is truly "the threatened return of the repressed." Those images however can also be stages of liberation from the racist psychosis of our era.

We are all connected intimately—neurologically, embryologically, historically, and by way of the collective unconscious—to the same shared human family. It is from the first generative minds of humanity that our first theories of consciousness, energy, and disciplined attention arose. Indeed it is in Kemetic Egyptian history and their theories of humanity itself that we find the first theories of the dynamic existence of the unconscious mind (Hourning, 1986). From Kemetic Egypt we find the first scientific studies of biological psychiatry and medicine (Finch, 1990; King, 1990). We find the first highly evolved theory of metaphysics and of consciousness that is not completely identified with the body but instead with the more subtle principles of mind and organization (Schwaller de Lubicz, 1961). It is also in ancient Kemetic Egypt that we find the first scientific and organized studies of the mysterious process of Kundalini. This luminous reality lies enfolded deep within the human body and consciousness and has profoundly affected almost every psychospiritual tradition from Asia, to Meso-America, the Christian revelations, and throughout the sacred mystical Kabbalism of the Jews. All this we shall study later. We mention them now as an overview to where we are going.

These ideas were spread by way of the trade routes to different parts of the world. Each area of the world took aspects of it, amplified it from their own perspective, and contributed to the shared richness of humanity. Some areas appear to have developed these ideas in isolation from others, or at least it would appear so on the surface. Our belief here, however, is that on a deeper level these ideas are sprung from a common soil, a common net and, like archetypes, manifest themselves differently in different contexts but always point to a common source. These various branchings or bifurcations within a common net lead in novel situations to new orders. This shared sea of emergent human consciousness, which is then able to affect the separate members of the race and the environment it inhabits, has been mythopoetically described as the noosphere (de Chardin, 1959). We take this mythopoetic description further and perceive it to be an operational and implicate order organizing principle capable of energy, information, and consciousness. For us, it is literally true *that we are one organism, that all human flesh is one, and that the opened inner eye inherently can see it.* A luminous interconnectedness within the system makes this possible.

At critical encounters, beginning civilizations such as the Renaissance European, the Greek, the Dravidian, the Olmec, and even the Egypto-Nubian were subject to the butterfly effect, or the "sensitive dependence on initial conditions." Given our root similarity on all levels, the generative "self-similarity of systems" was reinforced and expanded. It was not linear but nonlinear and yet cohesive and ultimately, though hardly directly, gave rise to a higher order. This we sense is the working of some deeper, more subtle, and implicate order unfolding in matter and evolution. These various diversifications have led to the dynamic mosaic that is the portrait of humanity today. The dawn of the Olmecs in Meso-America, the Shang dynasty and Fuhsi of China, the early rulers of Sumer and Elam, all had an Africoid connection. Pliny and other chroniclers of antiquity noted Blacks in Britain and early Greece. This in no way claims that these civilizations—the Chinese, the British, the Olmec Meso-Americans—were African simply because there was a creative mix and contact with African influences. That would be absurd and exactly the kind of idea held up to ridicule by those who either dislike or feel threatened by the "Afrocentric" perspective. Yet the reverse is often taken as true. The ancient Egyptians were predominantly African Blacks, as certainly were the Nubians and Ethiopians. Yet the scholars of the 17th, 18th, 19th, and 20th centuries find a bit of European influence in Egypt and Africa, and suddenly the roots of civilization become Greco-Roman or Mesopotamian! To be sure, just as the modern Germans, French, Russians, and English are all ethnically different but "racially" White, so were ancient Nubians, Egyptians, and other Africans of the Nile regions ethnically different, but nevertheless they were all Black by contemporary standards.

The structure of the ancient Egyptian language was not Indo-European or Semitic. It drew its linguistic structure from the interior and other regions of Africa. They were oriented to the South, the heartland and source of the species. No, what we are saying is that there is a common shared pool that sets the stage for nonlinear processes to unfold at crucial junctures leading to increased diversity and complexity. The first rise of Europe had many of its roots in ancient Egypt through the Greek transmission and the later Roman extensions. Then Europe fell into the Dark Ages after a period of creativity. After a sleep of nearly a millennia, the African genesis, amplified and transmitted by the Moors of North Africa, helped set the stage for the Renaissance in science and learning (Van Sertima, 1992). It is not that the European Renaissance is African! Rather there is a deep current of unfoldment that draws heavily from our shared genetic, embryological, and psychospiritual origin as an Africoid species in all its diversifications and surface-structure manifestations.

We now turn our attention to something that has been alluded to throughout this chapter. At various times and at various junctions we have suggested that there is a common route or an enfolded shared source of not only genetic, historical, and embryological significance, but also one of shared consciousness and shared receptivity to the world process. This we have referred to as the African unconscious. It is the substrata out of which all human variations of consciousness have unfolded. It is in essence the collective unconscious of humanity, the ideational and experiential inheritance of the entire hominid line arching back beyond even *Homo habilis* to the first adventures out of the trees on the edge of the savannas. Humanity originated in Africa and did not leave Africa until a relatively short time ago from an evolutionary perspective. Humankind is essentially an African species. It is African in developmental consciousness at its deepest levels. We now turn our attention to that idea and explore it in all of its various root manifestations.

2 THE AFRICAN UNCONSCIOUS

The collective unconscious does not develop individually, but is inherited.
—C. G. Jung, *Archetypes and the Collective Unconscious*
in *The Collected Works*

There probably exists in the mental life of the individual not only what he has experienced himself, but also what he brought with him at birth, fragments of phylogenetic origin, an archaic heritage. . . . The archaic heritage of mankind includes not only dispositions, but also ideational contents, memory traces of the experiences of former generations.
—Sigmund Freud, *Moses and Monotheism*

OLDAWAN: THE ANCIENT SOUL

THE oldest human soul is an African soul. Rooted in anthropology, biology, history, and genetics, the mysterious ocean that is human consciousness is at bottom collective, luminous, and genotypically African in its genesis. We have mentioned in the previous chapter that the oldest known human race is an African race. This leads us to the intuition that the oldest, deepest, and most primordial level of human consciousness is that mode of consciousness the hominid species has been most preoccupied with in its 2½ to 3 million years of existence. "Man," in some variation of his present form, was in Africa from 2½ to 3 million years ago and then as *Homo erectus* spread to the other areas of the world. Humankind carried out its first preliminary and earliest most sophisticated experiments within the African milieu. All the hominid variations, from the early and primitive lost pre-Australopithecines, to the Australopithecines we know of, to *Homo habilis* to *Homo erectus* and eventually to *Homo sapiens sapiens*, unfolded on the same continent shaped like a skull looking eastward on the planet like the mysterious sphinx. Their deep recurrent experiences, their racial memories are rooted in our own brains in a collective, primordial way. Indeed, from 2½ million years ago hominid ancestors experimented in some conscious way with their own mental landscape and with branchings and diversifications unfolded progressively more subtle forms of intelligence. These branchings, approximately 150,000 to 200,000 years ago, criss-crossed in a single female human being, dark and Africoid, on a forgotten savanna. Perhaps 188,000 years ago an Africoid male wrote upon every Y chromosome his own unfailing signature. In a very real way, the roots of the collective hominid and the human unconscious are really a primordial African unconscious.

The great pioneer Sigmund Freud was actually aware of this on some level. He referred to the collective unconscious as the racial memory. His library in Vienna was littered with artifacts from African and especially Egyptian history and anthropology. Freud was also ambivalent about this realization and revealed this on several occasions. He feared, as many do, the notion of a primordial African consciousness as the wellspring of human consciousness. He referred to it as the "black tide of Mud and occultism." It was perhaps the greater fear of the boundless unconscious, fear of the primordial darkness, and his own ultimate racial and egoic dissolution as a

European. Carl Jung referred to the collective unconscious as, indeed, we understand it generally today. However Jung was also aware from his own experience that he felt most in contact with his deepest, most elemental self when he was traveling the African continent. He left Europe several times with the intention of establishing a more universal perspective on this collective unconscious by studying the dreams of Blacks in Africa and in the United States. Many times he mentioned the uncanny experiences he had and the sense of some bottomless primordial memory underneath and foundationalizing his recent, emergent European memory. Despite his vision he was still like many Europeans, afraid of "going Black" and all that means for an ego identified as a White person. Recall that prior to 25,000 to 30,000 years ago, all *Homo sapiens sapiens* were Black and that "racial" diversification as we think of it today had not yet begun. The present-day implication of this, of course, is that beneath the wealth of contents in our shared or multicultural unconscious the primordial essence and genetic roots of our African dynamism dwells. Jung felt this deeper racial memory as his bedrock memory, and it unfolded within him a great peace and sense of unity between all the peoples of his planet. Many people have had similar experiences and insights.

This repression of the primordial African unconscious is an act of repression not only in Europe but also in Eurocentric science. It might be thought of as the collective "threatened return of the repressed." In the early Greek myths appears the motif of the "devouring sphinx," and we can see in this myth the fear of an ancient Kemetic Egyptian consciousness. This is associated with the earliest Greek myths and stories that allude to their origins as an Egyptian colony from Africa (Diop, 1991). The Greeks as a people did not come from Egypt of course, but strong early elements of their great cultural flowering did owe much to their neighbors farther to the south who had been flowering for millennia. It would seem that the Greek consciousness and Greek civilization, emerging from an early colony of Egyptians from their own mythohistorical point of view, was in some ways afraid of a slideback into its parent stock. This process of the emergence of classical Greek culture from contributions from Egyptian culture quickly arose around 600 B.C.E. However, it would be unfair to assume that the ancient Greeks were anti-Egyptian. If anything, they were very much pro-Egyptian and recognized ancient Egypt as not only the source of much of their own civilization but the source of civilization itself. Civilization is taken to mean not only medicine, but also the arts of writing, mathematics, astronomy, archeology, history, and philosophy.

The later Romans had a collective unconscious memory of ancient Egypt. In ancient Rome there were many cults of the "Black Madonna." These were variations of the earlier Kemetic cult of Isis, a cult which itself was even older than the Egyptians and originated in the Nubian civilization that was prior to the Egyptian civilization. As mentioned before, the cult of the Black Madonna in all its variations can be found scattered throughout Europe and the Near East. This is a manifestation of the memory and the influence of the collective unconscious in its African expression. As we shall see in future chapters, numerous luminaries of the Greek tradition actually studied in the Egyptian mystery schools and later translated directly the texts and philosophy of ancient Egypt into their own (Finch, 1990; James, 1954; Schwaller de Lubicz, 1961).

When the genius of Kemetic Egyptian civilization was rediscovered by Europe in the 18th and 19th centuries, this threatened return of the repressed was handled differently. Egypt was mentally and "scientifically" taken out of Africa and made an extension of European and Middle Eastern history and development. It became "Egypt *and* Africa." Along with this came a sudden interest in Indian culture and the Sanskrit language. The Indo-Aryan connection to India was heightened, and slowly a Caucasian genesis was seen in Hindu civilization. The indigenous African was erased from the teaching of history and the unfoldment of human civilization. This subtle psychological process continues to this day on a large scale. With a few notable exceptions, in the Eurocentric tradition it was simply inconceivable that a highly evolved civilization that gave light to the mind could have its genesis in a dark and mysterious world and then move in an African migration down toward the Mediterranean. This is despite the fact that the Romans did not come until Caesar, around 30 B.C.E., that the Greeks did not come in mass numbers before Alexander in 333 B.C.E., that the Jews did not come to be known before Abraham and Joseph, that the Assyrians, Phoenicians, and many others did not come until very late in the day. By that time the Kemetic lens of the human mind had already developed several written scripts, astronomy, medicine, mathematics, mummification, a form of biological psychiatry, a precise calendar, the pyramids, and by the 8th century B.C.E. in the 25th Dynasty, had made contact with peoples from southern India to the Americas. Such awareness must be repressed if you are to hold people in bondage and justify the belief that they are an inferior race. Otherwise, a deep disquiet disturbs the peace and the order of society is merely based on pure power, aggression, and savagery. This is incongruous with a self-perception of being a person or people of reason, enlightened and committed to the spiritual equality of all human souls in the community of God. Yes, all this must be repressed and replaced with a perception that is more soothing and justifying of one's actions and the "mission" of one's culture. And yet this deep memory does not stay dead. It is alive and gives rise to our deeper experiences and perhaps our earliest, most noble aspirations. It is within all of us and all of us are within it.

THE NATURE OF THE UNCONSCIOUS

Before plunging into the netherworld of the unconscious, it is necessary to say just what on earth is meant by the idea of an unconscious mind. Generally speaking, it means a dimension of mental life in which information is processed outside of conscious awareness. The recognition of this arches back to the ancient Kemetic idea of the creative flux out of which life and conscious awareness arises, the so-called Primeval Waters of Nun (Hourning, 1986). Parallel to it is their notion of consciousness descending in sleep and in death to an all-Black underworld of symbols, animals, forces, and dynamics, only to reawaken or be resurrected in the future. This is the all-Black underworld of their Amenta (King, 1990). In both instances, the priests, both male and female, were *conscious* of this agency of the mind, and it was fully integrated in both medicine and religion, e.g., use of hypnosis, trance, and dream interpretation. These dynamics were known in the Old Kingdom period!

The use of the unconscious reached its most evolved state in the so-called "sleep temples" of these ancient times. The techniques of initiation involved the strict observance of certain ascetic rules of diet, living, and self-discipline, and some systematic method of meditation. This was believed to intensify or awaken the spiritual impulse. In some sleep temples large but harmless serpents were present on the floor while the initiate lay half sleeping or in trance in the darkened room. This created a highly aroused state. During this time, the priest, male or female, would verbally guide the patient or student/neophyte, by means of hypnosis or other altered state of consciousness, through certain realms of experience and into deep trance. There occurred a temporary dissociation of the "I" or "ego" from consciousness. The unconscious or Amenta underworld of beings and forces were then manifest to some level of experience. The initiate's body, wrapped in grave clothes or other ceremonial garments and enclosed in the temple tomb after ritual baths and a thorough "interview" by the priest, hovered on the ledge between life and death. Many of the phenomena that now accompany the NDE, or clinical near-death experience, arose, including luminous experiences and the witnessing of spiritual beings. The dissociation between ordinary consciousness and numinous or spiritual experience was temporarily overcome by this intentional but temporary counterdissociation using trance and hypnosis! When the neophyte was awakened from the procedure, the priest would call forth the "traveler" between worlds in what was literally a ritual of resurrection. A mystical death had been experienced, and the neophyte now had a living memory-knowledge of his deeper eternal self that is projected into the realm of space, time, and matter. He or she had seen beyond the five senses and was "born again." These Kemetic Egyptian initiates were called the "twice born," who now had a direct contact with the great macrocosm of which they were a microcosmic reflection. They had ever so briefly "come forth by day." This was the journey and drama of Osiris, an adventure that we will return to later and find echoed throughout this book.

This ancient approach to the Amenta, or unconscious, began in Kemet and spread down the Nile and then throughout the Mediterranean world of Greece, Rome, and the Near East. At one time there were over 400 such temples to the god Asclepius. They existed from 600 B.C.E. to 500 C.E. The medical caduceus, a staff with a serpent entwined around it seven times, was taken from this period. The whole point, beyond physical-medical healing, was to "awaken" the sleepers to the deeper spiritual life existing in the unconscious depths of their experience. It was to *re-member*, to put back together again the consciousness of the finite individual material life with the infinite collective and luminous life of the great spiritual being. When this was accomplished, the neophyte matured into one of the "sons of light" and was capable of "coming forth by day and going forth by night." After the fall of the Roman Empire in the West, there was both struggle and cultural destruction and eventually a papal bigotry arose against these techniques, for hundreds of years driving them underground. For over a thousand years the knowledge was all but lost in Europe until the Enlightenment, when its scholars began to notice again that the mind was active on several levels at once. The personal unconscious is now an accepted mental terrain in science and philosophy. The deeper regions of this unconscious, the unconscious as experienced in the Amenta, however, is still taboo to much of Western science.

Leibniz, in his *New Essays on Human Understanding* (1704/1981), openly suggested that the human mind harbored an unconscious process that influenced behavior. He said, "there are hundreds of indications leading us to conclude that at every moment there is in us an infinity of perceptions unaccompanied by awareness or reflection." "The choice we make arises from these insensible stimuli, which, mingled with the actions of objects and our bodily interiors, make us find one direction of movement more comfortable than the other." It was also Leibniz who, in contrast to Newton and others, emphasized an interpenetrating and wavelike view of reality, a view that implies underlying rhythms, harmonies, and resonances as the ordering structures of the physical universe.

Before Freud, the psychiatrist Janet had suggested the clinical concept of dissociation, which deeply influenced James in America, and later Hilgard. Pierre and Jastrow, working in experimental psychophysical psychology, suggested the phenomena of subliminal perception, which was picked up by others researching unconscious learning and sensation. Helmholtz and others had introduced the idea of automatic processing and unconscious inference in perception (Kihlstrom, Barnhardt, & Tataryn, 1992). So by the time Freud came on the scene, there was much in the air about unconscious mental life and information outside of awareness that dynamically influenced human behavior.

When Freud arose, he had both a medical background and recent observations of dissociation and hysterical phenomena. He also, as we shall see later, had a foundation in certain currents of Jewish mysticism. His genius was the integration of these vibrant currents in a stunning new synthesis. In a crucial way Freud and the other Western explorers of the newly rediscovered unconscious helped reintroduce the "magical" level of the mind into a Europe whose vision and science were descending deeper and deeper into the three-dimensional world of materialism, where the soul is eclipsed and the essence of humanity was being reduced to the automata of matter, cause, effect, and the rigid space and time world locked in the senses. Einstein in his own way and at about the same time was effecting his own liberation with the exploration of the space–time continuum and transformations between matter and energy.

Freud's unconscious was one that fomented with passion, feeling, primitive impulses, and deep biological drives. In order to hold these in check, to keep the vibrant stream locked in "knots," required force, psychic force. Freud focused on the process of repression as opposed to dissociation. Yet even Freud acknowledged a deep "racial memory" that is inherited by the organism. In this way, he was connected with Jung, who embraced a "collective unconscious" of shared ideas, images, dynamisms, and archetypes.

Nonlocality and the Unconscious

Today, there is little disagreement that there is an unconscious agency in mental life. The question is how intelligent it is and what areas it covers. A good deal of experimental data suggest that nonconscious information-acquisition processes are extremely fast and set up programs that later quickly encode similar information (Lewicki, Hill, & Czyzewska, 1992). In the areas of clinical psychopathology, it is acknowledged that an unconscious agency of mental life can dissociate and exchange or transform one situation for another. These are the so-called dissociative and conversion disorders. Patients with brain damage or other organic pathologies are capable of discriminative responses that they cannot see, the so-called "blindsight syndrome," and, like sighted people, they are capable of certain forms of subliminal perception. There is a wealth of clinical, experimental, and theoretical information we could present on this that would take us far afield. The main thrust here is that the human mind has a dynamic hidden mental life that absorbs images and complex information, processes it on simple and apparently sophisticated levels, is capable of subtle perceptions that influence behavior, and has a deep, implicit memory of important and repeated situations.

This is equally so in the deep-structure syntax of language, for language and grammar, even universal grammar, has embedded in them the ideas, preferences, and intuitive apprehensions of reality. The unconscious here is, therefore, *not* to be identified exclusively with the Freudian unconscious, but rather contains or subsumes it. It also, like Jung's fuller conception, embraces deep and primordial racial memories that are passed across the waves and waves of human generations and are *implicate* or enfolded in each of us. The ego is a local and boundary-setting process. The unconscious or the ancient Kemetic Amenta is a nonlocal phenomenon. The basic "building block" of the psyche and soma is not the isolated, egoic "atom," so to speak, but rather the interconnected, nonlocal "quantum of action." Nonlocality is a feature of the everyday world! It is also, as we will see in the chapter on psychoneurology and the solar logos, an intimate feature of the nervous system and the brain! This unfolds different psychological and psychospiritual field dynamics from the intrapsychic, interpersonal, or even systemic model of influence and causality. The world process, including the psychological plane, is inherently transtemporal and transpatial.

This transtemporal and transpatial matrix of consciousness, energy, and information over duration and development appears to have a profound effect on the members of the matrix. The "wave" form, if you will, acts as an envelope over the separate "parts" of the system here, and the system itself is rooted in an Africoid phenomenon. The deepest images and memories are primordial and African, whether we like it or not. This includes the deepest primordial images of the familial unconscious. This is true for Europeans as well as modern peoples of African lineage! This primal Alajobi is peopled with the earliest memories of faces of the Blacks and Browns, or "moros," the parents of the human race. They are real and embedded at a certain level of the unconscious, almost like mental archetypes. We bear witness to these under extraordinary conditions, in ancestral visions, and in the vision-quest of indigenous peoples.

We accept and *extend* the tenets of the so-called cognitive revolution in psychology and science that subsumed the mechanistic-behavioral and purely physicalistic-reductionist mode of explanation. The new vision here suggests that these deep primordial currents *and* the emergent mental forces are actually causal and supervenient over lower-order brain and physical states. We *extend* it here to suggest that higher-order enfolded *consciousness* is prior to, all-pervasive within, and causal over even emergent *mental states* and actually arches into the generative order of creativity and consciousness itself. This is both the intimate scope and the subtle reach of the web we are all enfolded in, the African unconscious.

We know that our personal consciousness comes and then goes in sleep, in altered states of consciousness, in psychopathological conditions of various kinds, and perhaps in death. It is at least embedded in the world and also, it seems, emerges out of the unconscious. But so far we have not been able to "locate" it definitely anywhere in the brain. Certain regions are more densely associated with it, but it is yet uncertainly located in the brain. It appears to be inherently nonlocatable, at least on the personal level.

Also, human consciousness is at the very least embedded in the material world, acts upon and is acted upon by the material world but, again, so far is uncertainly located in the world. Excursions into neuroscience and cognitive psychology will not lead us to the front door of consciousness either, although we would come to know the general neighborhood quite well. The twin pillars of contemporary physics, relativity theory and quantum mechanics, both acknowledge the observing consciousness as an implicit part of the deep and lyrical equation with reality. Relativity reminds us that we cannot view the observer beyond or outside of the observed system and that this consciousness must be granted a specific and unique space–time coordinate in reference to the entire system. Quantum mechanics, from the other direction, suggests that the conscious observer must be present for the reality to be confirmed by the system at all (Kafatos & Nadeau, 1990). In both situations there is no local human consciousness with absolutely clear perception in space and time. Implicitly the "location" of consciousness must be outside the local corridors of space and time in order for transcendent perception to arise. Certain meditative disciplines and traditions and now recently certain suggestive trends in modern science intimate that consciousness and elements of human identity may indeed reflect nonlocal dynamics.

When we turn to striking phenomena reported in African religious disciplines and experimental phenomena, we will return again and again to this notion of consciousness as nonlocal. It is not so much that modern science is *confirming* these ancient phenomena, only that the philosophy of science is expanding to recognized dynamics it has heretofore found inexplicable.

A subtle but important point must be acknowledged at this juncture, and that is the double-edged blade of looking at anything through the eye of "the unconscious." Just as the quantum and relativistic physicists use abstruse mathematics to populate the universe with all kinds of exotic creatures and processes, only some of which are discovered to be "real" while the others remain only mathematical possibilities, so must we be careful in calling something not seen unconscious simply because it is theoretically possible. For that very humbling reason, the processes and experiences outlined in this book will keep referring back to the actual *lived experience* of students, teachers, and initiates of all the different disciplines we will mention.

So what are some of the basic principles we might discover if we were to take a bold exploration of the African unconscious? How might these be not only unfolded and differentiated from but also seen as the archetypal or enfolded root form implicit in other philosophical, scientific, and psychospiritual traditions? We will begin a preliminary exploration of this. It is by no means exhaustive, but tentative and suggestive in places. We hope to throw more light on this ancient and overlooked paradigm, a paradigm that was the prototype and the template of humanity's great arch up from primordial times into the light of current day civilization. What are its common routes, what are its earliest forms?

SOME BASIC TENETS OF THE AFRICAN UNCONSCIOUS

Civilization has given rise to different visions of and approaches to reality. These different paradigms can be quite scientific and also give rise to our deepest intuitions of the nature of light, consciousness, and reality itself. In the West, meaning primarily Europe and current-day United States, materialism has taken root as the fundamental notion as to the basis of reality. In other words, physical matter, including energy, is taken to be the primordial reality out of which all other things are composed, transformed, and evolved. In Asia, meaning primarily India but also China and Japan, the spiritual foundation is considered to be the ultimate basis of reality. Matter and energy are taken to be manifestations of spirit. These two world intuitions would seem to dominate the intellectual landscape of modern times. However, there is a third paradigm that is often overlooked but that has also guided humanity for eons. This is the approach of personalism, an approach more indigenous to the African intuition of reality.

In "personalism" the essence of reality is taken to be the personhood of persons, objects, situations, and forces. Personalism is not to be identified with archaic reasoning, but rather there is an emphasis on the "essence" of a person or a force. It implies a certain pantheism in nature. The notion of atheism is itself quite alien in this worldview (Asante, 1984). The world process is literally one of personalized spiritual forces interacting and interconnected with each other within a nonlinear causal matrix of space, matter, intentionality, and time. As one contemporary African sociologist has put it:

> I am strongly inclined to believe ... that there is an unwelt [worldview] characteristic of the African peoples wherever they may live in asuwada eniyan [socialized human life], and regardless of the climatic and physical condition. Africans, to my mind, perceive spiritual beings in the world around them.

They believe that the true substances—that is real selves of such objects as man, trees, rivers, hills, desertland, fishes, crocodiles, horses and the like—are these forces which continue in being after the physical forms of the objects have been rendered inactive somehow. As illustrations, they aver that when a fire is extinguished its real self is sheathed in ashes awaiting the next occasion to burst forth in flames; that when a banana tree matures, the real banana assumes new expiessions in offshoots, and that a tree when cut down by a wood cutter, comes out as a tender sapling. The capability of human beings to reproduce their kinds is merely one way of expressing the substance or realness of Human Beings. (Akiwowo, 1980, p. 17)

In this worldview is rooted the notion and implicit perception of continuous transformation, including the reincarnation of all beings high and low. It is what we will later look at as the Osirian process of eternal renewal, because, as it is expressed in the West African Yoruba traditions of Ifa and Orunmila, "the purpose of the human physical form is the transmission of certain spiritual values to the inhabitants of the Earth through human beings" (Akiwowo, 1980, p. 11).

Personalism, therefore, includes not only this intuition of spirit inhabiting and pervading material and temporal reality, but it seems to go beyond this to include as a generalized predisposition or mode of perception and cognition and therefore *experience* in the world, the proclivity or tendency to unfold an enfolded higher-order energy and informational matrix at times. This can be seen in the religious systems when an Orisha or Loa, by way of rhythmic entrainment, is unfolded into a more localized situation from a higher-order enfolded reality. This is again a form of the top-down mode of cognitive psychology mentioned earlier, which acknowledges that emergent states of conscious brain activity can come to control the activity of the lower states of activity that gave rise to it and, thereby, influence its behavior. But we ask, what if these "emergent states" are tapping into something, some intelligent energy that is hidden, ordered, and already preexisting? There would be interconnected fields, rhythms, levels of information, forms of intelligent communication. It would be to accept that there are systems of order and planes of intelligence both higher and lower than the human plane. Rhythm is reflected in the primary structure and ordering process of the universe (Cousto, 1990; Flatischler, 1990). Matter itself, from the quantum mechanical view, is a localization of waves and rhythms of probability superimposed upon each other but not absolutely located in one area, rather having its boundaries extended throughout the universe of energy and information. For the African sensibility, rhythm is fundamental and orders both the heartbeat and the orbits of the stars and planets, not to mention communal life and the "spirit world." It embraces a transpersonal and transcendental dimension of reality, a realm from which other phenomena such as healing, psi, and prophecy emerge within the context of a disciplined psychospiritual lineage. We will return to this theme again in later chapters. Suffice it to say this is not "primitive" in the simplistic sense, but in the sense of "prime" or first cause.

It was actually Auguste Comte (1830) who originally gave the notion of personalism a bad name by associating it negatively with the idea of "primitive and less articulate, irrational, and more archaic." Eventually this tradition became even more pejorative, e.g., inferior, antilogical, alogical, "impressionistic," "prelogical," etc. This arose in Europe during the heyday of logical positivism. It was also historically a time when the European powers were supreme in terms of military power and technological science, and had geopolitical and financial hegemony over the other parts of the world. However, the notion of personalism did not completely submerge in European philosophy. In fact we can find certain aspects of "personalism" in the philosophy of the great paleontologist, priest, and mystic Teilhard de Chardin. Here in this great Jesuit visionary and scientist we find the personal imbued not only in the day-to-day activities of humankind, but also in evolutionary philosophy and in the divine milieu.

The notion of personalism progressively finds more expression in clinically scientific events and day-to-day circles within the lifestyles of families. In other words, in families the personality or the personhood of another person is primary as opposed to their thinghood. From the perspective of personhood, no one person or situation or thing is ever ultimately separate or autonomous from any other thing. Psychological and emotional boundaries are a matter of emphasis or focus, not a matter of absoluteness. The so-called "participation mystique' is an outgrowth and natural expression of this dynamic interpenetration paradigm of energies and essences in the world process. This is most clear in issues surrounding the notions of blame, causality, and emotional influence as seen in both family therapy and family medicine practice. From this arises one of the fundamental differentiations one finds in the personalism view that is a manifestation of the African unconscious. In other words, the collective and familial emphasis on the web of identity and causality is highlighted as opposed to the more individual or egoic. One finds this in many areas of the African unconscious paradigm.

Diop (1991) and others have alluded to this numerous times. Looking at the collective and familial versus the individual and egoic, one reveals a number of interesting "dichotomies." In other words, if we took the collective and familial and placed this opposite the individual and egoic, we'd be able to notice very much an emphasis on the syncretic versus the analytical, the poly as opposed to the mono, the rhythmic as opposed to the melodic, the continuous as opposed to the discrete, the organic as opposed to the mechanistic, the inductive as opposed to the deductive, pattern recognition as opposed to discrete identities, and a sensory tactile mode as opposed to the mood of isolation and withdrawal. The oral tradition is emphasized over the written here, and it defines time in relation to interpersonal events in the past and future (White & Parham, 1990). These are of course simplifications, but they begin to give one a notion of the differences and the drift and the tone of the different approaches inherent and embedded in the African unconscious. Linda James Myers (1993), in her compendium of African-centered belief systems and paradigms, has succinctly organized this perspective, echoing some of the same dichotomies as Diop while placing an emphasis on the optimal functioning of the human mind and spirit. (See Figure 22.)

There are different streams that make up the African unconscious in terms of the psychological process. Nothing is foreign or alien to it, rather certain areas are emphasized more than others. From the African unconscious emerges an approach to dream interpretation and theory that has been elaborated in other works (Bynum, 1993). In the African unconscious, as we've just seen, personalism is emphasized and to some extent it enfolds both spiritualism and materialism. It is more than possible to do science in each of these worldviews. This will have profound implications for certain areas of psychology and the scientific process.

Personalism, spiritualism, and materialism each have a special strength and none are totally distinct from the others. They do, however, see each other differently. Spiritualism sees the world process as primarily a manifestation of transcendental intelligence—matter, energy, and mind all being projections of spirit into time and every manner of circumstances. As the great scholar-mystic and yogi, Sri Aurobindo, said "some people see Beings and others see Forces" (Satprem, 1968, p. 198). Materialism on the other hand sees spirit as either a myth or at best like mind itself, a mere energetic epiphenomenon of matter, while personalism is relegated to either "archaic" thinking or just plain primitivism. Personalism sees matter and spirit coexistent in every form as essences which, while eternally alive in some *transformation*, are subtle expressions of a great personalizing Being. It is again more than possible to do science *within* each worldview.

The Web of Transformations

One of the other primary principles or matrices of the African unconscious, as we said earlier, is the active perception of transformations in all of the life processes and creation. In other words, $E = mc^2$ is an active personalized perception of what is occurring in nature. Again, some people see Beings, others see Forces. In both paradigms it is an active *perception* of

FIGURE 22. Optimal Conceptualization: Methods of an Ancient Afrocentric Psychology.

Based on the philosophical assumptions and principles serving as the foundation of the worldview of ancient Africans, a conceptual system has been identified that empowers us toward the achievement of everlasting peace and happiness. When we value such an aim, it may be described as optimal. In the West, however, most of us have been socialized into a worldview undergirded by a conceptual system that is less than optimal, yielding racism, sexism, classism, and so on. This conceptual system is termed sub-optimal.

Described below are the differences between the optimal and sub-optimal conceptual systems and their consequent worldviews.

Assumptions	Optimal Systems	Sub-Optimal Systems
Ontology (nature of reality)	Spiritual (known in an extrasensory fashion) and material (known through the five senses) as one	Material with possible spiritual aspect is separate and secondary
Epistemology (nature of knowledge)	Self-knowledge known through symbolic imagery and rhythm	External knowledge known through counting and measuring
Axiology (nature of value)	Highest value placed on positive interpersonal relationships	Highest value placed on objects or acquiring objects
Logic (reason)	Diunital—emphasizes union of opposites (both/and conclusions)	Dichotomous—emphasizes duality (either/or conclusions)
Process	Ntuology—all sets are interrelated through human and spiritual networks	Technology—all sets are repeatable and reproducible
Identity	Extended self, multidimensional	Individual form
Self-worth	Intrinsic in being	Based on external criteria or materialism
Values guiding behavior	Spiritualism, oneness with nature, communalism	Materialism, competition, individualism
Sense of well-being	Positively consistent despite appearances due to relationship with source	In constant flux and struggle
Life, space	Infinite and unlimited (spirit manifesting)	Finite and limited (beginning with birth and ending with death)

Developed by Linda James Myers, Ph.D., this table shows many, although not all, of the conceptual and paradigmatic differentiations between present-day "Western" philosophical assumptions and those of traditional and ancient African conceptual systems. (Permission of L. J. Myers, *Understanding An Afrocentric World View.*)

constant transformations. This occurs in the creation of polyforms of rhythms in music, in the creation of shifting patterns in the production of textiles, and in the religious intuitions in the lives of practitioners (Thompson, 1983). The earliest known metaphysical and philosophical codification of an active perception of endless transformations in nature and human life can be seen in the Kemetic Egyptian text of the *Going Forth By Day*, more commonly known as the *Egyptian Book of the Dead*, written some 3,500 years before the birth of Christ. In this active perception of transformations in all of the life processes in creation, personal or egoic death is seen as real, yet an illusion to the soul and a radical shift in spiritual consciousness. There is an inherent belief in the levels of consciousness as reflected in the perception of the presence of deceased family members at different levels of subtle embodiment and our capacity to make contact with them. This is seen as a superstition or fear from the physicalistic and traditional materialistic point of view but is seen as a living reality from an Afrocentric point of view. We might also add that most peoples throughout the Earth also share this intuition. Embedded in this worldview—a worldview that gave rise to the first sophisticated medical science, architecture, the building of the pyramids, and mathematics—is the intuition that consciousness itself is implicit everywhere in nature and the world process. Consciousness is believed in living principle to pervade the spaces between the stars and the shifting dances below the quantum. In science, particularly in medicine and biology, it gave rise to the belief in the projection of healing to others and the belief in a living energy throughout the body that can be used by skilled medical and psychological practitioners. It gave rise to the use of sophisticated trance, elaborate herbs, and specialized medicines, both psychosomatic and otherwise, for the healing of the body. These techniques were later partially absorbed by the Romans and Greeks. It also significantly enough gave rise to the first codified notion of an evolutionary energy in the body, known as Kundalini.

In ancient Kemetic Egypt this active perception of transformations in all of the life processes and creation is seen metaphorically and mythologically in the dynamics of the earth and sky as intrinsically united. In other words, there is no body–mind split or inherent dissociation as one finds in certain other forms of Western and even Asian psychologies and spiritual traditions. The Hermetic tradition is intuited and rooted here. It's an intuition of an implicate order in nature in which each part reflects each other part in nature. An aspect or permutation of this finds expression again today in certain areas of science, such as David Bohm's (1980) implicate order as outlined in *Wholeness in the Implicate Order*. We see that it is the intuition that different aspects of the entire living, conscious field of life have reflected or enfolded in them all other aspects of the field, including the body and the wider environment. The ancient Kemetic Egyptians believed that a subtle seed of the pharaoh himself was enfolded in their own bodies and vice versa. From the myth of Osiris, they believed that the god's dismembered body was buried in sacred sites all over Egypt, binding the nation into one body and civilization, renewing its life and energy from time to time.

The upshot of all of this is that there is an intuition that there is a constant and active transformation of body, mind, and consciousness in the life process at all levels. Not only great trees, rivers, animals, and ancestors, but also inanimate nature itself seems to reflect or exhibit mental and spiritual qualities. Death is perceived as an illusion of the embodied soul and a radical shift in consciousness. In this worldview, consciousness is prior to and implicate in the body–mind, eternal, and all-pervasive. Individual essences or human beings participate and go through transformations within this greater sea of consciousness. It is all-pervasive in noumena and yet localizing in phenomena and therein personalizing in its specific aspects.

A Basic Aliveness in All Things

One of the other primordial matrices of the African unconscious is the belief, perception, and intuition of a vitalism in all things. In West African tradition, it is often referred to as "Ase," another form of conscious energy or shakti, and dwells in all things. It is what artists seek to evoke in their work and religious persons seek to manifest. Like rhythm, it is imbued with the sense of time and pattern, and is thought to be deeper than the three dimensions of an object, yet gives the object its life force. This can be traced in a formalized fashion all the way back to the *Egyptian Book of the Dead*. This vitalism can be understood as a heightened ability to experience the essence of the all-pervasive life feeling or the life current (Bynum, 1994). It has led to the valued and refined ability, particularly the familially or collectively heightened ability at times, to enter into trance states of so-called possession for healing and other purposes. The essence of things and the forces that bind and *mutually define* people are experienced as primary.

In ancient Egypt the vitalism of the king was associated with his or her capacity to rule in the royal line. It historically grew out of a cycle of eight years of a royal lineage. The origin of this is shrouded in history and no doubt the result of ancient tribal rites (Diop, 1974). However, the notion of vitalism or life energy or life intensity is primary in the African unconscious worldview. It also is subject to intense criticism when encountering a force or a civilization that has a more dissociated or hostile approach to the life current. In that situation vitalism is seen as "lower, dirty, primitive, sexual," and all the other negative connotations that one too often associates with darkness. In many European traditions, there is a subtle mood of isolation and withdrawal from this vitalistic life current. It is believed that ancient man was immersed in the unconscious and that therefore the rise of civilization is a matter of increasing *repression* of this unconscious and its vitalistic life current. For the Kemets it was not so much repression as sublimation and controlled direction of the life current. For the former the unconscious, especially an Africoid unconscious, must be repressed. For the latter it needs to be integrated and divinized by discipline and controlled tactile sensuality and rhythm.

This intuition or perception of life or vitalism in everything that exists is not confined to philosophy alone even in our own day. The founders of modern quantum mechanics felt that supposedly purely physical reality, including micro-objects, had a certain "animate-sentient"-like aspect. In other words, embedded in the primary constitution of the material world was a certain consciousness and life or initial capacity for volition and self-activity (Miller, 1991). This is to admit that consciousness and life are in a sense *immanent* in everything and that *biology has a more fundamental status than physics* in the world process. Human consciousness is a living part of a vast, interconnected community of spirit, information, and energy. This extends to the perception and belief from the African unconscious perspective in intelligences above and beyond ordinary human experience that are a fuller and still natural expression of evolutionary unfoldment. These forms of intelligence are believed to communicate themselves within the context of disciplined attention and bodily absorption within specifically designed ritualistic processes. Rhythm brings one into attunement with this vibratory matrix. This root intuition is what informs the African unconscious that personhood and spirit are in all forces, objects, and persons. Africans do not believe, as E. B. Tylor (1871) and other early Eurocentric scholars of Africa suggested when they talked of animism, that *every* object has a soul. Rather they tend to believe certain spirits can have specific objects as their abode or habitat and that they can be embodied or attached to material-energetic objects and through these objects exert their influence (Opoku, 1978). This notion and the transformations of consciousness will reappear throughout this book whenever this consciousness turns its attention to forces and interactions in the worlds, and whenever we talk of life force, a vitalism pervasive throughout the cosmos, we will look toward the current scientific idea of biological superconductivity.

Rhythm and Organization

Another primary matrix of the African unconscious is the apprehension or perception of rhythm or the propensity for pattern repetition as intrinsic in nature. We mentioned it earlier in reference to *personalism* and just now in the context of vitalism, but it requires a little more clarification. Rhythm is one of the great and powerful ordering principles in nature. There was believed to be a hidden consonance between matter, rhythm, harmony, and life, of interpenetrating forces and frequencies that bound the universe together. This extended from the stars to human life to the forces in the deepest interior of the Earth. In the external world this rhythmic sense and rhythmic apprehension of the universe led to the construction of the first exact calendars. It also led to the perception of cycles and cycles within cycles. This eventually gave rise to the intuition of the end enfolded in the beginning and the beginning implicit in the end. This opens to the eternal enfolded in time. Out of rhythm and cycles came mathematics and indeed the zodiac. All of these were later codified in the earliest forms of African science in the Kemetic civilizations of Egypt and Nubia.

In the external world this rhythmic sense can be seen in the "mystical trances" that are highly identified with the music of Blacks and dark-skinned peoples. We mention in this context also the whirling dervishes of the Muslim lineage, particularly the Zhikr. Each of these involves the repetition of certain rhythms, words, and so forth in a very intense regular fashion combined with breath and bodily gestures. When these are intensified, this leads to an oblation or eclipse of ordinary consciousness and the benign fixation of the psyche and other mental processes such that a transformation in consciousness can arise. This is similar to certain processes formalized in Yoga in which there is a fusion of concentration, contemplation, and stages of Samadhi so that eventually the emergence of a transcendental consciousness occurs.

Rhythm finds expression in the healing arts that use incantation and repetition of powerful phrases to affect mental and physical states. Like different radio frequencies that inhabit the same "space," the different rhythms of the body, soul, spirit, and "other" can coexist in the same space of the person, a person who takes as self-evident that he or she lives in a multidimensional universe. Rhythmic entrainment can also unfold these dimensions under disciplined conditions. We will have more to say about this later when we focus on trance healing and the bioinformational field of the body. For now we are outlining the rootwork of this paradigm.

In the context of rhythm giving rise to cycles, calendars, and mathematics, it is significant that the Egyptian calendar is the oldest and the most accurate until those of relatively recent times. It was in use prior to 4236 B.C.E. Rhythm and interconnectedness are the primary matrix out of which modern physics operates. Physics finds a certain parallel to these phenomena in the eastern or Asian forms of mysticism in which fluctuations, oscillations, and so forth are seen to be the literal "tissue of reality." The ancient classic, the *Tao De Ching*, is another variation of the subtle rhythms and cycles of nature and their reflections of the cosmic dance. When this basic apprehension of pattern repetition and rhythmic incantation is fully recognized and exploited, it will influence the process of insight and memory and group cognitive behavior and in the process lead to a revolution in the educational system of America's inner cities.

It has, no doubt, crossed your mind that rhythm and waves or wavefronts are much the same in the sense of their repetition, pattern creation, and ability to carry, store, and communicate information. It is implicit in this perspective that each person, each individual, past and present, regardless of surface phenotype, carries this deep rhythmic signature of an African origin. It is reflected in our genetic structure, our hominid morphology, our shared early Paleolithic adventures, and it is constantly recapitulated anew in our individual embryological unfoldment. These individual wavefronts, like all waves, are interconnected with each other and their hominid signature over time, and their repetition creates a holonomic sea of consciousness and information that sustains on a deep level the African unconscious. The rhythmic- or frequency-oriented apprehension of the world process is actually a direct path into the spectral domain of this holonomic vision of the cosmos. This includes our intuitions about bodily and terrestrial currents and forces that, while not presently accepted in the domain of scientific thought, are nevertheless enduring perceptions of natural occurrences and, therefore, worthy of our respect.

Magical-Religious Perception

Still another foundational intuition or matrix within the African unconscious paradigm is the perception of so-called magical-religious permutations in nature. Here different psychological boundaries are perceived to be exactly that, different and shifting. The practical fall-out of this is in the human encounter with the phenomenon of death. Death is a shift in consciousness, a transformation of one's self on the divine matrix. The belief in death is an illusion of finitude. For this very reason ancestor reverence, not ancestor worship, is known throughout Africa and many parts of the world associated with the African lineage. There is an active perception and an open embrace of the experience of "psychic forces" in reality, the *literal felt presence* of the essences of other personhoods. This is seen to be primitive and is anathema in contemporary Western scientific circles, but it seems to be the living reality for most peoples of the planet. The world is not a circus of dead matter and its chance and random permutations. Scientific materialism with its "faith" in reductionism, its "belief" that matter can ultimately be understood by mechanics and mathematics, and its "hope" that objective mind separate from the phenomena it observes can discover physical laws with an exact correspondence to physical theory and measurement—this scientific fundamentalism would have us believe all other thinking is but archaic thought. The totality of the world process is composed certainly of matter and energy, but also spirit and the essence or personhood of persons, forces, and other aspects of nature. There is a tacit acceptance of all of these—matter, spirit, and personhood—in a unified field within the African unconscious worldview. It is just that at certain times specific rhythmic vibrational dimensions are emphasized more than others. Spirit and personhood are not dissociated from the field of matter, nor are the others dissociated from each other. They are interconnected, each aspect implicating all others.

These motifs find beautiful, abundant, and recurrent expression in the oral and literary tradition of African peoples and those deeply affected by a sustained contact with people of African lineage, such as the Spanish and Portuguese of the Iberian peninsula and the Americas, including the Caribbean. African-American folktales speak of the people who could fly (Hamilton, 1985), of "supernatural" forces imbuing the world, psychic events, and epiphanies of the dead. Nobel laureate Toni Morrison's work breathes with this, as does the work of other literary laureates in this tradition, Wole Soyinka and Derek Walcott. Caribbean and Latin writers reflect the same currents, e.g., Gabriel García Marquez, Jorge Amado, and Isabel Allende. Many of these roots, no doubt, spiral into the collective racial memory of beliefs and hidden disciplines in Voudoun, Santería, psi episodes, OBES (out-of-body experiences), and lucid dream experiences. These practices and disciplines have always been terrifying to the Western world. In recoil from this dimension of the world process, they are simply dismissed as crude superstition and pseudoscience. But make no mistake about it, there is a deep and steep basis in fact here. There is also an empirical methodology that incorporates many disciplines within a paradigm of rhythm, vibration, and a field of consciousness totally coextensive with the realms of matter, energy, and spatiotemporal coordinates. This does not contradict modern science, it compliments it! There is a *mutability* in the boundary between self and other, between substance and force, between life and death.

The Ascending Force: Kundalini

One of the most profound aspects of the African unconscious worldview, we believe, is the openness to the phenomenon of Kundalini as the basis of religion, art, science, and metaphysics. Kundalini is literally the evolutionary force becoming conscious in man. This ancient force, associated with certain movements and energies of the braincore and spine in consciousness, was first uncovered in Kemetic science approximately 7,000 years before

Christ. It was later partially codified in ancient Kemetic science in terms of the eye of Horus. It has also been associated with light, the pineal gland, and brain neuromelanin (King, 1990). We'll explore these further in the next chapter. Suffice it to say here that it is the foundation of many aspects of the African unconscious worldview. If one looks at the heraldry of ancient Egypt, particularly the headdress, we find references to the luminous serpent of Kundalini many times. If we study the Pyramid Texts of ancient Egypt and their ramifications, we quickly realize that the science of Kundalini was well known in ancient Egypt (King, 1990). If we look to genetic, racial, and cultural connections with the other civilizations of African lineage, particularly those of the Dravidians in India, we find numerous references to the presence and the perception of the process of Kundalini. It was central to their Yogic-based religions in the ancient cities of Harappa and Mohenjo-Daro. This is all at least 1,000 years before the first Aryan invasions of northern India.

Communal Consciousness

Another one of the primary matrices or reflections of the African unconscious can be found in the emphasis on group or tribal or community consciousness as opposed to egoic or individualized or autonomous consciousness. We have alluded to this earlier. This emphasis on tribal or group or shared consciousness has very many practical aspects. In a very real way the approach is a much more ecological and relational one as opposed to an autonomous or atomistic one. Clinically speaking, in the approach one focuses on the wider environment both internally and externally. This wider environment includes not only the somatic expression of the body but also the health of the family, the community, and a person's relationship to the gods. There is a subtle bias toward nurturance and interconnectedness with the wider ecology, a relational and resonate affinity in one's perceptions with a deemphasis, but *not* negation, of objectification and market values. Because it is a highly personalized world and the consciousness is not isolated but rather localized in certain areas, boundaries are inherently permeable by other personhoods and so, clinically speaking, it is not a matter of "What is the matter with you?" but rather "Who is the matter with you?" Or, said in another way, "I am because we are and since we are, therefore I am." The emphasis is on racial and collective or community consciousness and it is seen as prior and primary to individuated consciousness. This is why again the individual or localized principle is seen to participate in a wider sea of consciousness that is prior to it and will exist after that individualized or more localized principle has gone through dissolution.

In day-to-day living reality, this finds its expression in terms of one's experience and perception of one's own individual identity and also the existence of one's community and family. The family unconscious, the shared field of experience that each member of a family participates in, is seen to unfold like a wave over at least three or four levels or generations. In other words, family consciousness is said to enfold not only the person *to be born* but also the *present living person*. But more than that, it said to enfold the *recent dead* or deceased in the family. This is known as "the living dead." In the West this has all kinds of negative connotations, but certainly it does not from an Afrocentric point of view. There are certain metaphysical beliefs and experiences about "the living dead" and family dynamics that greatly extend our conception of family and of individual identity (Mbiti, 1969). This family unconscious is said to spread out and enfold the recent or the living dead up to *at least four generations from the present living person*. Living human beings have enfolded in their own lives the reincarnated attributes and feelings of the dead. The family unconsciousness is seen to be an active, living, conscious principle that moves back numerous generations in time and also reaches forward to those who are not yet born. This dimension of familial consciousness emerges to us in extraordinary states of awareness such as vision-quests, death itself, and the clinical NDE where we are met in the immediate post-mortem state by deceased relatives and others we know by intuitive feel and kinship association. This occurs prior to our encounter with the luminous being beyond mental comprehension with whom we experience a vast panoramic life review. This family system, or Ajobi, is a constant theme in African life and scholarship. As the sociologist Akiwowo (1980) puts it:

> Ajobi refers to members of a family or a group of related families or several groups of related families, in a house, in a compound of dwellers, units in a village, town and so on. Ajobi also refers to members united by birth and blood who live separately in distant villages, towns or regions of the world, or a people in diaspora. According to the Orunmilaist perspective of mankind, all human beings, regardless of race, color, and religion belong to a primordial alajobi or common origin and therefore share the ajobi bond. This idea is expressed thus: Iya kan, baba kan lo bi gbogbo wa, (translated as one mother, one father gave birth to us all, humankind). (pp. 18–19)

This, of course, is the great, enfolding family unconscious. In the implicate order that enfolds us, we each have a minority representation in the other and in more intense localized family systems. This representation is an almost "inverse square" representation in terms of shared identity, imagery, affect, and ideation. We are, after all, beings in "energetic" relationships with each other. It is a dynamic, personalized matrix and a representation of the transformation of individualized consciousness.[1] This can be seen literally mapped out in particular sections of the Pyramid Texts and the *Egyptian Book of the Dead*. Indeed the *Egyptian Book of the Dead* can be seen as a codified projection of the transformations of consciousness after its release from local embodiment and also the transformations of consciousness that occur when the person or individualized principle of consciousness moves through the different levels of consciousness that are anterior to the body–mind.

In this last area we must mention that regardless of how alien it may seem to the Eurocentric point of view, the African unconscious believes that the living dead can be sent against another person with an evil purpose. We find a proliferation of beliefs in living sorcerers and witches who can use the vital forces spoken of earlier for evil. However, this is a very rare practice even when it is believed in. The community is believed to be ultimately hurt by this kind of malignant practice. The potential damage inflicted by these practices extends beyond the particular individuals who may be involved to the community of which that individual is a member (Mbiti, 1969).

In indigenous African belief systems the localized family unconscious, or Ajobi, is "guarded" or watched over by one or more of the deceased ancestors. Members psychologically and spiritually have a dynamic relationship with these ancestors, who in special cases have evolved in the unseen but coextensive spirit world with other natural forces to become the Orishas. This human intuition is pervasive in almost every non-European culture of today regardless of modern technological level (e.g., Yoruba, Japanese, Chinese, Australian Aboriginal, etc.). Before the invasion of the Indo-Aryans into Europe, the indigenous Europeans for millennia also practiced a form of ancestor veneration. Families were known to have a "family spirit" (Gimbutas, 1992). Most of this was swept away or crushed into repression with the conquest of the horse-riding patriarchal tribes. Yet deep in the interior of the African unconscious level of their own psyche, this dynamic intuition still lives.

Conductivity of the Life Force

Finally, we should mention one last principle of the African unconscious, the subtle presence of the above principles integrated into a belief in the literal movement of the life process by way of rhythm and vitality through the body. This is associated with light, bioenergy, and the life force. In modern terms we refer to this as bioconductivity. It has a certain affinity to more

---

1. On the deepest level of this family unconscious for all peoples, including the European branches of the great Alajobi, the primal members are "moro" or Browns and Blacks.

recent scientific notions such as biological superconductivity, which we will mention later. It is also highly associated with certain neurobiological and neuroembryological processes embedded in the human body–mind structure. We are referring to neuromelanin, which is present from the beginning of human embryogenesis and is highly integrated and subtle throughout the braincore of the adult human being. It is highly associated with the "energy line" that we see in Yoga and acupuncture. In further chapters we shall return to this last and vital area.

A Living Memory

So quickly then, how does this living system perpetuate itself in us? These deep structures of the African unconscious are both *inherited* and *transmitted* across the ages and generations. It is an informational and energy system rooted in the brainwork and the living tissue of culture in all its permutations that we both give to and take from. It is almost as though such a memory is stored vibrationally in both the body and the air! Imagine this. A message is sent to the moon at the speed of light by S_1 to S_2. It takes nearly three seconds. The person on the moon, or S_2, reflects this signal and sends the message back to S_1. Now imagine numerous persons at the S_1 area sending multiple messages to numerous persons at the S_2 site, at different times, and each is reflecting and sending back the messages, but somewhat differently and at different time intervals. Different signals and messages cross at different times. New information is added all the time. After a while the messages, in this somewhat linear analogy, are being "stored" in the seemingly empty or virtual "space" between them. It is, energetically speaking, somewhat like a conscious and living worldwide Internet, only more subtle and extensive in time, and everyone is inherently connected. All are taking and receiving from this "storehouse memory." The system, after a while, affects those who send and receive the messages. The system we are all plugged into feels alive and suffused with information and therein consciousness. This is how the system perpetuates itself.

SUMMARY

We have mentioned a number of basic principles that seem to be associated with the deep collective unconscious matrix of the African primordial consciousness. It is by no means a simple or simplistic affair, nor does any one area totally exhaust or preclude any other area. Rather they are processed and integrated with each other, and at different times different areas receive a different degree of emphasis. We have mentioned the emphasis in the African unconscious paradigm of personalism not as opposed to materialism and spiritualism but as enfolding them both. These are all worldviews and in various historical eras have given rise to the dominant scientific paradigms. We have mentioned that the collective unconscious is the inherited experiences and proclivities of humanity from the earliest times. Since the roots of humanity of the last 2½ to 3 million years have been primarily an African experience and present-day racial diversification has begun only in the last 25,000 years, we are suggesting that the bedrock or archetypal template of human experience, both genetic and conscious, is primarily an African-rooted apprehension of the universe. The collective unconscious in its deepest roots is the African unconscious. From the initial pre-Australopithecines of East Africa to *Homo habilis* to *Homo erectus* on through to present-day *Homo sapiens sapiens*, all the major transformations of the species have occurred in Africa. We have, therefore, emphasized the act of the perception of transformations in all of life and life processes and creations as an archetypal process that has reached human consciousness by way of the root and route of this primordial unconscious of humanity. This is enfolded in the areas of music, textiles, religion, the perception of death, and also the ultimate union of body and mind as opposed to the split dissociation of mind and body. The Hermetic tradition is the oldest known and still practiced tradition that amplifies and puts forth this worldview. It has profound implications for our perception of body, mind, and consciousness. We have also emphasized the inherent vitalism or perception of a life current pervasive in all things which have different manifestations at different times. Again the essence or personhood of things is amplified and taken to be the primary reality. We have also emphasized the basic perception of rhythm and cycles of nature. Not only did this give rise in the outer world to the earliest calendars, mathematics, and other associated sciences, but in the inner world it has given rise to the earliest metaphysical religions and theories of transcendence and salvation. Depending on your point of view, this "rhythmic" process can be seen in a negative context (e.g., dirty, primitive, sexual, etc.), or it can be seen as the cornerstone of life, modern science (especially physics), and philosophy. We've also at various times in this chapter mentioned the inherent magical-religious perception of permutations in the universe and how that affects the experience and perception of boundaries and the perception of death. This has direct bearing on one's perception of one's relationship through family members, including the not yet born, the presently living, and the deceased up to four generations. It has given rise to the earliest highly codified science of Kundalini. It's also given rise to the emphasis on tribal or family or community consciousness as opposed to individual autonomy in the egoic consciousness. Its various emphases can be either positive or negative and need not be confined to either or both.

Finally we mentioned that from our own point of view there is implicit in this a perception that the life current can not only move through the body by way of rhythm and vitalism but also can be consciously focused and is inherently associated with light, bioenergy, or bioconductivity. This has an affinity to certain current scientific notions such as superconductivity and evolutionary neurobiology, particularly brain neuromelanin development in embryology and biological superconductivity.

The African unconscious is the bedrock, the deepest rootwork of the primordial collective unconscious, the sea and ocean of consciousness that humanity has been immersed in since it left the hominid species on its own trek toward modern civilization. Each chapter to come in this book, be it the Osirian complex, the neurodynamics of psychoneurology and the solar logos, or the paths of meditation, explores a line of development about the evolution and unfoldment of mind toward the literal light of our embodied species. It is about consciousness and its trajectory in the cosmos. It is an open question whether the other ancient hominids who went into an evolutionary dead end may have also in a limited way shared this sea of consciousness. In all likelihood they did. Why they did not survive is a great mystery. Perhaps in some curious way they live enfolded within us. All we know is that so far we have survived, that we are all permutations of the same great familial stock, and that our apparent differences are like the differences of language, merely surface structure, and that at the deeper, more primordial level, we are all children of the African womb.

3

THE ROOTS OF MODERN SCIENCE AND RELIGION IN ANCIENT EGYPT

This civilization, called Egyptian in our period, developed for a long time in its early cradle; then it slowly descended the Nile valley to spread out around the Mediterranean basin. This cycle of civilization, the longest in history, presumably lasted 10,000 years.
—Cheikh Anta Diop, *The African Origin of Civilization*

When Herodotus visited it, Egypt had already lost its independence a century earlier [525 B.C.E] . . . . Ruined by all these successive invasions, Egypt, the cradle of civilization for 10,000 years while the rest of the world was steeped in barbarism, would no longer play a political role. Nevertheless, it would long continue to initiate the younger Mediterranean peoples (Greeks and Romans, among others) into the enlightenment of civilization. Throughout Antiquity it would remain the classic land where the Mediterranean peoples went on pilgrimages to drink at the fount of scientific, religious, moral and social knowledge, the most ancient such knowledge that mankind had acquired.
—Cheikh Anta Diop, *The African Origin of Civilization*

It now seems perfectly clear that the vast majority of pre-dynastic Egyptians were of continental African stock, and even of central-west Saharan origins.
—Basil Davidson, *Africa in History*

MEDICINE, MATHEMATICS, AND ASTRONOMY

Iн our own day, particularly in the Western world, science and religion have changed places in terms of which one decides what is reality and what is most likely just a fantasy. In medieval times religion was considered the true fundamental reality and science was theoretical, the fantasy world of eccentrics, philosophers, and dreamers. Now it is vice versa! Yet there was a time when this was not the case and the two worlds shared a different harmony. Kemet was such a place.

The cornerstone of Egyptian medicine for thousands of years far exceeded anything the world knew at that time in terms of clinical philosophy, detail, and sophistication in clinical treatment. The ancient Egyptians were known to have practiced surgery and trauma medicine (Finch, 1990). Obviously, to amass this kind of detailed information would take centuries upon centuries, not simply a couple of hundred years. There is a 2,400-year span of history between the standard field medical texts of the ancient Egyptians and the medicine of Hippocrates. If we simply extrapolate a little bit and assume at the very best that they took at least several hundred, if not several thousand more years, to develop this sophisticated medical science, then we are beginning to push back the dawn of Egyptian medicine to its earliest pre-dynastic times well before the beginning of the standard Edwin Smith and Ebers Papyri, back to approximately 6000 B.C.E. Some figures push this back to before 7000 B.C.E. (Finch, 1990). This again is due to the fact that the other scientific marvel of accuracy, the Egyptian calendar, was highly sophisticated in terms of the days of the year. It could even be used today, but was known to have been in operation by the year 4236 B.C.E.!

The most famous Greek physician of antiquity, Galen (130–200 C.E.), was known to have studied in the medical schools of Egypt and in particular in the temple of Imhotep in the early centuries C.E. in search of medical knowledge. He wrote numerous medical texts, of which only 83 or so have survived the transmission of the ages. The symbols of the legendary Greek physician and healing god, Asclepius, are known to have been descendant from the Egyptian tradition. Indeed it was adopted by the Greeks from the sixth century B.C.E. onward. Asclepiades of Bithynia was in this tradition. In his lifetime (124–40 B.C.E.) he spread the teachings in the Greco-Roman world and established an influential school of medicine in Rome. His wisdom and skill did not appear overnight! The knowledge and symbols of medicine, particularly the medical caduceus, are over 6,000 years old.

The Egyptians were writing medical textbooks as early as 5,000 years ago. Of the literally thousands of medical papyri that were written, tragically we have only roughly 10 known to our present time. These include primarily the so-called Hearst papyrus, the two Berlin papyri, the Kahun medical papyrus, the London medical papyrus, and the Edwin Smith and Ebers papyrus. The rest have all been destroyed or otherwise lost to history. The Egyptian temples of learning, which they called the "houses of life" or "per ankh," served not only as library and medical school but also as temple, seminary, and university. This was the foundation of the Egyptian mystery schools that spread not only throughout Kemetic Egypt but also farther up the Nile and into the interior of Africa. It was an extensive and ancient system of lodges and teachings that persisted for centuries until largely destroyed or sent underground by the edicts of the Roman Emperors Theodosius and Justinian in the 4th and 6th centuries C.E. These medical papyri reveal that the Egyptians, due in part to the art of mummification and battlefield trauma medicine, had a rather sophisticated knowledge of anatomy and physiology at least 4,500 years before the studies of the cardiovascular system by the English physician, Harvey (Finch, 1990).

The Egyptian approach to medicine resembled very much that of today. It involved a skillful questioning of the patient, close examination of the patient's body, taking of the patient's pulse, looking into the patient's eyes, and other standard medical practices. The Egyptian priest/physician also used specific herbs and bacteriological sources to fight various diseases. It is significant that the Egyptians practiced a certain form of neurosurgery known as trephination, or opening of the skull. Physically, it was done with precision to relieve chronic headache, epilepsy, and also compressions on the brain due to trauma. Indeed the Edwin Smith papyrus is really a collection of surgical and anatomical knowledge of the ancient Egyptians. The Egyptians dispensed prescriptions and medications for health. They had evolved over the years an extensive pharmacology of herbs and mixed medications to be given in prescribed amounts. The science of physical chemistry, again in large part due to the requirements for mummification, was well developed. This, of course, was the physical side of the science of chemistry (Kemetstry). They also used enemas, suppositories, infusions, and precise wrapping of wounds. These treatments and the numerous implements used later were dispersed and sometimes improved upon throughout the Mediterranean world and have been unearthed by modern archeology (Bliquez, 1981). Even Hollywood movies acknowledge this, as, for instance, the physician hero of the sword-and-sandals classic, *The Egyptian*.

These Egyptians had some knowledge of quarantine and also of the process of creating an immunity to certain diseases by way of inoculation (Finch, 1990). From archeological remains, tools, and recovered papyri, we know that not only did they possess a variety of other medical subspecialties (Sigerist, 1951) but that among them dentistry was a highly advanced art even earlier than the New Kingdom (1552–1069 B.C.E.) (Marion, 1996). The Ebers, Hearst, Berlin, Kahun, and Smith papyri make specific references to dental procedures.

In terms of the Greek physician Hippocrates, we must point out that much of what Hippocrates contributed was by way of transmission and translation. He was born on the island of Cos in the 5th century B.C.E., from a long line of family physicians and priests of Asclepius, an Egyptian sect, who had access to the Egyptian medical knowledge reflected in the Edwin Smith papyrus and others (Ghalioungui, 1973). He was clearly a gifted writer, teacher, and healing clinician who greatly contributed to medical science. Herophilus, an Alexandrian Greek of the 4th century B.C.E., is usually credited with the discovery of taking the cardiovascular pulse. However, again, if we look at the Ebers and Smith papyri dated 3,500 years earlier, we see the exact same technique. It is more than reasonable to assume that this great Greek physician had access to the ancient Egyptian medical text called *The Book of Heart and Vessels*. Also his contemporary, the other Alexandrian physician Erasistratus, who is often credited with first outlining the relationship between the central nervous system and its peripheral nerves, also got his information from looking at the ancient Egyptian texts. The library of Alexandria had over 700,000 volumes at one point, and the city was the intellectual center of the ancient world.

Many of Egypt's techniques and the wealth of its knowledge have only been exceeded in the last century in Europe! The Egyptians were aware of the relationship between the spinal cord and various difficulties of the viscera. They had more than 200 anatomical terms identified, of which nearly 100 are found of the Edwin Smith papyrus (Finch, 1990). They knew about dislocations of the spine. They also had a sophisticated knowledge of the localization of some brain functions. It is usually thought that the Egyptians, because they placed much of their emphasis on the heart and liver, knew very little of the brain. This is categorically not true. They knew of the functions of the brain, that the compression of the brain in certain locations led to the paralysis of specific areas of the body. They knew of the different levels or layers of the brain from the outside dura mater, to the pia mater in the middle to the arachnoid situated between the outer layer of the dura mater and the inner layer of the pia mater. They were quite specific about this.

The Egyptian symbol of medical practice, the healing serpent, was, as we said earlier, subsequently taken up by the Greeks. It was intimately associated with their psychospiritual beliefs and practices, as we shall see. The Greeks focused primarily on a physical and medical or material aspect of their knowledge of the Egyptians. They tended to ignore or perhaps not understand the more subtle psychological and psychospiritual aspects of Egyptian science and philosophy. They completely missed or at best knew very little of Egyptian "psychology," e.g., the concept of the dynamic unconscious as expressed in the Primeval Waters of Nun and the images and forces of the all-Black Amenta (Hourning, 1986; King, 1990). What little they knew of Egyptian psychology and psychospiritual discipline was relegated to the supposedly "dark sciences." The Greek gift was a preoccupation with deductive rationality and the selective transmission of this to Europe, especially to Rome. In the area of religious experience they appear to have performed a kind of spiritectomy and sought, at least institutionally, to formally separate science and religion. This tradition continues even into our own day, but it fails to recognize that this healing serpent embraced both science and religion or the spirit. We will return to this in our discussion of West African religions, especially Voudoun and Ifa. The science of Kundalini and its manifestations in terms of the ascent of energy through the body was largely ignored by the Greeks. We find very few indications of any Greek awareness of the Kundalini process other than indirect reference symbolically by way of the medical caduceus. However, this knowledge was well known to the Egyptians, particularly Egyptian priests and the royal family. It was also known and taught in the mystery schools of Yoga and Kundalini Yoga, in particular in Dravidian India.

We might list many other ancient Greek luminaries here who either studied directly the texts of the Egyptian mystery schools or the men who actually traveled and lived in Egypt for long periods of time. To be sure, there were many and they founded philosophical schools whose thought still influences our scientific thinking today. Their spirituality is couched, as we shall see, in scientific terms. The point, however, has been that the ancient Greeks were very open-minded, accepting, and learned an enormous amount from the ancient Egyptians. Sometimes they cited their sources in their texts, but often they did not. Other than cryptomnesia, we have no other understanding of why they did not report their sources other than the most obvious, simple blatant racism. Remember their cultural myth of the devouring sphinx and the threatened return of the repressed.

Rhythms, Numbers, and Calendars

From Egyptian mathematics came the first detailed studies of geometry and abstract mathematics. The so-call discoveries made by the Greek lumi-

naries such as Archimedes and Pythagoras are direct translations of ancient
Egyptian texts. We have very few papyri of that period left, but we do have
enough to support this fact (Diop, 1991). In particular, the papyrus of Moscow details the Egyptian knowledge of sophisticated mathematics. The Rhind
papyrus published by T. Erik shows that the Egyptians knew the exact formula for the volume of a cylinder, $V = \pi r^2 \times h$, and the sphere and parallelepiped. They calculated the area of rectangles and squares, as well as the
relationship between the area of a circle and its diameter. They also laid
down the basic functions of algebra and trigonometry, including quadratic
equations. These are found in the Rhind, Berlin, Kahun, and Moscow papyri.
What Diop and others call the Greek tradition of plagiarism apparently is
the case for not only the ones we've mentioned so far, but also for Thales,
Solon, Eudoxus of Cnidus, Pythagoras, Plato, Idocsus, Aristotle, Oenopides,
and many, many others. The Greek historians were apparently more honest.
We are told this by Isocrates, Strabo, Josephus, Plutarch, Diogenes, and
Jamblichus, all ancient writers and chroniclers of the day. Herodotus and
Diodorus of Sicily remind us continually of the fact that the ancient Greeks
not only studied but borrowed directly their discoveries from the ancient
Egyptians. This includes Archimedes and much of what is attributed to him.
Finally, before we leave the area of mathematics we note that the Egyptians
implicitly had the notion of an irrational number. The papyrus of Moscow
gives us, among other things, proof that the famous discovery by Archimedes
has to be credited to the ancient Egyptians. The exactness of the Egyptians'
knowledge of geometry was an ancient assumption and was only displaced
by relatively recent—that is, the last 300 years—of history. From the Greek
tradition it is assumed that geometry came to Greece not from Babylonia
but from Egypt (Diop, 1991). Anyone looking to study more deeply the
Rhind papyrus or the Moscow papyrus is referred to the brilliant work of
Cheikh Anta Diop in *Civilization or Barbarism*.

This insight into rhythm that first gave the human family an exact science of mathematics was not confined to the Earth, the cycles of nature, or
to the mechanics of the body. The stars, the planets, and the constellations
were also of keen interest to the ancients. They saw the cycles of the Nile
River reflected in the celestial river overhead, the Milky Way, and integrated
it into their cosmic religion. The pharaoh at death would make the great
journey in his solar boat, becoming one with the immortals who had preceded him:

> The winding waterway is flooded, the fields of rushes are filled with water,
> and I am ferried over thereon to yonder eastern side of the sky, the place where
> the gods fashioned me. . . . Orion's sister is Sirius. . . . I have come to my
> waterways which are in the bank of the flood of the Great Inundation, to the

place of contentment ... which is in the horizon. ... May you lift me and raise me to the winding waterway, may you set me among the gods, the imperishable stars. (Faulkner, 1969, lines 343–375, line 508 and utterance 317, line, 1760)

This region of stars, especially the three stars of Orion's Belt, was known as the Duát, and the sacred structures, especially the three great Giza pyramids and the sphinx, are in exact alignment with it. The sphinx is situated due east on the vernal equinox. There was an exceedingly close correlation of those astronomical occurrences in 2500 B.C.E. during the pyramid age, when they were assumed to have been constructed. However, by new, sophisticated, computer-simulated archeoastronomy of the ancient skies over Africa, researchers have found that there was also an exact conjunction in 10,500 B.C.E., when the older sphinx it seems may have been carved out of limestone by unknown others (Hancock & Bauval, 1996). In this mapping of the skies, the two huge pyramids of Dahshur appear on the ground to reflect and be in astronomical alignment with the two brightest stars in the Hyades region (Bauval & Gilbert, 1994). The reflection of the heavens on Earth, the Hermetic "as above, so below," is encoded in their sacred book of *What Is in the Duát*, the Coffin Texts, the *Book of the Dead*, the *Book of Gates*, and, of course, the oldest of them all, the Pyramid Texts.

As we said earlier, the Kemetic Egyptians invented the 365-day-a-year calendar with 12 months of 30 days each, plus five intercalculated days devoted to the gods Osiris, Isis, Seth, Nephthys, and Horus. There were three seasons with four months each, and each month had three weeks of ten days. It was off by one-quarter of a day a year. The solution was not our current leap day every four years, but a leap year every 1,460 years. This sidereal calendar was connected to the period of time that separates two helical risings of the star Sirius in the constellation Canis Major. Thereby the helical rising of the bright star Sirius every 1,460 years coincides with the rising of the sun at the latitude of the ancient city of Memphis! This sidereal calendar was in use prior to 4236 B.C.E. This close observation of the rhythm of the stars and planets was tightly woven into the internal structure of the Great Pyramid. All the planets and major constellations were known to them and written on obelisks, pyramid tombs, and megaliths, both in Egypt and beyond. They predicted solar and lunar eclipses by the Saros cycle where every 18 years, 11 1/3 days the Earth, moon, and sun return to their exact geometric alignment.

In Kenya at Namoratunga, a megalithic site in the northwestern part of the country, there are the ruins of an ancient observatory. It has 19 basalt pillars oriented toward certain stars and constellations (Lynch & Robbins, 1978). They are exact and date from 300 B.C.E. There are other indications of accurate megalithic calendar sites from eastern Africa developed by the first millennium B.C.E. But we must remember that Kemetic influence was felt from Dravidian India, across Africa, and into Europe. In England during their megalithic period, there was a strong Black Egyptian-Phoenician influence (Parrain, 1977). The model for the megalithic civilizations of Western Europe from 2000 to 1400 B.C.E. was Egypt. The astronomical and religious sites at Dolmen of La Ferté-Bernaud, the Men er Roeck, and England's Stonehenge all reflect a sophisticated astronomy and a connection with lavish funerary rites.

In West Africa the Dogon of medieval Mali seem to have been keen observers of the stars and constellations. We mention this here because, like the ancient Egyptians, they were deeply interested in the star Sirius. Their tradition is known to be at least 700 years old, but may be older. The Dogon observed and plotted the orbits of stars circling the star Sirius. But they also revealed the unusual nature of one of the stars, Sirius B, to be one of the smallest yet one of the heaviest in the sky. This second star is *invisible* to the naked eye. For the Dogon this star—Sirius B, or "po tolo"—is the most important star and has religious implications. The Dogon calculated the exact orbits of this star, which they somehow knew as a heavy star! All this was "confirmed" 600 years later by modern techniques of celestial observation. The Dogon documented this before the European Renaissance (Adams, 1983; Griaule & Dieterlen, 1986). Historical, mythological, and other data suggest a contact with ancient Egypt and related peoples, especially the 24th Dynasty. It may have been an independent discovery by methods we have yet to learn. Perhaps we shall never know. And then again, perhaps once something significant is discovered by human consciousness and then witnessed by many others, it can never again be completely forgotten, only submerged to be rediscovered again in some future time.

"Al-Kemit" and Alchemy

This tradition of science continued long after the defeat of the indigenous Egyptian civilization by the invasion of the Romans and later the subjugation by the Semitic migrations of the Islamic conquest. In Europe the influence of an earlier Kemetic science can be seen in the Renaissance works of Kepler and Galileo. However, there began to be more and more a gradual repression in Europe of the contributions of Kemetic Egypt and other parts of Africa. Hermetic thought was eventually believed to have been completely a creation of the Greeks. The new European canon forgot that in the ancient Masonic lodges of Luxor, Abydos, Abu Simbel, and other mystery schools that these sciences and philosophies had been taught continually for 4,000 years. In later chapters we will bring up again how the Hermetic tradition gave rise to the Masons, Freemasons, Roscrusians, and other mystery schools that had a direct bearing upon the structure and thought of the Founding Fathers of the United States. This was largely unconscious but can be seen to be a second African awakening in the West. While suppressed by the edicts of Roman Emperors Theodosius and Justinian and then later by the Arab jihads, it did spread, this knowledge, by circuitous and transformative roots into western Africa and into Europe. It crossed the waters with the second African diaspora. We mention this because in contemporary times there is an ongoing reintegration of the realms of spirit and science. Indeed we are coming to see that spirit and science are both embedded in matter and that matter is embedded in a wider universe that is a highly personalized universe. We are coming to understand that the dynamics of light itself are intimately associated with spirit and that the living spirit, for many traditions, is believed capable of being conducted through the body–mind in the subtle and the central nervous system by an ancient science. This is the solar logos, which we will turn to in future chapters. It involves the transmutation of the body by the dynamics of the spirit.

The "real" science was understood in ancient Egypt not to be simply a manipulation of matter and mentalized symbols, but rather the deep transformation of consciousness itself. In this original Hermetic science, which the invading Arabs called the "science of al-Kemit," it was not merely the transformation of base minerals into gold that was sought, but the actual transformation of human consciousness into the divine consciousness. It seems that both the Greeks and the later Arabs found only the physical *"chem-istry"* of the Kemets and did not grasp the spiritual science beyond the corrupted myth of "alchemy." This, we shall see later, is intimately related to the science of Kundalini. What Freud assumed to be a form or symbol of sublimation turns out later to be far deeper and a symbol for the translation from one level of manifestation in consciousness to another.

In ancient Egypt we find the first sign and source of the "science of Thoth." In later Greek traditions Thoth becomes Hermes, the author of the vast Hermetic corpus of scientific and esoteric works. Thoth is associated with the ancient sacred writings, and in Nubia and Egypt are found the first written languages of humankind in approximately 5300 B.C.E. (Diop, 1991). The Greeks, by an institutional spiritectomy, began the process of dissociating the notions of faith and intuition from reason in their conception of an orderly world process in an effort to create a science that sees the world more "objectively." Order was seen as an external phenomenon. In the process the Greeks may have lost some of their respect for revelation and mystery (Schwaller de Lubicz, 1961). We pointed out earlier many Greek luminaries who studied in Egypt. The temples of Helas, such as those at Delphi, Eleusis, and Delos, were modeled on the Egyptian mystery schools. It was in these ancient mystery schools—these houses of life, or "per ankh"—that humanity first, in a systematized way, sought conscious transformation and divine translation of itself. They were the first libraries for this study of the divine consciousness permeating the world process.

In ancient Egypt the pharaoh was seen as a symbol of the ordinary man's divine origin. Implicitly the ordinary man could see his potential perfection in the form that the pharaoh represented. This is another way to talk of the return of man's consciousness to its origin, which is light itself. The pharaoh symbolized the final trajectory to be realized by mortals, spirit fully awakened in man. This is anthropocosmos. It is out of this intellectual, cultural, and scientific environment that the first great theories of salvation emerged. This is particularly the case in the myth of Osiris, which is the great theory of reincarnation and resurrection. Here is the archetypal metaphor for the transmutation of man into "light" and how he returns back to his source and then emerges out of that source again and again and again. This great myth of Osiris was the fundamental myth of the ancient world for unbroken thousands of years. We shall return to it later in this book. For now we want to simply state that the Egyptian knowledge of medicine, mathematics, astronomy, masonry work, engineering, chemistry, and agriculture far outshined anything known in the ancient world continually for several thousand years. It raised the pyramids, studied and preserved the body by mummification, charted the movement of the constellations, and explored the watery, mythic unconscious 3,000 years before the birth of Christ. This knowledge was not merely localized in Egypt and the Nubian area, but spread both northward and southward into the interior of Africa. At one time this network stretched from the Dravidians of India, across the northern and middle width of Africa to its west coast, and across the 1,500-mile ocean on three natural currents to the Olmec peoples of the Americas. The preciseness, majesty, and size of the pyramids have not even been equaled in our own day. The pyramids were based upon exacting scientific formulas and were intimately integrated with not only their spiritual vision of the cosmos, including a precise astronomy, but also with their vision of the eternal spirit dwelling in humanity. We shall later point out how this Egyptian knowledge of the pyramid and the stellar process of the stars is intricately connected with other religious and philosophical beliefs throughout northwestern parts of Africa, particularly among the Dogon people of Mali. Their connections with the star Sirius is interwoven with the Egyptian knowledge of the star of Sirius. This in turn is intimately connected with their own beliefs about the luminous movement of the life energy embedded within each human being (Griaule & Dieterlen, 1986).

THE RISE OF THE MODERN RELIGIONS IN ANCIENT EGYPT

It is an irony of history that the three great religions of Europe and the Middle East, Christianity, Judaism, and Islam, did not originate there but rather had their genesis, like the human species itself, under more southern skies (Ben-Jochannan, 1970). Indeed the oldest of these, Judaism, which gave rise to Christianity, and the later Islam were nestled by ancient intuitions that arose and were first codified by seekers of the ultimate in the Nile Valley. It was a natural evolution.

Long before the memory of our time along the banks of the Nile's two sources, the blue and the white Nile, peoples began the cultivation of crops after millennia of merely gathering, scavenging, and hunting. This was perhaps 18,300 to 17,000 B.C.E. Over the eons they had migrated down these two branches. This was really the dawn of the Neolithic age. Here agriculture, the cultivation of the land, small herds of domesticated animals, and towns grew up. By the time of the great Fayum Lake settlements, crop cultivation was a way of life. The observation of the cycles of growth, maturation, harvesting, and planting reinforced the natural perception of seen and unseen cycles in the natural world. It would have been a small step to notice the planting of human seed in the body of women, growth and pregnancy, birth, maturity, then death and the symbolism of rebirth. With surplus food and a more sedentary life, spiritual reflection on these cycles would naturally arise. In the cycle of birth, death, and rebirth is the root of the intuition in the heart of the myth of Osiris. At some point the age-old ritual of the burial of the dead was infused with a new intuition, that of rebirth. The rise of this new cult, an intuition nascent throughout the world at that time, occurred here first. The Africans *wrote* this down in scripts, and it became the genesis of a new religion and a new idea in human consciousness. The idea was that life and light could move into the unseen realm of death, undergo a *transformation*, and reemerge in a new form. This was the intuition that $E = mc^2$, that matter is neither created nor destroyed but transformed from one state of existence to another. It infused the secret societies and "mystery schools" that had so profound an influence on spiritual life. This discovery of a new subtle order in nature was an advance over the idea of the spirit world with its vague forces and beings. This new cult, first to take root in the Nile Valley, occurred at about the same time as human civilization as we know it today arose (Budge, 1960)! These intuitions and epochal new spiritual ideas were written in papyrus and stone in the Coffin and Pyramid Texts of the Old Kingdom. The spiritual genius of these insights was to later percolate through the doctrines of Judaism, Christianity, and Islam.

If we look closely at the story of the Christian messiah, many of its roots are in ancient Egypt. Gerald Massy traces the archetypal Christian saga back to 10,000 B.C.E. along the Nile River. Finch (1990) shows intimate connections between the Christ myth and the influential drama of Osiris. Indeed the story of the life of Christ was not really codified until several centuries after his death. Many of the central figures in the story of Christ can be traced back to the mythology of ancient Egypt, particularly the story of the messiah, the virgin mother, and the virgin birth. One can even find the origin of the Semitic notion of the devil in the Egyptian cosmology. The nativity scene itself comes right out of the original Egyptian rites at the temple of Luxor. It is here that the avatar king of Egypt, called Horus, is seen to arise and be sent on a course to save humankind. We know that the historical Jesus left Palestine for some 18 years and did not return until much later. The Bible also suggests that he came from a family of several brothers (Matthew 12: 46–50). It is assumed in the Christian scriptures that Egypt was his home and that he traveled, if not throughout Egypt, at least to Egypt and much of the ancient world on the trade routes with Nicodemus, his wealthy benefactor. He is assumed by others to have studied at the ancient mystery schools of Egypt and perhaps traveled even to India. The Greek word "Christ" comes from the ancient Egyptian word "Karast," or "Krst," which was the anointed mummy identified as the reborn, re-arisen Osiris. The origin of the idea or the reality of returning from the dead is firmly rooted in the history of Egypt, particularly that of Osiris. Horus as the anointed one and a king and deliverer is also deeply imbued in the Hebraic tradition. The Egyptian "Krst" and the Greek "Kristos," meaning "the anointed one," are virtually identical. Finch (1990) goes into much more detail and draws striking parallels between the ancient Egyptian Osirian myth and its similarity to the modern Christian story. This is not to say that Christ was not the awakened avatar of Judea. Rather his origin and possibly even his very appearance are much more akin to the view of the Kemetic origin than they are to the contemporary image of a tall, blond, blue-eyed Christ who, in the Bible itself, however, is reported to have had "woolly hair" and "feet the color of bronze" (Revelation 1: 14–15). Finally it should be emphasized, as Finch does, that the first centuries of Christianity were evolved in the deserts of Egypt. The desert fathers of the Church wrote and rewrote the ancient texts and maybe changed some of the fundamental symbolism. The first large number of "Christians" were black and from the deserts of Egypt and Africa. The first symbols of Christianity were black.

In the first centuries after Christ the new faith was spread by North African converts who left their mark on its theology. St. Augustine, the bishop of Hippo (354–430 C.E.), was an African born in Tagaste, Numidia. In his three great works, *Confessions, On Christian Doctrines*, and *The City of God*, he laid out a vision and theological structure for the religion that even today is studied at a profound level. Two other African Church Fathers are notable here. Thascius Cyprianus, later St. Cyprian, spread the new faith aggressively as bishop of Carthage (249–258 C.E.) and was beheaded for this by the Romans. Also Tertullian spread the faith as a great scholar in his major works on *Hermogenes* and *De Anima*. Born in Carthage, North Africa, also (155 C.E.), he too suffered martyrdom for the faith. The point here is that orthodox Roman Catholicism is really *theologically* rooted in North African writers in the first centuries after Christ when religion was still "hot" with the fires of the Holy Spirit. We can only imagine what happened in later revisions of this ancient and luminous movement.

The influence of Africans on the spirituality of the Roman world before Christ had expressed itself in the popular cults of Isis and Osiris. In Rome itself these cults had numerous followers in every strata of society, from the common man to the emperor himself. Roman tombs of the wealthy and noble were carved with the symbols of Osiris; Egyptian and Greek physicians who trained along the Nile were highly sought after. But African influence was not limited to the world of the spirit.

Lucius Septimius Severus (146–211 C.E.) was born into a Romanized North African family. He was a warrior and governor before becoming emperor in 193. He and his Danube legions persuaded the Roman Senate to have him retroactively "adopted" by the dead Caesar Marcus Aurelius, of the great Antonine line. He was succeeded to the throne by his oldest son Caracalla, better known as Marcus Aurelius Antoninus. Caracalla, a name given to him by the Alamanni German tribes he fought against on the upper Rhine, is perhaps best remembered for the great luxurious and expensive baths he built on over 26 acres, plunging the empire into a fiscal crisis. He and his brother Geta had ruled together for awhile, but in 212 he murdered Geta and all his followers. However, during the reign of this Afro-Syrian warrior he also offered Roman citizenship to almost every free man in the empire. After ruling from 211 until 217, he was murdered by a usurper to the throne, Macrinus, when the emperor was on a campaign in Mesopotamia and Iran against Parthia in April of that year. Macrinus had been commander of the Praetorian Guard when this occurred and became emperor for a brief period. Eventually Macrinus himself was killed in 218 by Varius Avitus Bassianus. As Whites at times have sat on the throne of Black Egypt, so have Romanized Africans sat on the throne of Rome. So while the primary influence of Africans on the Romans was in theology, science, and the continual expansion of material civilization, they were also at times, including the times of Carthaginian Hannibal in Rome during his brief triumph in the Second Punic War, a political force that influenced the complexion of Western civilization. Their cultural, political, and religious influence would flower again during the time of the Moors.

Judaism

The roots of Judaism cross-fertilize and in many ways originate in the wider historical context of ancient Egypt. The most popular story of the Hebrews begins around 1700 B.C.E. with the migration of the shepherd later known as Abraham out of the city of Ur in the kingdom of Chaldea in the southern portion of the Tigris-Euphrates Valley of Mesopotamia. This region of the world at that time in history was largely inhabited by a melange of dark-skinned Africoid peoples. These are not exactly the Hebrews of today, but rather some of the first known historical records we have of their lineage. These were a tribal people and certainly not practicing the law of Moses, a historical figure who did not emerge until 500 years after Abraham. This person Abraham is seen to be the mythological fountainhead of the western Semites and in some Jewish traditions the father of the Egyptian people. The latter is obviously not true but rather a historical myth. Abraham is seen as the founder of both the Arab people and others. His first son, Ishmael, is the mythic father of the Arab people and his second son, Isaac, the father of the Edomites through Esau and finally of the Hebrews through Jacob/Israel. Ishmael's mother Hagar is known to have been a Black Egyptian (Finch, 1990).

The ancient Hebrews are believed by tradition to have entered Egypt as a group, merely 70 shepherds, organized in 12 patriarchal families in a nomadic culture, but then left some 400 or 500 years later over half a million strong and with an entrenched tradition of monotheism. Whatever may have been their real origin and entry into Egypt, which we will explore in a later chapter, we first hear of them approximately 1700 B.C.E. After this, history is somewhat unclear. How they became involved with the building of the pyramids is unknown. Whether this was by way of conquest, insurrection, or whatever is a mystery. They obviously did not design or create the pyramids. All we know from history is that they eventually became the political enemies of Ramses II and exacting tolls were taken against them.

It is at this time that a new crisis emerged in Egypt. With the development of monotheistic strains in Egypt, eventually reaching to the level of the pharaoh Akhenaton, who believed in the one-god notion, great turmoils swept through Egypt. After the death of his father Amenhotep III, this new boy pharaoh changed his name from Amenhotep IV, moved the capital from Thebes to Tel al Amarna, and, among other cultural, artistic, and political reforms, repressed the earlier religion of Amon. Whether Akhenaton attempted to bring Egypt politically together under a central universal religion, or was driven primarily by theological concerns, is another mystery. All we know is that in all likelihood Moses, who was born in, grew up in, educated in, and spoke in ancient Egyptian, eventually became a hero to the Hebrews. It is the opinion of Freud, Diop, and numerous others, including the ancient chroniclers Manetho and Strabo, that Moses himself was not Hebrew but rather a Black Egyptian priest. In all likelihood Moses was influenced by this political reform. He received his theological and academic training in Heliopolis. While monotheism already existed in certain aspects in specific areas of Egypt, particularly in the Sudan and Ethiopia, it was still primarily a minority religion. The Hebrews perceived themselves to be persecuted by the larger Egyptian population and sought to leave Egypt. They were galvanized and led in this process by the historical figure of Moses. Inspired by faith and great charisma, Moses led the Hebrew people out of Egypt. The messianic tradition of Moses became the center of this ancient Hebrew monotheistic religion. The Hebrews did not invent monotheism but were inspired by it, and it provided a powerful political and cultural identity around which to localize their emergent political and cultural aspirations. As it is repeated millions of times every year in the Pesach or Passover ceremony, "In Egypt did Israel become a nation." At a certain point even after Moses had led the Hebrews out of Egypt they rejected his monotheistic religion and returned to a polytheistic religion in the worship of the golden calf at the foot of Mt. Sinai. They paid an exacting price for this transgression. Since that time a covenant has been held culturally between the Hebrews and the monotheistic religion. We shall later see that this monotheistic religion had a profound influence not only on the Judeo-Christian tradition but also in the approach to science, particularly the science and practice of psychoanalysis.

It is quite possible that the enormous geopolitical changes in Egypt, especially the eruption of the volcano on the island of Santorini, were a cataclysmic event in the ancient world. The volcano sent dust and darkness over the Mediterranean for a considerable period of time and it must have seemed like the end of the world (Jaynes, 1976). This coincided with the literature of the 18th Dynasty in Egypt. It may have given rise to the messianic movement of the Hebrew prophets and their prophecy of doom. Akhenaton's later-composed hymn to the sun is a reflection of this earlier period. He talks about epidemics of ancient Egypt and sets up the background for the restorative and transformational messianic movements. This eruption on the island of Santorini also had its influence in Greek mythology and legends (Diop, 1991). Indeed the 18th Dynasty of Egypt was contemporaneous with the Mycenaean Greek period. It was held that Athens was founded by a colony of Black Egyptians led by the mythological Cecrops, who supposedly introduced the science of metallurgy, agriculture, and other knowledge to Greece around the 16th century B.C.E. As the first king of Athens, he was often portrayed to be half man and half serpent. This was about the same time that we had the emergence of Abraham. For 500 years the messianic tradition may have developed until the historical figure of Moses fulfilled the prophecy and led the Hebrews out of Egypt. The 18th Dynasty of Egypt, particularly latter phases of it ruled by Sakere, Tutankhamen, and others, was characterized by the rejection of monotheism and the return to the earlier Egyptian gods. This meant a displacement of the god Aton, who had come to reign under the protection of the pharaoh Akhenaton (1375–58 B.C.E.).

It would seem that this was a time that the Egyptians, who perhaps may have initially invited or at least accepted the Hebrews into their country, expelled them with all deliberate speed. It should be noted that in addition to carrying out of Egypt the idea of monotheism, an idea it did not enter Egypt with, and also given the fact they had entered as a group of 70 shepherds and left after intermixing with the indigenous African population for hundreds of years, in all likelihood the Hebrews who left Egypt did not resemble the other Semitic groups as much as they resembled the darker-skinned Egyptians of that period. It would be quite difficult for a tribe of 70 to intermingle for half a millennium with a vaster group and leave almost half a million strong without taking on some of the characteristics of the indigenous population. The Hebrews, it seems, left Egypt much darker in skin tone, and with a dynamic monotheistic religion.

Islam

The first we know of the Arab and Semitic migrations is from the decline of Roman influence in southern Egypt (Williams, 1987). As the Romans withdrew from Egypt to help check the erosion of their overextended empire, the Arabs and Jews, who were later called "Solomonids," were slowly moving into the southeastern region of Africa. As they moved into Ethiopia or Abyssinia, the indigenous Africans were pressed southward and further into the interior. It was the Axumite Arabs and the other populations in the region who developed the kingdom of Axum. In approximately 350 C.E. their armies destroyed Meroe and an epoch in history ended. From this center Arab migration moved farther and farther into Ethiopia and Egypt. There were periodic skirmishes and one army or another would take control for a short period of time and then lose it. However the Christian Church by this time was relatively well established in Egypt and was known as the Coptic Church. It also had its influence in Ethiopia, which had a strong influence of the Jewish or Hebrew lineage. The Arabs as a particular cultural group, however, did not receive great and overwhelming power until the arrival of the prophet Muhammad.

In 639 C.E. there was a Muslim invasion of unprecedented proportions. It came on the heels of a previous Persian invasion around 529 to 619 C.E. In 651 C.E. the Arab viceroy of Egypt decided to extend his power to the indigenous population in full regalia. The Arabs had been defeated by indigenous Black armies in Africa in 643 C.E. on the plains of Makuria. Eight years later the Arabs tried again. In 652 C.E. a peace treaty was signed between the Arabs and the indigenous Blacks. However, even though the peace treaty excluded Arabs from coming into Africa, little by little, more and more Arabs did. With them they brought Islam and also other aspects of Arab culture.

All this was a stunning reversal of earlier history. At one time a Kushite empire sprawled throughout Arabia. It was exemplified by the Adites of Ad, the supposed grandsons of Ham, the mythical ancestor of the Blacks. This empire was destroyed in the 18th century B.C.E. It is alluded to as the "earthly paradise" mentioned in the Koran. While the Kushite element regained control for a while, they eventually lost it again. More and more Arabs came across the Red Sea at Badl Mandeb to settle in Ethiopia. This was an area that had been known as early as 4000 B.C.E. to be a prosperous land. Different empires at different times ruled it, but its main commercial ties were with Egypt. Indeed it was around 4000 B.C.E. that the area of the Sudan and Nubia first transmitted its 12 hieroglyphs to Egypt that would have become its first embryonic alphabet. With the rise of Muhammad all of this went underground. The Arab jihads, galvanized by this new faith, emerged from the plains of southern Yemen, moved through Arabia, invaded Egypt and swept upward into North Africa, reaching all the way over to West Africa and Spain. They actively suppressed an indigenous religious consciousness and attempted to replace it with a more Semitic religion. Images of the indigenous people were denigrated. The Semitic conquerors seemed to have experienced a similar psychology as the Greeks, and that was a fear of the threatened return of the repressed consciousness of the indigenous peoples and their religion. The transformational science of al-Kemit simply became debased alchemy. And thus was lost a great religion. Make no mistake about it, Islam, Christianity, Freemasonry, and much of Judaism all have their origins in the indigenous consciousness of ancient Africa.

In summary, the ancient civilized world—that is, the world that we know from 5000 until approximately 500 B.C.E.—was centered around Egypt and the Sudan area. It had trade routes and other religious, cultural, and intellectual connections with the indigenous dark inhabitants of India all the way over to the inhabitants of the west coast of Africa and beyond. There is more than passing evidence to indicate that the influence spread deep into the interior. It was a source of the sciences of medicine, physics, chemistry, architecture, and astronomy of the ancient world. It is the cradle of the three major religions of the western part of the ancient world—Christianity, Judaism, and Islam. Judaism emerged out of the context of Egyptian history, galvanized by the figures of Akhenaton, Moses, and the worship of the monotheistic god, Aton. Christianity emerged out of the Osirian mythos, and has many of its major characteristics reflecting the mythical Osiris and his son Horus. The historical figure of Christ no doubt was partially educated in the mystery schools of ancient Egypt and the trade routes that united Egypt with the ancient world. Islam, a religion emerging from the insight of Muhammad, was undoubtedly influenced by the religious currents of Africa, particularly the east coast of Africa near Yemen. The particular dynamic historical forces at the time in connection with brilliant new intuitions of the divine in the collective unconscious led to the emergence of Islam in a fiery sheath across north Africa. It led to the suppression of indigenous peoples and the diaspora of African religions to the west coast of Africa (Asante, 1984). There from the west coast of Africa it would find submerged expressions in the secret mystery schools of West Africa. There are strong indications that some aspects of this philosophy and religion then spread to the New World many years before Columbus by way of seafaring voyagers from the empires on the west coast of Africa (Jackson, 1970; Van Sertima, 1976). And also, finally, the origin of Freemasonry, the Rosicrusian Order, and the Hermetic philosophies all arose from the ancient mystery schools of Egypt from the ancient valley of the kings, through Luxor, Abu Simbel, Memphis, and ancient Thebes. This ancient Hermetic order moved through not only ancient Greece and Rome but through medieval times all the way up to the Enlightenment in Europe. Its flame influenced many of the major figures of the Enlightenment in Europe and also the Founding Fathers of the American experience in government.

CONTEMPORARY SCIENCE AND THE ANCIENT
IDEAS OF FIRE AND ENERGY

There are certain seminal ideas in science and philosophy that have spanned the centuries and have a special relevance to contemporary science. We are referring to the notions of process and probability, atoms and energy, implicate orders and luminosity, and the idea of matter itself as light or bounded energy, notions which seem to pervade nearly all the disciplines of modern science. These too have their roots in an ancient soil.

In 700 B.C.E. the provinces of Greece were largely an unknown land. In one of its provinces, Ionia in western Asia Minor, colonized by the Greeks in the 11th century B.C.E., several luminaries arose who were to leave their imprint on the minds of humanity. By 700 B.C.E. Egypt was an ancient world.

On and off over the centuries Egypt had been a strong cultural and military presence in Ionia and other parts of Asia Minor. It had also practiced the mysteries of Isis and Osiris for millennia and from the pyramid cultures had worshipped fire or energy for eons (pyr = fire). From Egypt the mystery schools spread out over the Mediterranean and Near East. Zoroaster carried the mysteries into Persia and perhaps Greece; Orpheus carried them into Thrace. In each land the mysteries took on different forms and names as they integrated with the indigenous peoples. In Asia they took the form of Mithra; in Boeotia, that of Bacchus. In Crete, the form of Jupiter; in Athens, those of Ceres and Persephone. And in Samothrace, they took the form of the mother of the gods. The most spectacular of the Egyptian mysteries in transformation were the Orphic, the Eleusinian, the Bacchic, the Samothracian, and the Mithraic. All were pyr, or fire, worshipers, the forerunners of "energy worship," and preceded the Ionian luminaries by thousands of years (James, 1954).[2] These ideas permeated Greek and Mediterranean cultures. There is a subtle tendency in contemporary times, we believe, to separate the workings of the universe from the intentionality of the divine intelligence, to dissociate order and rationality from revelation. But clearly, a transrational intuition was at the root of these ancient insights and paradigms.

The early Ionian school saw the rise of Thales, Anaximander, and Anaximenes. Thales (620–546 B.C.E.) was a resident of Miletus. He taught that water (the Primeval Waters of Nun?) was the origin of all living creatures and that all things are pervaded by God.

Anaximander, born in 610 B.C.E., also in Miletus, is remembered for preaching that the origin of all things, both animate and inanimate, was ultimately the boundless or infinite space, the background emptiness of the universe. And Anaximenes, also of the great city, who died in 528 B.C.E., espoused the corollary view that all things arose from the air. These ideas on the origin of life and order itself are to a large extent permutations on age-old ideas expounded in the temples of the Nile at Luxor, Thebes, and Abydos thousands of years before these luminaries arose. In point of fact, many of them are explications of doctrines outlined in the creation story of Egypt of 4000 B.C.E. as recounted in the Memphite theology (James, 1954). The Memphite theology itself is written on a stone unearthed in Egypt and is currently housed in the British Museum. While dated from 700 B.C.E., its author testifies that it was copied from his ancestors' inscriptions ages earlier, when the initial dynasties were in Memphis, around 4000–3500 B.C.E. Its text has three parts—the first describing the gods of chaos; the second,

---

2. Note the derivations here: pyramid; pyromancy, or divination by fire or flames; pyromania; pyrogenic, etc.

the gods of order and form; and the third, the God of Gods through whose force material creation was formed. Part one in particular describes ten principles, four pairs of opposite forces, and two other gods that order both material and psychospiritual reality. These ideas moved down from the upper Nile and, like a rich delta, nourished the cultures of the whole Mediterranean basin. Asia Minor was part of the development.

The later Ionian philosophers, however, bring us even closer to these ideas that pervade contemporary science. Heraclitus (530–470 B.C.E.) was a native of Ephesus in the Middle East. He is credited in history with not only the idea that all of creation is in a constant flux driven by the laws of change and transformation, but that the primary or underlying element of this ceaseless, moving flux was fire or energy. In this philosophy we see the modern idea of a process universe. He taught that these changes were not random or chance, but rather driven by orderly laws and cycles. In other words, there is no real chance, randomness, or even blind probability, but rather law, sequence, and perhaps "hidden variables" that act on all matter and form. There was a hidden unseen harmony in all of nature that reconciled opposites, and this harmony was the expression of an incomparable intelligence or consciousness. The soul was part of this ceaseless moving and in its depths were dynamics peculiar to its own unfolding. Mind, soul, matter, and energy were seen to be interconnected and a kind of "undivided whole in flowing movement."

Anaxagoras (500–430 B.C.E.) was a native of Clazomenac in Ionia. His ideas complemented those of Heraclitus in many ways, especially in his notion that mind alone in the world process is self-moved. He expressed the view that mind or intelligence was the ultimate cause of motion or the world process and that this intelligent consciousness held the supreme power over objects, events, and persons.

Finally Democritus (420–316 B.C.E.), a native of Abdora on the Aegean, was the son of Hegesistratus. He is most claimed by history for his doctrine of the atom. His description of the atom as indivisible, colorless, tasteless, etc., but capable of aggregations into the innumerable forms of this world, is indeed one of the cornerstones of modern science. The atom's behavior influenced one's thoughts, life, and even the cause of one's death. There were also different kinds of atoms. Large objects emanate, or give off, atoms which account for our images of the things of the world which were received with our senses. Significantly enough, the mind or soul was believed to be composed of the most subtle and mobile of the atoms, the fire atoms, which were distributed throughout the universe in all animate things, especially the human body and mind.

These ideas, which are often believed to have suddenly arisen between 600 and 400 B.C.E., remind us of the ancient fire worship of the mysteries (pyr = pyramid = fire). They also bear a striking parallel to the Egyptian god Ptah, who according to Jamblichus, was the god of order and form in creation, the principle of structure, process, and intelligence who unfolded the material universe out the process of fire and energy. The distribution of these fire energies and atoms throughout the universe gave rise to the notion of interconnectedness among objects by way of emanations and harmonies, or even we might say "coupling strengths" and "radiant affinities."

In this last context the figure of Pythagoras is most important. Another pre-Socratic born on the island of Samos in the Aegean around 530 B.C.E., he studied the mysteries as an initiate for decades in Egypt, then returned to Samos. Eventually he migrated to Croton in Italy, where his own mystery school florished. Before he was unceremoniously expelled he further transmitted the Egyptian doctrines of the immortality, transmigration, and ultimate salvation of the soul, the theory of music and spiritual purification, and the hidden relationships between all matter, harmony, and the material universe. This last notion of harmonics, rhythm, and vibration is at the very heart of contemporary cosmic string theory, where the basic "strings" of the universe are conceived to be vibrating in no less than 10 dimensions, and their various harmonics unfold the dynamics of space, time, gravitation, and the structure of matter itself. In other words, the elusive unified field theory, except that there is no "field" per se, but rather a process of interpenetrating harmonics and rhythmic vibrations.

We said earlier that there is, we believe, a subtle tendency in Greek philosophy to dissociate order and rationality from intuition and revelation. This is apparent here when *laws* of nature are stressed over the *experience* of nature in these systems. The Greeks, as many people do today, sought to explain complex systems in terms of more "primitive" or simple structures, e.g., atoms, elementary particles, etc. Experience of the processes of nature, however, leads to a sense that systems and experiences have their own order and cohesion and cannot always be logically deduced from lower-order phenomena. In other words, the *direct spiritual encounter* tends to suggest experience in and of the divine, whereas a focus on laws of nature in which one's personal consciousness is abstracted tends to create the worlds of "inner" and "outer" and a sense of alienation from the universe. This tendency is gradual, not absolute, for in most personal senses these luminaries spoke of gods and forces, and indeed the gods of Mount Olympus were believed to take a personal interest in the motivations and affairs of the Greeks. Eventually, this institutional tendency led to a separative stance to the world process, an emphasis on seeking absolute laws of order abstracted from the personal consciousness. The world became more fragmented in terms of "inner" and "outer," body from mind, self from society, man from nature. It was eventually forgotten that many cherished scientific "laws" of the particular era are but limited tendencies within the realm of material experience. The laws merely point to the experience of matter and energy, which is actually always in transformation. The essence of reality is not manifest matter, but its form. "Form is emptiness and the very emptiness is form," says the Buddhist Heart Sutra.

It is significant that the Greeks did not elaborate on the "Waters of Nun" or the Amenta, the Kemetic terms for the unconscious. In fact, the Greeks and later Romans had no concept of the "unconscious" in their philosophy and science. Many believe this is because the Greeks did not penetrate that deeply into the mystery schools of the Nile. The gods of the Kemetic unconscious were Black and primordial, like the great ancestors of all humanity. To make contact with this level of the unconscious, the surface self must be surrendered or dissolved, at least briefly. There is no time in the unconscious and all is interconnected. Things can move at unbelievable speeds. Or, said in a more contemporary way, the speed of the darkness is faster than the speed of light. To be familiar and fully accepting of the unconscious, one must be able to deeply *identify with the darkness* and intuit paradoxically that it is full of light and fire. The great luminaries could do this but not describe the dance. One path, or pattern of the dance, leads into the psychospiritual union of opposites and unseen harmonies *beyond* intellectual or rational understanding and into deep identification with the dark and yet luminous transcendental source of revelation. The other path tends to see matter as primary, leads eventually to a philosophy of randomness and chance, the ghostly god of probability, the exhausted philosophy of existential angst and ennui. Personhood and spirit are the sisters of matter and energy. The path of materialism eventually arches toward separation from matter and nature, dissociation from self-ablating revelation and, yes, eventually the fragmentation and subtle toxicity of logical positivism.

There is a science of psychology buried here in these ancient ideas, germinal ideas first codified in the Memphite theology. "Fire underlies the life of the universe" was echoed by Heraclitus; "air as the basis of life" was stressed by Anaximenes; "the boundless, unlimited" universe of Anaximander; "water as the source of all things," espoused by Thales; the "fire atoms filling all space as the mind or soul of the world" of Democritus; and "the world-soul composed of fire Atoms" of Plato are each a germinal idea enfolded in the Memphite theology.

In the temples of Luxor and Abydos, the seven liberal arts were taught for the evolution and emancipation of the soul, a model later to be institutionalized in the academic university systems throughout Europe. The original Grand Lodge of Luxor, built near Danderah during the third dynasty by Pharaoh Khufu, was some 2,000 feet long and 1,000 feet wide. This oblong shape recurs often in secret Masonic temples from ancient times, through the Renaissance, to the American Founding Fathers, to the Freemasons of today. There were at least 18 known subordinate lodges of this Grand Lodge of Luxor scattered in places as far away as Rome, Crete, Zimbabwe, and India (Ben-Jochannan, 1972).

Even in the labyrinth of the early psychoanalytic notions of Freud and Jung can be found these ideas. From the anthropologist Sir Edward Tylor's *Primitive Culture* (1871), Carl Jung took the coined word "animism" from the Latin words *animus* and *anima*, and saw that it described the "life, soul, spirit" of the person and incorporated it into his emerging analytic psychology. Freud's libido idea reflected in mystical Judaism also parallels the Egyptian Sekhem, or vital force. Jung drew the concept of the archetype from the African scholar Saint Augustine's *Principales*. Both Freud and Jung knew that the Egyptians had studied magnetic healing, hypnotism, dream analysis, and the dynamic unconscious. Linguistic analysis even suggests that the Greek word for soul or "psyche," associated with the goddess Psyche, issues from the Egyptian "Khe" for soul and "Su" for she, Su-Khe (Massey, 1881).

We could go further in this vein but the thrust is clear. Here are embedded the ideas of process and change, energy and atoms, hidden variables and unseen harmonies along with a subtle interconnectedness and implicate order residing in all things. The Egyptians drew it in seed form from the observation of the stars, the planets, and the rhythms of the Nile over 6,000 years ago. The Greeks amplified it between 600 and 300 B.C.E. While they suspected the existence of the atom and knew through direct experience about "static" and the force of magnets, the early parents of Maxwell's electromagnetism, they surely also felt the force of gravity and knew that somehow the starry constellations were held in celestial patterns in space. The Romans learned it, the Arabs protected and expanded it, the Renaissance rediscovered it, and today it pervades the frontiers of our science. And yet from its origins on the Nile ages ago to its place in the academy today, it seems to have lost more and more of its primordial spirit among its practitioners if not in its theory. No, we do not worship "fire" today with rituals and secret formulas in temples attended to by the initiated priests. Or do we? Instead we worship the cult of "energy" with experimental equipment, esoteric formulas, and equations in laboratories attended to by specialists with advanced degrees in restricted disciplines in search of a great intelligence that orders the material universe.

The fact that this material universe itself, under certain conditions, transforms into new and higher orders of complexity leads inescapably to the intuition that the very heart of matter exhibits animate-like behavior and thereby consciousness. In some conditional states, such as superconductivity, which we will discuss later, matter displays unusual properties which suggest an "animate-sentient-like" aspect (Miller, 1991). Evolution, it seems, occurs not only in biological forms, but perhaps in matter itself. Consciousness and energy we believe have a deep and nonlocal marriage. The earlier more local coupling was between fire and the tissue of human attention that witnessed it. On some primordial level the ceaseless fire of the external world implicates that subtle fire of the inner world. Together they are the original energy. The ancients believed that this energy and the body were functionally related to each other and indeed were both connected to the Earth itself by some form of transformation. For this reason, in later chapters of this book, we will turn our attention to the *possibility* of this terrestrial relationship. This intuition is buried deep in the African unconscious worldview and is implicit in many others. We will look at some of the leading candidates in our present time that fit the bill for this "energy," including traditional sources and the more recent notions of biological superconductivity and geomagnetic fields. It is our strong belief that just as our science has moved from a deterministic-materialistic perspective over the last 300 years to a probabilistic-energetic one today, we are more and more compelled to recognize that consciousness itself is part of the equation and that perhaps consciousness is implicate, the very ground of being and, as such, is, like energy, transtemporal and transpatial in its very heart.

On some level *all* expressions of energy couple with each other. As the great physicist niels Bohr said, "Consciousness must be a part of nature or more generally of reality, which means that, quite apart from the laws of physics and chemistry, as laid down in the quantum theory, we must also consider laws quite a different kind—here we obviously have a case of complementarity, one that we shall have to analyze in greater detail" (quoted in Heisenberg, 1971). These two seemingly separate realms of manifestations, that of matter and that of consciousness, no doubt meet in some original form or source. Perhaps we would do well to look again at the original energy and its spiritual parallel and overcome this subtle dissociation of matter from spirit. To this end the next chapter is directed.

4 KUNDALINI AND THE SPREAD OF AFRICAN MYSTICISM

The Egyptian name for the cranial vertex is "wpt" which means "to open" . . . the symbolism inherent in the term "wpt" also signifies the "opening" of the higher cortical centers that correspond to the "awakened" state, in this way identical to the rising of the Kundalini Serpent of Tantric Yoga that climbs from the base of the spine to the top of the head during the course of spiritual exercises. . . . It is significant that among the ritual kings and traditional priests of Africa, their power is said to reside in their heads; even in the rural south of the United States, the successful Voodoo doctor is said to be "strong in the head."

—Charles S. Finch, M.D., *The African Background to Medical Science*

The arousal of Kundalini power is a dramatic occurrence. It is traditionally looked upon as a mighty process of purification that leads to the transcendence of the body and the mind in the culminating state of ecstatic unification of subject and object.

—Lee Sannella, M.D., *The Kundalini Experience*

KUNDALINI AND THE RELIGIOUS TRADITIONS

Iᴺ the mouths of the river valleys, around the shores of innumerable lakes, in the dense forests that stretched for thousands of miles, human beings for eons lived with an endless variety of snakes. Then the climate changed, the new migrations began, the tribes came down the blue and white Nile. Other peoples retreating from the new Sahara came from the West to the banks of the great river. In this foment over the millennia, civilization as we know it germinated on Earth. Hunting and gathering were eventually added to the new planting and harvesting and the Neolithic age began somewhere around 18,000 B.C.E. Towns and villages arose, then spread, as did trade and religious ideas. Always present, however, was the ubiquitous serpent.

We do not know when, but somewhere during this time the cults of the serpent, the bird, and the other natural life forms took on a new symbolic life in the mind of our species. Perhaps it was the Neolithic invention of agriculture that reinforced the natural observation of a seed planted in the earth going through a *transformation* over time and, though unseen, re-emerging and growing to fruition, then dying, that suggests the idea of life after life and a life beyond the illusion of death. In this was intuited the hidden evolution of the soul. It could not have escaped the eyes of our ancient forebears that the serpent was equally at home *above* the earth and also *below* the earth and the waters! The serpent, coiling with life and energy, every year would shed its old skin and return anew with force and power. Also each man, each male child born of women, had his own attached serpent in the form of a penis, whose erect action was associated with pleasure, elimination, and the mystery of creativity and regeneration in the same physical area as the female.

That other creature of the world and the imagination, the bird, was also woven into the mystery. Able to fly by some unknown magic, it became part of the legend of immortality. For thousands of years the cults of the serpent and the bird entranced the spiritual imagination of our species and helped us evolve a new intuition of ourselves and the world.

By the time the Sahara had fully formed, the Fayum Lake settlements and those of Lake Chad were replete with villages and commerce. A new religious consciousness was everywhere in the air on the verge of expression. The Ophidian cults of Africa had produced ideas and intuitions that on the trade routes had reached Indus Valley India by at least 3000 B.C.E.

The Indian system of Tantra drew not only ideas but also words and phrases from the Typhonian cults of ancient Egypt (Grant, 1979). The Indian word for power, or "shakti," in Egypt was the word "sekht" or "sekhmet," the very lover of the gods. The heroic Khart or sun god of light Horus or Hoor-paar-Kraat, appears later in the Hindu system as Kartikeya, the son of the sun god. The fire of the sun and the inner fire of the human body were equivalent in their regenerative power and capacity for transformation. Elaborate experimentation with the human body in this psychocultural contest eventually gave rise to all kinds of "disciplines" and religious symbolism. This was for operating in both the seen world but also the unseen inner spiritual, psychic, and astral realms of the initiated (Grant, 1979). Some, involving the effluvia and regenerative fluids of men and women—i.e., semen and menstrual fluids—became sacred or profane in the eyes of the uninitiated into the secret societies that were abundant during this period. Many of these disciplines survive today in certain hidden religions of Africa and Asia. They were fused in different systems with the animal powers, but the bird and the serpent remained the most prominent. Struggles between cults and the exchange of disciplines between groups over time gave birth to a new spiritual consciousness. The bird, the serpent, the seed, and the natural cycles gave way to the intuition and perception of birth, unfoldment, maturity, and death and then rebirth like the serpent who coils above and below this world. These experiments carried out in the intimate laboratory of the human body–mind gave birth to the cult of resurrection and Osiris and to the discovery of the inner fiery serpent who rises, takes flight, and transforms the world. In Egypt this fire snake was called the uraeus serpent; in the Indus Valley she was called the Kundalini. In both places she lived coiled asleep and at the base of the spine until awakened. *Every religion in its ascension bows to her.* The headdress of the first pharaohs, the first rulers of civilizations that arose with this new knowledge, had molded into it the royal falcon and the rising, resplendent serpent.

The phenomenon of Kundalini, of course, is not unique to the civilization of the Nile Valley. Peoples all over the Earth have encountered this mysterious spiritual and psychophysical phenomenon. The Kundalini and its representation as the coiled serpents of the modern medical caduceus are found among the early Blacks in ancient Sumer of 2000 B.C.E. Two lion-birds at the sides of a door or shrine appear from the reign of King Gudea of Lugash in the era of the Sumerian renaissance that occurred after the Semitic invasions. This caduceus figure becomes the staff of Hermes in other traditions, Hermes the guide to immortal life. The Incas of the Americas had an extensive mythological literature of Kundalini (Chaney & Messick, 1980). On the same continent the Mayan and seminal Olmec civilizations had an extensive knowledge of not only the solar expanse but also of mathematics and also, interestingly enough, of Kundalini. The Olmec culture appears to have had direct contact with seafaring African cultures, as was mentioned earlier (Van Sertima, 1976). Also, the Native Americans of North America had a certain knowledge of Kundalini. In addition to these peoples briefly mentioned, throughout every major religious tradition there are references direct and indirect of the phenomenon of Kundalini.

Judaism, Hinduism, Islam

In Judaism there are references to Kundalini and the third eye. It is also expressed in the symbology of the tefillin. The tefillin is a leather strap with boxes in which are written the primary laws of Judaism. It is wrapped around the top of the head and over the forehead in patterns that conform to symbolic numerology. It is also elaborately wrapped seven times around the hand and arms. There are four passages in the Old Testament that cite specific times and purposes for using the tefillin. In the book of Deuteronomy (6: 6–9), Jews are instructed to "use it as a sign upon your hand and a front between thine eyes." It is mentioned in the book of Exodus (13:16), where Jews are told to use the tefillin because "it shall be as a sign in thy hand, and as a thing hung between thine eyes, for the remembrance; because the Lord hath brought us forth out of Egypt by a strong hand." It goes on to say furthermore in Exodus that "a memorial between thine eyes; and that the law of the Lord always in thine mouth." It is essentially a way to know God. In the Kabbala there are numerous references to meditation, concentration, and the stimulation of the process of Kundalini. The mystical lineage of the Kabbala itself and one of its primary texts, the Zohar, has elements that can be traced to the ancient Kemetic mystery school system and the ten laws or commandments of Moses, which themselves were taken from the 42 laws of Maát and the Pillars of Osiris (King, 1990). Moses composed or began the composition of the first five books of the Bible, the Torah, *after* he left Egypt and most certainly wrote them in Egyptian, since Hebrew as a written language did not emerge until 500 years after the Exodus. The original texts were suffused with the Egyptian mysteries and the newer dynamic Hebrew vision. This system was imbued with the Kundalini mythos and disciplines which surround it.

The skull cap or the yarmulke—"kippot" in Hebrew—is worn to remind the wearer of eternal reverence before God and of the area at the top of the skull where Kundalini is said to enter into the higher domain of its evolutionary path (Krishna, 1971b; Mookerjee, 1982). All this should hardly be surprising since this knowledge was well known to the Kemetic Egyptian mystery schools and Moses, a Black Egyptian priest or prince, was schooled in the mysteries he learned at Heliopolis and wrote the early books of Judaism. Certainly this spiritual luminary's inner eye was open. In all of these the "eye" is associated with a luminous "inner vision" that appears to have an intimate association to the pineal gland (King, 1990). The Kemetic Egyptian as far back as the Pyramid Texts of 3200 B.C.E. referred to this as the Eye of Horus.

Hinduism, in its psychospiritual disciplines, is literally almost based upon the phenomenon and the power of Kundalini. It is mentioned in the Vedas. Also throughout the Upanishads of India we find repeated references to the phenomenon of Kundalini. Its most expansive expression is perhaps found in the lineage of Kashmir Shaivaism. In Buddhism there are numerous references to not only the third eye, but also to the phenomenon of Kundalini. This is most accentuated in the Tantric tradition of Buddhism. In Hinduism we see the symbolism of Shiva and Shakti intertwining with each other in the life of each individual. Buddhism, initially an offshoot of Hinduism, shows us the same phenomenon. In Christianity, whose cradle was Palestine and the deserts of Africa, there are repeated subtle references to the Kundalini phenomenon. Christ mentions "The Light of the body is the eye: if therefore thine eye be single, thy whole body shall be full of Light" (Matthew 6:22). This is in reference to the phenomena of Kundalini and the third eye and the necessity of a certain psychospiritual discipline. Many scholars even see the hidden workings of the Kundalini process pervading the entire Bible, especially its esoteric side (Elder, 1994). Surely the allegory of climbing Jacob's ladder (Genesis 28:12) is about Kundalini and the processes associated with it (Haich, 1975).

In Islam are references to the awakened fiery serpent. We know historically that when Muhammad was approximately 47 years old he became distressed by the unreligious life of the Arabs in his home, Mecca, and sought solitude among the hills of Mt. Hira. The faith has it that after 28 days of deep and intensive meditation the archangel Gabriel appeared to him in a vision and pointed to him as the chosen apostle of God. This tradition and methodology of concentrated attention is a very ancient one. It is comprised of a long period of silence and meditation, a discipline that ignites the latent powers in the body–mind, and then unfolds out of the process of highly personalized internal reality a luminous intelligent figure. This is an epiphany or divine manifestation. Within this tradition the prophet Muhammad is said to have become "enlightened," and began to share the message of his inner visions or revelations to others.

Muhammad is placed in the tradition of the great prophets of the Middle East—Elijah, Jeremiah, Ezekiel, Zoroaster, John the Baptist, and Jesus. Within Islam the school of Sufism is a mystical sect that worships the "inner science" in which various disciplines are used to awaken the third eye and work with the process of Kundalini. In many world myths, the Kundalini process is symbolically represented by fierce dragons and serpents (nagas) guarding the entrance to secret caves where either treasures or beautiful maidens are kept prisoners waiting for the strong, pure heart who will liberate them.

So, in essence, we see that the phenomenon of Kundalini is not unique to the Nile Valley civilizations. However, it is in the Nile Valley civilizations that we find the first highly sophisticated, sustained, and integrated practice of this powerful psychospiritual methodology in the transformation of human consciousness. These ancient "Kemets" practiced both physical and spiritual "chemit-stry" for natural science and also for the transformation of human consciousness into the divine. After the Roman and Islamic conquests, the science and its discipline were largely lost and misunderstood to be merely the "magical" transformation of base metals into gold, al-Kemit or alchemy.

So what is Kundalini and how is its phenomenon related to the body–mind and the progression of religious mysticism throughout the ancient and the modern world? We shall now look at the earliest known detailed references to a sophisticated knowledge of the Kundalini process and how it has transformed and yet remains the undercurrent of many psychospiritual traditions, secret societies, and other timeless methods of transformation of the human consciousness and body–mind.

KUNDALINI IN HISTORY AND SCIENCE

Kundalini is often referred to as "the serpent power." This is because in the worldwide experience of Kundalini in different times and by different peoples the phenomenal experience is one of a coiled energy, perceived in the form of a serpent coiled 3½ times around its base and residing in the lower part of the human spine. In some cases, it is 3,500 coils, a multiple of 3½. This inner perception of a coiled 3½ times around force with lines of energy moving in currents from it can be seen in Dravidian Indian representations of 2000 B.C.E., in Rajasthan drawings of the 19th century C.E., in Tantric Buddhist symbolism, in the sculpture and traditions of West Africa, in the imagery of the Olmec and Mayan Americas, in the mystical traditions of almost every known religion and civilization. Various methods and disciplines are used to awaken this dormant power and have it ascend, unobstructed, through the various levels of the human spine and brainstem to the top of the human skull in the seat of consciousness. The various obstructions and the ways of getting around these are the core of the discipline of Kundalini Yoga and all of its various manifestations. Symbolically there are innumerable references to this in different cultures. We've mentioned the

Hindus, the Kemets, and the Mayas. As widely separated as these traditions appear to be, the human body–mind is essentially the same and therefore the subtle, the psychophysical, and the neurological pathway through which the Kundalini phenomenon passes is archetypically the same for all humans. There are some disagreements in terms of the Kundalini process arising in which the Kundalini force is said to descend from higher realms of consciousness (Aurobindo, 1971). These are rather technical matters for emphasis in particular disciplines and are indeed important. There's also some minor controversy as to where the exact origin of Kundalini is in the body, that is to say, at the very base of the spine or several fingertips above the base of the spine. Phenomenologically, however, all sources, ancient and modern, are in agreement that the Kundalini phenomenon is associated with the spinal line of the body and generally in its ascent moves from the base of the spine all the way to the tip of the cranium. Most traditions work from the base upward, but a few, like the Integral Yoga of Sri Aurobindo, work with the *descent* of the consciousness force while the ascent of the force from the base of the spine occurs. When the Kundalini awakens in the traditional manner from the base of the spine upward, it is said to awaken with an enormous amount of power in its ascendance through the spinal line and through progressively penetrating the levels of consciousness is said to radically transform the individual consciousness and have it unified with the cosmic or the all-pervasive consciousness. (See Figure 23.)

Unification of the individual with the greater universe is referred to as "Yoga," or union. The symbols of this are often the Hindu symbols of Shiva and Shakti. Shiva is the imminent and all-pervasive consciousness, and Shakti manifests the energetic aspect of the phenomenon. In ancient Egypt a parallel process was symbolized in terms of Isis and Osiris in that they complemented each other and sought ultimate union. The Kundalini itself was referred to as the uraeus or luminous serpent. Undoubtedly due to thousands of years of experimentation, communication, and cross-fertilization of religious ideas along the trade routes, there is a similarity in ideas. Also given the genetic, historical, and phenotypical linkage between the Dravidian peoples of southern India and the peoples of eastern Africa, it is not surprising to find a striking similarity between their religious concepts and their philosophical experiences. A deeper look at the Australian Aboriginals, the close cousins of these Dravidians, would no doubt reveal a special form of the "union" or "Yoga" in their dreamtime religion and the disciplines associated with it.

In the Dravidian cultures of south India, we find numerous references to Kundalini even from their earliest cities of Mohenjo-Daro and Harappa. These, again, existed at least a thousand years before the Aryan invasions.

FIGURE 23. Ancient Symbols of the Dormant, Awakened, and Fulfilled Life Current.

AWAKENED

The Yogi seven chakras each associated with a plexus and a level of consciousness. This·is the symbol of the awakened current moving to the brain.

The flow of the Life Current awakened and fulfilled in the braincore.

DORMANT

The Mysterious Serpent - The medical caduceus and its seven centers each associated with a specific homonal and endocrine function. The current in its dormant state.

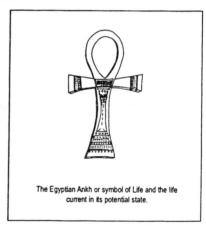

The Egyptian Ankh or symbol of Life and the life current in its potential state.

These are four expressions of the internal perception of the ancient and traditional life current that animates both somatic and spiritual experience. In Western medicine its forgotten origin is hidden in the medical caduceus, while its complete fulfillment is the Kemetic Egyptian ankh. (Copyright © 1999 Teachers College, Columbia University)

The naga cults of India have the coiled serpents that go back millennia. It is often assumed that the Aryans, spreading out from the Caucasus Mountains and invading northwestern India around the second millennium B.C.E., brought with them the knowledge of Kundalini. This is not true. Aryan invaders, after over a century of huge and fierce battles for supremacy in the Indus Valley, conquered the darker-skinned indigenous peoples, whose written script even in this day has not been deciphered, imposed a brutal caste system, and then absorbed their religion and translated it into the own Sanskrit language. The Aryan contribution appears to have been a particular gift for metaphysics and speculation. This, in combination with the primary experience of Kundalini as unfolded by the Dravidians, evolved into one of the world's most highly articulated disciplines for the arousal, maintenance, and ascendancy of this all-but-divine force.

But even before its emergence in India and then later in China and Japan, the phenomenon of Kundalini was well known and attested to in the Nile Valley of Upper and Lower Egypt. In the Masonic lodges of Luxor and Abu Simbel the discipline of Kundalini was well known. In numerous secret societies the phenomenon of Kundalini was integrated not only with astronomy and astrology but also with mathematics. The royal crown of the pharaoh with the serpent emerging from the third eye is a clear symbol of the uraeus and its significance to the ruling class. The same masters who built the great pyramids in earlier dynasties were initiates into the phenomenon, the inner fire, the order of Kundalini.

Kundalini is actually a descendant of the shadowy Ophidian or serpent cults of ancient Africa. It is from this "tantric" practice that this discipline originated among the Blacks and then spread to India. Gopi Krishna, the Kashmiri yogi and pundit of Indian mysticism, perhaps the foremost modern exponent of Kundalini, experienced its awakening and repeatedly made reference between its Hindu yogic expression and those of ancient Egypt (Krishna, 1978a, 1978b). Egyptian terms from their ancient Draconian or Typhonian cults are found in the Indian systems of Tantra (Grant, 1979). The word for "power," for instance, so central to the Tantras, "shakti," was known ages before as "sekht" or "sekhmet" in Egypt. She was the consort of the gods and was the fiery southern sun and sexual heat of the lioness, a symbol of African origin. The Khart of Egypt was the god Horus as a child. He is said to reappear in the Indian system later as Kartikeya, the son of the sun god. In addition to these and many more, the god On in Egypt was identified with the sun, and its name On became the Ong and Om of the radiant Vedas of India.

One cannot help noticing this primal sound Om and all its variations that go back so far, and the fact that some sounds, particularly the sound

Om, when focused as a vibration through certain substances, as Swiss researcher Hans Jenny (1975) did, create a specific, physical pattern—in this case, the pattern or Yantra, as it is known in India, of the Sri Yantra. In samyama Tantric tradition, it is the symbol of the law of manifestation or physical vibratory expression in matter. The figure is a circle filled with concentric squares and triangles, a kind of worlds-within-worlds symbolism or holonomic pattern, if you will. It is considered the mother of all vidyas or symbols. This should suggest something to us about the human mind's capacity to bridge or enfold the seemingly separate realms of matter and imagery and the world of sound while projecting and receiving energy in the process. After all, to feel a pattern in sound that corresponds to or awakens and makes contact with a physical pattern in matter, energy, and imagery is a projection and materialization of consciousness in the holonomic energy field that enfolds both. During this "translation" consciousness moves from the enfolded frequency/spectral domain to the unfolded space–time domain. Said another way, it moves from vibration to spacialization, i.e., "and the word was made flesh." When the pattern is personalized, it becomes the complex signature of the Orisha or saint that appears to the devotee or practitioner. It is not a hallucination, but an epiphany.

Kundalini has always had a close association with sexuality. At one time there were sexual practices connected with female priestesses in Dravidian India, and these later influenced the symbolism of the Tibetan Tantric tradition. It survived in various forms until around 1940, when these "temple dancers," called devadasis, were completely suppressed. In any event, through the several millennia of sustained civilizations in the Nile Valley a highly articulated and sophisticated understanding and integration of Kundalini took place. It was a fountainhead of their exacting mathematical and astronomical science. It was also intimately associated with the study of light. They possessed an elaborate symbolism of the light of the sun and the inner light of the body, which was symbolized by way of the phenomenon of the pineal gland. They were also well aware of the phenomenon of the unconscious mind (Hourning, 1986). They were aware of the earliest forms of cyclical hormonal influence on the body known to man. It is in ancient Egypt that we find the first sophisticated scientific knowledge of biological psychiatry (King, 1990). The Egyptians knew about the effect of sunlight upon the body, particularly as manifested by the hormonal cycle of the pineal gland. The pineal gland is responsive to light and has an intimate effect on the circadian rhythms and the biometabolism of the body. This intimate knowledge of symbolism, endocrinology, and states of consciousness was highly integrated into ancient Kemetic thought over the millennia of civilization.

When the Greeks entered into Egyptian culture, they took into their hearts a number of teachings from the mystery schools. However, they seemed to have missed or were not introduced to the phenomenon of Kundalini. This may have been due to their emphasis on the "rational" side of science and their recoil from transrational phenomena and experience. It may have been that, in keeping with the initial traditions of the mystery schools, students were under oath not to reveal to the uninitiated the mysteries of the sect (James, 1954). It may also have been due to their inability to either understand or endure the phenomenon of Kundalini. As mentioned before, Kundalini, once awakened, is an extremely potent force and tends to destabilize the uninitiated. Kundalini is an arational phenomenon, neither rational nor irrational. It is simply an extraordinarily powerful energetic movement that tends to radically transform the ego-structured consciousness principle. The Greeks, with their predilection for rationality and the mood of bodily doubt, perhaps had evolved no way of *sustained transcendence* of the ego except in brief periods of Dionysian and Eleusian cult ecstasy, when they openly worshiped and sought, like the Voudoun disciplines, to embody the gods. Egyptian science was founded on the phenomenon of transformation and transcendence. We find very little references in Greek philosophy to the particular notion of transcendence. There is a movement toward the dialectic, but always a dialectic in terms of the ego and the gods, which are always perceived as outside of the individual, i.e., on Mount Olympus, not in the heart itself, which the Egyptians did and went to such ends to preserve it in the art of mummification. It is in Egyptian religion and its mystical offshoots in Christianity, Judaism, and Islam that we find the notion of a transcendental psychospiritual force at the base of human existence and urging it forward in its evolutionary unfoldment.

HISTORY AND THE NETERS OF EGYPT

Exactly how was this notion of Kundalini manifested in ancient Egypt? What were its philosophical parameters and foundations?

In earliest ancient Egypt there was the notion of a one god and all of the gods being an aspect of this one god in various manifestations. There were harmonic forces in nature, often referred to as "neters." The Egyptians also had the notion of a "neter of neters," a boundless, incomprehensible intelligence and energy out of which the other lesser neters unfolded and interacted with different coupling strengths from time to time. In other words, there was a god of gods or an all-embracing deity of which there were various manifestations. There was also parallel or isomorphic to this the idea of a primordial conscious unmanifest energy of which all the other energies were various manifestations. A holonomic sea of conscious energy, if you will, that is in various degrees of phase alignment with the manifested or explicate order of material phenomena. Their harmonic conjunction with the affairs of Earth and humankind was the essence of justice, Maát, and "resonance." In this harmonic phase of alignment is hidden the foundation of their belief in what today we call magic.

Each neter and each particular aspect of god belonged to a certain theological system and could be localized in certain areas. Consequently different areas of the nation and its different peoples had different gods which they emphasized, but all the gods were part of the same pantheon. During periods of war, civil strife, and upheaval, these theological systems and gods cross-fertilized with each other. In various times the kings of Upper and Lower Egypt, even after Menes united the two lands, were known to make use of the different competing "gods" in different parts of Egypt. In the royal papyrus of Turin are named all the rulers of Egypt from Menes on.

In terms of the antiquity or the age of Egyptian science there is great controversy. The Kemetic Egyptians themselves dated their own origin to 40,000 years B.C.E. Diodorus of Sicily said that the gods and heroes of ancient times ruled Egypt for 18,000 years and then mortal man ruled for 5,000 years. There were said to be 23,000 years of civilization in Egypt prior to the time of Diodorus himself. Manetho gives 15,150 years to divine dynasties of Egypt and then 9,777 to the kings before Menes. This led to a combined history of 24,927 years of prehistory. Herodotus mentions 340 generations of kings and high priests who ruled Egypt before his arrival. There is obviously from these ancient accounts a long unknown history of Egypt. Other more modern researchers claim a high civilization in Egypt thousands of years before the birth of Christ or Buddha or Krishna, a time 10,500 years ago during the origin of the sphinx (West, 1970). It is during these undated, mythic times that Kundalini was first manifested and then eventually over the millennia codified as a highly technical psychospiritual science.

The list of neters and demigods who personified natural forces and ruled Egypt during the mystical period as reported in the papyrus of Turin are numerous. They include Tah, Ra, Shu, Geb, Osiris, Set, Horus, Thoth (who later becomes Hermes in the Greco-Latin tradition), and Maát (Schwaller de Lubicz, 1961).

The exact age of the origin of ancient Egypt we shall never know. However, given some of the fragmentary records, monuments, and stelai that have been left by the ancients, we can begin an educated guess and no doubt many of our guesses fall short of what is the true date. We must remember that the first exact calendar was in operation prior to the year 4236 B.C.E. In point of fact, as exacting as this calendar was, it had to be preceded by at least several hundred and perhaps a thousand years of observation prior to 4236 B.C.E.! A great civilization may have preceded the Egyptian civilization, as alluded to in myths and the text of *Serpent in the Sky*. We say this because a commemorative stele was erected between the paws of the great sphinx innumerable years before the Black pharaoh Thutmose IV of the 18th Dynasty arrived on the scene. This was around 1425 B.C.E. and he even had to clear the sand away in order to uncover and refurbish this great sphinx, which may have been there for thousands of years before that. The heavy water erosion marks around its base suggest that it was built at least 8000 to 10,000 B.C.E., when the Sahara was still a lush and near-tropical land of rivers and rain, not an arid desert. The sphinx, it seems, was an ancient symbol even in the days of the pharaohs.

The Mystery Schools and Kundalini

We mentioned in earlier chapters how after several millennia of sustained development that Egyptian Kemetic civilization was intermittently invaded by Assyrians (664–525 B.C.E.), partially conquered by the Persians under Darius the Great (525–404 B.C.E.), then Alexander the Great of Macedonia (332 B.C.E.), then the legions of Julius Caesar (30 B.C.E.), and was finally overcome and suppressed by Arab jihads (642 C.E.) under the influence of the Islamic revolution. Egypt and Nubia were also subject to periodic southern domination by the Ethiopians. When the Islamic conquerors came through northern Africa and descended into Egypt, they essentially conquered all but a few of the independent kingdoms of the Nile Valley (Williams, 1987). There was an active and conscious suppression of the indigenous Kemetic peoples and religion. The mystery schools were also under attack. Those that could not be absorbed into Islam were made legal outcasts. The captive Christian Church was under attack. The only place in the African continent where it survived openly was in the highlands of Ethiopia. The net effect of this was to drive the mystery schools, schools that had been under attack not only from the Islamic conquest but also from the earlier Roman invasions and the edicts of their two emperors, to an underground mystery school religion. It moved westward and became integrated into the secret societies of West African civilizations who already knew of its existence. In their context it reemerged in varied integrated form. Its symbols and its exacting sciences in some areas were lost, but there are certain remnants. These are particularly so in the symbols. We've alluded in earlier times to how the medical caduceus was actually a symbol of the earlier mysteries of Thoth and the initiate societies of Egypt. In West Africa the symbol of the medical caduceus and the secret societies of Kundalini were ex-

pressed in the symbols of the Domballah. This symbol is of a serpent twin-
ing seven times around a tree as it ascends to the top. This again is a symbol
of the rise of Kundalini to the higher centers of the brain for illumination.

The symbol of the earlier Hermetic mystery school had been around
the original idea of a primal ray of light and its corporification or localization into objects. In other words, the original vision was of all-pervasive
energy, light, and divine intelligence that became localized in a particular
object. This is another way of saying that light, when it becomes condensed
or contracted, becomes perceived as an object. This has an affinity to certain notions in contemporary physics. The Horian logos refers specifically
to the symbolism of the Eye of Horus. The reigning king in ancient Egyptian
times was a symbol literally of the mythical and mystically Hermetic order
and a reflection of the original all-pervasive light and its localization in the
pharaoh. This was the Horian logos (Schwaller de Lubicz, 1961). The pharaoh was a reflection of the capacity of the mortal to attain anthropocosmos.
Said in another way, the Horian logos symbolized the capacity of the human
to rise to the level of an immortal out of the unknown light by way of
identification with the king and thereby ultimately return consciously to
that light. This is reflected in the *Egyptian Book of the Dead*, better known
as the "coming forth by day and the going forth by night." *This going forth
literally represents going forth into human life and then returning to the all-
pervasive light.* Matter, in a real sense, is intuited to be concertized or enfolded, localized light. Matter, in other words, is repressed light and light is
the most subtle expression of spirit. The body of matter must be liberated
back into light. The death of the body is therefore the doorway to a greater
life. Or, as Aurobindo said, "the life you lead conceals the light you are"
(1954, p. 420). As we are coming to see in modern science, light is literally
nonlocal and interconnected everywhere and may indeed be, in some sense,
conscious or an expression of consciousness. This appears to be a reflection
of the real notion behind reincarnation and the endless transformations of
consciousness.

THE BODILY PERCEPTION OF THE LIVING CURRENT

One of the great and enduring symbols of the ancient Kemetic Egyptians was the ankh or the sign of life. The ankh literally means life force, and
the houses of life where the Egyptians studied were called "per ankh." If we
look closely at the ankh we see a cross, and at the top of the cross is a
elliptical circuit. We have mentioned elsewhere that this elliptical circuit
may be the perception within the body of a living neuromelanin current that
is a forerunner and a precursor of neurological development even in embryo-

genesis (Bynum, 1994). The ankh is the somatic expression in ontogenetic memory of our own embryogenesis or neural development in the womb and the organismic perception of the neuromelanin superconductive current and its residual anlage in the braincore. In embryogenesis, or the development of the human fetus, there are lines of force (Goldscheider, 1906; Lashley, 1942; Loeb, 1907) and perhaps the eventual template of a future human being's form and psychoenergetic substructures of future experience. This includes not only somatic experience but the potential direction of embodied human consciousness itself.

In later chapters we will take up in more detail our understanding of the relationship between Kundalini and the wider ecological and solar environment. Suffice it to say here that this neuromelanin nerve current, the common inheritance of all humanity, both genetically and somatically and therefore rooted potentially in the rudimentary neurodynamics of human consciousness, is present in embryonic form from the first stages of human development. It is organismically perceived as a current of living energy by those in states of deep meditation and in states of ecstasy or trance. This basic embodiment of the psychospiritual process manifested in terms of Kundalini is greatly amplified by certain disciplines. The meditative disciplines of Kundalini Yoga as exemplified in the Egyptian, Dravidian Indian, and later Hindu and Buddhist Tantric traditions are highly refined examples. The "circulation of the light" from the head down through the spinal line in a loop and "out" again, coordinated with the breath, is a well-known Taoist practice of China and Japan. Another example can be found in the rhythm-vibration-entrainment process that occurs within certain disciplines that we can find in meditative music and highly rhythmatized forms of trance induction as emplified by the !Kung people of southwest Africa (Katz, 1982).

We mentioned in Chapter 2, in reference to the primary matrices of the African unconscious, that one of its primary modes was rhythm-vibration. Rhythm and pattern recognition pervade the African consciousness. This basic mode gave rise not only to the perception of cycles in nature, but also to the earliest forms of codified mathematics and the perception of distant rhythms in the solar abyss. There is a direct linkage between the early development of the calendar, the rhythm of the stars, the rhythms within one's own body, and the rhythms of the environment, particularly the rhythm of the Nile over thousands and thousands of years. We have come to believe that the rising of this psychospiritual force reflected in the body–mind of the individual can be done by a number of rhythmic entrainments. In particular the rising of Kundalini or the stimulation of Kundalini by way of resonance and vibrations of the neuromelanin nerve current in music, particularly highly rhythmic music, can be seen throughout the secret societies of West Africa. It is even embedded in the genesis of music that permeates African diasporic music from the ceremonies of Voudoun and Candomble to the roots of jazz, rock-and-roll, and the joyous spirituals.

In many of the world traditions surrounding this phenomenon, the current starts in the toes and feet, then progresses up through the legs before it reaches the spinal line. Then from the spine, it rises up the back to the head then descends down the front of the body to end in the lower abdomen. In the process, individual consciousness is transcended at least briefly. It begins with rhythm. In other words, by highly rhythmic music in which the individual consciousness is eclipsed in the greater communal consciousness that is punctuated and organized by rhythm we see the stimulation of Kundalini. This is seen today in the West in the African American spirituals, diasporic music of the Americas and Caribbean, certain West African trends, and again in the traditions of the !Kung in southwest Africa (Katz, 1982). Rhythmic stamping of the feet is critical here, for it appears to initiate a pattern. It is interesting to speculate that this intense rhythmic entrainment of a neuromelanin nerve current may act as a resonant stimulator to superconductive capacities. This is interesting in light of the sense that the resonant affinity or the vibrant organism can then enter into, by way of entrainment, other more subtle and nonlinear vibratory modes. In other words, just as the ancient pharaohs were believed to enfold and represent within their own bodies the neters and the principles of the individual mortal consciousness, an implicate order, it is possible that this variation of a metaphysical concept continues to exist in the religions and philosophies of the widely scattered Diaspora of peoples of this tradition. In particular, the rhythmic entrainment of the neuromelanin nerve current may act as a resonant superconductor in a wider solar environment with the Earth, an Earth that is inhabited by other forms of intelligent consciousness than our own. This suggests an implicate order, a holonomic universe in which consciousness is pervasive on all levels. This touches back to the notion of a personal or personalizing and localizing universe in which the all-pervasive original light is corporified or localized into specific objects, places, and persons.

In the other Kiaspora-Diaspora religions of West Africa exist similar religious, philosophical, and mystical concepts. In rhythm and music is a literal discipline of this. In the West African religions of Dahomey, Nigeria, Benin, Senegal, Mali, Ghana, and other areas of northwest Africa, this phenomenon of rhythm and music is used to entrain the body and entrance the mind into a highly personalized and vibrationally conscious universe. In different places these religions and philosophical systems have different names. The most well known in that part of west Africa is the religion we have come to call Voudoun. This religion has spread with the diaspora of African peoples to the Americas. In Brazil and Cuba are variations in the religions of Candomble and Santería. In the Caribbean the religion of

Voudoun reached one of its highest and most intense expressions within that particular domain. There are variations of Voudoun in the New Orleans area in the United States. In the dance movements of these traditions, especially in the hip and rhythmic gyrations of the back and lower spine, there is a subtle stimulation of the Kundalini process, both individually and in a collective group mode. In this context the indigenous Black churches of the United States have a long tradition of deep rhythmic entrainment and spiritual possession as part of the worship service.

In Haitian Voudoun, the most direct expression of the Kundalini process is associated with the serpent god Domballah. The Domballah is directly associated with the return of animal or bossale (uninitiated) matter to the sun or solar principle through the rite of initiation (Rigaud, 1969). This solar principle of Domballah expresses the geometric perfection of the gifts of "the holy spirit" and the gifts are said to be seven in number. Many other variations of this motif and paradigm are seen in the serpent cults of West African history and civilization, especially in Dahomey. When Dahomey was raided by the French for slaves, the captured brought this religious belief and discipline with them to Haiti, Martinique, and eventually to Louisiana, whence it spread through the southern United States. The rites involved deep rhythmic music, incantation, bodily movement, and "mounting" or "possession" in the head by way of the bodily line. In days past, especially in Haiti and Dahomey, the serpent power was directly worshiped with a snake in a cage at the altar. This discipline was nourished by a myth from the Dahomey that a coiled snake supports the Earth with 3,500 coils above and below the Earth. The notion of 3,500 coils beneath the surface is the intuition of the Earth as a source of energy itself. There is an intuited gravitational vortex in the deeper regions of the Earth that creates "spirals" and shapes or warps space-time itself and our perception of space, time, and "distance." This energy field was believed to be directly experienced by human beings. This is a cross-cultural perception, as we shall see. The serpent itself was believed to have erected four pillars to support the sky, then coiled around them to keep them upright. The priestess would sit on the cage during certain parts of the ceremony and symbolically be penetrated by the god, leading to convulsions and the oracular power (Metraux, 1959). A collective delirium arose during the dancing and even those in the audience, including the few Whites who attended, were affected with physical and psychological reactions. Clairvoyance was one of the primary powers associated with the priest or priestess in the ceremony as the rhythm built to a climax. Seeing the serpent worshiped, the frenzy of the dance, the anomalous phenomena emerging out of the trance and being swept up by it themselves into a vortex of spiritual energy made many Whites see this as "the devil's music," an image that surrounds almost every new Black music in the West.

A Biomedical Model

What we are saying essentially is that there is a recurrent conscious and unconscious motif here of using rhythm, vibration, and entrainment to stimulate and on some occasions to awaken, albeit briefly, the process of Kundalini. This process then becomes magnified and moves through the body like a current of living energy, much as we see in the sacred dances and religious practices of the !Kung and others of West African origin. In the process of full "entrancement," the individual principle is eclipsed and brought into union or higher Yoga by way of a higher-order emergent principle. There is an association between the intense rhythmic process of the drum and other percussion instruments and entering into trance states.

This actually may be in multiples of 6 to 7 hertz (Hz) throughout the body. How this may be connected with the heart aorta and the function of the awakening of Kundalini in the model offered by Sannella (1987) and Bentov (1977) is of special interest. Here it is shown that the human heart's aorta sets up a standing wave in the body of about 7 Hz. This rhythmic vibration through the dense structures of the body, particularly the skull and cranial vault, converts this mechanical vibration into electrical ones, creating acoustical plane waves that reflect upon the third and lateral ventricles of the brain. This creates a hierarchy of other frequencies that couple or entrain with the original 7-Hz vibration. Such a vibrational system sends a current through the sensory cortex of the brain that is felt throughout the entire body–mind. Along the spinal line and in the brain, we believe that it may directly stimulate neuromelanin superconductive processes. This model is one of great interest because in both Sannella's and Bentov's model, when Kundalini is awakened, it is also integrated into the Earth's wider magnetic and solar fields. Between the conductive layer around the Earth called the ionosphere, about 80 kilometers up, and the Earth's surface, an electromagnetic wave reflects or vibrates back and forth at certain resonance frequencies. These Earth-ionosphere cavity resonance frequencies have been calculated by J. Toomey, C. Polk, and others at 7.8, 14.1, 20.3, and 32.5 Hz (Persinger, 1974). The lowest of these is almost 7.5 Hz, the same as that of the heart, especially in states of deep meditation. It is nearly identical to the velocity of electromagnetic radiation divided by the Earth's circumference (Bentov, 1977):

$$\frac{2.998 \times 10^8 \text{m/sec}}{4.003 \times 10^7 \text{m}} = 7.489 \text{ or } 7.5 \text{ Hz}$$

It is interesting in this light that the !Kung have an underlying musical (pulse) of 7 to 8 Hz and various variations on that theme (Katz, 1982). Given the higher incidence of "juvenile heart" or juvenile EKG patterns in the physiology in Blacks, it is interesting to speculate on the greater preponderance or possibility of this particular entrainment occurring.

In a harmonic model or analogy, higher levels of vibration tend to entrain lower-order vibrations. This is somewhat similar to the principle in cognitive psychology where emergent higher-order processes of the brain can come to emphasize an order and supervenient influence over lower-order phenomenon (Sperry, 1988). This is interesting in connection to a certain phenomenon that occurs in possession states. By possession we do not mean in its negative sense, as often seen in Hollywood movies. Rather we are referring to the phenomenon in which persons consciously, and voluntarily, enter into a profound trance by way of a traditional methodology and are guided by the coordinated discipline of the community such that they are eventually "possessed" or, better yet, actually "embody the gods." The embodiment of a "god" is referred to as a possession by Loa in Voudoun. Here literally the initiates have the experience of their body and consciousness being entered into by a god or being or force that exists on a higher plane or deeper, more subtle order. The nonlocal, by disciplined rhythm, becomes localized. In this connection we remember the words of the Indian yogi, philosopher, and luminary Sri Aurobindo, who said repeatedly that depending on one's own proclivities in deeper states of meditation, one either sees "beings" or one sees "forces," according to your disposition (Satprem, 1968). This is the case with other disciplines in which the individual enters into a long and profound study.

There are many dangers associated with this psychospiritual discipline, which is why it is done primarily in secret societies. It is a long, involved discipline and not to be entered into frivolously. The sudden and unexpected stimulation of Kundalini can be experienced like a severe panic attack, and therefore be very disturbing (Fox, 1994). There are a number of important preliminary technical disciplines that must be mastered, including the control of the breath, the mastery of attention, and the control of certain internal bodily "currents" or routes of energy through the body. The two main ones that were focused on in ancient Egyptian times and also in the Dravidian Indian technique of Kundalini Yoga involved primary pathways of energy on the right and left sides of the spinal column, often referred to as Ida and Pingala. These merged at the crown of the head. In ancient Egyptian science and mysticism they are referred to as the silver and the red crown, which also ended at the top of the cranium in the so-called double-uraeus serpents. The mummy skulls of the high priests and pharaohs like Tutankhamen had this woven on them in burial rites (Schwaller de Lubicz, 1961). The net effect of this Kundalini phenomenon and practice, both in ancient times and later times in West Africa, involved the literal earth-shaking second birth of the individual into a higher level of consciousness by way of radical transformation of the mind and consciousness in the body. This is a higher perfection or harmony of Maát. It is again literally the capacity to emerge into that level of consciousness that, as in the *Egyptian Book of the Dead*, allows one the ability to "come forth by day and go forth by night." It is to enter into the realm of constant transformation. This again is a primary matrix of the African unconscious.

This ancient science spread in its technical forms from the Nile Valley civilizations to those of the Dravidians of the Indus Valley of India. We see these in the remnants of their ancient cities, Mohenjo-Daro and Harappa, destroyed by the Aryan incursions from the North. As with so many other phenomena, once there's awakening in one place it tends to spread outward from that place to others. The phenomenon of Kundalini no doubt entered pre-Aryan India by way of the trade routes with East Africa. Silburn (1988) mentions how in pre-Aryan India, especially in Kashmir, a cult of the prestigious naga, both the divine serpent and lineage of mystical sages, was known to be in possession of an immanent science of an occult nature revealing a heavenly ambrosia and the capacity for a radical transformation of consciousness. The word "naga" appears in Kemetic Egypt in forms of Kundalini worship. Also there are a number of cities and sites in the upper Nile area that have the word "naga" as the root word. Underneath all of these, however, we find a striking parallel in terms of the technical discipline of Kundalini Yoga. This cannot be emphasized enough. The similarity is due not only to the same genetic origin of the peoples of Dravidian India and the Nile Valley of Africa, but also simply to the similar structure of the body–mind in all human beings. This we believe is a result of the neuromelanin nerve current present early in embryogenesis and reaching its full awakening in the adult human being by way of an elaborate and studied discipline. Melanin and the neuromelanin nerve current, we are suggesting, have the capacity to absorb light and to *transduce* other forms of light (Barr, 1983a).

The phenomenon of Kundalini is a worldwide phenomenon, perhaps reaching its highest level of sophistication and practice in the Nile Valley civilizations of Kemetic Egypt and later in the highly evolved pre-Aryan psychospiritual traditions of Dravidian India. Later civilizations and societies have perfected certain areas and others have totally forgotten it. However, it is a phenomenon rooted in the genetic and embryological body–mind of the human being and is the capacity of all human beings. When the Kundalini phenomenon is awakened by steady Yogic discipline, rhythmic entrainment, or other discipline, the heart and brain of the subtle anatomy of the human being are awakened and then entrained. This entrainment, by way of vibration, may very well enter into the wider ecological environment of the solar forces of the Earth. This is not a mystical notion at all. There is an interconnected living field of life called Gaia that encircles this planet and a geomagnetic field surrounding and infusing the Earth (Dubrov, 1978). Modern science has come to recognize that the Earth is a living phenomenon and not a dead piece of matter spinning in the universe. In that context we begin to recognize the Kundalini phenomenon as another energetic and living biogravitational phenomenon inherent in the localized form of a human being which, by natural extension, is also reflected in the wider living field of the Earth and its more localized solar environment. In the process of union or Yoga, the individual principle, by way of discipline and emergent intelligent vibratory interaction, is integrated into higher levels of vibration corresponding to the higher vibrational field of the Earth. The intuition of this can be seen rooted in numerous religions scattered throughout antiquity and modern times. We have merely traced its manifestation through one discipline out of Kemetic Egypt over to Dravidian India and then over to West Africa. As mentioned before, the Greeks, in their study of Egyptian disciplines and civilization, seem to have abstracted or focused primarily on the "rational" aspects of Egyptian civilization and seem to have either failed to understand, were never initiated into, or simply recoiled from the deeper, more subtle and esoteric aspects of their religious science and philosophy. What the Greeks did not understand, and what the Romans did not understand, they relegated to the "dark sciences." The knowledge and psychodynamics of the unconscious mind or Amenta eluded Greek and Roman civilizations for 2,000 years, only to be rediscovered by a son of Moses and the ancient Hebrew-Egyptian lineage, Sigmund Freud. And even Freud was aware of its lineage and had mixed feelings about it. He referred to his fear of complete emergence into the primordial racial unconscious as fear of the "black tide of mud, of occultism." Yet Freud was perfectly aware that Moses was in all likelihood a Black Kemetic Egyptian priest, was married to the daughter of an African priest, and that much of modern Judaism has its roots in the African soil (Diop, 1991; Finch, 1990; Williams, 1987). The Kabbala is the esoteric Hebrew study of meditation, the third eye, and the highly symbolized hidden force of Kundalini.

The symbol of a dormant Kundalini is the medical caduceus, first initiated by the ancient Kemetic Egyptians and later used by the Hermetic transformations of the Greeks. The sign of a fully awaken Kundalini is the Egyptian ankh. Both, we believe, are reflections of the organismic or inner bodily perception of the neuromelanin nerve current, that line from early embryogenesis that is highly sensitive to light, conducts a bioenergy through the body, and may have superconductive capacities. The phenomenon of a bioluminous energy, perhaps a form of biological superconductivity, moving through the physical and subtle body in specific patterns, is testified to by innumerable cultures from time immemorial and is directly observable to almost anyone who enters the psychospiritual disciplines. It is often thought of as the primal energy in our species and directly associated with evolutionary forces. It rises upward toward light and, in a sense, seeks to be united or reunited with light. What we are suggesting here is that neuromelanin, because of recent research findings and certain "neatness-of-fit" considerations, is currently the *leading candidate* that best correlates with this process in human experience. The superconductive capacity is a phenomenon of quantum mechanics and allows it, by way of the quantum potential, to enter into the implicate order of the biogravitational field of the wider solar and ecological environment of the Earth. If the Earth is a living intelligent system, then when the individual or localized principle is made to fall into union or integrate into the higher intelligent luminous organismic field, we have the science, practice, and ancient lineage of Kundalini Yoga. This lineage and this practice we believe are the foundation, underground swell, and ultimate trajectory of a human body–mind in its present localization.

PSYCHONEUROLOGY AND THE SOLAR LOGOS

So what is this biological and solar process common to all members of the human family? What are some of its physical and medical characteristics? For this we must focus a little more closely on areas mentioned earlier: embryology and neuromelanin.

Prior to crying, to walking upright, to talking with and sometimes at each other, all of us, regardless of race, color, or creed shared a great adventure. This was the journey from our earliest embryonic stage in our mother's womb, through complete fetal development or embryogenesis, to splashing onto the shores of a human birth. In the process of individual development or ontology we relived significant structural elements in the phylogenetic or group history of the race in evolution. This was so on the ancient African savannahs and is so today in downtown New York City. There is a clear connection between embryogenesis, light, human development, and the forms of intelligence.

During embryogenesis or the development of the embryo in the uterus, there is an interesting unfoldment. After conception the female egg begins to divide and multiply into a cluster of fetal cells called a blastula. The initial blastula unfolds three distinct layers of cells, the outermost level or ectoderm, the inner layer or endoderm, and the mesoderm. Each area of the adult human body is rooted in one of these three early layers of fetal cells. The ectodermal layer contains melanin in high concentrations throughout its region (Pearse, 1969; Pearse & Takor, 1976). Only 28 hours after conception, the ectoderm has moved into the interior of the blastula and begun to form a neural tube. During embryogenesis this neural tube develops into the precursor of the brain and spinal line. The neural tube unfolds into the spinal cord, the end of the tube or the neural crest mid-point develops into the brain, and very importantly, the cells along the tube evolve into light-sensitive melanocytes, which eventually develop into all the endocrine glands, e.g., pineal, pituitary, adrenal, mast cells, hypothalamus, thyroid, parathyroid, pancreas, and others that will develop in the gastrointestinal tract, lungs, and heart (King, 1990; Welbourn, 1977).

This initial unfoldment in space and time occurs, mind you, *prior* to the first heartbeat. It is the first localization of what is later a human life, the Horian logos if you will, the corporification of the primal light. All these cells, again, originated out of the melanin-dense ectoderm, and melanin itself is most sensitive to and also *absorbs* light. As an organic semi-conductor it has a very small band-gap on the UV-visible spectrum and absorbs photons easily, hence it is dark colored. This fetal development continues and seems to be guided by an unusual direct current that appears to continue throughout embryogenesis, guiding the development of the embryo from its earliest stages all the way through to its birth. In the earliest stages, it is intimately associated with the development of various melanocytes along the neural crest and spinal line (Barr, 1983). Indeed, there's considerable support for the notion that melanin and *neuromelanin*, or melanin located in the brain regions in particular, is a significant if not *the* significant organizing molecule during embryogenesis for the human being. This is true regardless of surface racial differences, since at deeper levels our biological and genetic inheritance issues from the same template. This, of course, extends into the brainstem itself. Small problems in development are quickly corrected even at the molecular level by the self-consistency of the organism and its "guidance system" so to speak. There is no doubt a form of quantum resonance behind this self-consistency.

This melanin and neuromelanin tract itself appears intimately associated with a certain aspect of the process of biochemilluminosity. This is the particular capacity of melanin and neuromelanin to absorb light and not re-radiate it out into the system. It absorbs photons and is intimately associated with electromagnetic phenomena. This, again, is what accounts for neuromelanin being dark or black. The absorbed photons are apparently organized into a more complex structure. This increasing complexity or negative entropy is the mystery of evolution.

Conductivity in organic substances is generally explained by electronic transitions (normally ionization) to create "holes" (empty orbitals) in long conjugated chains. Electrons, and thus the holes, can move along chains and hop from chain to chain. A hole is created in a photo-conductor when an electron moves from a bonding to an anti-bonding orbital upon stimulation by a photon. The difference in energy between these orbitals, termed a band-gap in semiconductor terminology, is the same energy as the photon (quantized). This value can be seen in the UV-visible spectrum. A true organic conductor has a very small band-gap, absorbs photons easily, and therefore is dark or black.

Since all systems of energy and life are ultimately interconnected with each other, both locally and non-locally, it is not unreasonable to assume that the subtle field of neuromelanin bio-conductivity is in some permutations intimately associated with the wider vibrational, rhythmic, and energetic forces and fields of the Earth, mediated most probably by the so-called "quantum of action." In particular we have noticed that in further human development there seem to be well-attested acupuncture lines or meridians that course through the body, suggesting the possibility of biological superconducting regions in living systems, since these acupuncture points and meridians are associated with high electrical conductivity (Dubrov, 1978; Maxey & Beal, 1975; Plonsey, 1969). A similar phenomenon is noticed in the nadis of Yoga (Motoyama, 1972). In both of these systems conduits or lines of energy are clearly demarcated to flow through the human body. In both the Hindu Yoga tradition and the Chinese medical tradition of acupuncture these lines of energy are intimately related to the subtle energies that are solar and geomagnetic through and around the Earth.

Neuromelanin may be a superconductor, that is, it has the capacity to enter into a particular state in which energy is conducted through the system with a high degree of efficiency (Barr, 1983; Cope, 1981; Dubrov, 1978). These lines of neuromelanin conductivity are present from the earliest stages of embryogenesis. Again, they are active *prior* to the first heartbeat. In fact, early on in embryogenesis there are perceived "lines of force" that evolve and later may unfold the forms and templates of human cognitive, emotional, and spiritual experience (Goldscheider, 1906; Lashley, 1942; Loeb, 1907).

Melanin itself is a universal pigment in living organisms, from the most primitive to primates and man. It tends to become localized in the major functional areas of the body. For vertebrates such as mammals and higher primates, it concentrates in the skin, ears, eyes, the central and peripheral nervous system, and very importantly, the diffuse neuroendocrine loci. This means the pineal, pituitary, thyroid, parathyroid, and adrenal glands. It is also found concentrated in all the viscera, liver, arteries, heart, GI tract, muscles, and sexual organs. It is present from the dawn of life and because it absorbs light or quanta, seems intimately involved with the earliest movements of the evolutionary adventure on earth (Altschule & Hegedus, 1972; Menon & Haberman, 1977; Sarnat & Netsky, 1981). It has the capacity to turn excited energy states into molecular rotation and vibrational or rhythmic patterns and vice versa.

Melanin is a rather "heterogeneous polymer," meaning its component molecules can and do show variability in terms of amount, type, and structure. This accounts for much of the uniqueness of each molecule. It is also rich in free radicals and metal ions. Its structure is remarkably stable and, therefore, resistant to change (Sealy et al., 1980; Swan, 1973). It can be thought of as a "basic building block."

An extremely interesting property of the melanin found in the brain, referred to as neuromelanin, is that it is concentrated within the neurons and glia located in very strategic areas of the brainstem, putting it at the intersecting crossway of *all* sensory and motor input–output signals. It seems to act as a "gate" to not only motor activity, but also emotional and cognitive processes. Barr and others believe that it serves as an integrative trigger molecule that partially regulates monoamines and neuroglia during motor and intellectual activity. It also increases in amount and richness with the gradual ascent up the evolutionary tree and is most concentrated in the highly functional areas of the brain (Bazelon et al., 1967; Bogerts, 1981).

For as yet unclear reasons, melanin demonstrates an uncanny facility for accumulating and binding with metals and other ions. This suggests an ability to activate key enzymes and thereby control cellular metabolism in general. It also bonds quickly and powerfully with vitamins and a number of important *consciousness* influencing drugs (e.g., hallucinogens, neuroleptics, amphetamines, cocaine, etc.). *It thus has a resonate affinity for consciousness* (Salazar et al., 1978; Tjalve et al., 1981).

Melanin is also known to have semi-conducting properties. This becomes relevant when the issue of information and memory storage processes is considered. The whole phenomenon of photo-conductivity shows that melanin inherently absorbs light and that its conductivity can change, even by a magnitude of ten (Filators, McGinness, & Corey, 1976).

In relationship to its place in healing and possibly in immune system function, it is known that leukocytes and tissue mast cells synthesize melanin. In the bloodstream these cells can deliver melanin in a "hormone-like" manner throughout the system quickly (Okun, 1976; Okun et al., 1972). We know that the brain has neuropeptides, but apparently so do the immune cells, such that the brain can communicate with the body's immune system. Melanin seems to be another news messenger, or rather to have neurotransmitter potentials and regenerative capacities.

Some researchers (Sarna et al., 1980) have studied melanin and oxygen consumption and concluded that the consumption of oxygen changes with light, pH, temperature, and type of melanin. This is important because the brainstem melanin system is critically involved in the regulation of breathing. Controlled breathing techniques, as occurs in Kundalini and Hatha Yoga, may affect the neuromelanin system and its neuroendocrine regulation. Remember, with the right stimulus, melanin can quickly increase its conductivity by a magnitude of ten! This may account for the tremendous rush of bioenergy through the system when certain processes are brought into play with the activation of Kundalini. Perhaps when the 7 Hz cycle of the aorta is reflected on the third and lateral ventricles of the brain, neuromelanin's capacity to convert mechanical energy to electronic energy amplifies the sensory current, and a coherent biological superconductive process arises that, by way of the quantum potential, interacts with both more local and nonlocal phenomena. Neuroscience is only now beginning to look seriously at the nonlinear systems that operate in the brain, and how these processes underlie numerous nonlocal modes of information transfer. When these nonlinear neurodynamics are more fully understood, a more comprehensive view of psychodynamics will emerge in which information and resonances will predominate. This is a vibratory universe!

Finally, let it be added again that the brainstem melanin system produces neurotransmitters. Actually these are better understood as neuromodulators. In any event they regulate crucial glands and organs such as the hypothalamic, neuroendocrine, and autonomic responses, which in turn affect the higher regulatory systems. This brainstem melanin system extends from the peripheral autonomic ganglia to the very top of the brainstem. If it is destabilized, there will appear both autonomic nervous system and immune system complications as well as mental and emotional instability (Jacobowitz, 1977; Mason & Docherty, 1980; Swanson & Mogenson, 1981).

Predictably enough, as quantum theory matures it has turned its gaze toward both the brain and consciousness itself. Nobel Laurette in medicine John Eccles sees quantum tunneling effects in the brain (Eccles, 1976), so does E. Harris Walker (1970). Physicists L. Bass (1975) and F. A. Wolf (1984) have drawn attention to the observation that a single neuron fired is accompanied by a legion of other nonlocal correlations of neuronal firing! Many others (Grinberg-Zylberbaum & Ramos, 1987, 1994; Lockwood, 1989) are moving in this direction. Sooner or later the nonlinear systems of the brain and the neurodynamics that are associated with them will be recognized by clinical science. When and if quantum theory becomes a complete theory it will naturally embrace the marriage of light and consciousness. This will extend our reach of understanding considerably and neuromelanin we believe is implicated in this.

In every human culture and civilization, with the possible exception of our own contemporary situation, wisdom and insight have always been associated with advancing age and experience. The wise man, the women of wisdom, were archetypally a generation or two beyond the norm. More if possible. In this light it is interesting that neuromelanin also increases in age with the normal brain, especially in the locus coeruleus and substantia nigra, which rest at the uppermost extreme of the human brainstem's system (Kaiya, 1980). It increases with age up to 60 or 70, then either levels out or very slowly declines. This may parallel the traditional capacity of the elders to "see within," to make contact with reservoirs of collective wisdom from the prior experiences of the tribe and race. It may also be the doorway to the great initiations.

5 THE OSIRIAN COMPLEX

For it is demonstrable that the religious concept of the "Christhood" was worked out first in the profoundly important and influential drama of Osiris.
—Charles S. Finch, M.D., *African Background to Medical Science*

The great change which took place in the religious views of the Egyptians a little before the beginning of dynastic history was, I believe, due entirely to the rise and spread of the cult of Osiris throughout Egypt.
—E. A. Wallis Budge, *The Book of the Dead*

To Amelineau we owe the discovery of Osiris' tomb at Abydos, thanks to which Osiris could no longer be considered a mythical hero but an historic personage, an initial ancestor of the pharaohs, a Black ancestor as was his sister, Isis. Thus we can understand why the Egyptians always painted their gods black as coal, in the image of their race. It would be paradoxical and quite incomprehensible for a white people never to have painted its gods white, but to choose, on the contrary, to depict its most sacred beings in the black color of Isis and Osiris on Egyptian monuments.
—Cheikh Anta Diop, *The African Origin of Civilization*

TO BIND THEM IN MYTH

THE African unconscious is the deep bedrock of the primordial collective unconscious shared by all human beings regardless of race, sex, or historical time. Indeed the African unconscious is the first sustained psychic structure that has come into the possession of humankind. Humankind's 2½ to 3 million years of ancestral experience in Africa before its migration out reinforced the genetic basis of the African unconscious. Despite surface skin and phenotypical differences and permutations of other kinds in language, customs, and beliefs, in the depths of the deepest collective unconscious it remains essentially an African human creation. In this chapter we will explore how this African unconscious has given to humanity its oldest and perhaps its deepest and certainly its most long-lived and continuous structure and mythos for the transformation of human consciousness. We each have an intimate affair with this level of consciousness and with the all-pervasive consciousness as it is localized and "conducted" through the body–mind. Light and intelligence are implicated on all levels, from birth to death to what little we know of the life beyond this. The dynamics of personality unfoldment are largely a function of how this "current of living energy" is navigated by the psychological structures both "above and below" the ego (Bynum, 1994), an ego that too often eclipses the literal light of this primordial ground of all being, consciousness itself.

In the Osirian myth of ancient Kemetic Egypt are embedded and implicate the intuitions of the eternity of the soul, the "fall" from paradise, reincarnation, birth, death, and transcendence played out in a human life. The myth of Osiris held the imagination of untold millions of human beings for at least 5,000 years before the birth of Christ (Budge, 1961). It was the source of constant nourishment and the assumed and intuited trajectory of human consciousness. It grew out of the numerous fertility gods and other agricultural cults that arose with the new Neolithic age of the Nile Valley. The Ophidian cults of the serpent and the shadows throughout this period nurtured the genesis of the emerging intuition of *transformation* throughout the seen and unseen world that took hold of the human mind and imagination. In the process it gave rise to a new perception in nature that filtered its way into religion. Millennia of observation and symbolic imitation of nature gave rise to dances that reflected the behavior of animals for sure, but also the structures and cycles of the stars. The Nile River was seen reflected in the "winding waterway" of the Milky Way overhead. The three great pyramids at Giza were laid out in a reflection, astronomically speaking, of the three stars of Orion's Belt. The lion-bodied sphinx was laid out to look due east on the vernal equinox into the constellation of Leo, all reflecting an esoteric theory of eternal life in the cosmic region called the Duát . This was the great leap in human consciousness that eventually showed itself in the cult of Osiris. It swaddled human beings in a sustained and living myth from the cradle to the grave and beyond. In the symbolic and visionary experiences of the great "sleep temples" of the ancient world, it was reenacted innumerable times. In the middle kingdoms of West Africa's secret societies it was played out over and over, complete with ritual burial and resurrection from the tomb. In this chapter we will see how this primordial myth and system implicitly structures our consciousness on an intimate level even today.

The *Egyptian Book of the Dead*, or the "coming forth by day and the going forth by night," appears to be a collective unconscious metaphor, map, and psychic legacy of the human body–mind in its involvement with progressively more subtle levels of matter, energy, and consciousness. It is a reflection of humankind's ageless encounter with beings, intelligences, and forces that implicated and reflected life on various levels. The inner workings of the *Egyptian Book of the Dead* can be seen in different religions throughout Africa, India, and the Caribbean. It is also profoundly implicated in the Christian myth and we shall see that Christianity has many of its origins in this myth (Finch, 1991). When we say myth we do not mean fantasy or imagination. We mean a living map left by an actual person as a way of apprehending a meaningful and intelligible psychic and conscious order in the universe. It exercises a higher-order controlling influence over more apparently subjective and random permutations of human consciousness. We shall see in the Osirian myth and complex a model, structure, and spiritual metamorphosis that encompasses not only one's somatic expression as a human being but also one's psychological, psychic, and ultimately spiritual reality. It is a myth that has spoken to humanity through the millennia. Its symbolism percolates through the different symbols that we have mentioned in earlier chapters. This mythos treats the human body–mind as a living metaphor of transformation, of literally spiritually speaking $E = mc^2$. It is found in cultures as widely disparate as the Greek, Indian, Japanese, and Christian. One even finds aspects of it in the Islamic religion, particularly around the notions of death, resurrection, and the hero's spiritual journey. All of these were firmly entrenched in the mind and imagination of humankind for thousands of years before the Greek myths.

There seems to be a need in humanity through its collective and individual evolution for a mythos that can touch on all the phases and levels of human existence, from matter to psyche to spirit. A great universal myth is indeed needed to embrace all the realms of human experience. All these realms of existence and endeavors need to be reflected through this myth such that it is completely rounded and applicable to nearly every significant aspect of life. This includes not only the physical, the emotional, and the familial, but also the religious, the heroic and virtuous, the cultural, and the divine aspirations. Many other powerful and useful myths in humanity have already been elaborated and cover part of the territory. They will be mentioned presently in a somewhat ascending order in terms of the dimension of experience that they appear to be most applicable for explaining.

THE FAMILY OF HUMAN MYTHS

The Oedipus myth and the Electra myth are taken from Greek mythology and would appear to be powerful and excellent meaningful models of our relations as human beings around issues of power, sexuality, and tragedy. The Oedipus myth was used by Sigmund Freud in a brilliant way to explicate the dynamic operative between parents and male children within the family unconscious system. His model was an intrapsychic one as opposed to a systemic one, as we see in the family unconscious system (Taub-Bynum, 1984). However, the relationship between a son and his mother as expressed explicitly in the Oedipus myth, or the relationship between a father and his daughter as seen in the Electra myth, are dynamic and real in the everyday life of people today, especially those engaged in the structure of a nuclear family. They did reflect a paternal Greek family system and to a large extent the pattern of a European familial structure. However, they are also in less degree applicable to other familial structures in different cultures.

The story of Job in the Bible has been used by Carl Jung and others (Jung, 1953). Jung used this story as a myth in an engaging way to explore the human psyche's involvement with the powerful emotions of guilt and innocence, sin, loss, and redemption. It is a Biblical myth taken from the Jewish Semitic tradition. It too deals with issues of power, guilt, sin, and redemption, as does the Oedipus myth. However, the Oedipus myth deals more explicitly in modern form with sexuality, where the myth of Job does not. The myth of Job deals more incisively with issues of ethics, faith, and redemption than does the Oedipus myth. However, neither one deals with the issue of spiritualization and resurrection—or for that matter the intuition of eternal life.

The Midas myth deals with issues of power, greed, and remorse. It focuses on essentially the futility of attaining an illusory goal. The fulfillment of Midas' crude wish turns everything into gold. Gold may be beautiful, but it is cold and lifeless. It is a metaphor for how the realization of a crude ideal can lead to "frozen motion," to death, to the denouement of diseased desire. In other words, whenever things are touched and turned into gold it makes everything that one touches inanimate and no longer life-giving. Midas eventually was made deeply unhappy by his success. In this way the myth deals very powerfully with the issues of power, greed, and remorse.

The myths of King Arthur and Beowulf in northern England and Europe are ones that cover the dynamics of heroism and courage. In them are elements of the search for the true spiritual secrets of life. However, more than anything else they are stories of courage, commitment, and heroism in life. They are stories of the individual principle striving to move beyond itself but still captured primarily by the heroic dynamics of the ego.

The myth of Icarus is the myth of one's flight toward godhood but ends in partial failure. In the flight of Icarus, the hero is first exhilarated by his capacity to soar upward, to escape, but he moves too close and too quickly toward the sun. In the process the wax that held together the man-made wings begins to melt and one of the heroes plummets from the sky into the waters of death and the unconscious. It is the young, untested, or undisciplined son Icarus who falls. His more mature father Daedalus remains focused in mind and heart and thereby escapes his predicament of being isolated on an island in the sea. It is he who makes it to the mainland and salvation. It is a myth of soaring human achievement with a tragic flaw, what we might call egoic inflation. On a more subtle level it might be seen as a divine impulse but not harnessed enough by emotional discipline such that the light toward which it is moving eventually destroys it and it crashes into the sea.

And then there are histories and myths of the great messiahs and prophets. These include Krishna, the Christ, Buddha, Muhammad, and numerous others lost to history. These are collective expressions of humanity's encounter, aspiration, and recognition of the divine immanent within itself. It is at this final level that we begin to see the Osirian mythos. Osiris was, like Christ, Muhammad, Moses, and the Buddha, a real person and figure in the world. Abbé Emile Amelineau (1850–1916), while excavating at Om El'Gaab near Abydos, found the actual tomb of Osiris. He is painted black to signify not only the underworld but also how he looked. All the early Egyptians gods were painted Black for this reason on the tombs of the deceased. The Greeks and Romans followed this custom, tacitly acknowledging the origin of their beliefs. Until the coming of the Osirian doctrines, the life beyond death for the Greeks and Romans was the gloomy shades of Hades.

The Osirian mythos includes the saga of his son Horus and the Horian logos mentioned in earlier chapters. It is the story of the recognition of the original prior light of the divine consciousness, the corporification and localization of light, the loss of this all-pervasive light by "the fall" into matter (Lucifer into darkness, into Set into Satan), and then the passion and restoration to this light in the dynamics of resurrection. This we hold is an intimate human dynamic. It may even be related to the luminous current, the biological superconducting luminous current that is with us prior to birth in embryogenesis and connected to the cosmos by the quantum potential, moves out after birth into its multiplicative forms of the human encounter, becomes the ultimate aim toward which consciousness and light are directed while living an embodied life, and then becomes the template trajectory of human consciousness back into light after the transcendence of its localization in the body–mind. The *Egyptian Book of the Dead*, like its later cousin the Bardo Throtol or *Tibetan Book of the Dead*, is directed toward helping the recently deceased, that person who has either left or transcended the dense body–mind and whose consciousness is now free to wander the plains of existence untethered by the constraints of localized, physically embodied consciousness. The real self may be ultimately nonlocal and outside of space and time.

The completeness of this Osirian myth in terms of its capacity to embrace all levels of human endeavor and consciousness is quite striking. It begins with the god-birth of Osiris, also called Ausar in some traditions, follows him through evolution, death, and back by resurrection to the godhead. The all-pervasive, intelligent light from which he originally comes is localized, lost, and then found again. It is literally the "light" and human adventure in consciousness throughout the realm of Earth and matter. Its embodiment is the Horian logos. It is literally $E = mc^2$, the light of consciousness itself, all-pervasive prior to the body–mind and all particularizing experience. When Osiris reawakens or is resurrected, he transcends the collapse of the local wave-packet of light into matter and reawakens to the all-pervasive nonlocal reality of consciousness. He is the father and progenitor of his son Horus, the solar hero at war with the dynamic forces of good and evil. One immediately finds an affinity here to the Buddhist perspective and intuition of intelligence and enlightenment as prior to human incarnation. Indeed the Buddha, Osiris, Krishna, Christ, and others are manifestations of the human aspiration and capacity to reawaken to its luminous origin and trajectory.[3]

This myth in its various forms is played out among the peoples of the earth. It originated in the dark-skinned Kemetic peoples of Egypt. It is the primordial underground mythos of Western consciousness as expressed through the Christian myth. As we shall see, the Christian myth in many

---

3. Krishna and Buddha of India, the Black Osiris, and the Christ with "woolly hair" and "feet the color of bronze" were clearly men of color. Perhaps part of their primordial spiritual genius lay in being able, through discipline, to touch upon this Black and paradoxically luminous inner current.

ways parallels the Osirian myth, a myth that is much older by several millennia. Much of the Osirian myth is about divine communion and resurrection. It is at the heart of the ancient and sacred science of the Kemetic Egyptians (Schwaller de Lubicz, 1961). What, then, is this myth and how is it relevant to our living experience even in our own day?

THE OSIRIAN MYTH, THE OSIRIAN JOURNEY

Many writers in history have chronicled the legend of Osiris. One of the most famous is the brilliant but somewhat flawed rendition by the Greek writer Plutarch. Clearly this legend was active and alive in his own day. It was also translated from the Egyptian hieroglyphics by Wallace Budge in his book, *Osiris and the Egyptian Resurrection* (1961). In it are all the personages of good and evil forces, high and low, in the process of transformation. It existed as a guiding belief at least 4,000 years before Christ. The oldest sources of written information we have about the extraordinary life and myth of Osiris are the ancient Kemetic Egyptian Pyramid Texts. In all likelihood, the Osirian cult arose just prior to the First Dynasty of Menes from the earlier pre-dynastic ideas rooted in their collective unconscious.[4] The cult of Osiris then spread quickly with the consolidation of the First Dynasty. This new teaching asserted that the body itself of the dead was a sacred vessel out of which a *future* radiant and eternal body would be resurrected and made to live in the divine domain. It went beyond the notion of burial and life after death of the earlier religion. It taught, perhaps in an evolutionary leap, that the deeper, real human spiritual body was luminous, eternal, and moving toward something higher than before. *This new belief was nearly coincident with the rise of civilization as we know it!* This last point cannot be stressed enough.

After that period in history, particularly later in the 19th and 26th Dynasties, we find numerous references to the myth of Osiris along with praises and hymns to Osiris. We find numerous references to the myth of Osiris in later Greek and Roman times written on tombs and temples. As mentioned earlier, there was a large and powerful presence of African religions in the Roman Empire, including Rome itself. The myth and the cult of Black Isis, who was the mythic wife of Osiris, and the Black Madonna and others were quite prominent in Roman times. The face and figure of Osiris

---

4. The exact date of Menes' First Dynasty, which unified Upper and Lower Egypt, is unknown. That he was a Black African is undeniable (Diop, 1974). Champollion says 5869 B.C.E., Mariette suggests 4455 B.C.E., Brugsch gives 3893 B.C.E., Petrie gives 3892 B.C.E. (Budge, 1960). The most conservative date is 3200 B.C.E.

is almost universally painted in black. While we in modern times have as yet uncovered no one doctrine that includes the entire myth of Osiris, we find its references scattered throughout the different papyri and texts uncovered from the tombs and houses of life of ancient Egypt. This myth and the archetypal ideas woven through it remained essentially unchanged from the earliest dynasties down to the time when the Copts embraced Christianity after the spreading of the faith by St. Mark the Evangelist in Alexandria in 69 C.E.

Elements of the Osirian saga found their way into Judaism, especially in the motifs surrounding the personal, moral lineage of the balancing of good and evil deeds after death in the heart. This judgment-redemption theme, with its emphasis on the personal moral tone, appears to have come to prominence among certain sects of the Kemetics, and may have been taken with them in their Diaspora out of Egypt. It certainly figured heavily in Christianity. It is the opinion of Budge and others that the early Egyptians, who were the racial descendants of the ancient dark Africans of the interior and the drying savannas to the west of the Nile, fused together the beliefs about Christianity and the symbolism of Osiris. Many of the themes of Christian belief had already been practiced in the temples of Luxor for a thousand years in terms of belief in a superhuman royal history, e.g., annunciation of spiritual conception, divine birth, baptism, public teaching at the age of 12, and others. The early African Christians saw the Christ as the highest expression of the pharaonic mysteries, the final "reconciliation of Set and Horus" and human incarnation of the divine consciousness in the flesh. It was the embodiment of the god of gods, the "word made flesh." We will find in later chapters a similar syncretic process and tendency toward embodiment of the gods when the African diasporic peoples of the slave trade integrated the Christianity of the European variety with their own indigenous West African faiths and trance technologies to create Voudoun, Santería, Candomble, and other expressions in their passage to the Americas.

According to Plutarch, Budge, and others, the myth of Osiris is focused initially around his birth. According to them the Egyptian goddess Nut, the wife of Ra, was apparently beloved by another, whose name was Keb. When the god Ra discovered their relationship, he became enraged with his wife and declared that she would not be able to have a child in any month or in any year. Then the god Thoth, later referred to as Hermes, who also loved Queen Nut, supposedly played at tables with Seline and won for the queen a seventeenth part of each day of the year which, added together, made 5 whole days. This is significant in terms of the fusion of Egyptian mythology and science, because these 5 days were joined to the 360 of what was then used as the calendar year. It was supposedly upon these first 5 days that Osiris was brought forth. In fact, the myth says that others of the royal line were born on the other 4 days: Horus, the son of Isis and Osiris, on the second; Set (Typhon, the evil one) on the third; Isis, his wife, on the fourth; and Nephthys, the sister of Isis, on the fifth. The family unconscious takes on mythic dimensions in this foundational epic of early civilization.

At the moment of his birth, legend holds it a great voice was heard to proclaim that the lord of creation had incarnated on Earth. In the course of time Osiris became king or pharaoh and devoted himself to civilizing his subjects and showing them the crafts of society and refinement. He established a set of laws that men might worship and be in right relationship with the gods. He is reported to have made Egypt a great peaceful and flourishing land. He then set out on a messianic quest to instruct other nations of the world in this civilizing manner. During his absence his wife, whose name was Isis, ruled the state of Egypt so well that Set, who later appears as the evil one or the devil Satan, was unable to do Osiris, his rival, any harm. When Osiris returned to Egypt again, Set is supposed to have plotted with 72 comrades and also with Aso, the queen of Ethiopia, to betray and murder Osiris. They secretly plotted and got the exact measure of the body of Osiris and made ready a chest exactly his body size, which was brought to his feast banquet hall when Osiris was present together with other guests. By a manipulation, Osiris was induced to lay down in the chest, which then was immediately closed by the evil Set and his fellow conspirators then quickly put upon the Nile and floated to the sea. According to Budge these things happened on the 17th day of the month of Hathor, when Osiris was either 28 years old or in the 28th year of his reign. The first to know about this were the mythological creatures, the Pans and Satyrs, who dwelled in the land of Panopolas. Eventually the tragic news was brought to Queen Isis at Coptos, where she reportedly, in distress, cut off a lock of her hair and put on mourning apparel. (The word "Coptic" comes from the word *Coptos* and indicates the original inhabitants of Kemetic Egypt.)

When the queen put on her mourning apparel, she went into deep grief and set out on a great journey to find her husband's body. In the process of her journey she discovered that Osiris had been sexually united with her sister, Nephthys, and that Anubis, the offspring of their union, had been exposed to the elements by his mother as soon as he was born. Isis tracked her husband with the help of Anubis and other dogs and even brought up Anubis as her own guard dog and attendant. Soon after this she reportedly learned that the chest carrying the body of Osiris had been carried out by the sea to the ancient religious city of Byblos, where it was gently laid by the waves among the branches of a tamarisk tree. (*Byblos* is the origin of the word "Bible.")

The branches of the tamarisk tree in a very short time had grown into a large and magnificent tree, enclosing the chest bearing the body of Osiris inside of its trunk. The king of the country, having admired the tree, cut it down and made it into a pillar for the roof of his house. Thus within the pillar of the house of a king in a distant land was contained the sacred body of Osiris. When Isis heard of this she went to Byblos and secured admission to the palace disguised as a nurse. She was a nurse to one of the king's sons. However, instead of nursing the child, Isis gave the child her finger to suck and each night put the child in the fire to consume his mortal parts. The queen of this distant land happened once to see her child in flames and cried out and thereby in some way deprived this child of immortality. The queen then spoke to Isis, who revealed herself to the queen and told the queen her long story. Isis begged for the body of her dead husband, Osiris. The queen gave the body and the chest to Isis. Isis then opened the tomb of her husband, saw his body, and her anguish was apparently so loud and forceful that she destroyed one of the royal children that night by way of her terrifying screams.

Isis then brought the chest by ship back to Egypt, where she opened it and embraced the body of her husband while continuing to weep bitterly. Isis then saw her son, Horus, in Buto in Lower Egypt after she hid the chest in a secret place that no one would find. However Set, the evil one, was hunting one night by moonlight and happened upon the chest and recognizing the body immediately seized upon it and tore it into 14 pieces, which he scattered up and down the length of Egypt. When Isis heard of this travesty she took a boat made out of papyrus and sailed down the Nile in search of the 14 fragments of Osiris' body. Wherever she found one, there she built a tomb. The tomb was the center of the city's life. The city came to honor the bodily fragment of Osiris. Thus the fragments of Osiris' body were symbolically located in key sites over the body of Egypt. The head was at Abydos, the ear at Sais, the dorsal spine at Mendes, the left hand at the island of Biggeh near Philae, and so on (Schwaller de Lubicz, 1961). There is even evidence from the Pyramid Texts, the Coffin Texts, and texts that contain the Memphite theology, the so-called Shabaka Texts, that astronomically speaking some of the pyramids are laid out on ground to reflect the symbolic image of Osiris over the body of Kemet (Hancock & Bauval, 1996). This is an image of Osiris on the Earth as well as the heavens.

Anyway, by this time, the child of Osiris and Isis, whose name was Horus, had grown up. Horus, knowing of his father's betrayal, set out to avenge his death against the evil Set. In this family argument, many battles ensued. Eventually Set, the evil one, lost. Horus took Set prisoner and commended the prisoner to the control of Isis, the queen. However, for unknown reasons, the queen let evil Set go. Horus, in his rage, tore from the queen's head her royal crown. However, Thoth gave her a helmet in the shape of a cow's head. Two other battles were fought between them and eventually

Horus, the solar hero and messenger of light, was victorious over the darkness of the evil one, Set. He becomes pharaoh, the son of the great father Osiris.

Ultimately Osiris returns to the abode of the gods in the Duát, a region in the sky along the "winding waterway" of the Milky Way. He is reunited with the prior light and consciousness. Each Horus-king who follows him after death seeks to return, by the way of the solar boat and the guidance of the mysteries, to this cosmic ambience. The celestial Duát was reflected in the sacred structures exactingly built on Earth! When Osiris disappeared, he was preparing for rebirth, a kind of astral rebirth, just as his star, the star Sirius, disappears for 70 days then reappears out of the Duát (Hancock & Bauval, 1996).

This was the story of Osiris told largely from the writings of Plutarch, the commentaries of the Pyramids Texts, and the authority of Wallace Budge. Osiris was the god-man whose sufferings and death the Egyptians hoped to identify with and thereby rise again in the glorified spirit–body. Osiris was the one who conquered death. The dead are identified with Osiris the mummy, who again is painted black to signify his origin and the unconscious underworld of death. However, Osiris, the mummy, is a reawakened or resurrected mummy. Thus from a luminous divine dimension before birth, Osiris is embodied as a god-man. He goes through a number of sufferings and deaths. There are issues of family dynamics and alliances, betrayal, illicit romantic involvements, deceit, and loyalty. Eventually battles of good and evil over the body of Osiris and its destiny occur. We find this mythos not only written in the Pyramid Texts and tombs of ancient Egypt but also on the coffins of the later Greek and Roman period. Clearly what is done for the identified spirit of Osiris is also done for the recently deceased. There is a psychological fusion of the deceased with the destiny of Osiris. If Osiris liveth forever, so doth the deceased. It is therefore easy to see how this myth, one that had been sustained in the Egyptian collective unconscious for thousands of years, was made to absorb the myth of Christ in his life. The forces of good and evil, betrayal and the supreme deliverance are all there and only need active assimilation to become whole.

The Osirian cycle of an embodiment, loss, and then resurrection and return to the divine intelligence is essentially the human drama at all its levels. It is the saga of involution and evolution, of the descent of spirit into matter and the reawakening of this unconsciousness to its divine origin. The idea of the luminous spirit returning to the divine intelligence is expressed by the West African Yoruba in the verb "to die" or *ku*, which also means "to become a luminous spirit" (Lucas, 1948). They are not alone in this belief, a belief that suggests the unfoldment of consciousness from deep within the implicate order and its return after a period of corporification in the Horian logos. Issues of family loyalty, betrayal, the embodiment of the spirit, the destruction of the body, the resurrection of the body, moral conflicts, and spiritual illumination are all embodied in this great heroic journey. The family dynamics of Oedipus and Electra are played out in the Osirian myth. The dynamics of Job, especially ethics, sin, guilt, and redemption, are played out in this myth. The myth of Midas, especially around issues of power, greed, and remorse leading to the denouement, are played out. The flight of Icarus toward the divine state but fallen short of that is also played out. The heroism of King Arthur and Beowulf, the motifs of courage and sacrifice are played out. And finally the prophetic and messianic visions of Christ, Krishna, Buddha, and Muhammad, all seeking salvation and transformation, are played out in this great universalizing myth. Indeed the dynamics of light and biolight itself in its corporification in the human body–mind, its loss, and its eventually refinding or redemption through the second birth are played out in this myth. The completeness of this Osirian myth for the realms of human development is quite striking. One goes from the divine birth, through evolution, through loss, back to the recaptured god existence. The literal light of the human adventure in the realm of Earth and matter is played out in the dynamic of the Horian logos. Horus is the "local" hero on the battlefield of good and evil. He is light collapsed from the all-pervasive and transcendent realms of consciousness. Osiris is his progenitor, his root from the transcendent domain who returns to it at the end of the saga. The Buddhist notion of prior enlightenment even before human embodiment is implicit in this great world-affirming myth. It is not about *denial* of the body, but rather *complete acceptance of embodiment* with the tragedies and ecstasies inherent in this drama, and then finally the transformation of this whole process on the luminous matrix of the primordial African unconscious.

IMPLICATIONS OF THE OSIRIAN COMPLEX IN CULTURE

In the myth of Osiris, his body is dismembered into 14 pieces, 13 of which are spread out all over the land in specific sites. The 14th piece is lost forever. That is to say, while 13 pieces are recovered of the 14, the last piece, the 14th, is lost. This last piece is the lost phallus. Beyond the obvious Freudian symbolism, the Osirian phallus in the hymns to Osiris is associated with reincarnation, the sacred seeds of life, the union of the here and the hereafter. It is significant that these 13 pieces spread out over key sites of Egypt are mythically said to represent the body of Osiris in the different parts of the divine Egyptian or Kemetic body. They are implicate over specific sacred regions throughout legendary Egypt, and Egypt was itself believed to have sacred connections to the planets and stars. In later Greek and Roman times the idea emerges that different parts of the human body are indeed related to different aspects of the solar constellations, including the planets and the stars (von Frantz, 1987). We find in this system that different parts of the human anatomy—the heart, the spleen, the liver, the brain—are all reflected in the different planets and stars. This strikes us as, perhaps, an intuition that the body is an implicate order reflection of the universe, the microcosm reflecting the macrocosm. In other words, a microcosm of the universe is implicate in our own bodies. We find similar beliefs in the divination practices of peoples throughout the Earth, especially those of the Dogon peoples of Mali, who trace their lineage and cosmology to pre-dynastic Egypt. It is striking in this respect because the Dogon people, by way of their own conscious connection with the ancient lineage of Egypt and their own theories about how the physical body is related to the body of the solar system, have been able to use this methodology to track the pathway of stars for 5,000 years that were not known to modern astronomy until the last century (Giraule & Diertelen, 1986). The process by which this may have been done may be intimately connected to the process of opening a supersensory channel in the brain that is amenable to contact by way of the techniques of the hidden or sacred sciences (Krishna, 1972). The Dogon believe in a kind of implicate order universe because the physical world is held to be the dynamic product of a far more deep and primary level of reality which is constantly giving birth to the material world and then reenfolding it after some period of time. The cosmos is literally a vast, interconnected, living organism, with only its densest aspect manifesting as the material world we see. Within it, phenomena of all kinds appear, disappear, transform, and reappear.

Resurrection is an indigenous notion manifested in a number of different African religions (Mbiti, 1969). In these indigenous African religions immortality is a given, just as implicit immortality is a given in Buddhism. Also, interestingly enough, in many of the indigenous African religions we find a partial resurrection in certain psychological aspects of the deceased. In other words, it is not uncommon for members of a family to take significant note of certain psychological personality traits in a person that were quite pronounced in ancestors who died several generations earlier. This is a reflection of the family unconscious mentioned earlier, which stretches out several generations from the time of the loss of the deceased (Mbiti, 1969). Throughout African religions we find numerous references to the Osirian motif.

From this point of view, the Osirian point of view, human life is a series of endless transformations. "Death" is really a perception of discontinuity in the world line of the body–mind. It is an illusion. A human incarnation is essentially for the purpose of a progressive and successive unveiling of consciousness in evolution. A human existence is intimately associated with being and is a manifestation of the divine being itself. This being passes into bodily form for three purposes. It is for existence itself, the perfection of a human life. Being is also incorporated in the human form as an animating effect, which implicates the souls of all other forms. This too is for the purpose of the progressive unveiling of consciousness through transformation. The third aspect of this is the being's essences of origin, the spirit of oneness which solicits return into this unity and death and beyond so that the forces are complemented both by their origin and by their final completion (Schwaller de Lubicz, 1961).

This is even seen in a somewhat pathological context today by psychologists, psychiatrists, and other clinicians who encounter suicidal patients. In the psychodynamic life of these clients, particularly when they are in an acute or psychotic state, there are numerous references to reunion with a lost family member, of rebirth and reincarnation. These arise out of pain, hopelessness, and turmoil. The thought/perception of transformation out of their pain is associated with "peace." This is why, when the patients feel "calm" after deciding to kill themselves, the clinician must be especially careful. Unfortunately, this generally pathological expression of Osirian perceptions and tendencies is how contemporary medicine views intuitions of reincarnation and life beyond the body. The other negative examples include the motifs about demonic possession found in popular movies and novels about "the mummy," vampires, etc. Despite its psychiatric distortion, however, it remains a true and deep intuition of the great cycles and transformations in the natural world.

In the Ifa tradition of West Africa, the expression of this belief takes on the trappings of a certain kind of theory of spiritual evolution. In a long chapter or Odu of the Ifa oral tradition, or ese-ifa, titled *Irosu-Wori*, by Olamiwa Epega, it is suggested specifically that all human beings (awon eniyan), by the laws of necessity, must return to earth (aye) after death, having spent some duration in the bardo or afterlife or heaven (orun), until by the cycles of these heaven-earth, earth-heaven movements over time and incarnations, each human attains a certain amount or degree of goodness (ipo rere na) (Akiwowo, 1980). It is at the very root of many African traditional religions and the Orunmilaist lineage in particular. Innumerable good things are believed to exist in this heaven and these are yet to be brought into material existence in obedience to certain other laws of necessity, even though the human imagination cannot yet conjure up all these goodnesses. With spiritual evolution the capacity for manifesting greater and greater degrees of goodness, intelligence, and light increases. Indeed this particular lineage, which expresses it as the process of Orunmila, Olodumare, and Oduduwa, says that man is a manifestation or emanate or unfoldment of the divine being from whom all beings emanate. Humanity's special mission is to incarnate into material existence progressively greater and greater degrees of goodness for the things and beings of Earth, as was foreordained by the genius of creation (Akiwowo, 1986). Is this not matter leading to life, leading to mind, leading to spirit? Is this not the god in man reawakening to itself?

This leads directly to two particular forms or theories or paths of liberation. In effect the literal existence of being itself informs a surviving principle in the midst of human transformation and continuity. At death there's a resurrection and oneness, a moving into the primordial light in which all of one's prior experiences are known. This includes earlier experiences in the present life and also lifetimes in the past. In the short or direct path this can occur immediately at death. Here one immediately thinks of the *Tibetan Book of the Dead* and the directives given for realization of the Clear Light at the moment of death. The second path to salvation is the Horian or Christian path, where, through many incarnations, one eventually reaches enlightenment. This demands numerous incarnations on the Osirian or indirect path (Schwaller de Lubicz, 1961). We will go into more detail about these in the last chapter. Suffice it to say here that in the Osirian myth there is the foundation for Egyptian, and later Greek and Christian, psychospiritual metaphysics. It includes the particular teachings of the mystery schools surrounding the incorporation of light and the conduction of living light or bioenergy through the body. This is contained in the disciplines identified with the Eye of Horus, the child of Osiris, and Isis. In pre-dynastic times there were various cults and "academies" in religious centers in Kemet who held power and priestly knowledge unknown to others. The followers of Horus were among the most famous and were associated with architecture and astronomy, that is to say, the study of structure and light. The doctrine of the eternity of life is more associated with the specific myth of Osiris. Also connected with this myth of Osiris is the notion of the implicate order of the specific or individualized life principle and its greater implicate association with the wider ecological, social, and material environment.

SUMMARY

The Osirian process or the Osirian complex is an all-encompassing myth, model, and spiritual metamorphosis that touches each level of the human life cycle. Unlike other myths, such as the Oedipal myth or even the myth of Job, the Osirian myth covers issues concerning every level. These include the somatic level of embodiment itself and the woes and terrors that are inherent in physical embodiment. It covers the individual psychological principles and conflicts of an intrapsychic and interpersonal nature. It encompasses the familial unconscious and the dynamics that play out in family processes, as seen in the dynamics of Osiris, Isis, Horus, and their various encounters with other gods and forces. It incorporates the heroic myths of courage and flight up and beyond one's source. In other words, it encompasses the myths about King Arthur and Beowulf. It involves the ecstasy and failures of Icarus. Finally it encompasses the mythos of a divine birth, human life, tragic death, and eventual resurrection by way of love, loyalty, and commitment. It engages the prophetic messianic adventures of Krishna, Christ, Buddha, Muhammad, and the other great light bringers to the human collective experience. It goes from the prior light to a god-birth, through evolution, to a return or reunion with the primal or fundamental pure light, and includes in the process all the accompanying tragedies and triumphs. It is essentially the psychic and mythological drama against which the dynamics of $E = mc^2$ in the human embodiment are found. Osiris replaces Oedipus in the great drama. A corollary of it can be approached in the great Hindu Indian saga of the Mahabharata. Here historical, individual, familial, and divine and spiritual forces come into conflict in the human embodiment around great moral and archetypal principles. Indeed there's a certain similarity between these two panoramas of the human story. The ancient Nile civilizations of Egypt and the great Indus River Valley civilizations of southern India have a great affinity to each other. It is perhaps no accident that the themes of both can be seen in the work of their authors. In the case of the Mahabharata, we know that its author, the poet Vyasa, was aware of the themes current in Hindu culture and wove them into a magnificent tapestry. The authors of the Osirian myth are lost to prehistory. In each case, however, both partake of the eternal and its manifestations in the realms of light.

6 THE AFRICAN RELIGIONS IN THEIR DIASPORA TO THE WEST

Ritual contact with divinity underscores the religious aspirations of the Yoruba. To become possessed by the spirit of a Yoruba deity, which is a formal goal of the religion, is to "make the god," to capture numinous flowing force within one's body.

—Robert Farris Thompson, *Flash of the Spirit*

The supervenient control exerted by the higher over lower level properties of a system, referred to also as "macro," "molar," or "emergent" determinism operates concurrently with the "micro" control "from below upward." Mental states, as emergent properties of brain activity, thus exert downward control over their constituent neuronal events . . . micro determinism is integrated with emergent determinism.

—R. M. Sperry, "Psychology's Mentalist Paradigm and the Religion/Science Tension"

Perceptual experiences may on occasion however reflect the spectral energy/ momentum potential more than they reflect space–time configurations. . . . When the spectral dimension dominates the production of a perception, space and time become enfolded in the experienced episode. Time evolution ceases and spatial boundaries disappear . . . the episode is often referred to as spiritual . . . an effective union is envisioned between perceiver and perceived.

—Karl H. Pribram, M.D., *Brain and Perception*

ROOTS IN KEMETIC EGYPT

S EVERAL times previously we've mentioned the profound influence of religious teachings in the Nile Valley on later and other West African religions, nations, and societies. These religious teachings were codified in the *Egyptian Book of the Dead*. In this classic of the "coming forth by day and the going forth by night," there is a long and detailed history of the Upper Nile birth of this ancient Kemetic faith and psychospiritual tradition. In the *Egyptian Book of the Dead* are contained the early systemized ideas concerning reincarnation, transmutation, transmigration, transformation, and other seminal notions and intuitions. In this book are also contained ideas on divine judgment, morality, heaven and hell, balance between inner forces of the self and nature, and other fundamental ideas that have informed the religions of the West. Also contained in this seminal book are more "technical" ideas on trance, bardo states, and other references to nonordinary states of human consciousness.

In the pyramid of Unas were found the religious texts concerning the Kemetic Egyptian beliefs about the afterlife. These are called the "Pyramid Texts" (King, 1990). The actual contents of the Pyramid Texts were painstakingly carved on the inner walls of the tomb in limestone. The pyramid of Unas was among the great buildings of the ancient Kemetic Egyptian empire. This pyramid of Unas was located on the plateau in the great valley. Its passageway was 666 meters long and 6 meters wide. Inside of it the limestone walls were covered with magnificent bas-reliefs reflecting every form of religious life, craft working, and other scenes from day-to-day Egyptian life. The burial chamber itself was lined with limestone on three walls. The west walls and the ends of the north and south walls encasing the sarcophagus were made of alabaster. One of the principal symbols inside of the tomb was the ankh. Sometimes this ankh was known to designate the "sap of life," meaning milk, and sometimes it represented other forms of life (Schwaller de Lubicz, 1961). Here were detailed all the necessities of both earthly and post-mortem life from within the Egyptian conception of the psychic and spiritual universe. The great Osirian journey that was enacted by each human life is magnificently portrayed on the walls of this tomb. It is as if one entered the great collective unconscious of humankind and saw in seed form all the great motifs and archetypes of human conceptualizations spread out in a magnificent, highly technical, and sophisticated mosaic.

The Osirian myth that sustained ancient Egypt and its surrounding environment for several millennia established a firm conceptual and emotional foundation for the later myth of the Christian ordeal. This is particularly so in the great myth of Osiris in his rising from the dead (Ben-Jochannan, 1970; Budge, 1960). In the great conceptual and literary mosaic of the Pyramid Texts of Unas written on its limestone inner sanctum are written the ideas that were later to be the foundation of Judaism as espoused by the great Egyptian prophet and priest, Moses. There are 42 laws of Maát in the great Egyptian tradition. The 10 Commandments of Moses are 10 precepts taken from the 42 laws of Maát (Asante, 1984; Finch, 1991). The notions of judgment, heaven and hell, retribution, and redemption are contained here in the Pyramid Texts and *Book of the Dead*. The roots of Christianity and Judaism, and also the founding notions of Islam, are here.

Africa, particularly Kemetic Egypt, actually *exported* early religious ideas to the rest of the world and not the other way around as first thought by the Europeans (Diop, 1974; Jahn, 1961). With the suppression of this indigenous religion by the onslaught of an invading culture—i.e., Islamic Arabic influence—this religion was pushed underground, only to flourish again after numerous permutations and syncretic fusions in distant areas remote from Egypt. The great sphinx of Cheops with its prominent Africoid features, particularly the nose and lips, was defamed by the armies of Napoleon in Egypt, no doubt in an attempt to erase the memory of the preexisting indigenous people's faith and political memory. This is an example of a threatened return of the repressed. Just as Hermes Trismegistus is a later Greek transformation of the earlier Kemetic teachings of Thoth (Diop, 1991), so are the later West African religions such a mixture of indigenous ideas and syncretic transformation of these other basic ideas. Rooted in their transformation are symbols and a syncretism. This symbol and syncretism finds its most direct expression in the ways that European Christianity was fused with the indigenous African religions during the slave trade to the Americas. Early Eurocentric writers, infused with evolutionary theory, saw African "personalism" as a "primitive animism." This was perhaps a colonialist and political way to denigrate the indigenous, intensely felt vitalistic religions of the early peoples (Tylor, 1871; Spencer, 1885). In particular, Spencer saw the religions of Africa that manifested a certain form of personalism as simply ancestor worship, a primitive cult of the dead as opposed to ancestor veneration (Mbiti, 1969). The implicit assumption is that the prior is inherently the product of a more archaic mentality and culture. We have only to point to the Dogon people of West Africa in the area of Mali, however, to challenge this wholesale perception. These people, who consciously traced their descent from pre-dynastic Egypt over 5,000 years ago, and who also apparently had the knowledge of a sophisticated astronomy, in some areas far in advance of Western science until only recently, also practice a form of ancestor veneration and believe in communication with the departed spirits of these ancestors. Their science and religious worlds are very close to each other. There are numerous other examples in science and medicine of this trend (Finch, 1990). This is merely to emphasize that the notions of "primitive" and "archaic" are often politicized terms to control the imagery and the process of colonialization, both intellectual and political. All these primordial ideas in religion and consciousness studies can be found in seed form and sometimes magnificently explicated in the seminal doctrine of the Pyramid Texts and in the *Egyptian Book of the Dead*. This is why indigenous Black African Egypt, ancient Kemetic Egypt, is the reference point, the classical civilization of Africa, just as the antiquity of Rome and Greece is the classical civilization of Europe.

WEST AFRICAN RELIGIONS IN THEIR DIASPORA

In addition to the Dogon people of Mali, there are a number of other direct correspondences between the religions of ancient Kemetic Egypt and their expression by way of West African peoples. Sometime during the middle dynastic period there was a great exodus from Egypt for unknown reasons. With this movement there came ideas rooted in the older Kemetic records. Egypt had extensive contacts with not only the Middle East, but also Ethiopia, India, Greece, even the outer banks of England, and also West Africa. Yoruba myths and legends overtly suggest an Egyptian origin of their nation. Asante and others have pointed out how after 5,000 years of civilization from Egypt and Nubia, particularly the great teachings at the temples of Karnak and Luxor, and the extensive mystery school system of ancient Egypt, that the Arab jihads swept out of Arabia and overran North Africa, driving the indigenous Egyptian language and religions underground. There then occurred another subsequent dispersal of these indigenous mystery schools, founded in the "houses of life," to various other parts of the continent, preparing for their eventual reemergence in the secret societies of the Yoruba Ifa divination, the Shona Mbira, and many others. These systems continued in the oral tradition with the integration of African medicine, theology, and agriculture. There are striking parallels between Egyptian cosmology and the west African Ifa worldview. Jahn (1961) says in *Muntu*, as does Mbiti (1969), that no African traditionalist can imagine medicine separated from its vital interconnectedness with philosophy, theology, agriculture, and the other necessities of life.

In the ancient city of Ile-Ife, the focal site of their spiritual tradition in the West African Yoruba world, seasonal celebrations are carried out in which, through Ifa, the correct power alignment of one's life with the lines of power across the Earth is believed to be correlated. The intuition of a great and unknown power radiating from beneath the Earth is an ancient human experience and was even an idea put forth in one of the oldest texts, the Memphite theology of Kemetic Egypt (James, 1954). These tract lines of power are called Ley lines in China and are used by the Ifa priest, called a Babalawo or "father of mysteries," to determine which Odu or archetypal spiritual form is most manifest in one's life and consciousness. One's entire life is seen as fused or integrated with the life and forces of the living Earth. This wholism and essential interconnectedness of phenomena on all levels is implicit and implicate. This wholism in religion, and in the other systems we have pointed out earlier, particularly around issues of reincarnation and the other basic ideas contained in seed form in the *Egyptian Book of the Dead*, can be found in the indigenous religions of West Africa. Asante refers to this vision and intuition of unity as the Sudic ideal of harmony, which can be achieved in rhythm, one of the tenets of the African unconscious. This leads to the African American mode of transcendence in the West. This is the case with Cubans, Haitians, most Brazilians, Jamaicans, many Ecuadoreans, and, of course, a large proportion of the African American citizens of the United States. Underneath the various religions, the same idea and the same basic psychospiritual rhythm in process predominates (Asante, 1984).

In Nigeria and other parts of West Africa the large and vital nation of the Yoruba peoples has been most influential in this area. But in addition to them other groups have given rise to different religious conceptions that have influenced psychospiritual disciplines in the West. These religious conceptions and disciplines that are transformations of the original paradigm of the continental religion include Voudoun, Santería, Candomble, Macombe, and recently in the United States what is termed Quanza. To these should also be added variations of this central rhythmic and psychospiritual tradition, such as the samba dance in Brazil, the Shango Cuban folk religion, the Brazilian folk religion Mbanda, and, of course, Myal, a Jamaican religion. Indeed a larger number of dances stemming from Latin America, such as the samba, the rumba, the mambo, and even the tame cha cha cha, are derived from the religious dances of Voudoun (Ashanti, 1990). (See Appendix C.) When rock-and-roll, rhythm-and-blues, and gospel *consciously* turn their attention to the rhythms and chorus of music felt to be permeated with the signature of the Orishas, their powerful ancient discovery is even closer to everyone. For it has the power, at least briefly, to literally eclipse and transform bodily felt consciousness.

Many of the slaves brought to the Americas were priests or Babalawos in their own communities. They crossed the oceans with their divination system intact, some with the divining chain around their necks. This is how there is so much underlying similarity in the spiritual paradigm we have mentioned. The traditions, many of them, did survive to be transmitted intact (Akiwowo, 1992). As a consequence of this dispersion, the undercurrent of Orisha worship of spirit and ancestors is scattered everywhere, but not randomly. Among the Haitians and Jamaicans, there are devotees of Voudoun and Shango. The Yoruba of Brazil tend to be devotees of Macombe and Candomble. Those in Puerto Rico, which had a large influence on the United States, tend to be devotees of Espiritismo, while those of Cuba tend to be devotees of Santería and Palo. Among the Dominicans, there are devotees of Luases and so on. Much like ancient India, there are different regions that emerge with devotees to a particular sect of Hinduism, yet if one looked deeper into the structure of the faith, one would find the genius of Shiva and Shakti, of Brahmen and Kundalini in the rootwork of this great religion. It is much the same here with the different sects and localized manifestations of the paradigm. Underneath there is a vast, interlocking network of images, concepts, and dynamic energies cross-fertilizing each other. All these religions are counted upon during critical archetypal phases in life to point the way for understanding and transcendence.

ETHNIC DIASPORA TO THE WEST

By the end of the last four voyages of Columbus, the idea of the slave trade had taken root in Europe. The year 1492 saw the Jews of Spain cast into exile again, and the Moors finally driven from the Spanish part of the peninsula. In 1503 or 1506 Bishop Bartholome de las Casas of the Roman Catholic Church persuaded King Ferdinand and Queen Isabella of the newly reunited Spain and the pope of Rome to institute the infamous slave trade. The first victims were the Black Moors who refused to convert after 1492. The first big slave port was Haiti in the Caribbean. Over 4,000 Moors were delivered there for las Casas. The tide of history had changed. Europe had arisen again and was spreading out. Spain, France, England, Portugal, and even Belgium had seen the wealth to be found in the cultivation of the new lands.

At first the indigenous peoples of the Americas were subjugated, but they died quickly of disease, hardship, and wholesale murder. Those that survived fled deeper into the forests. Europe needed to look elsewhere for cheap labor to work the fertile lands and mines. Africa provided an ideal setting and the transatlantic slave trade grew rapidly. In all, from conservative estimates of 10 to 15 million to perhaps some 30 to 40 million

Africans were stolen from the mother continent and shipped under hellish conditions to South, Central, and North America and the Caribbean. The European powers most involved in this profitable trade were the Spanish, Portuguese, French, Dutch, and English. The Jews were involved to some degree as middlemen and bankers in London, Paris, and Amsterdam (Faber, 1994). On the continent itself, the Arabs were serious investors. However, it should not be forgotten that the Africans themselves traded in slaves, usually as defeated tribes and armies. They were instrumental in this odious practice, led raids into the interior, and initially profited greatly from the misfortunes of their brethren. Some, like King Almammy, hated the business and refused to let their people participate. However, many did not. By the time they realized the full tragedy and scale of the practice on the race itself and tried to stop it, it was too late in the day, and millions had been stolen and transported, never to see Africa again. At least 7% of the exodus poured into North America. This human current came primarily from the west coast of Africa, but even within this area, some ethnic groups were more represented than others. *By the middle of the 18th century, a third of the people of African lineage resided outside of Africa.* They brought with them their ethnic heritage and their own take on the ocean of African religious thought and experience. (See Figures 24, 25, and 26.)

Herskovits (1924, 1958) identified numerous cultural zones in Africa and certain cultural patterns that survived the ordeal of slavery. Later researchers have been even more detailed on the areas where specific ethnic and cultural groups were taken (Holloway, 1990). From the basin of the Senegal River to the Niger River, delta groups such as the Mande, Akan, Mandinka, Wolof, Bambara, Fulani, and Balante were taken. Also stolen were the Yoruba, Nupe, Fon, Ewe, Edo-Bini, and others. Further south along the central African coast came the Bakongo, Bambo, Ndungo, Luba, Luango, Ouimbundu, Loanga, and Malimbo. A small percentage of these were Muslims, literate and schooled in the Koran. They were actually the first footprints of Islam in the Americas and left written records of their passage (Austin, 1997). In general, as far as North America is concerned, the upper colonies of New York, New Jersey, Rhode Island, Connecticut, Massachusetts, etc., tended to receive the peoples of West Africa. The southern colonies tended to have an infusion of peoples from central Africa. This is due partly to the colonists' beliefs about certain slave grouping, e.g., the Whydahs (Fons), Nagoes, and Pawpaws were preferred because they were "cheerful and submissive," the Mande because of their existent familiarity with rice, indigo, and tobacco cultivation, and the large Senegambian groupings because of their skill in carpentry, blacksmithing, and lumberjacking

FIGURE 24. Diaspora to the Americas.

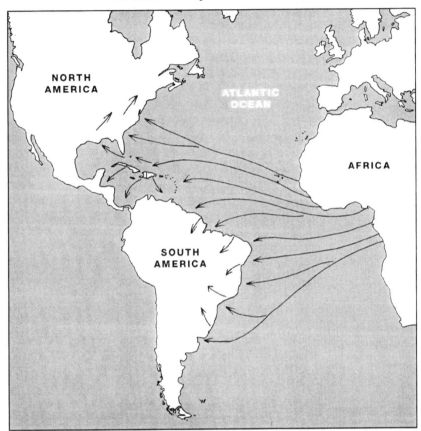

The vast majority of Africans captured and brought to the New World were transported to South America and the Caribbean. They were brought primarily by the Spanish and Portuguese. France and Holland tended to dominate the Caribbean basin, although the English were also present. At different times dependent on European geopolitical events, various powers dominated the trade. (Copyright © 1999 Teachers College, Columbia University)

(Holloway, 1990). In the sea islands off South Carolina there came peoples from Sierra Leone whose Gullah dialect so profoundly influences the English speech patterns of southern Americans, both Black and White. In the 1930s researcher Lorenzo Turner discovered over 3,000 words of African origin in the Gullah dialect (Turner, 1968). These speech patterns are still evident today (MacNeil, 1986).

FIGURE 25. Diaspora to the United States and the Caribbean.

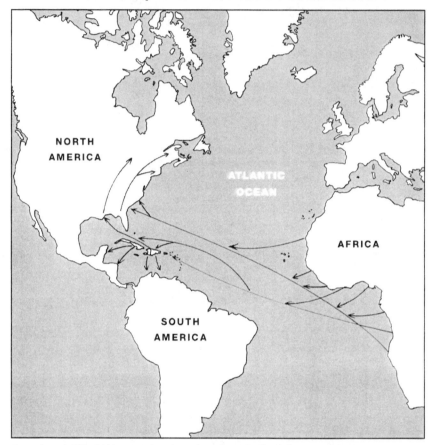

Approximately 7% of Africans enslaved were brought to the North American colonies and early United States. Even after the importing of slaves was outlawed by the new U.S. Constitution in 1808, slaves were brought in from the Caribbean. Britain banned the slave trade in 1807 and slavery in the West Indies in 1833. Most new Latin American nations banned slavery from their inception. Emancipation came to the United States in 1863 and to Brazil in 1888, the last in the hemisphere. (Copyright © 1999 Teachers College Press, Columbia University)

In South and Central America, the ethnic trends were somewhat different. More Africans from the central coastal region went to South America. There are heavier traces of the Congo basin and Bantu-speaking peoples and their religious practices there. But this is not absolute, for we can see traces of the Fon of Dahomey, the Ashanti and the Yoruba in the northern parts of South America and the whole of the Caribbean archipelago (Jahn,

FIGURE 26. The Guinea Coast.

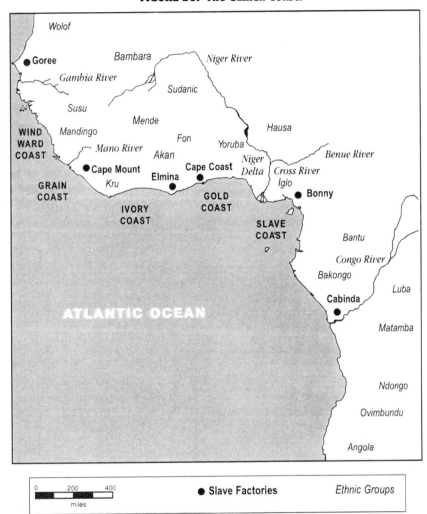

The slave trade was a holocaust that lasted for centuries. By the middle of the 18th century, a third of all people of African lineage resided outside of Africa. Africans and Europeans died in this malignant trade. Most who came to North America were captured from the ethnic groups along the Guinea coast. (Copyright © 1999 Teachers College Press, Columbia University)

1961). The presiding colonial power, dominant commercial trading lanes, African internal wars, colonial preferences for ethnic groups, religious politics, and other factors each influenced the current of human flesh from Africa. When Columbus made contact in 1492 with San Salvador, the era of the great states of West Africa was in decline. The empire of Ghana was largely memory, even though its state religion of the serpent-spirit Ouagadou-Bida lived on. The state of Mali was in ruins, the kingdom of Songhai was soon to fall, and though the seven original "Hausa" states were prosperous, they were loosely organized and remained so until the end of the 18th century. However, the tide had turned. After nearly a thousand years of empire in western Africa during Europe's medieval and Dark Ages, bleeding African internal wars and the expanding second rise of Europe led to the slave trade. In 1492 the Songhai emperor Sunni Ali of West Africa died, the Jews were driven from Spain, and in October of that year Columbus reached the Americas. There then began a mass syncretism of old, new, and novel that swept through the African religious consciousness and rooted its pained genius on this shore.

IFA, THE UNCONSCIOUS, AND THE IMPLICATE ORDER STOREHOUSE MEMORY

Many of the commonalities that underlie the religions of these diverse groups are seminal ideas rooted, or at least reflected, in the earlier Pyramid Texts and the *Egyptian Book of the Dead*. These commonalities include an understanding of spirit possession, trance states, family-rooted reincarnation, transformation, and transmutation. They occur in the conditions of group work, rhythmic entrainment, and other psychological and psychic influences. We have mentioned before our belief that the process of Kundalini is intrinsic and constantly manifested in these situations. It is literally a situation, both psychophysical and psychospiritual, that prepares the way for the rhythmic entrainment of the individual principle with the collective principle. This in itself prepares the way for the higher-order "embodiment of the gods" that is believed to be manifested in trance states, particularly in the Western Hemisphere as expressed in Voudoun, Santería, and Candomble (Deren, 1989). Much of the origin of this system and its commonalities in Voudoun, Santería, and Candomble can be seen embedded in the African Yoruba Ifa lineage.

Ifa is a system or corpus of knowledge with 256 sections or chapters. Each chapter has numerous other commentaries in it, at least 16, sometimes more. They are organized around 16 symbols called Odu. See Figure 27 of Ifa oracle of West Africa-binary principal. This living library of knowledge

FIGURE 27. Ifa Oracle of West Africa-Binary Principal.

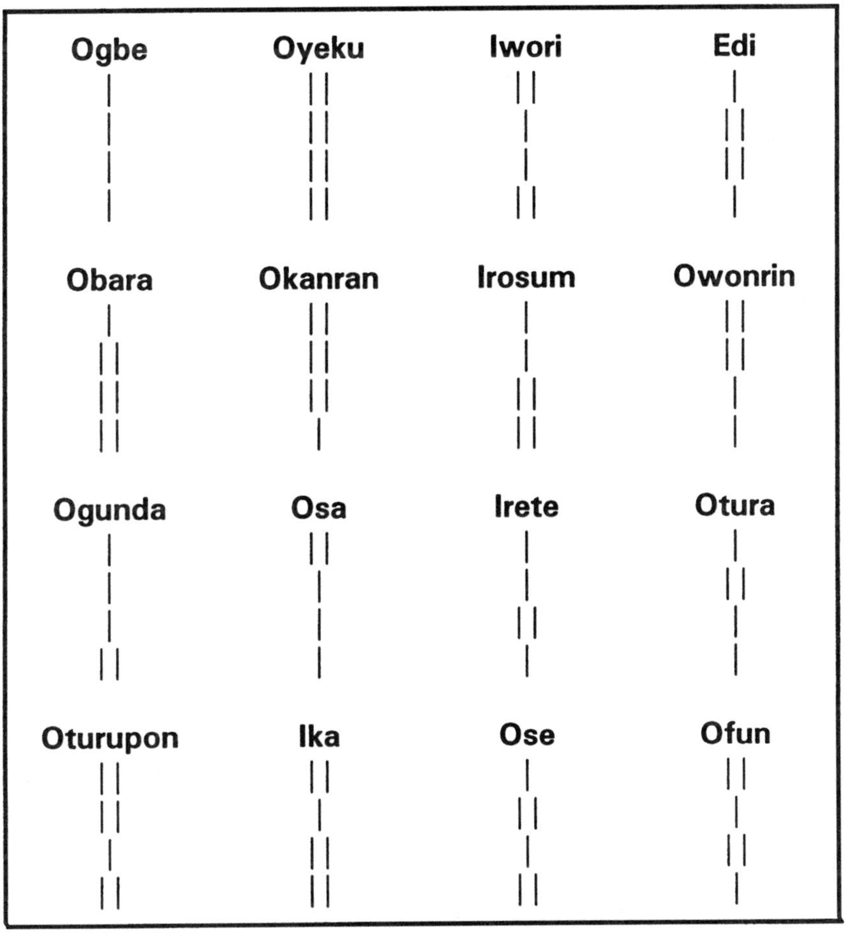

The 16 binary symbols that comprise the Ifa divination system are capable of 256 (16 × 16 = 256) patterns. They are similar and may have an historical connection with those used by the ancient Essene sects of Palestine and the 64 hexagrams (64 × 4 = 256) of the Chinese I Ching binary system. The Ifa and I Ching both show a similarity to pre–cuneiform patterns of expression. (Copyright © 1999 Teachers College Press, Columbia University)

and way of knowing is taught, without variation, from generation to generation by the initiates of the order. They are known as Babalawo or "father of the mysteries." While Orisha and Ifa "possession" are somewhat different, there are obvious similarities. Generally, Orisha possession is associated with an ecstatic experience accompanied by music and dance in praise of the Orisha. The Orisha are ancestral spirits and forces of nature that are personalized in human communication.[5] Ifa possession can be more "cool-headed possession" or ori tutu with more subtle bodily engagement.[6] Both involve verse or incantation, be it a praise song to the Orisha or the recitation of a particular Odu by the Babalawo. The Babalawo spends much of his day in recitation of the spiritual verses. This keeps the tradition alive in the community in a vibratory way. In both cases, however, the powers of the creation or the ase, it seems, is made to move from the base of the body to the top of the head to nourish the inner head or ori. This is accomplished by various forms of sacrifice, ritual, prayer, and actions (Abimbola, 1992) including ultimately it seems subtle forms of sacrificing attention itself to the inner head or ori. The practice at times also includes animal sacrifice that is believed to symbolically "wed" the union of man, nature, and Orisha together by blood, the expression of life force. In this way, the covenant is constantly renewed. Blood and breath touch spiritual forces. The spiritual forces induce the ori to turn its attention back and up from survival needs (lower chakras) ultimately to salvation. In Ifa theology, this ascent, or actually reascent from the original "descent" of the force, is described as the ascent of Obatala's ase from Ile back to Orun or Orunmila, the master of expansion and contraction. One of Orunmila's praise names is Eleri-Ipin, meaning "witness to creation." In India, we might say Shakti is returned to Shiva. In the Indian tradition with its roots deep in the Dravidian lineage of Yoga, we can also recognize the deep rhythmic call and answer in music employed in groups to attempt to awaken the Kundalini. This includes the African American gospel music and spirituals at their best. When this occurs, the ori of the devotee is elevated into the mystical or unitative conscious state of lae-lae, which is believed to transcend the cycles of birth, death, and thought itself. It is similar to a brief episode of Nirvana (Nirvikalpa Samadhi, actually) and Turyia but highly active emotionally and physically. In either case, the psychobiological technology of Kundalini Yoga is seen to underlie those diverse disciplines and beliefs.

This expansion and contraction is really another intuition or expression of the idea that light contracts to form matter and that matter expands to form light or energy. Both are ultimately transtemporal and transpatial in nature and are unfolded from the same spiritual source, consciousness. Both

---

5. The *ori* is both the material and spiritual head of the devotee. When the *ori* is full of life force or ase, and stabilized over time and practice, the ori briefly becomes the *ori-ase*, the *ori-sha* or *Orisha*. After death, they become personalized forces of nature or *Orisha*. When alive, they are thought to be able to "come forth by day and go forth by night" because their life force is full of god.

6. Note the motif of being "cool" or "cool pose" among the African American population, especially males.

are implicate in all forms. Even the material universe is thought to be pervaded by both the familiar contracting force of gravity and also some mysterious kind of antigravitational force emerging from space-time itself that seems to expand space. The system of Dafa is the graphic representation of this spiritual system and it is employed by the priest, the Babalawo, to "read" one's path in Ifa. An elaborate ritual is employed in the process. The Babalawo believes and perceives a kind of energy-information field surrounding the life and soul of the individual that binds them together with their family and their own destiny from life to life. The process or method uses a binary system to unfold the particular pattern. It requires many years of training to recognize and interpret all the patterns. There are 256 patterns, each of which is a specific expression of the ways that the expansive and contractive forces manifest in nature. The 256 symbols appear to be the same ones or very similar to those used by the divination system of the ancient Essene sect of Palestine prior to the arrival of Jesus the Christ (Fatunmbi, 1991). It also has a striking correspondence to the other binary system of personal destiny, the Chinese *Book of Changes*, or the *I Ching*. The *I Ching* has 64 hexagrams: 64 × 4 = 256. The Essenes were a Mesopotamian sect with ancient Sumerian and Black Elamite-Akkadian elements in their tradition. The characters of the binary *I Ching*, like those of Ifa, have a pre-cuneiform style to their expression. Both purport to tell the devotee of their unfoldment on Earth and their deeper destiny in the unseen heavens. There appear to be both mystical and historical connections at work here in the 256 patterns. (See Figure 27.)

Each of the 256 patterns, or chapters in the Ifa literary corpus, is associated with a specific verse in Ifa scripture (Abimbola, 1975, 1976). It is the most intricate, elaborate, and systematized oral literary tradition in Africa. In a sense, these forces that it speaks of are unconscious but manifest in one's life in a dynamic way. They are believed to reflect the enfolded order of the universe and it is believed that the order of the universe is reflected in us. In other words, the macrocosm is reflected in the microcosm, which is a living process, a vast literally organic unconscious. The Kemetic Egyptians referred to their dynamic unconscious as the Amenta (King, 1990) and the Primeval Waters of Nun (Hourning, 1986). The dynamic unconscious is conceptualized in this Ifa system sometimes as the Ayanmo concept, a system that incorporates one's primal choices in life as we enter this particular incarnation, and our potential future that may unfold as a consequence (Morakinyo, 1983). The paradigm subsumes the idea of the unconscious similar to Freud and the notion of existential choice within the wider spiritual context of birth, death, and the rebirth cycles, or what we might call the Osirian complex.

Ifa is held to be a living repository of knowledge and wisdom that the priest, by way of training and long experience, can enter. It is an interconnected field of relationships and information that manifests in its 256 ways or patterns of unfoldment. In this sense it "structures experience" or reality for the Babalawo, who, we must remember, perceives all things and beings as permeated with life, energy, and consciousness. Everything and everyone has personhood. In this sense it is like a living holographic field of interconnected relationships enfolding past, present, and future. The constant attention of generations of Babalawos keeps feeding the system, and the system is constantly feeding them. This unconscious realm in Ifa, therefore, incorporates more than the intrapsychic unconscious. It reaches deep into the collective unconscious and transpersonal realms of knowledge and experience. In this way, it is believed that Ifa can reflect upon the full cycle of a human life, e.g., choices prior to embodiment, the struggles of life, family and decisions, the entanglement with supernatural forces, and one's destiny in death and beyond. Osiris in his full context. Its perfection in life along with rhythm, vitality, and force is thought to be the perfection of character itself and in large areas of West Africa becomes the ideal or essence that underlies the aesthetic sensibility in sculpture, art, and related endeavors.

All of these religious notions have a long lineage not only in the West African religions but in varying degrees throughout different African religions spread over the continent in the West, South, and Southeast (Mbiti, 1969). We are currently witnessing a rebirth of these indigenous earth-spirit religions and their sensitivity and emphasis on ecological, wider psychic, and psychological integration. It should also be mentioned that these religions overtly and nonapologetically embrace psychic influences in the process of healing. We find these latter expressions only in very small and to certain extent radical movements in Christianity and Islam. However, in the religions of the diasporic peoples of West Africa they are right in the center along with other major principles of the African unconscious. There is no inherent dissociation between the psyche, matter, spirit, and other ecological and wider systemic influences in these religions as one might find in the predominant religions of the Europeans. Consciousness and life force in personalized occasions are seen as more primary than matter. Everything has an "animate-sentient-like" aspect to its nature and, therefore, on some level is alive. Biology is more fundamental than physics.

In this connection we would emphasize certain principles in particular. As mentioned earlier, vitalism in African religions is a very powerful principle (Mbiti, 1969). This is not a "primitive" or "archaic" process. Rather this is a primary apprehension of the basic aliveness of the world and the universe. For the African sensibility, the universe is a living force, an intelligent, conscious organism and matrix that one can relate to in a highly personal manner. It is an inherently multidimensional and interpenetrating process. Frequencies of living energy or consciousness are perceived as focused and localized in objects and enfolded in events that themselves are embedded in the always living matrix of consciousness. Things are imbued with this "animate-sentient-like aspect" whose signature is knowable by certain disciplines of human consciousness. Therein, tacitly, everything is alive! This "basic aliveness" is taken at face value in the spiritual traditions of Hinduism and Buddhism. In point of fact, it is taken as a basic reality in most religions of the world and only finds itself an outlaw in the secular lens of certain metaphysical assumptions in the currently Eurocentric canon of science. However, with the integration of an ecological point of view, including a recognition that the Earth is a living process, this notion of the individual's consciousness as being ultimately estranged from a nonliving world and universe is beginning to be eclipsed. This elemental "contact" is made, of course, by way of trance or what is called possession.

A SCIENCE OF DIVINE COMMUNION: THE PSYCHOSPIRITUAL DYNAMICS OF EMBODIMENT OR "POSSESSION"

Whether it be the Orisha or the Odu, each form of discipline is quite specific about the nature of the "entity" that "possesses" a devotee. The Orisha and the Odu are seen as personifications and patterns of spiritual energy and the devotees themselves are always in the position of "energy" in reference to the material world. Each one of the Orishas and each particular Odu has a personality or signature pattern that differentiates it from the others. One's life may be consecrated to a particular Orisha at birth by the family in that lineage. From then on the Orisha serves as one's guide in life and one worships it with an altar, appropriate sacrifices, and so forth.[7] (See Appendix A.) In the Ifa focus, there is certainly the Orisha that one honors, etc., but the most personal god is one's own ori or inner head. Even the Orishas in Ifa are said to have their own ori.

---

7. Some believe this close association between family, Orisha choice, and "active" practice of the disciplines is because the Orishas express evolutionary forces. Over generations, the familial psychic energy has been embodied by many individuals throughout many separate lives and deaths. The psychic energy of the Orisha, however, lives outside of ordinary space and time, past and "future." It dwells, they believe, in that realm that is continuous and, under certain conditions, is projected into the realm of space, time, matter, and form as we know it. It is like the great dreamtime of the Australian Aboriginal peoples. This energy of the species has moved with us up through the evolutionary adventure from the earliest days of *Homo sapiens sapiens*, and perhaps from the chaotic dawn of the hominid line. The energy of the familial generations collects in the head or ori, and can be contacted when the ase is made to unite with it. Therein, the word "ori-sha" or "ori-ase." In its mature form, its energy interacts with other natural forces and energies in nature and the environment.

In each situation, however, there is an elaborate ceremony prior to actual embodiment or possession. Purifying baths, fasting, prayers, and other means, including sacrifices, are used. Sacrifice is believed to bind together the forces of both good and evil supernatural forces and energies for a brief while and thereby bring order to a disordered situation (Abimbola, 1992). As the ceremony progresses, there is the recitation of verses in Ifa and/or rhythmic verse incantation and music and dance in Orisha worship. Over time the dance and prayer-verse incantations become more intense. Dancing and rhythm lead, in a large-group context, to rhythmic entrainment. Each Orisha has a signature call and dance. With increasing intensity, sometimes lasting hours, and also occurring in special grooves or other holy places and at special times when lunar and Earth energies are believed to be most powerful, an *entrancement by entrainment* occurs. The central nervous system has been greatly activated and the autonomic nervous system has been aroused. Consciousness has been harnessed by the events and even intensified. The rhythm and dance, in the case of Orisha worship, has led the devotee to the point that the rhythm begins to guide the motoric and autonomic responses of body and brain. The energy is experienced as ase "arising" in most cases, as it is in the Hindu traditions, to the head or "ori," but also to "descend" in other disciplines. The latter are more associated with the hidden female or Tantric traditions sometimes suppressed by the male-dominated Babalawo practices. At a crucial juncture the individual principle of consciousness is eclipsed, much as the eclipse occurs when a multiple personality or dissociative episode occurs, except here this is done with intense group support and is not pathological, but voluntary. There is a paradigm and it is of "embodiment" and the localization of consciousness.

Soon another intelligence speaks through the devotee in the case of Orisha possession. For the Ifa Babalawo, the incantation of the derived verses leads to the realization of the Odu's meaning and power, its forceful personification of divinity, if you will. The Orisha's style accompanied by physical movement and dance is actually closer to the classical medium or channeling methods than the Ifa Babalawo. The individual self or "I" is oblated with the Orisha, not necessarily with the Babalawo. The Orisha's embodiment allows it to speak to others in the group; the Babalawo speaks to the devotees about their specific situation. The Babalowo sees the realm (above) of Orun and the reflected material world (below) of Aiye while observing the enfolded lives past and future of the present localized self. In Orisha discipline the self of the devotee dissolves in or is absorbed by the manifestation of the god or Loa. The personal consciousness becomes the vibratory expression of an intelligent force. The Babalawo's consciousness becomes a conduit for the nonlocal consciousness of the divine forms and patterns of nature. While both believe in good and evil supernatural forces and witches, the Orisha worship seems to have had a greater influence on the subsequent development of the Voudoun tradition as it is found in Dahomey and Haiti in somewhat different forms.

When the "possession" is over in Orisha worship, the devotee is tired, etc., and has no memory of the details of his voluntary possession. The continuity of the Babalawo's consciousness has not been interrupted. Healing is accomplished in both circumstances. Contact with greater realms of knowledge and consciousness is held by all. It is the hero's journey, and he has returned to the world from another realm with a gift. This is in keeping with the ancient traditions and in it one can hear the lineage of the Gnostic, the Hermetic, the Kabbalistic orders in their power to initiate the devotee into the realm of the gods. In fact, Joseph Campbell (Deren, 1989) and Milo Rigaud (1969), among other scholars of world culture and mythology, see in these "possession" states, especially in one of the major derivative schools, Haitian Voudoun, the crisis of becoming "full of God," much the way the mythology is preserved in Greek and Roman literary documents. In both the archetypes are awake and actively experienced in the body (Deren, 1989). Vestiges of the Orisha "possession" practice can be seen today in the Pentecostal, Baptist, and "santified church" traditions of many African American communities. Some traditions are deep and close expositions of the original lineages, including the recitation of Ifa verses and their application to present-day circumstances in the United States (Gleason, Aworindo, & Ogundipe, 1973). In the future when science and spirituality have beautifully merged in a more luminous civilization on Earth we will look back upon these days as our own Dark Ages, the centuries when scientific materialism executed an Anschluss on world thought and nearly buried or forgot the spiritual visions of the world. These disciplines of initiation and other myriad practices of becoming "full of God" will be seen as the traditions that kept alive the paths to illumination and *direct* contact with the realms of light and intelligence presently beyond us. Like the Irish monks and Islamic scholars after the fall of Rome, they will be remembered as the ones who kept the light of the deeper learnings alive, and when the time was right, helped us to usher in our own renaissance.

Ubiquitous in these ceremonies and practices is a preoccupation with the energies of the serpent power or Kundalini. In the United States, but even more so in the Caribbean and South America, especially Brazil, the symbolism and actual interaction with serpents in the past has been widespread. African healers were known to associate their practices and presence with serpents in the most complex and sometimes "disturbing" ways to both European and African devotees. Individual and group trance often involved snakes, ecstatic trance states, erotic dance, and episodes of "possession." Because it was frightening to Europeans, it was often outlawed, and so continued to be practiced in secret. It was seen as pure witchcraft by the Europeans, and yet they were also secretly and repeatedly drawn to it, attesting many times to its real power to influence mind, body, soul, and even objects in the environment. The native South American and Catholic-influenced cults were sometimes open to Whites who had been initiated or allowed a "tourist's view" of events. The genuine African mystery sects, however, remained secret and did not admit Whites (Bastide, 1978). This is why even today the serpent-symbol psychotechnology of Voudoun is still alien to Whites and taught from master to student only after considerable preparation. There is a real and experienceable power embedded in this psychospiritual discipline that has to do with bodily energy, trance states, and certain paranormal agencies that only unfold under specific conditions. One must approach this discipline with the utmost caution and respect. "Possession" is a real phenomenon and not the expression of regression fantasies, archaic thought, or delusional states.

A clinical perspective from the "inside" of Voudoun practice can differentiate the various "signatures" of possession. An exploration here would take us far into the Kemetic origin and convoluted history of Voudoun. We also cannot explicate the psychotechnology of Voudoun here for obvious ethical and political reasons. Suffice it is to say that the practice is still strong and widespread throughout Africa, the Americas, and the Caribbean. An excellent clinical exploration of Voudoun and medicinal rootwork is found in *Rootwork and Voodoo in Mental Health*, by K. F. Ashanti (1990). Of particular interest is its integration with psychotherapy and its conception of how psychological forces and herbal remedies effect the psychic field and the life force of the individual. Ritual and symbolic ceremony are crucial in the disciplines of psychospiritual possession.

Kundalini itself is associated with the hidden "female" energies in this lineage, a tradition somewhat suppressed by the patriarchal system of the Babalawos, but retained by the secret women societies (Drewal & Drewal, 1983). The Irete-Meji Odu in the Yoruba tradition especially relates to this. Calculated in an esoteric way, the Odu has 3½ lines corresponding to the 3½ coils of the sleeping mother Shakti Kundalini. The energy in this lineage is thought to "descend" into the cauldron of the solar plexus during possession, as opposed to some traditions in which the energy is experienced as rising (Torres, 1994). The breath and internal body "locks" are nearly parallel to phenomena observed in Kundalini Yoga practice, especially at the perineum, navel point, and throat.

It seems as though the ceremony prepares the conscious and unconscious mind for brief release from the normal modes of consciousness. Especially in the case of the ecstatic Orisha worship, the central nervous system and autonomic nervous system are significantly engaged and the brain receives a tremendous rush of bioenergy from the body. In some cases of bodily worship of the divine, as with the !Kung of South Africa, Kundalini is awakened and slowly made to ascend to the top of the head. The areas of the brain that generate the sense of space and time are held in check or neutralized, leading to a perception of timelessness and eternity. Some neuroscientists suggest this very process when they say that:

> Perceptual experiences may on occasion . . . reflect the spectral energy/ momentum potential more than they reflect space-time configuration . . . one such occasion results when excitation in the frontolimbic formations greatly exceeds that in the posterior cerebral convexity. Frontolimbic excitation can be induced by internal neurochemical stimulation or by external methods such as concentrating on . . . stimuli provided by a mantra, for example. When the spectral dimension dominates the production of a perception, space and time become enfolded in the experienced episode. Time evolution ceases and spatial boundaries disappear. An infinity of envisioned covariations characterizes the episode. Therefore, the episode is often referred to as spiritual in the sense that, as a consequence of practiced inference, an effective union is envisioned between perceiver and perceived. (Pribram, 1991, pp. 272–273)

A kind of top-down cognitive psychology unfolds where the mind exercises a supervenient influence over the body and brain (Sperry, 1988). This occurs in meditation, whether it be induced by rhythm, a mantra, or another repetitive mode that holds the mind fixated and directs attention back upon itself. At this point we believe subtle energy and intelligence can unfold from potential and nonlocal realms into the plane of human awareness. The Orisha and the Odu can be understood as forms of nonlocal intelligence that is structured in subtle energy processes capable of being experienced by human consciousness under the appropriate circumstances and employing the correct psychophysiological and attention-focused methodology. The emergent states opened by specific psychospiritual disciplines provide a kind of temporary bridge to these higher interpenetrating intelligences, usually beyond our everyday perception. When the group is integrated and orchestrated by rhythm and incantation, a collective consciousness and memory are unfolded. The group, already having a shared, local history with each other, by repetition and rhythmic coordinated activity appear to be able to create an evoked potential of the brain's emergent forces that then operate down on lower-order individual psychic and somatic processes. "Collective memory is a set of mental images linked on the one hand to the motor mechanisms of rites (although going beyond them) and on the other hand to morphological and social structures. Hence remembrance is precipitated whenever the assembled African community regains its structure and reactivates, in the linking of roles, the ancestral motor mechanisms" (Bastide,

1978, p. 248). This group process has the undeniable power to affect body and mind, and indeed to open mind and consciousness to what is above and beyond it. Literally the embodiment of the gods. These forms of nonlocal intelligence appear to have a specific signature embedded in music and bodily rhythmic entrainment. How does this express itself in the psychology of religion?

THE WEST AFRICAN PSYCHOLOGY OF RELIGION

West African lineages greatly accentuate certain principles in their spiritual vision. What Parrinder (1951) and others found and what indigenous African scholars of these psychospiritual disciplines today continue to witness is a paradigm emphasis on dynamism, vitality, life force, power, and energy as the matrix of psychospiritual reality. These imbue the relationship with the chosen or inherited divinity, e.g., prayer, invocations, praises, dances, etc. The idea is to deepen or amplify the sense of life force. This increased sense of life force is to enhance one's power or vitality in life, to increase one's family, to avoid death, disease, and destruction. It is not about getting into the next life, although an afterlife is accepted. No, it is about intensifying and enhancing *this* life, *this* body, *this* existence. To increase one's emi is to amplify one's life force. One is in the position of "energy" with respect to life. Significantly enough, the disciplines of rhythm, dance, breathing, and community entrainment are designed to bring this emi or life force up the spinal line and into the head or ori. An accomplished practitioner is regarded as one who is "strong in the head." This belief pervades the West African paradigm of religion.

This life force is perceived in everything, and at critical junctures and in particular processes can become not only personified, but also personalized. While there were and are significant differences between tribal groups, some principles can be understood to underlie this diversity. First, there is a belief in a transcendent, benevolent divinity, who very often is far removed from the small affairs of people. This is the creatrix, the primal source and root manifestation of the world process. There is also a widespread belief in a number of immanent gods to whom a person must pay sacrifice in order to keep life strong and to keep the god active. Belief in the power of spirits animating things, forces, and beings in nature is quite common. These spirit forces are perceived to affect the day-to-day life of men. Coinciding with this is the belief in priests, priestesses, and others who can influence these spirit forces for positive and negative reasons through their training and "medicines." Some of these training disciplines, especially those involving dreams, visions, diagnosis, and the use of herbal medicines will be the in-depth focus later in this chapter under "Training and Initiation."

As stressed earlier, there is a profound and bodily-based belief in the direct experience and realization of the divine by way of "spirit possession." Each Orisha or Voudoun spirit has a particular rhythmic and dance "signature" recognized by each member of the many secret societies. This whole paradigm is one in which the life essence is seen to pervade the entire world. Biology and consciousness subsume physics. The world process is a discontinuous gradation of spirit, personhood, and matter localized at various times and in specific objects and forces out of the rhythmic flux and foment of existence.

This power and life force are believed to be implicit and active in all things, animate and inanimate. This is not necessarily "animism," but rather a radiant consciousness and dynamism pervading the world process. There is a hidden, all-pervasive power and force that interacts with human consciousness in different "coupling strengths" depending on one's relationship, skills, and psychospiritual discipline. This is how African "medicine" is thought to operate in the traditional context. Natural herbs, the vibratory power of the "name" of things, the inner structure of things and their relationship to corollary forces can be manipulated by consciousness. Things that are intimate or have had an intimate contact with the person—such as personal belongings, bodily parts, e.g., hair, blood, saliva, etc.—are believed to still have a resonate affinity or "sympathy" or similarity with the person and, in a sense, can psychoenergetically represent that person in certain spiritual equations. This is a philosophy of life force and dynamism that has an implicate order paradigm as its guiding assumption. The physical body is the localized body in which are enfolded the subtle and other bodies of the spiritual anatomy of one's beliefs and practices.

Witchcraft is the skillful manipulation of these forces for evil purposes. Embedded here is the importance of representative and localized bodily aspects of the person, especially blood, hair, and sexual products. In terms of sacrifice, blood is felt to carry the life force to the divinity or spirit world, which can then be recycled back to the person who does the sacrifice for more power and vitality. There are, of course, innumerable variations on this theme, but the underlying paradigm is a shared one. In this context, a witch is believed to be able to manipulate, capture, or, in some cases, "eat the spirit" of a person by skillful manipulation of these symbolic and actual objects that have a resonate affinity with the victim. This is the dark side of this practice. To the outside observer, of course, steeped in purely intrapsychic psychodynamics and logical positivism, these notions may raise an eyebrow or two. Direct experience of the phenomenon, however, with its sense of dread and skin-crawling uncanniness, we guarantee you purges the system of intellectual doubt!

The light side of this force, on the other hand, leads to community healing, altruistic sacrifice, and communion with the divine. It can also serve to ward off the evil force of the witch and circulate this spiritual force through the divine and back to the person. When the blood is spilled in sacrifice or another offering is made, an immaterial or energetic essence (ase) is believed to be liberated, directed, and by circulation is reamplified through the body–mind and life context of the practitioner. A clear distinction is made between the outer sacrifice and the inner essence of a thing. This is not archaic or concrete operational–level logic, but rather a certain psychoenergetic and metaphysical stance on hidden forces and spiritual equations that we have seen earlier stated in the Kemetic texts of Egypt and, to some extent, the later Greek philosophers. The Ionian school worshiped the hidden but all-pervasive energy that was imbued with the divine intelligence and force and gave rise, by way of emanation or unfoldment, to the objects, beings, and forces of this world. The background radiation or sea of light-energy in this universe is all-pervasive. Personalized consciousness and life force capable of "transfering" sacrificed energy by way of activating specific "coupling strengths" through the power of ritual and symbolic psychoenergetic formulas are known to the initiated disciplines. The forces of *this* world, including the physical body, are to be amplified, not negated or denied. There is no ascetic, body-negative tradition of withdrawal here, but rather energy enhancement, vitalism, and psychoenergetic discipline as far as the priest is concerned.

This is not to say that there is no tradition of the essence or "soul" of the person having dynamics beyond the body. Indeed, it is believed that the body can be invaded and inhabited by other intelligences, taking with it the "personality" of the person to a hidden place in the spirit world. Variations and nuances on this paradigm are numerous, of course, as are the number of "souls" enfolded in one person. Dependent on the cultural belief, there can be three or four types of souls in one person. In general, however, the "soul" is associated closer to the outward, social personality of the person and all their conflicts, etc., while the "spirit" is generally associated with the more inward arch toward the divine. Naturally there is an *unbroken continuum* supplied by thoughts, breath, and memories. There is no Cartesian dualism between mind and body here. As a consequence perhaps there is a marked tendency to associate feelings to bodily parts and states (Morakinyo & Akiwowo, 1981). This may lead to greater somatization and symbolization of the body, and perhaps to the belief that other minds can influence your body. It is really more a matter of localization than discrete either/or categorization, with each ethnic group and theology providing its own coloring to the perception. In this context, contact with ancestors, out-of-body experiences, dream-body travel, and all their related dynamics provide a matrix of events and transformations in life and death. This includes the belief in the capacity of the witch's soul to feed upon the soul or spirit of another person and the ability of the practitioner of "black magic" to evoke the soul of a living person into a jar or bowl of water, stick pins into it, and have the person fall ill of the soul, which then affects bodily health.

It is also believed that witches can send out their own souls in a dream, their own personal Khaba, causing nightmares, pain, injury, and confusion to the sleeping soul of another person. This is because it is often believed that the soul wanders from the body in sleep and is more vulnerable to attack and less protected by the deeper residing spirit of the sleeper. Some believe a wandering soul actually initiates the dream and can even be slightly separated from the body while awake. A sudden sensation of touch or being watched is actually a perception of a slightly separated soul from body. Again there are shadings and gradations of difference and metaphysical sophistication between ethnic groups and within ethnic groups between critical thinkers, practitioners, and lineages. However, all seem to share in the tangible perception of an elastic, mobile, and multifaceted inner soul of force and power, an aspect of which transcends the body and denser mind and is implicate in the divine, imperishable spirit of the Creator. In a very real sense, the practicing witch takes Bell's Theorem of Interconnectedness quite literally. That which has been connected with an object at some point in the past will always have some resonate affinity with it in the future, regardless of distance! Nonlocality. In the special case of the witch there are first these local then nonlocal connections to personal objects of the victim. The witch then "evokes" a negative process in the shared field by way of imagery and rhythmic/vibratory means, then projects this evoked potential to the victim, just as the healer does. The problem for the witches, however, which the healer does not have, is how to create a negative intention and image, but then not get caught by their own negative "medicine" that they are sending. The so-called boomerang effect. Part of the secret here is when and how to cease "effort." Quantum mechanical research in neuroscience already suggests that nonlocal evoked potentials are a real phenomenon in human interhemispheric communication between persons already in some relationship with each other. Some aspects of witchcraft appear to be older, non-Western demonstrations of this phenomena (Grinberg-Zylberbaum & Ramos, 1987, 1994).

Souls, Dreams, Spirits, and Vampires

As you can see, dreams have a special role to play in so-called witchcraft. However, dreams also have a crucial place in the nonpathological relationships, especially in the case of communication with family members and the ancestral realm. Unlike ego-psychological models of dreaming with their emphasis on the dynamics of regression, unconscious conflicts, wish fulfillment, day residue, brain biochemistry, neural misfirings, etc. etc., the West African and Kemetic understanding of dreams is that they often carry messages and communication from soul to soul and that dreams literally *live* in the souls of people. The boundaries of the soul are not rigid. Even more so in death. The ancestor, whose spirit is no longer as rigidly confined to three-dimensional corporeal existence, is believed capable of sending information and messages to the embodied soul more easily than in terrestrial life. Communion with the ancestral realm, especially during crucial times, is therefore an accepted reality. Remember, if you cannot think it, certain phenomena cannot happen nor can you perceive them when they do occur! These are some of the hidden dynamics of the soul that on some regions of the Earth have not been forgotten.

The spirit is different from the soul yet shades into it. Evil comes to the spirit by way of neglecting the taboos and divine laws. The spirit is the real protector of the body and soul. The spirit is what truly rules one's life, and the spirit of an ancestor is often inherited or reincarnated in the child. When the spirit departs, death has arrived, unlike the soul, which can wander in dream states and beyond. The spirit has a secret name and must be guarded with care, for it reveals the inner structure of the person, which can be misused by others. This is the real basis of trust when we say "you have my word on it." Your spirit is what you construct a temple or shrine to and is very often associated with the head and sometimes with the right side of the heart, but other locations are possible, e.g., the blood, pelvis, etc. The human spirit is an aspect of the divine or the great spirit that pervades the creation and into which one is reabsorbed at the end of the full incarnation cycle. This spirit therefore is differentiated from the understanding of the soul for this worldview, even though both inhibit the body of the same person and have different dynamics. This spirit has a certain affinity to the Kemetic Egyptian "khu," or spiritual soul, which is imperishable and dwells deep within the "sahu," or spiritual body (Budge, 1960).

In connection with Kemetic Egyptian ideas and influences, Parrinder (1951) and others (Breasted, 1912; Petrie, 1914) point to the belief in an oversoul or kind of guardian or guiding soul that seeks to favorably influence the destiny of a person in life. These European writers compared this soul force to the Kemetic Ka. For the Egyptologist Breasted, it was a "kind of superior genius intended to guide the fortunes of the individual" (p. 52) throughout all his life and adventures. For Flinders Petrie, this Kemetic Ka was "an ancestral emanation which was associated with each man from birth, and, by its superiority would guide and help him through this life and the next. . . . The dead person lives with the Ka, who expels the evil that is before him and removes the evil that is behind him" (p. 24). This idea finds expression not only among the peoples of Nigeria, but also of Togo, Dahomey, Ghana, the Ivory Coast, and parts of Senegal. It is sometimes associated with an ancestral spirit, a totem animal, or other guardian spirit. In the Ifa lineage, the Ifa oracle itself is regarded as a protecting agency and destiny. It reveals the innermost mind in the head or ori to the person in the divination process and helps him manage and balance the forces and functions that unfold through life for his success and evolution. Many different ethnic groups, such as the Ibo, Aba, and Yoruba, share this vision, and permutations of it are found among Ibibio, the Jukun, the Hausa, the Kentu, the Ba-ila, and many many others. The principles are rooted and recorded in the oral traditions of West Africa and stretch beyond 3000 B.C.E. (Bascom, 1969).

At death, of course, the body, soul or souls, and spirit are no longer integrated. Like the Kemetic Egyptians, most traditional African religions believe in some from of metamorphosis or transformation of the identity. The *Egyptian Book of the Dead* has 14 chapters on the ways of metamorphosis into other life forms and also the translation into the gods of light and the divine domain. The different ethnic and religious lineages have beliefs that range from changing into certain totem animals (Kanga-Bonou and Bouro), to kinship ties with different animals (Agni and Baoule of the Ivory Coast), to direct movement into the spirit world of the ancestors. Beliefs vary widely about the transformational process. Most believe that witches can transform themselves into various animals, usually birds, dogs, or cats. Dangerous and vicious animals are often thought of as witches. Benevolent animals are often seen as helping ancestors. Needless to say, this belief in transformation or metamorphosis includes great plants such as ancient trees, powerful rivers, holy groves and meadows, and beautiful mountains that radiate grace and power.

Finally, we may say something more deeply about witchcraft if for no other reason than the pervasive belief in its operation and the inferences we can draw from it about the operation of the mind beyond its localized somatic and space–time coordinates. For witchcraft, sorcery, and black magic are almost universally associated with the African mind, almost always in a pejorative context despite its presence in all human cultures and its psychological presence at some level in every human consciousness.

Sorcery is generally believed to be the conscious manipulation of spiritual forces for good or ill. One can go to a sorcerer to employ his skill. Witchcraft, however, is almost universally employed for negative or evil purposes. As said earlier, it is often believed that the witches can eat the souls of its victims by way of black magic, invading their dreams, or seducing them by way of hypnosis and dreams. The practices occur at night and are unseen by others unless the rites occur in a witch's meeting or sabbat.

People can become witches by witch seduction, in which case they come to "own the soul" of their victim. Just before their own death, however, they must "free the soul" of their victim lest they themselves come to harm. Before freedom, however, the soul of the victim can be made to perform evil deeds and the witch feeds on them by a kind of spiritual vampirism which increases the witch's vitality and extends his life.

Curiously enough, witches travel in many ways, e.g., the back of animals, snakes, etc. However, they are very often associated with the ability to "fly about at night," especially in dreams. Flying imagery is often associated with lucidity in dreams, and the body rigidity observed in some witches in their trance is associated with the out-of-body phenomenon. We will say more on this later in the section on "Training and Initiation." For now we want to emphasize that when the witch's transformed body is injured by those who hunt or fight these witches, a wound or bruise is thought to appear on that part of the witch's human body. These wounds can be seen only with the special eyes of the medicine man or his medicine, but many believe that at night there is a red glow associated with their presence and aura. They are at their evil work of attacking their victims, sucking their blood, stealing babies, sometimes even unborn babies from their mother's womb, and replacing them with dead ones! They help destroy crops, poison relationships, etc. Given the problems associated with rapid urbanization, the usual community restraints and alternative explanations of such phenomena are declining in many instances and these beliefs are increasing.

A few groups like the Azande believe that all witches have a subtle "witchcraft substance" in their bodies which they radiate out to their victims and which can be physically located in their bodies when they are captured or killed (Evans-Pritchard, 1976). This "witchcraft phlegm" is believed to capture, immobilize, and control victims until their souls are taken from them and devoured in an incorporeal vampirism.

Sexuality plays a part here. Many, but not all, groups believe that witches are usually women. Older women may have extended their own lives by incorporating the vital essence of others, either by theft or business. The Hausa believe a witch's power, for good but usually ill, can be bought. Young men especially bring them requests, and their visits have an unclear connection with sex, death, and visits to the underworld dwelling of the witch (Evans-Pritchard, 1976). The Ibo also believe that witches are primarily women, as do the Bambara and others. The Kassourna of the upper Ivory Coast believe hereditary witches are usually women, but they may be men.

When a witch is captured in the act or is accused by the community, it turns out that they themselves are sometimes unaware that they are practicing witchcraft. In other words, someone can be unconscious of their skill and behavior. This means, like classic poltergeist phenomena, there is the possibility of unconscious PK (psychokinesis) operating. They may confess anyway, but a tacit acknowledgment of dissociation, fugue states, and unconscious processes is accepted. Then a course of therapy for the victim is undertaken. While good and strong men may be immune, many people must take precautions. A special charm or fetish, a secret place or hidden pot to place one's soul in times of weakness or danger, etc., can be used. The Ngizim of Bornu have a rite to return the stolen soul to the victim after it is "located" by a diviner and put in a special calabash of water. Others have different cures.

The smaller and more family-interconnected and intense the community, the higher the reported incidents of witchcraft. No doubt family pressures and animosities, hostile primary process imagery in dreams, community belief, and a group-supported kind of hypnotic induction accounts for many of the cases. This is intensified in the cases of polygamy. This family unconscious process is reinforced by the fact that most believe that witches can harm only their own relatives and children. This is not the belief in the case of the sorcerer or black magician. In the case of the classic witch, however, we cannot overlook the possibility of the multiple personality who is able in different states of consciousness to exercise effects on conscious and psychic energy unavailable to the average mind. After all, the multiple personality is capable of dissociation, fugue states, deep trance, and also quite distinct personality styles, each style accompanied by distinct psychophysiological tendencies, including brainwave patterns (Bynum, 1994).

MEDIUMS, DIVINERS, AND THEIR FORMS OF SPIRIT POSSESSION

The traditional African religious intuition tends to believe in and also observe an energy and information field around all things, especially human beings (Somé, 1994). The paradigm accepts that all things are in some sense alive, and remain alive despite their apparent manifest transformation in the energetic field of space and time (Akiwowo, 1980). These transformations are observable to the initiate and trained eye and are of course open at times to different forms of influence.

"Spiritualism" is a basic accepted reality, experience, and tenet in these West African religions. Atheists and albinos are exceedingly rare in the climate of Africa. The world is tacitly recognized to be a process that occurs within an all-pervasive universe that, largely unseen, is infused with life and consciousness in continuous transformation. Mbiti (1969) and others have made extensive reference to the fact that in West African religions in particular there is a highly respected and highly functional place for mediums and diviners of all kinds in this religious universe. This seems to be especially so in the societies like the Ashanti, Baganda, Ewe, Fon, Yoruba, and others. Within this context there are different kinds and levels of mediumship. These mediums may work with the diviner or a medicine man, but their roles are quite separate.

In the case of the traditional medicine men, after a consultation with the patient and then divination based on an established system of clinical observations, assessment of crucial relationships with family, society, and the ancestral realm, an intervention occurs, often accompanied by a psychospiritual technology of one form. The cause may be attributed to primarily physical ailments. However, the cause may also be perceived to come from psychological dynamics, astral influences, spiritual causes, or other esoteric influences. Treatment is then offered based on this understanding. This can be counseling based on familial and extended relationship considerations, healing rites in the ancestral realm, diet changes, exercise or fasting, or a combination of herbal medication with these and prescribed sacrifice. The herbal medication may come from his own herbal garden or be purchased in the market. When you travel to the herbal market in Ile-Ife, you are likely to see a vast assortment of herbs, animal objects, and "things" quite alien to the Western mind which are clearly understood by the indigenous healer. When an evil influence is divined, either medical herbs and/or sacrifice is prescribed. The list of herbal medications is quite extensive among traditional healers, and medicines are quite specific to the clinical situation. They can be extraordinarily powerful (ase) in altering the consciousness and experience of the patient and also in confirming the theory of "causation" behind the illness. The specialist in herbal medications is required through training to know thousands of specific herbal combinations for not only their traditional medical value, ones that Western-trained physicians also employ for antibacteriological etc. treatments, but also to know the various combinations and proportions to effect other clinical changes. These may be used with incantation with the belief that words and images are vibrationally related to objects and situations in space and time (Makinde, 1988; Oyedipe, 1993). This is why imagery and rhythm are so important.

The skilled use of rhythmic incantation, the repetition of personally meaningful or egosyntonic phrases, and the emotional expectations built up upon seeing the healer, from even a traditional Western perspective, at the very least create a therapeutic technique which is like autogenetic and hypnotic procedures routinely used by the behavioral medicine clinician in the treatment of psychosomatic and various pain disorders. There is a great deal of word play. It harnesses the power of the unconscious, the autonomic nervous system, and the immune system at critical junctures. They will also use placebos at times, but it is clearly more than just placebo! Mutual trance will often spontaneously occur. Healers or medicine men in the West, however, do not go into trance while in treatment, or if they do they keep it to themselves.

In some cases diviners or medicine men may be possessed and temporarily become mediums, but not necessarily so. During the mediumship the person "loses" his or her being or senses and becomes simply an instrument for the embodiment of the spirit. He or she can be held to act or speak or sing according to the wishes of the Loa or the spirit, seemingly without necessarily doing damage to themselves. Many unusual and sometimes dangerous acts can be performed, and yet the medium is not hurt. In each of these cases there is a massive activation of the autonomic nervous system, an eclipse of personal consciousness, and a focus of attention inward in a way that seems to radically outshine the previous egoic consciousness. Interestingly enough while most medicine men are men and most diviners are men, most mediums are women.

These mediums are usually associated with priests and temples or shrines. This is especially so in the secret societies. These mediums may be trained by priests in the village or by village elders. They may or may not be married. Their training, like any other specialized discipline, can last from two to four or five years. During the actual "possession," all manner of intense and sometimes shocking behavior from a Western point of view can be noticed. However, this is largely culturally relevant. During the actual "possession" the medium may manifest one or several different personalities, and then communicate with the community that has gathered for this occasion. Thus when they manifest the particular spirit or Loa, they can behave like a pregnant woman, a warrior, an animal spirit, or any other particularly informative personalization. This motif of "spirit possession" appears to be one of the defining characteristics of both diasporic West African religions and their indigenous African expression (Hall, 1990). Generally speaking, the African medium is felt to be under the direct control of the Loa or spirit, whereas for others, such as the Native American shaman, the spirit may speak through them but the shaman retains control. In the case of highly gifted mediums or others, they may hold annual festivals in adoration of their particular god.

Some forms of possession are associated with witchcraft. Here it is believed that a demon or spirit has entered the body of a person against his or her will, the spirit often being that of an ancestor. Voluntary possession is more common, however, and the person uses a specific methodology for the effect on her community. Thus, again, witches may become so unwillingly and unconsciously. Interestingly enough these demons, while considered at times evil spirits, are not identified as a Lucifer, etc., or the great being of evil as is found in Christianity and Islam.

For a witch's possession, the public exposure of the situation is said to destroy the power of the possession. This is in marked contrast to the public possession of mediums, whose power in this context is actually increased. The standard psychiatric explanations of dissociation, hysteria, primitive regression, etc., do seem to explain much of what is seen. However, regardless of how controversial it may appear to be, at times these mediums do seem to be able to demonstrate various phenomena that have been associated with anomalous information or psi capacities, especially ESP, PK in healing, and precognition. Others appear capable of brief episodes of clairvoyance, remote viewing, and many other abilities thought latent in many people and to which modern experimental parapsychology now gives considerable attention (Jahn & Dunne, 1987; Targ & Puthoff, 1977; Vasiliev, 1976). While often dismissed as pseudoscience by contemporary science, these phenomena nevertheless remain enduring experiences to those directly involved. The medium's "trance" can be mild or highly agitated depending on "who" seems to be possessing her. The different Orisha have different styles and agendas. And as said above, sometimes a medium can be possessed by a series of spirits in progression whose presence the medium acts out. Other persons in the community may communicate with the medium at this time.

Some mediums, like those of the Ibibio, claim at times to be possessed by anything from animal spirits to totem animals such as a wild pig, leopard, or snake, but, by and large, it is possession by an ancestral spirit, an Orisha god or Loa. In this context, it is no wonder that near death it is believed that a priest or priestess can transfer the consciousness to a relative or devotee. There is a faint similarity to the Tibetan practice of Pho-wa, or the transference of consciousness, here, except of course that Tibetan Buddhism denies the very existence of an unchanging personal soul. The spirit may lodge itself anywhere, but the most common places in the body are believed to be the solar plexus, the stomach, and the blood. At times extraordinary powers of strength, physical healing, and anomalous communication do occur in these heightened states of emotional, psychological, and spiritual arousal. No doubt some psychospiritual process or "mechanism" underlies much of this space, time, psychic boundary, and identify-transforming process.

In the West African disciplines, many of which derive from the Ifa model and lineage, there appears to be a working with the life current or Kundalini in a way that interacts with forces associated with the Earth. In other words, in the dawning stages of Orisha spirit possession, the human ori, associated with the spiritual energy in the head, is linked with the ori or spiritual forces in the Earth. These forces are known as Irunmole, and they provide the medium with the experience of time as it is projected forward through evolution (Fatunmbi, 1991). As the trance or possession deepens, the medium's consciousness at such high energies with so much momentum begins to fuse or flow in a grand unification into other personalized forces or deities such as Imole, Irunmole, and Egun, into the realm of lae-lae, a condition that seems in many ways parallel to but not identical with what in Yoga is called Turyia or Samadhi.

In Ifa there are 256 Odu and their accompanying Ese-Ifa chapter expositions (Abombola, 1976). Odu is understood to be radiant spirit that generates form in the universe but itself is formless. From it the forms are unfolded, implicit in everything, and are enfolded again after manifestation. It is as though the involution of spirit into matter is accomplished by the descent and expression of the Odu in material reality. The differentiated Orishas manifest the Odu in all their frequencies. Light is spirit itself, and all the different colors of light are expressions of spirit. Since all light is contained in white light, all the Orishas in a personalized way are believed to be linked with Obatala, the force and deity who formed or molded the material universe. He is personified as dressed in white clothes, and each implicate aspect of creation is believed to contain an aspect of his power or ase. Interestingly enough the male Obatala in the Ifa creation myth didn't finish the job of creation because he rested. His female aspect finished the job. Both male and female are associated with the shape and symbol of the spiral-shaped snail shell held by the Kemetic Egyptians to be the most common pattern of growth exhibited by nature and a representative of the "golden mean." It is recognized by Ifa as the key to unlocking the real forces and powers of creation (Fatunmbi, 1991). This spiral's affinity to the serpent power is striking, as is the fact that such spirals are associated to other Earth or geomagnetic forces studied by ancient and contemporary science. Suffice it to say here that the medium's methodology is to enter trance by way of a specific Orisha's disciplines of diet, behavior, etc., and allow the "possession" to deepen his or her consciousness by way of personalized forces which are capable, like subatomic interactions, of shifting places and identities with each other. Here knowledge of universal forms is accessible. In Yoga this storehouse of knowledge and infinite possibilities is known as the Akashic Records, in Buddhism as the Alayavijnana; in Ifa, as we have said, it is Dafa. In healing practices the priest makes a connection between events and things or forces in the patient's life and certain vibratory sounds or words that are connected to these events in space and time which are enfolded in the Dafa[8]

---

8. Contemporary technological science has created an example of this in the form of the Internet and the World Wide Web. The former, however, reaches into the continuum of past-present-future, into the deeper primordial and archetypal forms, the realm of the trans- or superconscious. It subsumes the latter, and the latter is a projection of the expression of it. The latter technological forms are presently confined to the world of "data" and electronic processing.

(Makinde, 1988). From the "many-worlds" of possibility in the quantum mechanical analogy there is believed to be a kind of "collapse" of the wave-packet into the actuality of the devotee's life context which can be seen and understood by the Babalawo. This is accompanied by music and group participation. A variation of this is being possessed by energy or the "n/um" and "!kia" in the tradition of the !Kung people of southwest Africa (Katz, 1982). Whereas the former is initiated primarily by music, group support, and the incantatory power of the word, or "Nommo" (Jahn, 1961), the latter is initiated primarily by hours of music and group rites to "heat up" the energy. The latter may also be a more direct stimulation of Kundalini than the former (Sannella, 1987). The energy is said to sleep in the stomach and, when awakened, to rise through the spinal line until it reaches the brain, where it dissolves or transcends the egoic consciousness in a wave of ecstatic energy and intelligent light. It is used for healing, has a clear spiritual base, and, interestingly enough, is believed to run in families. The experience in *both* contexts is suffused with potentially unpleasant episodes and dynamic psychophysical energies rushing up from the deeper levels of the unconscious, both personal and otherwise. When the possession experience is over, the person often awakes with complete amnesia of what occurred.

TRAINING AND INITIATION

During the training of mediums the neophytes may practice the "imitation of death and resurrection" as part of the training process (Mbiti, 1969). This means going so far as to be wrapped in death clothes, buried in a tomb for a while, and ritualistically resurrected after going through an experience of intense visions and contact with the spirit worlds usually dissociated from ordinary waking consciousness. This is the saga of Osiris made deeply personal in the embodied life of new priests. Like others practicing and preparing for the priesthood, they may make sacrifices, have their head shaved, drink from specialized instruments, go into certain trance states, and change their sexual and dietary habits in accordance with the discipline. In some contexts powerful, vision-inducing herbal medicines are taken during initiation which, like LSD and other psychoactive agents, stimulate deep ancestral and even phylogenetic memories, including the memory of one's birth and what are believed to be prior life experiences. The Ibogaine root is only one example. It stimulates a kind of life review and serves a similar purpose as the Ayahuasca vine medicine used by Peruvian shamans in the remote Amazon in terms of seeing spirit forms and visions. In the African context, elaborate preparations and training are necessary before the initiate is allowed entry into these mysteries. Africa is suffused with secret societies. These prescriptions are not simply "taboos," but guides to keep one on their path. Music and incantation that go back centuries help the initiate, who is in an altered state, remain stabilized and somewhat protected from rather powerful and sometimes disturbing visions and experiences. Not everyone is successful! Often a new language is learned which later can be seen in the work of the medium during possession. Sometimes a new name is actually taken on by the medium in training. And when they receive their complete training there is a graduation acknowledged by community, friends, and family. The candidates may then resume "normal life" and practice their profession, returning to the temples and training sites during special occasions.

It is quite significant for the tradition of mediums, priests, and other highly religious and spiritualized religions and practitioners throughout Africa that the tradition of priests to enter trance is much stronger in West Africa than in other parts of the continent (Mbiti, 1969). This has had a profound influence on religious sentiments in the West, since a large percentage of indigenous peoples who were brought to the Caribbean and the United States were taken from these particular groups in West Africa, e.g., the Fon, Mandinka, Ashanti, Yoruba, etc. In the collective unconscious of African Americans we may find a higher degree of historical religious consciousness.

Strictly speaking, priests are religious servants associated with specific temples and shrines. They officiate in funeral services, puberty and ancestral rites, and the worship of spirits and divinities. They are also the keepers of the collective memory and guardians of the society's moral values. They actively participate in the vast unseen world of the religious universe, a universe that subsumes nearly every phase of lived and ancestral life. From the various peoples mentioned earlier, the Yoruba, and others, we would add those of the Ankore, Igbo, Akan, Shona, Baganda, Basonga, Sonjo, and others whose ancestors were brought to the New World. An interesting study of the African unconscious as manifested in the West might be had by a study of the African antecedents in terms of religious intensity in this area. This particular psychic and psychological tendency might then be traced through many forms of African American culture, religiosity, and philosophy (Holloway, 1990). This might make it much easier to understand how both the ideas of "homeopathic magic," "contagious magic," and other dynamic psychic processes are more easily accepted by large numbers of African Americans than by other groups who were also not native to the American situation, that is to say, peoples from Europe and other parts of the world.

African spirituality in general differentiates between the forms of "magic," witchcraft, and sorcery. We will return to witchcraft in a moment, but first let's look at "magic." "Fetish objects" of the gods and goddesses, of course, are no different for the African traditionalist than the fetish objects of the Christian cross and saints, the Islamic Ka'aba worn by the faithful, or the Judaic Mogen David star worn around the neck. They are psychological associations and are not necessarily "charms." True "charms" are believed to express dynamic power relationships. Charms and actions based on the *similarities* between things, such as images or dolls, etc., assume that "like produces like" or that an effect resembles its cause. It is the so-called homeopathic magic. The magic that is called contagious magic is based on the belief that objects once in contact with each other can continue to act on each other at a distance even when physical contact has been severed. This is similar to Bell's Theorem in quantum mechanics which some relativistic physicists, on first learning of its nonlocal implications, felt was some kind of "spooky action at a distance." Contagious magic operates in the principle on contiguousness (Opoku, 1978). Body parts, fingernails, personal clothing, and objects mentioned earlier fall into this category. These objects help generate occult forces and spirits. It is not so much that *every* object has a spirit, but that spirits inhabit many objects and can leave or travel from those objects. During training and initiation this is learned. It is also learned how to contact the ancestors and other spirits for good or evil.

It is believed that witchcraft can be acquired by either heredity or *contact* with certain powerful objects or spirits or people; also, it can be purchased in some situations and even acquired from demons against one's will! Needless to say, part of training and initiation is learning how to protect oneself from harm. In sorcery a powerful potion is created by the magician or sorcerer. In witchcraft it is believed to be mind-to-mind influence.

To the mind accustomed to material rationality and logical positivism, these notions appear absurd. Yet belief in and experience of these areas are widespread and enduring. As the European explorer and writer in this area said, "European psychology has not yet fully investigated the extent of the influence of mind over mind, and it is not impossible that Africans are more sensitive and skilled in these matters than we are ourselves" (Lucas, 1970, p. 333).

One of the more controversial areas of belief, especially from the contemporary Western and logical positivist perspective, is the active belief in so-called witchcraft and sorcery in these lineages and disciplines. However, when the neophyte begins these practices, the vast majority do not seek to practice witchcraft and most never do. But their experience and training convince them of the absolute reality of these practices. This is because the "experiences" of initiation are really experiential experiments within the paradigm that tend to confirm or refute the validity of numinous and anomalous phenomena according to the specific criterion and methodology appropriate to the context. The empirical method and the canon of necessary replication of "data" are not limited to the experiences of the physical world. All human knowledge systems, from so-called objective science to mystical revelation, work this way (Bynum, 1996).

We mentioned a little earlier in this section that the neophyte goes through behavioral rituals of death, burial, and rebirth into a new consciousness that is accompanied by intense visions of the spirit world and the unconscious (Somé, 1994). These experiences ratify certain vectors within this paradigm of reality. Take for instance those who choose to specialize in dreamwork. They may work on dream analysis with Ifa trance divination and a form of free association to the dream. And then again therapy may involve direct interpretation, some emotionally satisfying ritual sacrifice to "seal" the seen and unseen worlds together, and resultant directives to change behavior in the physical world with family or neglected ancestors. This is brief therapy carried out on the basis of "insight," affect, and behavioral change. Some doing dreamwork take a different path.

Lucid Dreams, Out-of-Body Experience, and the "Traveling" Experience

It is incontestable that practitioners of witchcraft and so-called sorcery actively *believe* in their experiences. These experiences have the subjective ring of certainty to them, and their effects can be "observed" by how waking reality can be interpreted by them and the community. There appear to be three overlapping methods whose experiences validate the paradigm the witchcraft worker or sorcerer uses in this form of more active dreamwork. They are a form of lucid dreaming, practices similar to Yoga nidra and the more controversial OBE, or out-of-body experience.

Lucid dreaming is the experience of becoming awake and aware while dreaming. Doubted as a reality until recently by Western science, it is now clearly established as a fact (Gackenbach & Bosweld, 1989; Garfield, 1974; La Berge, 1985). In other parts of the world it has never been doubted. The techniques are varied but all involved awakening and stabilizing consciousness while dreaming and then executing certain behaviors in the dream, all of which are intensely visual, tactile, and auditory. Often they contain *more* real feeling than the waking state yet have the fluid images, emotions, and space–time elasticity as the most intense dream. Their experience is profound. To some extent these practitioners believe and, therefore, perceive and experience the dream, as the Australian Aboriginals, as an objective state as real as the waking state. The Australian Aboriginals refer to it as the Dreaming (Bosnak, 1996; Cowan, 1991) or the Dreamtime. By the use of rituals and other mental disciplines, the practitioners consciously awaken in the dreamstate and have the decided experience of travel and transformation. In this method there is a brief separation and *eclipse* of the observing ego between falling asleep and the experience of what we call the dream.

There are also practices learned during the training period that are very similar to the meditative discipline of Yoga nidra. In this method the practitioner learns to go from waking to sleep to intense conscious dreaming *without* the loss of the individual principle of consciousness. This sleeping trance method involves ritual entrance into sleep from waking and holding fast to consciousness as the observing ego goes through various visual, auditory, and kinesthetic transformations. Often relaxing the body in a sequence that follows the sensory motor cortex outline of the body's motor homunculus is useful in keeping a tight rein on consciousness (Bynum, 1994; Saraswati, 1976). There are also several other methods for this entering of the dreaming state consciously and without a discontinuity in awareness (Evans-Wentz, 1958; Satyananda, 1985). The net result is the intense perception of the world process that is experienced as visually and kinesthetically real and valid. This direct experience and the resultant bodily and visual perception of "traveling" in a fluid space–time is not interpreted as going to sleep and dreaming so much as entering another realm of existence through secret disciplines and sacred rituals, then operating on the basis of the perceptual dynamics of this new realm.

Finally, for some mediums and sorcerers, there is the third discipline, which seems to be an OBE or out-of-body experience. This is the most difficult for the Western sensibility to comprehend but nevertheless is experienced as authentic to the practitioner. There is even scattered laboratory and "scientific" support for the phenomena (Rogo, 1978). The actual subjective experience is of either a conscious exit from the physical body in trance or the intentional "projection" of the principle of consciousness out from the body to some other location in the environment, usually in the same space–time. It is differentiated from the lucid dream and the Yoga nidra experience on the basis of the "exit" sensation. The exit is facilitated by ritual, mental-visual disciplines, certain internal rhythmic movements, and incantation. There is a discipline to generate the internal bodily perception of the psychological locus of consciousness slowly spinning within the physical body and moving upward until it exits the corporeal self. The location in the physical body for the perceived "exit" is crucial, since it will pattern the environment one travels to and to some degree the "character" of the other conscious entities one believes and perceives they encounter. *These disciplines take years to learn and it is highly ill advised to practice them without a skilled teacher!* The world encountered is a vibratory, conscious, and diversely "populated" spiritual ecology which has the distinct capacity to unsettle one's usual sense of self and personal boundary. There is an unmistakable sensation of "travel" and vivid imagery specific to the patterning and demand characteristics of the situation. As is said in Raja Yoga practice, "all the body is in the mind but not all the mind is in the body." This belief system and the practical disciplines associated with it may have been highly evolved in Dahomey and other parts of West Africa but is widespread throughout sub-Saharan Africa and was known to the Kemetic Egyptians of 3000 B.C.E. Again, the place of rhythmic incantation, sympathetic or resonate affinity to others, trance, and heightened intentionality, along with visual and mental disciplines, are an essential part of one's training.

When this vivid, fluid, and conscious state is achieved and stabilized by whichever practice, the intentionality associated with it gains agency and can operate in the world. For many African groups that part of the self called the Khaba, or covering of the soul in ancient Kemet, and the so-called etheric and astral body in esoteric Western psychology comes into play.[9] This region or frequency modulation of the system is believed to be the area responsible for sensory perceptions, rhythm, and the life force of the breath and circulating blood. It is aroused by sacred ritual, rhythmic drumming, and movement. As in ancient Kemetic psychology, the Ba, or breath of the soul that animates the living body (often symbolized by a bird that travels), and the Ka, or the system's bodily expression that lends it a necessary stability in space–time and the realm of matter, come together and complement each other (Akbar, 1984). The Ba and Ka come together in the Khaba and through the disciplines of sacred ritual and rhythmic modulation by drums, a "spirit possession" or opening and elevation of consciousness is achieved. In this elevated state the shared living memory of the ancestors and Orishas, the Ifa implicate order storehouse memory, is accessed, usually for healing but, yes, in some cases for witchcraft. "Possession" is a contact with forces to open and expand the self and communion; witchcraft is manipulation of certain forces in this matrix. "Possession" uses vivid imagery of the collective to elevate the spirit, often invoking the common symbols and objects of all in the work. Witchcraft manipulates objects that have or had a personal resonate affinity with the victim, e.g., their hair, personal clothing, special possessions, etc., to focus the malevolent imagery and intentionality of the witchcraft worker.

Rooted in the above is a basic intuitive understanding of rhythm as a higher-order organizing principle that has the capacity for the transcendence of the individualized localized identity principle and its hierarchical integration with emergent intelligences above the individual self. It also forms the foundation for an implicit understanding of a shared identity at a certain stage of experience. We can only speculate on the possibility, during intense trance states with massive autonomic nervous system arousal, the height-

---

9. Technically the etheric body is closer to the energy body, while the astral body is more associated with our emotional dynamism. But vibrating in the multidimensional and interpenetrating universe of ourselves, under certain conditions they can be made to move into a nonphasic relationship with the usual body–mind and thereby operate with different dynamics.

ened focus of attention and consciousness, and the eclipse of the individual consciousness principle, for the possibility of communication on subtle levels by way of superconducting transmission and emergent cortical and energetically structured intelligent processes not normally perceived during the traditional awaking state. This area deserves further study and attention.

SUMMARY

We have focused in this chapter on certain basic tenets of the African religious phenomenon as it dispersed after the Diaspora to the West in particular. We have seen how the roots of not only Christianity, Judaism, and Islam are implicated in seed form in the early *Egyptian Book of the Dead* and the Pyramid Texts, but how the suppression of this paradigm and its reemergence and syncretic integration with West African religions of the Yoruba and other peoples are later transformed into religious movements. These then went through still another transformation in terms of symbolism and syncretism during the Diaspora by way of the slave trade to the Americas. Under the impetus of European Christian political forces the indigenous religions we have mentioned found a way to fuse by way of syncretic integration the basic tenets of the religions of Dahomanian Voudoun and the Yoruba influences with those of Christianity. The results are the various dual images we find in the Haitian Voudoun religion, Santería, Candomble, Macombe, Myal, and others. There is a nonprejudiced acceptance of personalism in the capacity for intelligence to manifest itself in terms of spirit and force in the universe. This is true of the indigenous African peoples, especially the Yoruba, Fon, Ashanti, Mandinka, and other West African groups from which large numbers of African American populations were originally extracted. In a real sense significant aspects of the ancient African mystery schools survived through the secret societies of the Diaspora and exist both consciously and significantly on an unconscious level in the consciousness of the diasporic African peoples of not only North America but also the Caribbean and South America. In particular we find in the African American unconscious a high relevance and reference for the personal encounter between God and men. Here religion, in the small details of daily life, is a profound and intensely personal matter. We can see this in even the early Western studies of African religions done by Evans-Pritchard (1965), Lienhardt (1961), and Parrinder (1961). It is emphasized again that in the African tradition, as in the African unconscious matrix, there is no separation or dissociation of the religious and spiritual intuition from endeavors in the areas of science, medicine, agriculture, architecture, and the other significant domains of life, both large and small.

There are some 3,000 different African "tribes," each with its own rituals and beliefs. These different tribal nations have increased in size in different times and decreased in size in other times. There is a lineage between many of them back to pre-dynastic Egypt, as noted in the Dogon religion and others in West Africa. We are moving quickly toward a day when the prejudices of logical positivism as expounded by Auguste Comte (1830/1974) will be transcended and we will begin to recognize the contributions of this ancient lineage in modern science. We no longer hold the self-assured prejudice that religion is a progression from "primitive animism" to the notion of one god outside and above us and a clockwork mechanistic science. This is a false reading of evolution.

Someday there will an open recognition that there is no inherent separation between the religious or spiritual divine, science, agriculture, and the other domains of humanity. These are all variations of the human endeavor, implicate and interacting with each other. This is to return to the ancient African consciousness perspective in which there is no formal separation between the sacred and the secular, between the spiritual and the material. Religion and spirituality will again be seen to pervade all levels of life. In Africa there is not even a word for religion in some societies, since the notion of religion and the divine is so all pervasive (Mbiti, 1969). Religion, like spirituality and eventually science, will be seen to be community-based. Just as many in our contemporary society do not know how not to be technocratic, we will eventually again return to the point where we will find it odd and quite strange not to be deeply spiritual and see that spirituality is inherent in all aspects of our life. When this is eventually combined with the deeper understanding of science, mysticism, and luminosity, we will focus our newly won insights from an ancient past on the sacred task of healing in all its manifestations. This is the gift and the promise in the ancient legacy of the West African religions and their Diaspora to the rest of the world. This indeed is the great ankh, the great mystery of the life. Transformation after transformation after transformation.

7

FREUD, JUDAISM, AND THE LIMITS OF PSYCHODYNAMIC INSIGHT

The man Moses, the liberator and lawgiver of the Jewish people, was not a Jew, but an Egyptian.

Sigmund Freud, *Moses and Monotheism*

Scholem holds that Sabbatianism, encountering the emancipation of the Jews in the 19th century, passes into a rationalism which tends to conceal its Sabbation origins. After the French Revolution it was the Sabbatian groups still within the Jewish fold that fostered the movements toward reform, liberalism and enlightenment . . . most important is the fact that Sabbatianism, as a form of mysticism, shares with rationalism the conviction that the world reality, all reality, may be apprehended by, and encompassed in, thought. And as for our relating this to Freud, Sabbatianism encouraged concern with the forbidden areas of human experience.

David Bakan, *Sigmund Freud and the Jewish Mystical Tradition*

THE JEWS OF ANCIENT EGYPT: THREE THEORIES OF ORIGIN

THE historical origins of the Jews are shrouded in mystery. It was the firmly held opinion articulated by the ancient writers Tacitus, Eusebius, Celsus, Strabo, Plutarch, and Diodorus of Sicily that the Jews were originally a group of Ethiopians and Egyptians who migrated out of the Nile Valley to settle in Canaan (Finch, 1991). According to the great historian Manetho (after Josephus), there were at least two or three exoduses out of Egypt by the Jews, one involving a remnant loyal to the defeated Hyskos invaders who returned to the Canaanite city of Jerusalem, then called Hierosylma. The other was a small band of downtrodden and defeated Egyptian religious dissenters led by the great rebel Egyptian priest of Ra named Osarsiph, the "son of Osiris." He is reported to have also led his people into Palestine. It may well be that the later Hebrew writers and chroniclers fused the two episodes.

Manetho equates the Biblical Black Moses to the "son of Osiris" named Osarsiph. It is he who is credited in history with the moving of the Hebrews toward monotheistic religion and away from the Egyptian "polytheism" (Finch, 1991). From the 42 principles of Maát, which are really the 42 negative confessions from the *Egyptian Book of the Dead*, Moses distilled most of the 10 Commandments. His sect, it seems, was particularly sympathetic to the personal-moral dimension of the tradition, very concerned with the moral balancing of good and evil in the heart and the associated dynamics of judgment and redemption that was later to be echoed by their prophets. In addition to being a military man and an inspired prophet, he was obviously a well-trained scholar and priest. He was the spiritual leader of a nation yet reportedly had a speech impediment and needed Aaron to speak effectively to the masses. Despite this he could be a terror to his enemies, supposedly by divine injunction sending plagues and misfortunes to the sons and family of his enemies. (See Appendix B.) This highly educated "prince of Egypt" was schooled in the classical tradition of Egypt and so therefore wrote or began the oral tradition not in Hebrew but in Egyptian script five books—Genesis, Exodus, Leviticus, Numbers, and Deuteronomy—collectively called the Pentateuch, and fused his genius into the destiny of Judaism. When he helped the seven daughters of the priest Reuel at the well in Midian after his flight from Egypt, he was described as "an Egyptian [who] delivered us out of the hand of the shepherds" (Exodus 2: 16–19). Clearly he was not an Arab or a

European, and indistinguishable from a Black Egyptian. Except for the Hollywood convention that all the royalty of Egypt were White, in the cinematic version of this story Moses is also tacitly indistinguishable from the Egyptians, never learns their script, and only when he comes down from the mountain with God's laws written do we see the Hebrew letters. The truth is really right before our eyes if we open them and see without bias.

It is reasonable to ask, given the relative rigidity and conservative structure of Egyptian society, how likely is it that a highly educated priest or even "Prince of Egypt," after years of privilege, would write in the language of slaves. Even Alfred the Great of England, who did so much to initiate English "literature" in the ninth century, still had to start with a Latin script. If Moses were a "priest of Ra," he would still have come from the aristocracy and so, again, would have written in classical Egyptian script. Contemporary Biblical scholarship reveals three or four schools of thought in the Old Testament, including the priestly tradition; the Elohistic tradition which, in the Torah, says the Elohim in Genesis unfolded Creation itself, and the Yahwistic tradition (Buttrick, 1984). Sometimes Deuteronomy is held as a separate tradition or "school." These all came largely after Moses. With the death of Moses, his followers no doubt continued his traditions both orally and in written form, because the first authorized edition of the Torah is only written down some 300 years later, at the direction of the great prophetess Deborah. The text was then "edited" and revised for at least half a millennium, until it came down to the Hebrews of the 5th century B.C.E., who had it fairly intact. The Yahwistic tradition is the 9th century B.C.E., the Elohistic is the 8th century B.C.E., and the priestly is the 6th century B.C.E. (Buttrick, 1984; Finch, 1991). If Moses wrote, or more likely *initiated*, these traditions, then they would have borne the stamp of an Egyptian style, which his followers would have kept for centuries.

According to Manetho, the 3rd century B.C.E. priest-scholar who chronicled both the Hebrew story and the history of the pre-dynastic rulers of Kemet, these "uncleaned outcasts," as they were described, were driven out by the Egyptians. The Hebrews had grown in numbers and were no longer simply laborers and shepherds, and could potentially become a hostile army under certain conditions. This whole political and cultural movement was partially a reaction to the pharaoh Akhenaton and the new monotheistic religion of the sun god Aton, which was eventually defeated. A universal state religion would have served to unify his newly expanded empire and capital at Tel al-Amarna in 1396 B.C.E. The Jews were historically committed to this religion but fell into disfavor when Akhenaton lost and the religious hierarchy and priesthood regained ascendancy of the pharaonic authority.

The origin legends of the Hebrews themselves say they are the descendants of Abraham in Mesopotamia. The Sumerians had created the city of

Ur, the homeland of Abraham, and there it is said he flourished and seeded the Jewish faith. By 1500 B.C.E., Mesopotamia was thriving with many city-states. Under Ramses II, the Kemetic armies invaded Canaan and brought the Hebrews into Egypt. Ramses II had defeated the Hittite King Muwatallig and his 40,000 troops at the battle of Kadesh, which by the way he almost lost. He then pressed the Hebrews into service in order to build the city of Pi-Ramses on the eastern Nile delta. By this time, of course, the pyramids were already old, and the sphinx had been reconstructed several times during the ages. Actually, the first distinct records we have of the Hebrews is in 1222 B.C.E., where they are defeated by the Egyptian armies of Pharaoh. The records seem to indicate that it was not Ramses II but Merneptah who, on an expedition to pacify Palestine (Palestiou), brought back the Jews to Egypt as slaves. This is inscribed on the "Stele of Israel" and the first time in recorded history the Hebrews are mentioned (Diop, 1974). However, the records are incomplete because they were rumored to be captives of Egypt for 430 years, but Moses is said to have delivered them from pharaoh in 1250 B.C.E. It is most significant in this context, however, and something repeated every year by millions of Jews reciting the Haggadah during the Passover Seder service, that it was in Egypt (Africa) that "Israel became a nation!" In any event, after emancipation, they went back to Canaan and built a new nation. They were part of the wave of diverse peoples that moved in the Middle East of that period.

By 1200 B.C.E. Canaan saw the invasions of the "sea peoples" and mercenaries of Egypt. The region was in flux. Refugees flooded in. The Philistines, their traditional enemies, were part of this invasion. More refugees came. The Hebrew refugees from this human tidal wave fled inland and fused with the older, more settled Jews and became strong. By 1100 B.C.E., the religion of Yahweh was dynamic and spreading by conquest and conversion. Around 1120 B.C.E. the Israelites chose a king to unite the separate and scattered tribes. He was Saul. After Saul came King David, who is also credited with uniting the tribes. David leaves an empire. Solomon then came to rule huge areas of the empire. Egypt was in a period of decline. The empire of Solomon required taxes, conscription, and even forced labor, which led to social unrest. By the time of Solomon's death around 920 B.C.E., internal political pressures had increased and eventually led to the separation of the empire into two states, Israel in the North, and Judah in the South with Jerusalem as its capital. This is another era of scattered tribes and national suffering. Barbara Tuchman (1978) and other historians believe that eventually Rehoboam, son of King Solomon, lost the kingdom of Israel and the 10 tribes forever. The stress of the era led to epochal prophets. It is during this episode of spiritual tension and collective turmoil that the righteous voices of Hosea, Isaiah, Micah, and other prophets of doom wandered and echoed through the cities and country-side calling on the people to repent.

Egypt emerged from its decline, and the Mesopotamian states grew bolder. More war came, more successors, more defeats. Then in 586 B.C.E. came Nebuchadnezzar, the destruction of the temple, the sacking of Jerusalem, and the Babylonian captivity. It was during this episode of the recurrent scattering of the tribes that the exiled leaders composed the Old Testament of the Bible (Torah) and the God of dynamic history was born.

Still another view of the historical origin of the Jews has the Jews fleeing famine and coming into the Biblical land of Goshen, which was the Nile Valley of Egypt, as a tribe of only 70 nomadic shepherds grouped in 12 families during the Biblical time of Joseph and leaving during the time of Moses around 1250 to 1400 B.C.E. at over 600,000 strong (Diop, 1974). As we stated earlier, if the clan came in at only 70 members and intermixed with the populations for over 400 years, then when they left they certainly looked more Kemetic Egyptian than otherwise. The Bible describes the Egyptians as the sons of Ham, clearly Blacks. In fact, the first son of Abraham, the "father" of the Jewish people, was Ishmael, offspring of Hagar, the Egyptian who was the handmaiden of Sarah, the wife of Abraham (Genesis 16: 1–6; 21: 9–13). We do not know which of these three accounts is the true story since Hebrew as a language did not become codified until three centuries after the official exodus from Egypt (Finch, 1990). *All we really know from these three origin stories is that the Hebrews at one point were compelled to leave Egypt, left Egypt with a monotheistic religion, looked much more like the indigenous Kemetic Egyptians than did the Hyksos or other peoples of Asia Minor, and certainly were deeply imbued with the philosophy, religious practices, and the symbols of the collective unconscious imbedded in the language of the ancient Egyptians.* They carried with them the seed and the genius of Egyptian religion and added to it their own particular genius. This was to flower thousands of years later when, after a period of contact with another group of Africans, this time the Moors of Spain, they are cast out or exiled again and the scattered tribes give rise to the mystical Kabbala.

Branchings Within the Family Tree

As the Jews expanded in Israel and mixed with more Semitic peoples, they became less Africoid in appearance. Later, as they moved into Europe, the Ashkenazi branch became even more European in physical appearance. In contemporary times, a significant percentage of Jews identify themselves as "White." Historically of course this has not always been so. Throughout the ages what held them together was a great and unifying idea and associated cultural practices. This, as we shall soon see, included a particular written tradition of scholarship, distinct ingroup religious practices, and certain familial values that were portable and, thereby, allowed them to wander through varied cultures, yet maintain a remarkable cohesiveness.

This last point about being portable is important. To be sure, the Africans and the Jews have a long and shared convoluted history. At times the Kemetic Egypto-Nubians and the Jews have been allies, as when the Sudanese Pharaoh Taharqa, the son of Pharaoh Piankhi of the 25th Dynasty, led an army into Mesopotamia and saved the Hebrew army on the battlefield of Palestine against the Assyrian Sennacherib (II Kings 19: 9). The great monument known as the column of Taharqa in Karnak records this battle and alliance. Then at other times they have been rivals, such as when the Arabs and Jews, the latter often called "Solomonids" by history, moved into areas of northern Ethiopia together as allies against the Africans, as the Roman episode crumbled and its legions were withdrawn to other places in their besieged empire. In 350 C.E., the Arab, Jewish, and other armies overran and destroyed Black Meroe. Ethiopia split into three states, Nobadae, Makuria, and Alwa. In between these dates the Jews were laced throughout the history of northern Africa. They were slaves of the Kemetic Egyptians for 430 years, then "liberated" by Moses. Captured by the Assyrian King Sargon II in 721 B.C.E., some of the Hebrew "tribes" were lost, since only 10 of the northern tribes are recorded. In 586 B.C.E. came the Babylonian exile, when king Nebuchadnezzar carried them off and destroyed the temple and Jerusalem. Then Cyrus conquered Babylon and allowed them to return and rebuild the temple under Zerubbabel. Then came the Persian domination, 538–332 B.C.E., which was eventually destroyed by Alexander the Great. The Ptolemies, Seleucids, and Egyptians from time to time invaded or menaced Israel. Then came the Romans under Julius Caesar and finally, in 70 C.E., under the Roman general Titus, Jerusalem was invaded again and the Jews scattered. Some went to southern Arabia, some through Egypt down to Ethiopia, and some to West Africa, where many believe they made contact with the Hausa, Ashanti, Yoruba, and Nok (Ammi, 1982). Some migrated up from North Africa into southern Spain. And some traveled northward into the steppes of Russia and even in small groups to the shores of India. They took on the look of the indigenous peoples there, exchanged ideas and practices, but always retained their portable religion, the monotheistic religion of the first liberator Moses. In the Western world they become clustered into three primary groupings, the Ashkenazim, the Sephardim, and the Mizrakhim. The last group, the Mizrakhim, settled in Greece, Turkey, the Balkans, and portions of the old Ottoman Empire.

This scattering of the Hebrew tribes is chronicled in their written portable history by their scholars. As we shall see in the European Middle Ages and the

Renaissance, this scattering of the tribes is integrated into a mystical vision of reunion and redemption. Being outcast from Egypt, then outcast from Israel, then outcast from medieval Spain, etc., led to a philosophy of exile as the worst nightmare of the soul. It became tied in with earlier notions of expulsion and, in a strange way, the vision of the collapse of history itself and, therein, the birth of the Western messianic urge in philosophy and psychology.

In medieval Europe, things were no better for the most part. The systematic hatred and vile persecution of the Jews became an entrenched part of the psyche of Christian Europe. This was despite the fact that Jews had never attacked any European civilization, that they were the so-called "chosen people" of their sacred book, the holy Bible, and that for a few Greeks and Romans in the New Testament of the Bible, there were no "White" people even noticed and written about in the book! During the medieval period Jews and women, too, were demonized. Jews were commonly portrayed as treacherous dissidents and greedy money handlers who infested the Christian landscape. These images percolated through art, literature, church sermons, and popular homilies (Gregg, 1997). Periodically it was open season on the Jews. The late Byzantine Empire saw mass murders of the Jews, as was the policy during episodes in the Crusades. Hatred and cyclic expulsion were common: England in 1290, France in 1306, Spain in 1492, Portugal in 1497, Frankfurt in 1614, and Vienna in 1670. Anti-Semitic pogroms were quasi-official in the Ukraine in 1648 and 1767, Odessa in 1871, Russia in 1881, and finally the city of Kishinev in 1903. Unlike African Americans during slavery and afterwards, the Jews did not appear to revolt or race-riot or otherwise overtly strike back at their tormentors. In these somewhat "passive" responses, the Jews were killed off with few consequences for the oppressor. Unlike Blacks, Jews did not riot or violently rebel and others generally did not physically fear the Jews. These episodes in their shared history find expression in their deep-seated fears of extermination. Nothing, of course, approached the Nazi Holocaust.

After the defeat of Germany during the First World War, scapegoating psychology had increased. The supposed plans of world Jewry to financially conquer the world were made popular in numerous pamphlets, most notably Alfred Rosenberg's 19th-century book *The Protocols of the Elders of Zion*. It gave credence to old hatreds and laid the foundation for the crematoriums of Dachau, Auschwitz, Bergen-Belsen, and the other hell realms. As a text of pure evil it ranks with the infamous Malleus Malefacarium, the cruel bible of the Inquisition which itself was written in 1496, a few years after the Jews were exiled from Spain. Over 25 million people perished in the Second World War. Some 5,900,000 Jews were murdered, 72 percent of Europe's Jews and 85 percent of Poland's. These episodes did not occur in Moorish Spain between 700 and 1400 C.E., nor were there such mass incidents in the parts of Africa where Jews lived, or for that matter in India, where some Jews had migrated.

What we will do in this chapter is draw parallels between the ancient Kemetic Egyptian contributions, those of the Hebrews who left, and their psychological and sociocultural relevance to a present-day form of science and cognition that had its roots deeply in Jewish scholarship and mystical thought. This fusion of Jewish mystical thought and scientific thinking in the latter part of the last century culminated in the brilliant inventions and investigation of psychoanalysis led by Freud and a close circle of Jewish intellectuals and illuminates (Bakan, 1958/1990).

It is significant that the word "Bible" is derived from the word *Byblos*, a city in the ancient empire of Egypt noted for its religious firmament. From the 42 laws of Maát codified by the Kemetic Egyptians, we can see the outline of the 10 Commandments of Moses (Asante, 1984). The ancient Egyptians in certain situations practiced the rite of circumcision. The word "Yahweh" is itself a reflection of an Egyptian lunar worship cult (Finch, 1990). That Moses was actually a Black Egyptian priest is not only supported by the ancient writers but also by none other than Sigmund Freud in his book, *Moses and Monotheism* (1939). When Freud came out with this book, he was greeted with almost universal anathema. However, the courage and insight of this great modern Jewish prophet and scientist cannot be ignored. Freud went far beyond the prevailing paradigm of material rationalism of his day and looked at the internal, mental, unconscious world and the deep racial memories that it keeps.

One last comment about the Jews of antiquity and the family of Moses. Classic Jewish religious teachings mention quite clearly that Moses' second wife, Zipporah, the daughter of Jethro, was a Kushite and that the siblings of Moses, Aaron, and Miriam had significant difficulty with his wife (Numbers 12:1). This is only covertly presented in the story of Moses that we see in the popular press and in movies. However, it is true. There were clearly family and sibling issues in the family of Moses concerning his marriage to someone of a different *ethnic* but not different *racial* group. All of this leads us to support the idea that Moses himself was perhaps not an ethnic Jew by birth, but rather became a hero of the Jews of the same larger racial group for both political and cultural reasons.

JEWS IN THE AMERICAS

For over a thousand years, Jews were the "niggers" of Europe. After the Roman Empire became officially Christian, the Jews were the only religious "minority" on the continent. Pressure increased to convert to the Roman

Catholic religion. Occasional massacres by mobs, Crusaders on their way to fight in the Holy Land, and local political bloodletting made life as a Jew a dangerous occupation. Still, life went on despite expulsions and persecutions. These contingencies, as we shall see, were woven into the intimate pattern of familial, financial, and shifting political alliances. Armed resistance was suicidal for them, so they either left the country, stayed in the ghettos, or converted. They looked, acted, spoke, dressed, and worshiped differently from the Christians of Europe, and so became their universal whipping boy, absorbing many of the usual disowned bodily and moral projections. This did not happen in Moorish Spain or in the African lands where the Jews lived.

The first Jews to come to the United States arrived during the colonial era. They were Sephardic Jews from Spain and Portugal, who had experienced persecution and murder under the Visigoths from the 6th to 8th century, then tolerance under the Moors, then renewed persecution under reunited Christian Spain beginning in 1492. Money and property stolen from Jews helped finance Columbus' voyages to the Americas. There were some 2,000 Sephardic Jews in the 13 colonies at the outbreak of the American Revolution. Like other European groups, the Jews, to some extent, were financially and structurally involved in the African slave trade in both North and South America, especially Brazil, West Africa, and Europe (Faber, 1994). They had financial holdings in several of the large northern European trading houses. They did not, however, invent the slave trade, nor did they control it, nor were there many large Jewish plantations.

The expulsion of the Jews from Spain and Portugal helped establish triangular links among the American colonies, Amsterdam, and Brazil. The Dutch in Brazil, Surinam, and Curaçao had a high Jewish element in the sugar plantations for a brief period. In the southern United States in 1830, there were 140 Jews among the over 57,000 slaveholders who owned 20 or more African slaves. The British Royal African Company, which transplanted the highest number of slaves to the New World, and the Dutch West India Company were *not* dominated by Jewish financiers. Jewish money was perhaps 1.6 to 2%, or at most 5%, of the wealth of these companies that trafficked in human misery and flesh.

After the Revolution, the Sephardic Jews were gradually overtaken by the Ashkenazic Jews, especially the German branch. These new Jews were scattered throughout northern and eastern Europe. The Sephardic Jews did not die out, however, some even going west. The German Ashkenazic and Sephardic Jews progressed well, immigration was steady, and by 1880, there were some 500,000 mostly German Jews in the United States. They were peddlers, semiskilled workers, and garment makers, many located in New York City.

By 1880, Ashkenazic Jews from Poland and later Russia began to arrive in large numbers. As a new group, they were looked down upon by the more established German Jews. Intermarriage was rare. Socioeconomic differences were strong. The usual ethnic identity dynamics around feeling embarrassed yet identified with, protective of and also wanting to help and "advance" the group all occurred. There were even religious and cultural differences, as well as differences in language and many values. However, the underground shared identity persisted. These new Eastern European Jews had begun to come on the tides set in motion by the most recent episode of cyclic Russian persecution. Used, then abused, then used again as tax collectors, then hated by the masses, then used as scapegoats again by everyone in Europe, the Jews saw America as a promised land. Catherine the Great of Russia, in 1781, established the Jewish Pale of Settlement, where the Jews had to live, thereby further limiting Jewish freedom. They were restricted from going "beyond the Pale," and could face death or have their children kidnapped. In 1881, the new czar again violently attacked the Jews, and over a 40-year period, 2 million Jews, clearly a third of all the Jews of Eastern Europe, came to the United States. Half were literate and largely urban.

They, too, crowded into already overcrowded slums. True, there were no official pogroms, no kidnapping and stealing of children to convert them to Russian Christianity, no group murders with little legal recourse, but there was discrimination, as with all new groups. Still, some deep cultural values and styles were quickly and usefully adapted to the American system. These were themes woven into the fabric of Jewish family and social-intellectual life on the new loom of the American experience. The reverence for learning, even among the poorly literate groups, flowered in the United States, leading many into the legal, medical, and other professions after a generation as semiskilled laborers. Skills as urban businessmen and financial managers expanded and took root in the unusually tolerant American soil. Jews, perhaps, advanced faster then any other group. This, in turn, led to more money, better education, and a premium placed on scholarship, business, and scientific pursuits. This progressive and literate approach, coupled with a fierce and living collective memory of ethnic oppression, led, perhaps, to a general embrace of liberal causes politically. American Jews, particularly those from eastern Europe, were very influential in the early days of American cinema. They began to provide a new common and collective canvas of images on which the American experience was painted. For the most part they projected a rational, progressive, and humanistic vision of America, in keeping with other liberal trends. Today they are highly represented in most phases of cinema production, from writers to producers to studio heads to directors. There was and is, however, an ambivalent identification with the history of African American oppression for subtle and complex reasons. Jews were prominent in progressive social movements in the United States, especially the early civil rights movements. Jews are, even today, highly represented in traditional liberal causes, as spiritual seekers, and especially among the young and alternative sexual life-style experimentation. As a group, they tend to be quite diverse and also quite sensitive to issues of oppression and survival. Even though Jews were only 2% of the American population, they were often 40% of the non-black freedom riders and their supporters in the civil rights movement. In general they feel fairly optimistic about America because it has been true to its promise of freedom and opportunity for them despite episodes of anti-Semitism. We will return to this later.

Whether for religious reasons or other, the Jews in their slums had a lower incidence of alcoholism, group violence, and disease based on sanitary conditions than other groups (Sowell, 1981). Religious practices around food and an emphasis on cleanliness, even in prayer situations, may have contributed to this. Also "dialogue" with the oppressor group tends to decrease actual violence. This value placed on verbal dialogue, dovetailing with certain religious and education values and styles, may have combined with these other trends to forge a unique ethnocultural and cognitive patterns in the Americas for the Jews. Because of a history of persecution, there tended to be a liberal and progressive political spirit among them, but also always a deeper ambivalence as to their real and permanent status. This reflects a perpetual sense of vulnerability. After all, as late as the 1940s in a modern European state, Nazi Germany, within a few years millions of "assimilated Jews" could be officially murdered and few in the world seemed to give a damn.

FAMILIAL PATTERNS AND THE COGNITIVE STYLE OF PSYCHODYNAMIC THINKING

The question as to whether culture and behavior influence cognitive styles is as much a philosophical debate as a scientific one. In such an atmosphere, any kind of absolutism is atavistic. When a group phenomenon of any kind is measured, reflected upon, or merely observed, trends and tendencies emerge out of the chaos. This is as much the case in quantum mechanics as in epidemiology. Diversity and specificity are as comfortable with each other as unity in complexity.

No one would argue that Africans have not developed a different use of the dream than did Native Americans, even though biologically the dreams all arose from the same place. In fact, African Americans, when in contact with European musical instruments—e.g., brass instruments, piano, bass, etc.—created a unique idiom, jazz. In the area of medicine and ethnic groups, epidemiology studies reflect significant differences in groups. Beyond factors such as nutrition, climate, environment, socioeconomic forces, and related influences, genetics also has an influence. There is a significantly higher incidence of sickle cell anemia in African Americans than others; a much higher incidence of Tay-Sachs disease among East European Jews than others; a higher incidence of manic-depressive illness in some populations, etc. Finally, groups may have powerful cultural and cognitive styles that influence behavior and conceptual systems. These are all different aspects of our unity in diversity and the contributions we all make to the human family. A strong group or ethnic style—e.g., African American idioms creating jazz, rock-and-roll, etc.—can often lend its genius to other groups to be either taken in, expanded, restyled, or whatever other permutation. This influence arises out of the group's history and cultural dynamics, familial style, and both overt and covert values and aspirations. We believe in a diversity of cultural, cognitive, and intellectual styles (Galtung, 1981) that can, at specific junctures of history and climate, lead to a dynamic creativity and novel insight.

It is also abundantly clear that a "diversity" of cognitive styles is a dynamic, changing process and that abstractions about a hierarchy of intelligence based on race and ethnicity is both embarrassing and absurd at best. Before World War II, Jews scored significantly lower on intelligence tests than average Americans; now they score higher. In fact, IQ scores for many immigrant groups new to America—e.g., Greeks, Portuguese, Poles, Italians, etc.—were lower than "average." With socioeconomic advancement and smaller families, the scores increased. Today, the highest scores are found among the Asian groups, particularly the Japanese and Chinese. We must move beyond these diversions and embrace the genius of diversity in order to look at the deeper currents of identity and intelligence that infuse this process.

Psychoanalysis, arising as it did in the last century with Freud and his followers, is an extraordinarily brilliant synthesis of not only the then-contemporary scientific ideas, but also of deep and esoteric Hebrew spiritual teachings and also some of the folklore of Jewish culture, particularly the culture expressed in Europe (Bakan, 1958/1990). In particular, we draw your attention to the Talmudic methodology of seeking the source of truth that is assumed to be hidden in the source text. A great deal of value is placed on seeking out the "original meanings of things" in the Talmudic methodology. In addition there is a *high value placed on endless interpretations and commentary on the processes of the original text*. We also find in a study of Jewish culture and Jewish family styles certain themes that seem to reappear in or parallel the methodology of psychodynamic thinking.

One of the brilliant contributions of psychodynamic thinking is its elucidation of psychosomatic and hypochondriacal symptomatology. We note from certain researchers that hypochondriasis is a common clinical presentation among Jewish populations, with Jews, somewhat more than many other ethnic groups as a style, often complaining about their symptoms and constantly seeking out medical drugs and doctors. However, even in the process of doing so there is often observed a sigh that signifies that they really did not expect any better treatment from life (Zborowski, 1969). This capacity to understand suffering from a cognitive and intellectual point of view can be seen as a hallmark typifying many aspects of the Jewish family constellation and its values. The idea is that suffering is a fundamental part of life and is a shared value in both family and culture (Hertz & Rosen, 1982), or as the popular Yiddish aphorism says, "Shver zu zein a yid" ("It's tough to be a Jew").

In the Jewish family and culture, a great deal of honor and value is placed on a learned man. He is often called a "lehler" and a "hacham." This in all likelihood was due to the fact that Jews placed a high value on learning given the fact that *learning itself was portable* and the Jews of necessity by way of systematic and brutal persecution were always on the move. Portable learning also kept the tradition alive and helped bind the nation together in a kind of culture of shared mentality, just as Ifa and other hidden religious traditions did to the slaves brought over to the Americas. In the ghettos and small towns, or shtetls, of Eastern Europe, prestige, authority, and respect came from a deep study of the ancient texts and commentaries (Dimont, 1978; Zborowski & Herzog, 1952). Success was often measured by intellectual and academic achievement, leading, in modern times, to an emphasis on being a professional, social status, and money. "My son, the doctor." This is rooted in the ancient honored tradition of learning and the study of the Torah.

Michael Lerner (Lerner & West, 1996) points out how the Roman-Hellenistic society that militarily subdued Judea as conquerors tried to impose the value of the gymnasium on the Jews. To be a warrior or sportsman in Hellenistic society was a high value, the worship of the body. The Jews rebelled against this. To be a "real man" in a society in which one cannot really compete, one became a scholar, a reader of texts—primarily the Talmud with its complex interwoven laws and its seemingly endless, obsessive textual debates. In this way one demonstrated his prowess in the field of the written word and its interpretation. It was also a "safe" pursuit to the ruling army and society. Lerner suggests that after 2,000 years of this cultural milieu at the hands of one ruler or another, that certain verbal and intellectual skills became highly valued and refined, exactly the same skills that make for success in a modern capitalist state in which one has some moderate degree of freedom. While in some contexts this mildly obsessive intellectual style can become a kind of "questioning neurosis," in the disciplines of law, business, and science it can become a great tool navigating the waters. In the United States and to some extent in Europe, this verbal intellectual form of educational achievement was later transmuted into society to include secular study, even sometimes to the exclusion of religious study. The student was expected to not merely be good, but to excel (Rosenberg, 1965). Thus in the wider cultural and familial context of constant persecution, harassment, and endless insecurity and movement, a very high value was placed on financial, intellectual, and educational achievement, which are each portable and hopefully cannot be destroyed.

In the Middle Ages of Europe, this learning was focused not only on intellectual pursuits but also in the narrow external world that they were allowed by way of usury and money. This led to the emphasis historically in Europe of the Jews being allowed to lend money, since Christians were barred from doing so. The practice of moneylending fell to the Jews specifically because the Christians felt the practice was "dirty" (Marcus, 1960; Tuchman, 1978). The perception was thereby nourished that Jews were "unclean" and un-Christian, but of course rich. This led to the inevitable persecution and brutal anti-Semitic outbreaks against the Jews, particularly during financially and historically difficult times. Often this malignant rage was sponsored and directed by the European governments for their own needs. The Spanish Inquisition and expulsion of 1492 and the Holocaust of World War II are merely the most egregious of these periodic episodes. For Jews money, jewelry, and other valuables were liquid and thereby could be accumulated and moved very quickly, something that land obviously could not be. In order to survive and deal with endless persecution and harassment, certain styles by necessity became reinforced in Jewish culture much more so than others and survive as a cultural motif up to this day. More than anything else, learning and scholarship did.

For any oppressed group, it is a survival skill to understand the mind, behavior, and emotions of your oppressor in order to protect yourself when needed. The Black house slave turned this into an art. The Jews turned it into a science. A high value is placed on "dialogue" if at all possible with the oppressor for Jews. In the United States there is also a none-too-subtle message for a Jewish son to seek to be a doctor, a lawyer, or a successful businessman. These skills, again, are portable. In the United States, a relatively "safe" environment for Jews, these dynamic forces have led to both socioeconomic status and "White privilege" but also to the perpetual sense that one is still vulnerable and that it could all vanish in a political crisis. For an African American, the parallel message is to seek to be an athlete or entertainer (often music or comedy). In both cases, we can see the cultural and political-historical roots and rewards for such pursuits. On the plantation, the emphasis was on physical prowess, stamina, and amusing the master with slave antics and sometimes music. Teaching, reading, writing, and invention were dangerous activities, often even against the law. Even after emancipation, educated African Americans were viewed as "uppity Negroes" most likely to be organizers of resistance to the system and therefore watched closely with suspicion. Many were lynched in the shadows of Jim Crow, making the status of an educated Black man perilous. Cornel West believes this has reinforced a certain anti-intellectualism among African Americans (Lerner & West, 1996). Look for yourself. There are today only a handful of famous African American doctors and scientists, while there are correspondingly many entertainers and athletes of genius. Their towering figures can be seen on buildings overlooking our largest cities. They rush at us everyday on the television in commercials and sports. Children and adolescents, Black and White, have the walls of their rooms covered in their images! Yet how many famous basketball, baseball, football, track and field, etc., superstars are Jewish? On the other hand, how many scientists, doctors, and scholars are Jewish? One of four Nobel prizes in the United States has been won by a Jew (Sowell, 1981). Jews are highly represented on university faculties. These trends are reinforced by family values, mass cultural imagery, and economic opportunity. In both groups, there is the motif of the forced Diaspora and the sense of being "captive exiles in Babylon."

This shared feeling of alienation from the dominant culture, constant tension and testing, plus a painful history of overt brutal treatment by Europeans drew many Jews in the United States to African American trends, especially in music and art. Again, Jews in Europe served the same psychic functions as the Africans did in the United States. Jewish elements can be found in Tin Pan Alley music; the swing era of Benny Goodman, Woody Herman, Artie Shaw; the music of George Gershwin's *Rhapsody in Blue*, *An American in Paris*, *Porgy and Bess*; the songs of Irving Berlin, Stoller, Leiber, etc. (Steingroot, 1994). The list can go on. African Americans, on the other hand, deeply identified with the Biblical "stranger in a strange land" and sought a Moses, a deliverer from slavery. The shared history is deeper than we know, and it includes religious and psychospiritual traditions of the Black Hebrews, the Rastafarians, and several others. Some even see it in the structure of Jewish klezmer music and jazz, with their "pentatonic, Lydian modal, blues or minor scale, a vocal approach to instrumental timbre and improvisational and rhythmic elements which is more fully developed in jazz" (Steingroot, 1994). Jews of course were not the only group to mine the vein of genius embedded in African American music. During the 1920s and 1930s alone, the cross-fertilization of European "classical" and emerging American jazz led to schools such as "Novelty" and others in which Gershwin's *Rhapsody in Blue*, *An American in Paris*, and *Concerto in F* appeared. Add to this Dana Suesse's *Afternoon of a Black Fawn* and *Jazz*

Concerto in D Major for combo and orchestra; Aaron Copland's *Clarinet Concerto*, Stravinsky's *Ebony Concerto*, Zez Confrey's "Kitten on the Keys" and "Humorestless" (a musical twist on Dvorak's *Humoresque* and "Negro" music imitator Stephen Foster's "Old Folks At Home"!), and many others, and you see quickly how the vein was richly exploited by non–African Americans of a wide spectrum. It continues in almost every form of American music. One great difference between Blacks and Jews in particular in the Americas, however, is that the Blacks were forbidden to learn the written and symbol language of their culture, were intentionally kept politically disorganized, had their families owned and sold off on a financial whim, and were overtly discouraged from the traditions of scholarship and science. These trends, again, were allowed to the Jews of America, and it is reflected in our society today.

Perhaps as a result of some of these cultural and political dynamics that survived in Jewish families in particular, in terms of learning, argumentation, and intellectual pursuits in the study of the Torah and Talmud, we find a cognitive style in which a great deal of emphasis is placed on the verbal examination of various interpretations and meanings in order to arrive at the understanding of the original intent of the feeling or argument. In the Jewish family the parent is often looking for the child to be an "illui," or genius. In the orthodox or religious community, the little illui who can deliver learned discussions of the Hebrew texts, or drushas, is highly praised. There is the famous passage in the Zohar in which Rabbi Abba and the other Rabbis turn to a young boy for elucidation of an esoteric "midnight" issue. They hope the child will speak and clarify, will be the voice of the lamp (Scholem, 1949). This tradition, we believe, has some relevance to the value placed on "insight" and the collective family unconscious origin of psychoanalysis. In Jewish families, the children's insights and opinions are highly valued especially at the Sedar, and it would not be unusual for parents to take great pride in the contributions of their children to the solution of a problem (Hertz & Rosen, 1982). Many believe that this, in addition to other issues, such as less clear-cut boundaries between parents and children, has led to an emphasis on verbally expressing thoughts and feelings much more so than in other ethnic groups. Indeed, expressing thoughts and feelings emerges into a method of catharsis and becomes an important aspect of family interaction. Thus the emphasis on self-expression, high achievement, verbal skills, and interpreting phenomenon, and also the willingness to express pain and anger, form a pattern typical of Jewish families. Zborowski (1969) indicated in his *People in Pain* that Jewish Americans more than any other ethnic group seemed to enjoy the opportunity to express their negative feelings in a doctor–patient type of relationship. It was seen as an expression of intelligence and compassion. This in combination with an intellectual tradition of interpretation, and seeking the intent and the original meaning of things, can lead to a certain style that is, we believe, conducive to the intellectual culture of psychoanalysis. At its worst it becomes a form of obsessive thinking. At its best it becomes a method for deeper study.

ROOT TECHNIQUES OF PSYCHOANALYSIS AND MYSTICISM

In the Hebrew tradition, both the tree of knowledge and the tree of life stood in the Garden of Eden. The tree of knowledge gave the fruit of rationality and reason, the tree of life gave vision, spiritual teaching, and direct contact with the luminous divine. For centuries these two currents flowed through the ocean of Jewish mystical thought. The flower of Jewish mysticism, however, Kabbalism, has many of its roots in the fertile soil of early and medieval Spain. The Moors, we said earlier, brought in new ideas, new foods, new technologies, and new sciences into a sleeping Europe and set the stage for the Renaissance. From India, the use of the zero made higher mathematics possible. Trade in ideas and technologies was encouraged in Islam, ideas often explicitly outlawed by the Church in Europe. The range of the Moors' commercial contacts stretched from India in the East, to Spain in the North of Europe, to below Timbuktu and Mali in the heartland of Africa. The Jews, as scholars and merchants, were protected in Spain by the Moors. These Black African Moors also had access to older African traditions, especially those in West Africa and Kemetic Egypt, which they, no doubt, discussed with the Jews. These practices included the methods of Ifa divination, the creative recombining of symbols and sounds in disciplined states of meditation, solfege, and a positive religious association to trance states and being "possessed" by a luminous intelligence, what is sometimes thought of as becoming "full of God." In the more cognitive mode, the psychoanalysis of the early Freud is an offspring of this long tradition.

In particular there is a technique in the Kabbalistic tradition going all the way back to Abulafia in the Middle Ages in Spain in which there is methodologically an interpretation of content based upon making certain *associations* to the original meaning of things in order to elicit the hidden truth. Abulafia was born in Spain in 1240 C.E., over a thousand years after the dawn of Rabbinical Judaism and its greatest founder, Rabbi Akiba, in Palestine. He spent his youth with his father in the study of the Torah, commentary, Mishnah, and Talmud. He reportedly studied Maimonides' great book, *The Guide for the Perplexed*. He also immersed himself deeply in the Kabbalistic tradition, particularly the Sefer Yetzirah (Bakan, 1958/1990). Significantly enough, in his early thirties Abulafia became interested in the prophetic spirit and in mysticism. He believed that the inner forces of man were bound in as a result of his ordinary daily activity. In Abulafia's writings there is an explicit emphasis on understanding various locks and knots that keep the human being from making complete contact with the wider mystical cosmos. His mysticism led him to seek to overcome these knots. This, of course, is a form of Yogic meditation.

The techniques of untying these knots involved particular physical postures, controlled breathing, and mental states in Abulafia's methodology. When successful, the initiate had progressively less contact with the world of the senses, in some instances even severing all ties to the senses, like the formal practices of pratyahara or sense withdrawal of Yoga. This condition stimulates the harmonious movement of thoughts toward one of nearly pure thought, like the movement of pure music that is without words, but dense in perceived pattern and meaning. This meaning apprehension, then, leads one to a fuller participation in the secret hidden name of God, the word that is the unseen but all-ordering vibrational matrix of the universe (Scholem, 1941/1974). It was a powerful technique. Perhaps because Abulafia was not a trained rabbinical scholar, but rather self-taught and gifted, his system was not chained to the tribal limits of religious Judaism. His method was open to the world and indeed this Kabbalism opened humans to the world beyond it.

The other great branch of Jewish mysticism was and is Hasidism, perhaps the most pietistic movement in Judaism, founded by the Baal Shem Tov, Israel ben Eliezer, in the 18th century. It began in the Carpathian border areas of Walachia, Volhynia, and Pololia among the lower classes, and was partially a reaction to the collapse of the Sabbatian messianic movement and domination by the wealthy, privileged upper-class Jews of Eastern Europe. With a charismatic leader, it spread quickly, emphasizing intense religious devotion, humility, joy, and purity of heart, and above all, *direct contact with the luminous Divine in estatic song and dance.* The Baal Shem Tov, whose name meant "master of the good name," due to his knowledge of the *secret name of God,* taught, like Jesus, with parables. Some of his later followers added Hasidic folk tunes called niggunim to the method. The devotee sought to perceive God immanent throughout all manifest nature. Eventually, after the passing of the great Baal Shem Tov, elements of his doctrines were integrated with the more formal doctrines of Isaac Luria's Kabbalistic teachings by his successor, Dov Baer of Mezhirich.

In mystical Judaism, both early Kabbala and later Hasidic teachings, great interest is placed on experiences of light, which are associated with wisdom (Steinberg, 1993). The Kabbala itself with its 22 "paths of concealed glory" is partially rooted in the Sefer Yetzirah and the tree of life is, upon deeper reflection, actually an esoteric map of consciousness itself. The emphasis on a strong ethical and moral base prior to mystical practice is again similar to the early lower rungs of various Yoga practices of Kemetic Egypt and India. This prior moral structure is necessary if later powerful energies are to be unleashed in the soul's ascent. These Kabbalistic mystics report experiences of automatic asana or postures, pranayama or breathing patterns, sounds and holy wind and unusual abilities becoming manifest. The spheres from the Kabbalistic tree of life becomes luminous and appear to be similar to the Indian chakra system. (See Figure 28.) Above the "head" and deep within the secret "heart," the Kabbalists see luminous beings and forces, and focus this through their own cultural lens. These observations and correlations appear to place Kabbalistic mysticism within the great cross-cultural tradition of the Kundalini phenomenon, and show it to be another branch of the ancient hominid science of transcendence. Abulafia, on some level, was no doubt aware of this.

David Bakan (1958/1990) sees in the writings of Abulafia the origin of the psychodynamic theory of repression and the role of the ego in repression. In addition there is a particular interpretative method based on taking "liberties with the letters of the alphabet." We remember that this is also a technique that the ancient Kemetic Egyptians used with numbers and letters (King, 1990). "The pharaonic texts are rich in examples of litanies playing a magical role through repetition of sounds in words and through wordplay" (Schwaller de Lubicz, 1961, p. 167). In other words, during the process of interpretation while meditating, the letters of the text are separated and recombined; new themes arise by way of this combining and separating. *There was a sustained belief in the inner mystical logic of letters.* Intuition and revelation are superordinate over reason and ratiocination. We see this tradition even in Kabbalistic interpretations and traditions today. In Abulafia's method, he came to believe that these reformulations and these reinterpretations based upon association and recombination were not merely "whimsical" but corresponded to a hidden and deeper logic that reflected the original intent of the writers of the sacred texts. We find this parallel, again, very similar to the "logic" that Freud would find in understanding the symptoms and dreams that emerged from the unconscious. Remember that the unconscious was not the original creation or discovery of Sigmund Freud. The ancient Kemetic Egyptians were well aware of the dynamic process of the unconscious (Hourning, 1986; King, 1990). Also, there is a tradition in Western romantic thinking of the unconscious, particularly in the writings of Arthur Schopenhauer.

This operational use of the unconscious in both Kemetic and Hebrew mysticism can be traced back to the time of the pharaohs between 5000 and 2000 B.C.E. in the dynastic period. The pharaohs were initiated into the mysteries of Ra, the earlier solar principle of evolution from light. Some 1,500

FIGURE 28. Kabbalistic Tree of Life.

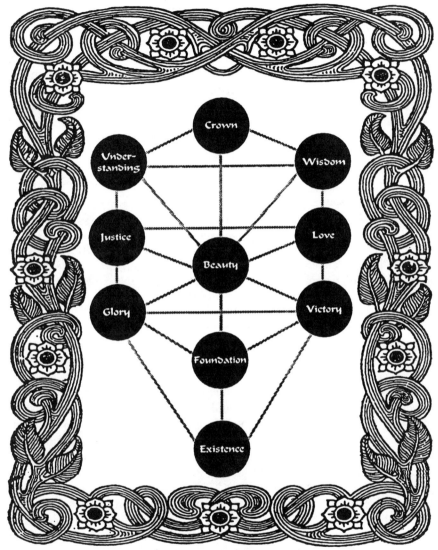

Each sphere on the tree of life is symbolic of a special power, and the appropriate meditation on each sphere is believed to help that special being-force-capacity to radiate and fulfill itself. It is similar to the Yogic chakra system in terms of the progression of subtle energy and states of mind. (Copyright © 1999 Teachers College Press, Columbia University)

years after the beginning of the dynastic period, the dominance of Ra was challenged by another solar deity named Aton, which involved a political crisis in which the Hebrews were eventually to be politically and theologically embroiled. When the Jews left, they took this with them. What is crucial is that the Exodus from Egypt may have gone toward Israel with some element moving toward the western parts of Africa. This is because in Ifa there are so many striking similarities to ancient Egypt cosmology and some aspects of early Hebrew mysticism. There appears to be a striking similarity between the divination systems of Ifa and the Ancient Essene sect of Palestine. The number systems are too close for mere coincidence (Fatunmbi, 1991). Both are based on the same 256 marks used to organize the manifest forces of nature. These suggest a root system of which there are many interconnecting branches, some of which, through the Kabbala and other sacred writings, reached into Abulafia's time. During his day the Moorish-Islamic caravans had contact with the medieval West African empires of the interior and the coast. The Ifa system was known to have been in active use in these regions and to have traveled along the trade routes with other ideas and goods. The Black Hebrews have their own chronology of dispersion and influence from ancient times to areas in Egypt-Ethiopia and West Africa, especially to the West African peoples of the Ashanti, Yoruba, Nok, Hausa, and Songhai (Ammi, 1982).

A second and extremely important method in Abulafia's work was the process of "jumping and skipping." In this process the "interpreter" uses a method very similar to free association to move from one concept to another. It is not completely "free association" but rather moving from one association to another by way of certain rules (Scholem, 1941/1974). Each new move opens up another new move and new area. The "logic" is a certain kind of formal logic, not necessarily material in is nature. However, within these new spheres the mind may freely associate from one situation and image to another. The jumping unites the different elements and guides the associations. This can lead to rather unusual results and leads to a deepening or a "widening of consciousness." This jumping and skipping, called dillug and kefitsah by Abulafia, brings to light "hidden meanings" in the mind and "it liberates us from the prison of the natural sphere and leads us to the boundaries of the divine sphere" (Scholem, 1941/1974, p. 136). Indeed all the other methods are seen as preparations for this particular method.

This practice was partially known to the early Hebrews of Egypt when they left with the priest, Moses, during the Exodus. Moses was a "prince of Egypt" and a scholar of the great traditions of the temple Per Ankh at Heliopolis. It is highly unlikely he choose to express his deepest thoughts in the script of a slave people of the era. Hebrew as a written script did not appear until 300 years after the Exodus, and so the jumping and skipping and taking liberties recombining letters has some of its roots in the Kemetic language (Schwaller de Lubicz, 1961). The later Hebrews both seemed to *retain* and significantly *expand* this series of techniques, and added to the wealth of human mystical literature. In some sense, it may be an attempt to reach our roots as a species and speak the Mother Tongue.

In the process of doing these series of practices, the "interpreter" puts himself in a quiet and meditative state, almost a state that we might describe as "evenly suspended attention." This technique of "evenly suspended attention" was later taken up by Sigmund Freud (Epstein, 1984). It is also interesting in this context that it has a certain affinity to the Buddhist meditative tradition of Vipassana, where one's mind is completely opened to whatever emerges from it. By continuing along in this process the mind becomes more intense and focused in the moment. The belief is that the stronger the intellectual movement within this current, the weaker would be the person's external degree of concentration. As the mind becomes more intensely and internally preoccupied it becomes less concerned with external processes. This has a striking affinity to the Yogic techniques of sensory withdrawal, contemplation, and absorption, called dyhana.

This methodology intensifies the internal state and at the very least awakens energy along the spinal line. As we said earlier, when external sensory withdrawal occurs, it is similar to the Yogic technique pratyahara, and the "awakened energy" is called pranothana. It may evolve into a full Kundalini awakening, but if this occurs there must also be a transcendence of thought itself, including mental associations and interpretations. The *failure* to do this leads to heightened verbal associations and mental insights, but also to more anxiety and ambivalence in emotional style and a tendency to cultivate obsessive ideas in relation to the flow of life energy.

In Abulafia's method, the inner intensity leads, when successful, to the full union or Yoga of the human intellect at its highest stages with the wider cosmic field of influence. The flow of this energy into the vessel of the self, the hidden heart, floods it with the prophetic vision. This is accompanied by techniques of breathing and is parallel or an expression of Yoga (Scholem, 1941/1974). Certain postures, as we said, are sometimes spontaneously assumed in this technique, along with a conditioned state of consciousness that opens to what is beyond it. The spiritual forces of the universe are contacted "above" the usually enfolded realms of order in consciousness. The vibrational affinities established by the techniques open the practitioner to seven levels or planes of experience. The intelligent forces are personalized according to the lens of lineage and history, but the phenomena behind them are the same. The Kabbalistic seers sees angels and others, the Tantric yogi sees dakinis, the Christian sees the saints, and the Ifa diviners and disciplines see the Orishas and may even embody or be possessed by them. In each case, the resonate vibratory state of the individual consciousness has been transcended and a way toward that which is beyond it is opened.

Cultivating a sense of "awe" is critical in this method. Cultivation of this *sense of awe* has a psychophysiological as well as psychospiritual manifestation. It awakens the energies associated with Kundalini and is similar to the generation of the great bliss in Tantra and the Mahamudra lineage. In Ifa, the sense of "awe"—and sometimes during initiation, "aweful"—is generated. When the sense of "awe" in Ifa is stabilized at the highest level, the devotee enters lae-lae, a form of Turyia or Samadhi. Behind them all is the luminous serpent mother Kundalini.

Finally, in Abulafia's kabbalistic writings and, especially, in the relationship of the student to the Kabbalistic teacher, we find an extremely important precursor to the idea found in psychodynamic thinking of "transference." In the process of deep scholastic study both the teacher and the student become fused in a higher relationship and identification with God. When this is successful it ends up paradoxically as a transcendent self-identification. In this state the man and the Torah become identified in classical Jewish mysticism (Scholem, 1941/1974).

David Bakan finds in this tradition a tendency to become absorbed in introspective analysis, particularly self-analysis. In the best traditions this technique can be seen as a way to cleanse the conscious and the unconscious mind. It breaks away the "knots" separating the inner principle from the divine principle. However, more than anything else, we are drawn to a striking parallel between this method of cognition and thinking and the later analysis of the transference relationship. Given that Freud was a Jew in the tradition of 19th-century European Judaism, lived in a Jewish community, and was aware of Jewish persecution and Jewish history, it is not unreasonable to believe he would be at least unconsciously aware of these phenomena. David Bakan is of the opinion that Freud knew very well what he was doing and that if he put an overt emphasis on the fact that this was Jewish philosophy in the guise of science that politically speaking psychoanalysis in anti-Semitic Vienna would go nowhere. Freud believed in a collective racial memory, a universal language of dreams, and did not want to be limited to ethnopsychiatry. He used the tools of this lineage, the expertise of a medical scientist, and the eye of a poet to look more deeply into the soul of every man.

The Berakoth and Zohar

The sirens of attention in Jewish intellectual thought often sing in the tradition of multiple interpretations of situations and meanings. This idea of a multiple interpretation is contained in the Berakoth (Simon, 1948). This is particularly noteworthy in connection with the interpretation of dreams. We already knew that there were many connections between Freud's psychoanalytic theory of dream interpretation and the traditional views of dreams scattered throughout the classic Jewish religious texts (Frieden, 1990). In the Berakoth, however, two fundamental principles of dream interpretation are rather significant. The first one is that all dreams have meaning. This is an assumption that is deeply held in the tradition. Dreams are believed to implicitly have within them the germs of wish fulfillment, word play, sexual significance, and, above all, are deeply symbolic, with streams of good and evil impulses present in them. The second basic principle is that the *interpretation* of the dream itself has priority over the dream originally. In other words, the interpretation of the dream might be more important than the actual dream itself. This again is a reflection of the high value placed on seeking not only the original intent and hidden meaning of things in reality, sacred scripture, and now dreams, but also on the extensive commentary itself. This reinforces a tremendous belief in dream interpretation and a belief that, as Jung later said, an unanalyzed dream is like an unopened letter.

In the Berakoth, as far as this mystical tradition is concerned, word play is an intregal and extremely valuable method in the search for the hidden meaning of the Torah. Each word is believed to have latent content or meaning. As said in the Zohar, "how assiduously should one ponder on each word of the Torah, for there is not a single word in it which does not contain allusions to this supernal holy name, not a word which does not contain many mysteries, many aspects, many roots, many branches" (Zohar III, cited in Bakan, 1958/1990, p. 172). The Torah is written in such a way with vowels and consonants that many interpretations can be made. Finally in the Zohar, one of the primary texts of the Kabbalistic tradition, which began around 1200 C.E., and probably was written by Moses de Leon, there are many references to plays on numbers. There are plays on words formed by the Kabbalistic methods of exegesis, plays on the value of numbers called *gematria*, and a deep involvement with symbolism in the search for the original meaning and intent inherent in this cognitive approach to reality (Bakan, 1958/1990; Scholem, 1941/1974). These enfolded symbolic meanings of the letters, words, and sentences and their correspondences based on certain numeric values assigned to them is also believed to be discerned by the notarikon and temurah methods in addition to gematria. Temurah in particular talks about things or ideas and their opposite or negation being enfolded in the same word and only differentiated by the sound emphasis when spoken. Things could easily mean their opposite in other words, a phenomena observed in the ancient Egyptian language and felt by Freud to be one of the dynamic ways the unconscious operates. It is the search for the origin of things in language transformations and symbols. We believe that it is even a search through the innumerable funnels of speech for the river of the Mother Tongue. The Zohar, you see, is really the book of splendor, the book of radiance! It is the mystical heart of the Kabbala.

In the Zohar and Kabbalism in general it is believed that there is a

> veil before the light of God. In the veil are the souls, deeds, and the past and future of the universe itself. The self in this universe is a vessel of the infinite light of God, or En-Sof. This vessel of the self is already full and perfect as it is. The "work" in the world is to transform the vessel itself in order to manifest even more of the divine light. This filling of the vessel will increase its capacity and by this paradox become involved in the co-creation of the cosmos. Indeed, the body and mind are the vessel of the light of the soul, so . . . strengthen the vessel! (Cooper, 1994)

If one's eyes are truly open, angels are everywhere reveals the book of splendor! Each blade of grass has an angel hovering over it murmuring "grow, grow." Each thought creates an energy bundle that reverberates throughout the universe. Every word and movement of the being creates an angel, some skillfully created, some not. "Nature" you see is but the shadow of God (Cooper, 1994). This teaching revelation has imbedded in it the ancient Hermetic insight that "as above, so below," a vision rooted in the ancient world. The deep-core messianic tradition then is really about the end of human history as we know it and the breakthrough to a new world consciousness. This is the real message of the Christ, of Osiris, of Elijah, of the Zohar and Kabbala! The Mishna, Midrashim, or oral teaching stories, and the Talmud had all been studied a thousand years before the Zohar. But the Zohar captured the soul of the faithful. It saw spirits everywhere. It held that prior to creation, there was an accident and the divine was scattered. All people, including the Jews, were scattered and in exile from God. The scattered each had a divine or celestial spark of spirit in them. To be whole again, the scattered sparks need to be recovered. Righteous behavior led to the restoration of the sparks, and this was redemption. This vision awakens deep archetypal currents in all peoples.

There is one final area that we would make mention of that seems to have significant influence on this tradition. In the Jewish mystical and intellectual tradition, particularly in the Sabbatian tradition,[10] there is the doc-

---

10. Sabbatai Zevi was a messianic figure in the Jewish communities of the mid 1600s. A charismatic personality who could move the masses to religious ecstasy, under pressure of death he converted to Islam and disillusioned thousands of hopeful Jews. This messiah failed in the supposed dawn of the new millennium in 1666. This caused a profound negative reaction to blind religious faith that found expression in a new faith, rationalism. However, this crisis did begin social and religious reforms which filtered into political currents in the liberal enlightenment of Europe (Bakan, 1958/1990).

trine of the necessity for the descent into evil in order to attain spiritual liberation. It is a doctrine which has implications for both the 19th-century Victorian approach to sexuality and also the notion of going "down into the unconscious." This is exactly what psychoanalysis did—it went down into the sexual and into that which was "below." The belief was that this full exploration, undeterred by fear or suppression of the truth, would lead to the real truth and to illumination. *This form of mystical tradition and belief shares with rationalism the conviction that reality, all reality, can actually be understood, approached, and completely comprehended in thought itself* (Bakan, 1958/1990). From our particular point of view, this seems to be not only the brilliant and pioneering legacy of psychoanalysis; but also this belief that all reality can be apprehended in thought reveals implicitly the limits of the psychoanalytic vision and insight. For it identifies reality with thought. It is our assertion here that thought is but one of the many manifestations of reality and that there are many other forms of understanding that can coincide with thought that are sometimes superior to the methodology of thought for apprehending the radiant texture of reality.

The last point should be emphasized. For it directly gives rise to the parallel notion in psychoanalysis that everything sane and rational can be understood within the confining structure of the ego. It implicitly assumes that what is "beyond the ego" is by definition regressive. It is by definition regressive and irrational. The world, it is assumed, can be understood by the ego and that all that is not ego is primitive or archaic. Implicit in psychoanalysis as practiced by the early practitioners is the view that the ego is the highest level of human cognition, development, and experience. This notion of the ego as the highest manifestation of human consciousness and intelligence leads inescapably to the position of psychological dualism, reductionism, and a dialectical approach to reality. We mentioned in earlier chapters that dualism and the dialectical approach were amplified in early Greek philosophy but were only one form of Kemetic philosophy (Diop, 1991; James, 1954). Kemetic philosophy certainly did have the seeds of dualism and dialectical thinking, but given the transcendental basis of that older approach it was not limited to dualism or dialectical thinking. The dualism and dialectical thinking, which were amplified by the Greeks, was done at the expense of the dissociation of revelation and the spiritual impulse from reality (Schwaller de Lubicz, 1961).

In the mystical writings of the Jewish seers there is a great and healthy elevation and recognition of pan-sexuality. This is the case in psychoanalysis (Bakan, 1958/1990). Also in psychoanalysis we see, arising directly from this view of pan-sexuality, the notion of sublimation. Sublimation as understood by Freud is the changing of the sexual or libidinal impulse into "higher" forms. These higher forms of expression in psychoanalysis are understood as rationalism and insight, and they are believed to be best expressed in terms of thought and words.

Given the view that what is inside of man is held inside of man by external forces, and also given the political and historical position of the Hebrews, particularly in Europe, an inherent "conflict model" of man, society, and culture arises. There is no bedrock or inherent concept of harmony or Maát except as it expresses itself in ultimate conditions.

Because there is an inherent conflict model, a basic belief in dualism and reductionism, and a belief that the ego is the highest form that the human being can manifest, there tends to arise in psychoanalysis at its limits a denial of the sublime dimension to human experience. This is not the case in the Jewish mystical traditions, but it is in primarily Jewish intellectual thought. In Jewish mystical thought we do not find a denial or ambivalence of the psychic dimensions and the religious dimensions. However in psychoanalysis, with a few notable exceptions, we find by and large not only a denial but outright hostility to the psychic and the religious.

Psychoanalysis and psychodynamic thinking became attractive to the new intellectuals of the 20th century in Europe and the Americas not only because of its brilliant synthesis of insights and methods but also because of other historical forces. Formal religious belief, be it Catholic, Protestant, or Jewish, was under attack by the powerful forces of materialistic science. Belief in the unseen and unmeasurable was reduced to mere superstition by the Eurocentric canons of Western science, especially logical positivism. Psychoanalysis offered a return to mystery in the language of science. In the quiet chambers of the analytic office *the ritual of confession*, especially of hidden sexual and other unwanted "sinful" feelings, images, and memories, was conveyed to the analyst. The analyst relieved personal "guilt," expiated the bad, and the client did some sort of penance—e.g., express feelings to others, change one's lifestyle, *pay* the analyst. This all unfolded from the peculiar genius of the methodology and opened up the swampy inner landscape of the unconscious to the healing sunlight of analysis.

INSIGHTS OF PSYCHOANALYSIS

What do we have from this brilliant pioneering fusion of early-20th-century scientific rationalism, Jewish mysticism, and Jewish cultural and family life? In psychoanalysis is the first modern European use of an ancient concept, the dynamic unconscious. The hidden or unconscious level of mental life here has a certain affinity to the Kabbalistic "sud," or secret, mysterious level of existence. The sud level of "insight" is believed to be hidden in the words and story-like teachings of the mind. These ideas go back for hundreds of years. Freud's genius and the genius of those surrounding him led to an intense exploration of this ancient phenomenon of the hidden unconscious using the age-old skills of Jewish intellectual and mystical disciplines. Their elucidations of this led to the foundation of psychoanalysis, the most modern new religion of the 20th century. There is much more here than just "the gloomy wisdom of godless Freud." There is even a journal, the *Journal of Psychology and Judaism*, partly devoted to the exploration of this in Jewish family life. Freud's work uncovered the primary defense mechanisms or knots that bind and guard the ego. These "security operations," as H. S. Sullivan (1953) called them, were seen as absolutely necessary for the besieged ego in a hostile world, society, and culture. Also in psychoanalysis we see the elucidation of the ego model of human development. It has become a bedrock of insight and in our day remains the definitive model of the middle level of human consciousness. We say middle level, because it does not explore in full depth the levels of the collective unconscious "below" it, nor does it fully address itself in any adequate way to the levels of the transconscious "above" it. However, it deals exactingly and brilliantly with the midlevel of human experience, the ego. It also deals perceptively and creatively with the level of the individual unconscious and its process as expressed in certain dream states, dream work, and dream phenomenon.

Psychoanalytic propositions are divided into two subdivisions, one "dynamic" and the other "genetic." The dynamic refers to underlying unconscious motivations for current everyday behavior. The genetic refers to the same behavior but believes the behavior to be the result of, or at least deeply influenced by, earlier experiences of infancy and childhood. Some would think of this as an "environmental" influence. Both the genetic and dynamic are seen by the clinician in the day-to-day life of the patient fairly easily. It's the *metapsychological* propositions of psychoanalysis that seem to go beyond the observable clinical data. These are "models" of energy transfer, "aggressive" energy, "tension reduction," instincts as behavioral determinants and the *inherent* conflict model. Its surface description models of energy dynamics are out of date and limit its application to wider field and psychospiritual dynamics. However, as shown in Chapter 2, the dynamic existence and operation of the unconscious mind in information processing, memory, and motivation is no longer seriously challenged. But that doesn't mean that the unconscious accounts for *all* motivation, psychopathology, or neurosis.

Psychoanalytic theory says that psychopathology arises as a reaction to unconscious conflicted aggressive and sexual wishes which threaten to awaken traumatic anxiety in the individual, who then tries to ward them off with various defensive operations. When successful, there is no problem. When these defenses and "security operations" fail, there emerge unwanted derivatives of these wishes and anxiety in the form of complex symptoms, e.g., neuroses, phobias, obsessions, etc. Both dynamic and historically recollected genetic data generally support much of the *observable* behavior. This is the level at which psychoanalysis has been at its best, the level of defenses and conflicted intrapsychic processes. Some experimental studies in subliminal activation and hypnotically induced conflict have tended to strongly support the dynamic and genetic propositions of psychoanalysis (Silverman, 1976).

Psychoanalysis has magnificently elucidated the process of dissociation. It has made clear the dynamics of regression and repression. Finally it has done an extraordinary and pioneering job in the elucidation of the psychological processes of projection, identification, substitution, displacement, and a plethora of other psychological dynamics that we see in the day-to-day life of the vast majority of human beings. Its roots are rich in one ethnic group but it touches deeply upon universal human dynamics and thereby goes beyond ethnopsychiatry.

There are, of course, subtle and numerous "inconsistencies" among Freud the founder and practitioner of this system, psychoanalytic theory itself, and several of its more famous patients, including wolfman, Dora, and others. A full review of these would take us far afield (Crews, 1993). However, despite even these obvious shortcomings, the paradigm has demonstrated a remarkable durability in the face of seething criticism.

Because psychoanalysis and psychodynamic thinking address the midlevel of human consciousness but not the lower and deepest collective unconscious terrain, nor the sublime transpersonal and transpsychic levels, it is not a full theory. Because of its reductionist lens, it does not understand episodes of spiritual "possession" and sees only "regression," not the emergent states of interpenetration and transcendence. In many ways psychoanalysis can be seen as form or a kind of special theory of relativity as opposed to the general theory of relativity. This is an analogy, but hopefully it makes the point. It is also significant that Einstein's pioneering work in special relativity also emerged at roughly the same time as Freud's pioneering work. This we do not think was any accident. We might say that for Freud, mind was repressed body and that for Einstein matter was repressed light. Both revealed a dynamic relationship, and both pointed the way to freedom.

Essentially then psychoanalysis—brilliant, pioneering, courageous, and overcoming many odds—still does not go far enough. It has within it the seeds of its own transcendence. Freud's concept of "evenly suspended attention" is very similar to the transcendental techniques of Vipassana meditation in Buddhism (Epstein, 1984). Sublimation as a concept is embedded in the mechanistic and hydraulic model predominant in 19th- and early-20th-century mechanics. However, if we look closely, we see that sublimation itself is really a vitalistic concept. It is closer to the mystical ideas of Henri Bergson and the élan vital than it is to the mechanics of 19th-century hydraulics. Indeed because both are deeply spiritual and vitalistic concepts, they have more affinity to certain notions we find in the African uncon-scious than they do to 19th-century mechanism. For Freud this vitalism was seen as a highly individualized and encapsulated process intrapsychically within the person as opposed to a more localized or corporealized expres-sion of a vaster psychic process. In all honesty to Freud, however, we must make note of the fact that Freud did believe in a "racial memory," a univer-sal language of dreams, and that intuitively he was aware of mystical cur-rents. He repeatedly denied it within himself, but over and over we see Freud returning to this. Freud had an on-again, off-again, on-again love affair with the study of parapsychology. Freud belonged to a parapsychological society, and in different times in his works alluded to parapsychological phenomena, "oceanic feelings," and other phenomena (Bynum, 1993). How-ever, perhaps for political reasons, Freud made a crucial decision that in order to keep psychoanalysis within the "scientific tradition" he had to clearly avoid such overt study. In this last area, that is to say, the "racial memory," Freud was intuitively in touch with the Mahayana Buddhist tradition of the Alayavijana. The Alayavijana is the "storehouse consciousness" of the Mahayana Buddhists that contains the seeds of all ideas, experiences, and forms.

Freud was deeply influenced by the secular and spiritual traditions of the Hebrew sojourn, particularly in the West. He was also deeply imbued with the mainstreams of scientific thinking in the early part of the 20th century. Interestingly enough, Freud did not follow deeply the scientific cur-rents in the early part of the century concerning physics but he did concern-ing biology. If he had looked more closely perhaps at the currents of early-20th-century physics, particularly relativity theory and quantum mechanics, he may have formulated psychoanalysis in a very different way. As it was, he was profoundly influenced on an unconscious level by the teachings of Jewish mysticism, particularly the Kabbalistic style of seeking the original meaning and interpretation of things, derivations, belief in a recombination of letters, symbol interpretation, and the entry into certain states of atten-tion for the interpretation of phenomena. He believed profoundly in dream interpretation and that all dreams had levels of meaning and sometimes multiple levels of meaning—that is to say, a latent and a manifest meaning (Bakan, 1958/1990). Many writers have drawn a parallel between Freud's use of certain methods also used in the Kabbala and perhaps the Kabbala's actual derivation from ancient Kemetic Egyptian forms of religion (King, 1990). The skipping and word play, the taking liberties with loose associa-tions in an either emotionally aroused or distilled state of mind that one finds in some Jewish mysticism and techniques in psychoanalysis, the preoc-cupation with numbers, names, and hidden forces, all have an echo in ancient Egyptian traditions. It is an attempt to elucidate the extended subtle field of meaning, information, and form in the divine equation. The apprehension of the hieroglyphs is based on a total field grasp, not of isolated bits of meaning. It is closer to the sense of an interconnected field, not its atomistic units. There is a direct lineage between the methodologies of the ancient Kemetic Egyptian teachings, especially those taken out of the traditions begun by the messianic savior Moses and later Hebrew philosophical and spiritual teachings, and perhaps those of the Ifa West African tradition. These are directly linked to the teachings of the Hebrews when they left ancient Egyptian under as yet unclear auspices, and whose written languages was not codified until at least 300 years *after* the Exodus. Thus, while their oral traditions may have been in Hebrew, their early written teachings were most likely in Egyptian text!

On some level Freud must have been aware of this and found it unsettling. Freud notes, in a very famous conversation, that he wanted Jung not to study certain areas of African history and intellectual thinking. In his conversation with Jung, Freud made note of his dread of the "black tide of mud, of occultism." He was having this conversation with Carl Jung in direct reference to Jung's exploration of the collective unconscious and also areas called occultism (King, 1990). Jung was very close to overtly making a connection between the collective unconscious and the African unconscious. He knew about this implicitly and he recounts many times how in his studies of Africa and in his studies actually carried out on the continent of Africa, in 1925 in Kenya and Uganda specifically, that he somehow felt primordially at home and remembered seeing what he knew from ancient times (Jung, 1965). Who knows, perhaps in some ways Jung was more courageous. Even he, however, psychically recoiled from the full acceptance of this dynamic reality that lives below the surface of the European "White" identity. Jung may have rushed into the deep dark waters of the African unconscious where Freud and the angels would fear to tread.

SOME PARALLELS BETWEEN JEWISH MYSTICAL THOUGHT AND ANCIENT KEMETIC EGYPT

Many elements of modern Judaism, particularly its mystical strains and its spiritual traditions, have certain roots and affinities in the mystery lodge traditions of ancient Egypt and even some elements of Ifa in West Africa. Monotheism in particular was pointed out by Freud as one of the unusual traditions that the Jews left ancient Egypt with. There are also a number of parallels between the 10 Commandments, or the 10 laws of Moses, and the older 42 laws of Maát (Asante, 1984). But more than this, there are a number of other striking parallels.

Judaism has always nurtured the belief in law, and Christianity matured in this soil the idea that the law itself was love. Hillel, the head of the Sanhedrin, the supreme council of Israel in the first century B.C.E., was asked by a critic once if he could teach the whole of the Torah while standing on one foot. The story goes that Hillel replied "What is hateful to yourself, do not to another. That is the whole of the Torah; all the rest is commentary." This exoteric connection is obvious. There are however also esoteric connections and affinities.

First of all, in the West African tradition of Ifa, as mentioned earlier, there are 256 symbols used to organize the forces of nature. These Odu appear to be the same symbols used by the Essene sect of ancient Palestine just prior to the arrival of Jesus the Christ. The Kemetic priests of Egypt believed that nature could be understood by understanding the nature of sound and the study of the proportions embedded in their overtones. This led to the development of what is called *solfege*, the use of sets of syllables which represent musical relationships. The lineage of combining and then recombining symbols in states of unitative conscious experiences is at the heart of the mystical Kabbala and, yes, even some aspects of psychoanalysis. It is the very root of the Ifa system.

In the Kabbala are certain other parallels to Egyptian religion. In the Egyptian mythos we find the god Ptah signifying the "fire fallen into the earth." This seems to be parallel to the "fall" into Earth of the Kabbala's faithless archangel Lucifer. This parallel finds its expression in Christianity. But also in addition to this we find the reversal of this god or fallen angel, as the path of Hotep, which some scholars believe clarifies the deeper meaning of the ancient "amen-hotep," or the *reversal* into Amen of the fire fallen into earth translated into a spiritualized version of that fire and its reversal and, therefore, of redemption (Schwaller de Lubicz, 1961). This would be a reversal of the Hebraic and Christian fall from heaven. In other words, inherent in the Egyptian system is not only the fall but the possibility of redemption and resurrection. This is a reflection of the Osirian myth. Remember that Osiris had a divine birth, had a "fall" into a human life, went through sufferings and family dynamics of various kinds, including betrayal, and eventually died but then was resurrected or redeemed and returned to the realm of light. He did so by way of spiritualization in resurrection. This is connected with the saga or the dynamics of his son or offspring Horus. Horus is the liberating eye of light held in the darkness of matter, Satan, or Set. It is the same Satan that we find in the Hebrew and later Jewish texts.

This "fall" and the notion of Satan have roots in an even older story, the so-called history of the fall of Atlantis as retold in the ancient mystery lodges of Egypt and later Tibet. It is neither a Christian nor Jewish vision of the fall. The Biblical "fall from paradise" in the theosophical account was brought about by the Luciferic adversaries of the celestial hierarchies, who, it is said, were successful in severing human consciousness from the guidance of the macrocosm and allowed it to become capable of both personal resolve and evil. Human consciousness was therein susceptible to its cravings and passions. This led to being overinvolved in the wheel of physical existence and the material world. The spirits of the earth-bound consciousness then took over. These Ahrimanic spirits, the second hierarchy of this trinity of evil, severed human consciousness almost completely from the vision of the whole macrocosm and trapped it in the three-dimensional world of measure, number, and weight. Ahriman chained human consciousness to the delusion of the physical world as the only real existence. In this way, the Atlantian mythos goes, Lucifer and Ahriman became the two mighty obstructions of human evolution, the blinders to the true destiny of human consciousness (Blavatsky, 1888/1966). The only escape was through some form of redemption.

The original codified model of redemption is here in the Kemetic Myth. For in the dynamic of Horus, Horus is the divine light, the corporification that is born into and carried along sensorily in time. Horus is literally the son and the manifestation of the primal light of Osiris. There are numerous other references to these parallels and reversals (Schwaller de Lubicz, 1961). They are too many and too numerous to be a coincidence. They reveal a striking parallel between the roots of ancient Christianity and Judaism and the primordial spiritual and intellectual grounds of Kemetic Egypt in the ancient world.

The idea of redemption is here. Near the end of the Book of Daniel at the end of days, "the people shall be delivered . . . many of them that sleep in the dust of the earth shall awake, some to everlasting life, and some to shame and everlasting contempt" (Daniel 12:1–2). This is echoed in the Ethiopic Book of Enoch written in the first century C.E., where are mentioned the "day of judgment" and "the last day," when the righteous ones would enter their kingdom. These ideas echo the vision of Kemetic Egypt millennia earlier, because while not in the Torah or among the beliefs of the Sadducees, they were nevertheless present in Isaiah and among the Pharisees (Johnson, 1987). These ideas were germinated by the Osirian resurrection mythos with its dramas of judgment as outlined in the *Book of the Dead*.

Osiris was considered the archetypal hero and liberator, the ideal avatar and messianic force who reawakens human consciousness to is divine origin. The body of Osiris was destroyed or *exiled* from its unity, and scattered throughout the land as the mythos goes, and was only partially *redeemed* by great love, in his case the love of his wife, Isis. For the Jews who were exiles and outcasts from the royal place, the "body" of the nation was scattered. Each fragment of the scatter was a divine spark that would some day, by love and discipline, be reunited. By the time of Isaac Luria's Kabbalism in Europe after the medieval outcast or exile from Spain in 1492, this story of exile and redemption was elevated to the status of a great personalized myth. Man is seen as ultimately a spark exiled from the great fire of the divine itself. Each Jew in each land was a repository of this spark, this piece of the original perfectly incarnated man, or Adam. This was the exile of the soul through the lower worlds of matter and even animals, the transmigration of the soul. Redemption was the return to the light of En-Sof and union, or the great Yoga, the restitution of all things back into God, the primal light and logos. This is the messianic seed that is rooted in all philosophies of spiritual exile, be it in Egypt or Babylon or the world stage itself. No doubt at a future date after some great cataclysm of our species, we shall again seek some kind of unspeakable redemption in languages and places far beyond the Earth. In the present age, we have a dawning scientific knowledge, based in archeology, anthropology, morphology, and genetics, that *Homo sapiens sapiens*, and most likely the germ of civilization itself, is rooted in our modern repression and devaluation of African consciousness on the world stage. Human consciousness must turn back upon itself and recognize the African genesis in the deep reservoir of the human spirit. Once beyond this psychospiritual contraction of racism, we expand as a species.

SUMMARY

So what can we say at this point about Judaism, psychiatry, and the limits of psychodynamic insight? First, the insights of psychodynamic thinking are not *merely* an elaboration of Kemetic ideas but represent an original and far-reaching contribution. This chapter began with a brief look the historical context of Judaism. An extraordinarily long and complex history of political and cultural oppression, expulsions, resettlements, cyclical pograms, and mass migrations reinforced a sense of perpetual vulnerability. In the 20th century alone more Jews have been overtly and systematically murdered in a brief episode of official slaughter than any other single group, including Blacks, Chinese, Cambodians, and Armenians! This has profoundly shaped cultural and family identity. We saw how the cultural, social, and familial background of 19th- and 20th-century Judaism, including cognitive style and family unconscious dynamics, contributed to the stream of psychoanalytic methodology. We saw the way the brilliant intellectual and mystical tradition of several streams of Judaism contributed to the methodology of psychoanalysis. We then went on to see some of the original elucidations of psychoanalysis, including the internal knots of defense mechanisms, the new and expanded mapping of the unconscious, and the contribution of the ego model to human development. We observed some of the limits of psychoanalysis, including its apparent conflict model of man and society and its denial of intelligent levels of cognition and consciousness below and above the ego. Psychodynamic theory did not invent or discover the unconscious. However, it took it considerably further in some directions than even the Egyptians. We saw how the entire methodology of psychoanalysis was not created primarily by Freud but rather has roots that reach back over the centuries to the Middle Ages and further. Psychoanalysis has many parallels to the Jewish mystical tradition, in particular those of Abulafia and others in the Middle Ages. There are certain parallels between the methodology of the Kabbala in particular and certain technical approaches of psychoanalysis. There are even older historical connections between certain Jewish mystical traditions and those of Kemetic Egypt. Certainly psychoanalysis is not merely a rendition or rehashing of ideas embedded in Kemetic science and philosophy. It is an original and far-reaching expansion in many ways. It also, however, has inherent limits, in particular the belief that the world process can be apprehended in thought alone. The Jewish mystical tradition is divided on this issue; psychoanalysis is not.

We have even seen some parallels between the historical roots of Judaism, the Exodus, and certain ongoing intellectual concerns of our own day. We mentioned how Freud himself was an ardent believer that Moses himself was a Black Egyptian and not a Jew. We mentioned that the origins of the Hebrews in Egypt is unclear. Whether they were indigenous Egyptians and Ethiopians who, coming by way of political involvement with monotheism and the rise of the Aton cult under the patronage of the Pharaoh Akhenaton in the 18th Dynasty of Egypt (1580 to 1350 B.C.E.), were eventually politically ostracized or whether the Jews were a variation of invading Semitic armies such as the Hyksos, is still unknown. The Biblical legend is of 70 shepherds in 12 families in a peaceful, pastoral migration into Egypt. We do know that the Hebrew Bible in all likelihood had some of its historical roots in the ancient city of Byblos (Diop, 1974). We also know that Hebrew as a language was not codified until at least 300 years after the Exodus and that therefore the ancient Hebrews in all likelihood spoke, wrote, and chronicled much of their history and perhaps much of their religious mystical techniques in the Egyptian language. Though the Jews are often historically believed to have come into Egypt as a clan of 70 shepherds during the time of Joseph and to have left some 400 to 500 years later close to more than half a million strong, in all likelihood they looked significantly more like the indigenous Kemetic Egyptians than they did other Mid-Eastern-looking people today.

Finally Diop and others are of the opinion that during the powerful and fomenting 18th Dynasty in Egypt there was an extraordinary eruption of a volcano on the island of Santorini. This is believed to have given rise to many of the catastrophic events and messianic prophets and movements of that time. The Biblical Exodus may have been a political and cultural fulfillment of the messianic message that had been initiated by this catastrophic explosion on this island. Diop and others are even of the belief that the myth of a lost civilization of Atlantis is rooted here. This, however, is more controversial. What we do know, however, is that these events occurred in roughly the same historical period, that the Jews when they left Egypt were obviously profoundly influenced by Kemetic culture, thought, religion and intuitions of the divine, and that they left Egypt with a unique and illuminating gift, the belief in monotheism. In many ways, the psychoanalytic tradition in the 19th and 20th centuries was a rediscovery of the ancient Kemetic Amenta and the Primeval Waters of Nun, the dynamic unconscious. Jewish mysticism no doubt rediscovered and borrowed tremendously from the bedrock mysticism of the ancient Kemetic tradition. It also expanded this considerably. It contributed an original and thought-provoking new synthesis to science and Western civilization. One of those scholastic and revolutionary contributions was, in fact, the method of psychoanalysis. Psychoanalysis with all its brilliant illuminations of our subterranean consciousness also reveals, because of its own subtle clinging to thought and verbal production in innumerable ways, its ultimate limitation as a science of consciousness.

8 THE PRESENT CONFRONTATION IN THE AMERICAS

For a Black man survival in America depends in large measure on the development of a healthy cultural paranoia.
—William H. Grier and Price M. Cobbs, *Black Rage*

The myth of the bad nigger is part of the collective unconscious.
—Frantz Fanon, *Black Skin, White Masks*

I believe that we are lost here in America, but I believe we shall be found. . . . I think the true discovery of America is before us. I think the true fulfillment of our spirit, of our people, of our mighty and immortal land, is yet to come. I think the true discovery of our own democracy is still before us. And I think that all these are certain as the morning, as inevitable as noon. This glorious assurance is not only our living hope, but our dream to be accomplished.
—Thomas Wolf, *You Can't Go Home Again*

THE MILIEU OF RACE IN THE NEW WORLD

BETWEEN the voyages of Columbus and the first two decades after the American Revolution, anywhere from a very conservative 10 million to perhaps 40 million Africans were forcibly taken from Africa to the Caribbean and both the Americas (Holloway, 1990). This massive Diaspora occurred primarily from the west coast of Africa, but there were lines of forced immigration even from the interior and the east coast. Africans from deeper in the interior were captured, brought to the coast, and sold, primarily by other Africans. From the North of present-day Senegal, all the way down to the bottom of present-day Angola, a vast exodus or Kiaspora occurred. During this infamous middle passage, stolen Africans by the millions awoke in a hell realm that lasted for centuries. In the wooden bowels of huge sailing ships flying the ocean like great white birds of prey, they plunged forward over and over into mountainous foaming waves of icy waters filled with sharks trailing them, waiting for the dead and excess human cargo thrown overboard to become the next meal. Chained together row after row by iron and terror, sick, filthy, rebellious, and religious, they endured the long voyage toward unknown destinations, women and children, too, in unspeakable heat. Of the conservative 15 million over the centuries who were forcibly taken, a mere 10 million or so actually survived the journey. A third died in horrid captivity waiting for transport. From 15% to 30% died during the Atlantic middle passage. It was one of the largest waves of forced migration and one of the greatest crimes in world history, a great disturbance in the force of a people.

This malignant trade took its toll in European lives as well. Sailors and soldiers were the usual victims. Sometimes only 50% of the initial crew returned, while 25% deserted. Mortality rates were sometimes 220 or so out of a 1,000! Clearly nearly one out of five sailors died each slave voyage, and perhaps 13% of new troops and planters in the West Indies succumbed to strange tropical diseases and "fevers" for which they had no immunity (Curtin, 1969). This placed a drain on a European society that in turn was bleeding an African one to near death. Only the bankers and merchants thrived. The huge loss of British lives and eventually the sheer repugnance of the trade were crucial elements in why the British finally began to criminalize and militarily suppress this filthy practice.

The peoples who were taken from the west coast of Africa constituted the second migration of Africans to the New World. The first migration occurred long before Columbus (Van Sertima, 1976). These were originally seafarers and traders from the empires of the west coast, particularly the medieval empire of Mali that reached to the northwest coast of Africa. At one time the Mali empire controlled the lands stretching from the "Guinea" coast to the Sudan. The medieval scholar Ibn Fadl Allah Al Omari in this book *Masalik el Absar fir Mamalik el Amsar* (Van Sertima, 1976) records Malians, most likely the Mandinkas, during the rein of the emperor Abuba Kari II traveling by sea to the Americas in 1311–1312. However, as we saw earlier, there are signs of an even earlier Egyptian 25th Dynasty contact with the foundational Olmec civilization of old Mexico.

This second migration radically dwarfed the first. The peoples taken in the Northern Hemisphere were the peoples of the lands of the Yoruba, the Ashanti, the Fanti, those from Dahomey, the so-called Bantu, and others. This wave after wave of human migration carried within it also the seeds of a genetic, historical, and biological reality that enclosed and enfolded what we have been referring to throughout this book as an African unconscious.

There are at least two manifestations of this collective unconscious, the individual manifestation and the collective manifestation. In this chapter we will explore both the individual and the collective manifestations and not only how they played themselves out in recent history but also how the dynamics of recent history, particularly the dynamics of forced labor and slave history, play themselves out in the psychodynamics and sociocultural dynamics of today. For indeed today is only the last and most recent chapter of an epic, genetic, and spiritual adventure in consciousness, full of tragedy and triumph, that began untold eons ago on the shores of the ancient lakes of east Africa and the gorges of the Rift Valley.

Obviously slavery was not invented by Europeans. In fact the Arabs of northern Africa first introduced the Europeans of Portugal and Spain to the financial benefits of Black slavery. Arab merchants had traded in White slaves in North Africa for centuries. Assyrians, Chinese, Egyptians, and many other peoples of antiquity used slaves. The Romans first used the word "slave" in connection with the "Slavic" peoples, whom they colonized. They were White, of course, but the term came to include all peoples in bondage. However, in the Americas, it was eventually based solely on race and color. The first bondsmen in the United States were Englishmen, i.e., rogues, debtors, paupers, etc., the dregs of English society. In the 17th century, they were primarily Scots, Irish, Germans, and even Swiss who had been kidnapped or made prisoners for some crime. White children were also stolen and sold into indentured servitude if, as too often occurred, they were abandoned by their families. Some Europeans sold themselves into slavery for two to seven years for passage to the colonies.

The Spanish and Portuguese had moved into North Africa during this time, and they followed a practice of the Arabs. These three groups used religion as a rationale for "saving" Africans from their "heathen" and "infidel" worlds by taking them into slavery. The growth of the sugar plantations and rum trading (the legal drug trade!) in the New World made slavery even more profitable. The indigenous Native American or Amerindians quickly died off from the new diseases or suicide, or were intentionally exterminated by the European powers. In Africa and this New World the Africans were one of the few peoples the Europeans were not able to exterminate! By the 17th century the Dutch, English, and French had conquered much of the Caribbean and expanded the trade—the Dutch in St. Eustatius, Tobago, and Curaçao; the English in Barbados and Jamaica; the French in Guadeloupe and Martinique. The first African slaves in the United States came in a group of 20 aboard a Dutch warship to Virginia in 1619. White bondsmen eventually were freed and the Indians died or escaped back to their familiar haunts in the forest. Eventually slavery was confined only to Africans.

The slave populations were concentrated in the southern states even though the bankers and merchants of Boston, Newport, and other northern cities participated in the trade. This was especially true after the American Revolution, when the thirteen original states grew in number. The big plantations were in the Deep South, i.e., Mississippi, Louisiana, Georgia, and South Carolina. However, in Georgia nearly two-fifths of the White families had slaves; in North Carolina, Tennessee, Texas, and Kentucky, one-fifth; and in Maryland and Missouri, one-eighth. Most states, like Delaware, had only one family in thirty or fewer with slaves (Stampp, 1956).

The first "slave" Blacks were Africanized in the sense of knowing that they came from a country quite different in climate and other features from the Americas. The first ones were also, like other bondsmen, freed legally after their period of servitude was over. They participated in many areas of community life, professionally and even politically. They brought labor and skills, particularly agricultural ones, to the developing economies of the colonies. Native Americans, Jews, and other Blacks at times also owned Black slaves. Blacks owned more than 15 times the number of slaves owned by Sephardic Jews in North America. Intermarriage between Africans, Europeans, and Native Americans occurred frequently, as did the offspring of these unions. There were, indeed, many potential models of development in seed form for the politics of race in the Americas at that time, and the one of lifetime slavery based on skin color was by no means inevitable (Bennett, 1962). This "choice," however, of eventual Black slavery set in motion over time a psychocultural and spiritual nightmare that even into our own day is alive and violently present.

By the time of the American Revolution, Blacks were fighting on both sides of the rebellion. At the outbreak of armed hostilities Lord Dunmore, the British governor of Virginia, promised freedom to all male slaves willing to fight. Thousands of slaves deserted their plantation masters and battled. At Kemp's Landing in Virginia they defeated the ranks of White soldiers. Soon Washington and his generals were forced to reverse their earlier position and let free Blacks fight for the Revolution. Blacks were afterwards in every major confrontation in the war. They served as soldiers, spies, and the whole spectrum of roles (Bennett, 1962). In an irony of ironies the two sides were even rumored to have faced each other in battle. After the war, thousands were freed and thousands more ran away from the plantations.

Flowing in the background and souls of the millions who lived this era of history was the life story told in the music; an almost evolutionary strength was found in the music. Gospel music, the fountainhead of Black music in North America, began in the slave songs, field hollers, and call-response style Africans brought with them. The field hollers too came from West Africa. This music, almost always religious, went through several transformations far beyond the scope of this book. Suffice it to say that by the 18th century the early fusion of field hollers, slave songs, and songs with multiple encoded messages evolved into the camp-meeting spiritual, the sorrowful songs of slavery, and eventually the ecstatic jubilee spiritual. After legal slavery was over, it moved into the missionary and revival songs of the early 20th century. Eventually came the kind of gospel songs we hear today, which themselves flowed into the blues, parts of jazz, several other streams, and eventually today's rock-and-roll and soul music. This music, of course, has found its way into the American psyche and is so pervasive that even White racists listen to it fervently now and have their own favorites. But music was not the only stream of the African legacy that poured into the national soul.

The Africans brought to the Americas eventually exercised an influence on the speech of the peoples where they lived. Because the captured ethnic groups were intentionally mixed together by the Europeans in order to keep communication and rebellion low, the Africans developed a kind of pidgin English, a mixture of English and the indigenous tongues that they brought with them to the Americas. In North America, this pidgin English and Gullah dialect helped create the dialect and accent of English spoken eventually by Whites and Blacks in the southern United States (MacNeil, 1986). For poor Whites, sometimes their lives and diets were as miserable as those of most slaves.

Slave food, by and large, consisted of an allowance of corn meal, or hominy grits, some salt, and bacon. If there was a garden, one might grow something. Fruit was rare. Scurvy and other diseases were quite common. Slave quarters were dingy, run down, and often near the lowlands, where water, swamps, and other situations helped the spread of mosquito-borne malaria, tuberculosis, typhoid, and other diseases, including cholera. Near the coastal areas the diet was more varied with seafood etc., but by and large foods such as eggs, fruit, fresh meat, milk, and a variety of vegetables were exceedingly rare. The slaves were forced to make do with what little they had or what was left over. This was especially so for the vast majority of field slaves. The slaves hours were from sunrise to sunset six days a week. Some slaves did have small gardens and in some cases could trade with each other. Washington bought from and sold items to a few of his slaves. At his death in 1799 the plantation was some 8,000 acres and housed 439 slaves. It was large but not the largest. The Carters of Virginia owned 1,000 slaves! While most American slaves were illiterate, a few could secretly read and write (e.g., Frederick Douglass). Some slaves were even overseers and with permission could travel and conduct business for the plantation. These, however, were the exceptions. The overwhelming masses lived in squalid, hopeless poverty and resentment.

For house slaves the situation was somewhat better than for field slaves. A well-kept slave made a master look better to the other Whites in society, so such slaves had better clothes, better food, etc. Also a sick slave was less valuable, and so minimal medical care was provided. Again, the house servant fared a little better and, as you might expect, was generally more loyal to the master. Rarely did the field slave have adequate clothing, lodging, shoes, furniture, bedding, or diet. Most clothes were made of homespun cloth and natural dyes. Their cabins were often very near the site of the overseer's house, where they could be closely watched.

At various times, in order to keep up their financial investment, masters rehabilitated the slave quarters. Fresh water decreased disease, as did an annual cleaning, a fireplace, and waterproofing by elevating the structure above the ground. Despite this, however, the life of the overwhelming majority of millions of slaves was bleak and soul-crushing, to say the least. Still, the "peculiar institution" grew. For a while after the American Revolution it seemed slavery might die a slow natural death. However, Eli Whitney's invention of the cotton gin in 1793 made cotton king and slavery an even more profitable business. The die was cast. An uneasy truce settled in but was broken many times. There were over 250 slave revolts recorded within the United States (Aptheker, 1943). Numerous others were not recorded. The first occurred 94 years before the landing of the *Mayflower*, near the mouth of the Pedee River in South Carolina. A Spanish colonizer, Lucas Vásquez de Ayllon, in the summer of 1526 lost control of his slaves after illness and discord weakened his settlement. He withdrew to Haiti, leaving behind the rebellious Africans and their Native American allies (Bennett, 1962). This was the first permanent settlement of Africans and non–Native Americans in the New World! There were other rebellions to follow.

Haitian slaves under Toussaint L'Ouverture rebelled and successfully freed themselves after the American Revolution. Their victory weakened Napoleon's hand such that he sold the Louisiana Territory to Jefferson in 1803 for pennies an acre, a move which doubled the size of the United States. Blacks were burned and hanged in New York City after a rebellion in 1741. There were many other rebellions, led by Gabriel Prosser, Denmark Vesey, Nat Turner—all unsuccessful militarily, even though Whites were killed in the rebellions. Some visionary Whites could see that slavery was a cultural and moral time bomb and tried to either free Blacks legally or else transport them back to Africa. In 1822 the American Colonization Society founded a colony for freed Blacks which in 1847 became the Republic of Liberia. But the guerrilla war in America continued. Some slaves in the rebellions escaped to the bayous, some to the Indians, some to other states. These failed militarily, yes, but they created a constant fear and subliminal terror for the slaver holder. At any moment a slave might rise in revolt and murder, poison, or in some way terrorize the master and his family. This fear led to edicts that outlawed playing drums, since the drum could be used for long-distance communication as they had been in Africa. The spirituals as a result often became encoded with messages since they were allowed in this Draconian world. The "limbo dance" shared a similar fate. It was made illegal by slave holders because it was a powerfully evocative dance performed by the African priest of the Obyah rites. Plantation owners, often outnumbered by their slaves, feared that the dance stimulated heathenism, cannibalism, and "black magic" in the African soul that might erupt and overwhelm the system, bringing on not only political rebellion but a spiritual nightmare of the worst possible kind.

An Uneasy Truce

This was indeed a complex time for race relations. On the one hand Whites worked hard to reinforce the notion of Black inferiority in society, in religion, in law, and in mass cultural imagery. Yet at the same time there were indications of another countervailing current even in the midst of horrid chattel slavery. In every southern state except Virginia, South Carolina, and Georgia, free Blacks could vote until 1812. In a 1705 Virginia statute, a master could kill a rebellious slave and it was not even a felony since the slave was the master's property. By 1788 the statute was repealed and killing slaves became a form of murder. It is recorded that two of Thomas Jefferson's nephews were legally prosecuted for this kind of crime (Rosen, 1996). So we had both more and more legal controls and restrictions on slaves over time, yet there were also more and more laws on the books that attempted to "protect" these very same slaves. Contempt and fear coexisted with paternalism and noblesse oblige throughout the antebellum period. Perhaps this uneasy dilemma was nowhere more apparent than when it came to "understanding" the mental and physical health of the slave.

When a slave did show signs of rebellion, it had to be dealt with, either by force or "insight." By "insight" we mean medical knowledge and psychiatry. Slaves often had symptoms with high levels of "mental instability," "brain fevers," and suffering "under an aberration of mind" (Deutsch, 1840). Stillbirths and mysterious crib deaths occurred three times as much to slave women as to free women. "It was a prevalent notion that Negro women 'were not subject to the difficulty, danger, and pain which attended women of the better classes in giving birth to their offspring'" (Stampp, 1956, p. 316). Compared to White women, these Black women were believed to experience little pain in childbirth (Dye, 1912; White, 1799). Excess force and the harness of slavery therefore did not cause as much pain! Hernias were very common. There were many, many cases of mysterious "fevers," odd "chills and fever," all of which decreased the slave's capacity to work the field (Stampp, 1956). Diseases were rampant at times and moved in cycles for Blacks in many areas. Observers like J. T. Hicks in 1836 Natchez recorded that "the hearse has been running regularily bearing dead bodies from the Negro market to the publick cemetery" (Stampp, 1956, p. 297). Strange outbreaks of dirt eating by slaves occurred and was called Cachexia Africania, which was really an expression of dietary deficiency in slave life. These, of course, were understood to be the result of simple biological inferiority or morbid "Negro consumption" resulting from a naturally weak mind (Cartwright, 1852, 1858). There were a few "hospitals" for sick or insane Blacks, but treatment could vary widely depending on the psychiatric diagnosis or medical condition. Naturally the "Negro diseases" were different from White diseases, and so a cure for a White man might injure or kill a Black (Cartwright, 1852). Such "hospitals" were usually on the plantation, but some were run by physicians in Charleston, Savannah, Natchez, Montgomery, and New Orleans.

Mental disease took a curious turn. When slaves perpetually did poor work, damaged property, or showed endless irresponsibility on the job, their "rascality," as the master referred to it, was medically diagnosed as Dysaesthesia Aethiopica. This condition explained their "mischief," which fooled you into thinking such behavior was done "as if intentional," since it was assumed that deep down the slave really responded well to slavery. Another mental disease, called Drapetomania, caused such simple, healthy, happy darkies to suddenly run away! The symptoms were a "sulky and dissatisfied" attitude. If no physical problem was found, preventive "treatment" consisted of an early form of behavior modification, which was severely "whipping the devil out of them" *before* they ran away. Such "insight" and psychiatry went hand in hand with medical-political ideas. As the great Civil War approached, these ideas were questioned more and more, but still held the day.

There were of course other devices used for more recalcitrant slaves. These ranged from metal tongue depressors locked in place, arm and leg shackles, heavy neck collars with bells and spikes, occasional bodily mutilation for runaways, torture involving insects (especially bees, wasps and stinging ants), plus a whole list of medieval dungeon pain instruments used by the overseer and "specialists" in slave behavior. Hanging, disembowelment, and burning alive were employed in cases of unforgivable behavior like murdering Whites or inciting rebellion.

Sex, of course, occurred between the races, mostly white masters and Black slave women. Both Washington and Jefferson had offspring from slave women. The full range of dynamics in male/female relationships occurred, but the vast majority involved sex between the conquered by the conqueror. Some slave women were openly bought and sold specifically for this purpose in the marketplace. This was a privilege of the wealthy classes of southern gentlemen. Sometimes, they were long-term and emotionally complex relationships, such as that between Thomas Jefferson and Sally Hemings (Bennett, 1962). These relationships were tolerated out of powerlessness, passion, need, the whole range of human dynamics around bondage. In some cases, love was a significant force; in most, lust, power, domination, and a peculiar weaving of *extended family unconscious dynamics* were involved. Such unions spawned all shades of color and social politics associated with it, not only in the United States but in all the Americas. Blacks became the "uncles, aunts, and mammys" of White families. It was also not even uncommon for a White master–Black slave liaison to produce dark-skinned offspring who stayed on the plantation, as in the cases of U.S. presidents Washington and Jefferson. A few slave families lived on the plantations for generations. The reality of having one's own son or daughter as a slave in the racial caste systems further deepened this pained and extended family unconscious matrix.

In all fairness to Washington, he did come to realize near the end of his life that slavery was an overt evil and wrote in 1797 that "I wish from my soul that the legislature of this state could see the policy of a gradual abolition of slavery." Still, he freed only one slave at his death; but instead of selling them in his will he kept and cared for his and his wife Martha's slave families on the plantation after his passing. He also provided in his will that they could learn to read and write and "brought up to some useful occupation agreeable to the laws of the Commonwealth of Virginia" (Toler, 1996).

The role of a slave apparently could be complex and subtle on many levels for both master and servant.

White females during this time were limited to familial roles either largely controlled by men or else in a state of scornful limbo reflected by both men and women. For sure it was a better life than the one for Blacks and Indians, but it was certainly not an exalted state. In general a woman could not own property except as it passed through her father or husband. She could not vote or hold public office or for that matter appear too forceful in public situations. It was perceived by Whites and Blacks to be "unwomanly" and an embarrassment to the family. She had only a few roles open to her re-gardless of her socioeconomic class. If unmarried, and this was rarely the case (1 to 3% were "left" unmarried), she could be the frail passive sufferer, idealized, asexual, and pure. She could be, at least for a while in her youth, the "belle" who flirted with the young men and drove them to do noble deeds in war or politics and harvest. She was often a plantation owner's daughter or the scion of a well-to-do family in polite society. In the worst of circumstances, however, she fought off evil, lecherous men and proved she had spirit. These were all acceptable roles in society and plantation novel literature. The unacceptable roles were the "spinster" who was left over after the harvesting by men, or, of course, the sexually and morally polluted "fallen women," who was usually lower-class. Married women by contrast were wives and good or bad mothers who taught religion and ran the house (Tracy, 1995). The widow's status cut across all categories and classes. Most, like their Black slave counterparts, were in a kind of vast, genteel prison, where the shackles lay in the mind and financial structures underpinning a medieval society while their blood flowed for centuries into a hot plantation soil tilled and sweated by Blacks.

From time to time, great leaders arose who risked everything to help slaves escape to the North. The Underground Railroad conducted thousands of slaves to freedom and many Whites, especially abolitionists and Quakers, helped. Harriet Tubman, a Black woman, returned secretly to the South numerous times and led over 300 slaves to freedom. Sojourner Truth did likewise, as did many, many others. In the North, abolitionists Frederick Douglass, William Lloyd Garrison, and others gathered forces. The tide slowly turned. By the time of the great conflagration, slavery as an institution was in deep trouble on almost every ground, although still economically viable. By the end of the Civil War, 188,000 in Black regiments had fought, died, and helped change the map of the United States. Some had even fought in the Confederate Army during its last desperate hours! Even after the war, at least 5,000 died in lynchings, in group attacks by displaced Whites, and through organized pogroms by southern reactionaries. Some soldiers went west and became the 9th and 10th U.S. Cavalry or Buffalo soldiers, as they were named by the Comanche, Cheyenne, and Sioux warriors they fought in settling the West. They protected the migrating American populations and for nearly 30 years made up 20% of the uniformed American forces in the area (Leckie, 1967; Black Heritage Collection, 1992). This was the frontier, mind you—Texas, Kansas, and New Mexico. This occurred during the era of Reconstruction, the Ku Klux Klan (KKK), the federal abdication, Jim Crow, lynching, and all the legalities of the Emancipation Proclamation and 13th, 14th, and 15th Amendments, and the blood of battle. Race and race dynamics, however, go deeper than written law. Its power issues from forces and images in the unconscious.

REFLECTIONS OF BLACK IMAGERY IN THE NEW WORLD

After Columbus' four historic voyages, institutional slavery, at that time only a mild aberration in European cultural and financial institutions, became a massive cultural and historical undertaking. Given the Christian faith of Europe, but also the burgeoning power and pressure of an expanding capitalism, and perhaps a memory of recent experiences with a second dark invader into Spain[11] and lower Europe by way of the Moorish invaders of Spain from northern Africa, there was deep ambivalence in European circles concerning the African presence. In the Copper and Bronze Ages between 2500 and 1500 B.C.E. huge stone monuments of the Egyptian mastaba type began to appear in southern Spain and Malta. They appeared to be cultural imitations from African influences farther south. In the time of the Romans, the African was associated with the origin of civilization, ancient wisdom, and Osirian cults of spirituality in Rome. Antagonisms were not based on color or race, but fear of conquest. Hannibal, the Black Carthaginian, actually invaded Rome and ruled for 10 years before political intrigue led to his demise and eventual suicide. Hundreds of years before him, African armies had entered parts of Spain and created kingdoms that held sway over the region for a century (Van Sertima, 1991). So the two groups had met several times before on the plains of history.

African mystery schools had flourished in Rome until the edicts of the emperors Theodosius and Justinian in the 4th and 6th century C.E. The dark presence of the African Moors changed this in both the popular and educated European mind. The Moors, remember, were initially primarily North and West African Blacks who embraced Islam. A smaller percent were Arabs.

---

11. Some scholars believe that the first dark invader was the Grimaldi Negroids over 40,000 years ago, who were the genetic basis of the later Alpine, Slavic, and Nordic peoples (Diop, 1974, 1991).

They ruled the Iberian peninsula of Spain and Portugal for 700 years. In Spain and Portugal, after the expulsion of the Africans, a conflict arose between the egalitarian spiritual perception of being common brothers in the body of Christ and the potential financial power and rewards of chattel labor. This seemed to be expressed primarily by certain circles within the Catholic Church. The Catholic Church benefited enormously both financially and geopolitically from the imposition of slaves into the New World. The image of Africans in the European unconscious began to undergo a radical change. Europeans first attempted to enslave the indigenous inhabitants of the Americas. For various reasons, including their massive death due to disease and outright slaughter, the indigenous population did not endure slavery well. The European naval powers then turned their engines of capitalism toward the plunder and the exploitation of the indigenous peoples of West Africa. Spain had defeated the Moors in 1492, expelled the Jews in the same year, by that October had beached Columbus in the Caribbean, and knew that the last African emperor, Sunni Ali, had just died. The axis of world power was changing again.

At this time many of the African empires that had been strong for centuries were geopolitically in decline. These included the ruined empires of Ghana, weakened Mali, and numerous others.[12] Songhay, after 1492, was soon to fall with the death of its emperor, Sunni Ali, even though it rallied one more time. The empires were fragmenting, small wars proliferated, and a spiritual darkness swept across the inner landscape of once powerful and prosperous medieval West Africa. Europe, on the other hand, was rising a second time from its Dark Ages. In addition to Europeans involved in the slave trade, there were also Arabs and Africans who sold other Africans into slavery. Few Africans knew the kind of hell realm they sold their brethren into for profit or revenge. Often the Africans sold into slavery were a remnant of defeated armies, destroyed cities and villages. Men stole other men, women, and children for profit and sometimes revenge. Each European culture had a somewhat different political, financial, and religious constellation that dealt with the slaves differently. But let there be no doubt that slavery was an abomination in North America, in the Caribbean, and in South America. In order to rationalize slave taking, a new image had to be nurtured of the captured Africans, an image of savagery, sexual license, mental inferiority, and a soul in bad need of saving by a superior people. The unconscious changed.

---

12. Not all European nations were directly involved in the African slave trade. Those who prospered were primarily the naval powers of Spain, Portugal, France, Holland, and England. They built on an earlier system utilized by the Arabs, with a significant portion of the enterprise actively supported by indigenous African nations (Davidson, 1968; Jackson, 1970; Williams, 1987).

In North America slavery became institutionalized in an uneasy system. It was the "peculiar institution" (Stampp, 1956). Despite numerous slave rebellions, unpublicized revolts and uprisings, and escaping of slaves, the slave trade continued to flourish uninterrupted. Eventually slavery[13] of the dark-skinned peoples became an accepted way of life. Historically, there had been a slave trade, especially in European women, by Arabs for their harems in northern Africa and the Middle East. This actually contributed to the lightening of the Black populations of the area, especially Egypt. However, ever since the successful rebellion of the White "slave" armies of the Mamelukes against the Arabs between 1316 and 1323 c.e., mass slavery in Africa and the West became associated almost exclusively with Blacks (Williams, 1987). This, psychologically speaking, helped put more distance between the Arab and European slaver and their "property." The unconscious imagery of virtuous pure white versus evil dirty black became enshrined. European philosophical and political opinion shifted and molded to adjust and assimilate this financially lucrative but evil fact of life. However, the deep contradictions inherent in Christianity, the emerging ideas of the Enlightenment, and the simple overt human brutality of slavery continued to stimulate an uneasy ambivalence in the minds of the Europeans. In the minds of Africans it was an abomination completely unthinkable. Thousands died of suicide. Only a third of those captured even made it on the slave ships across the ocean. Once in the New World many escaped into the interior, made alliances with the Indians, or disappeared entirely. This occurred not only in the emerging United States, but also in the Caribbean and in South America. This abominable institution eventually for geopolitical reasons reached its ends. However, the legacy of slavery and the psychological dynamics of the slaver and the enslaved continued and continues into today in the shared unconscious shaped by recent history.

Before we move any further, we should mention again two significant facts, since they have influenced unconscious racial imagery. First of all, historically speaking, the Spanish had been invaded, conquered, and then ruled by the dark Moorish African invaders from Mauritania for over 700 years. In point of fact, the Moors invaded even southern France while overrunning the crumbling Visigothic kingdom of Roderick. Under the command of Abd-al-Rahman they were defeated at the Battle of Tours or Poitiers in 732 c.e. by the Franks under the command of Charles Martel. It was a small battle in terms of the size of the conflicting sides but a historic one because it drew the outlines and stimulated in many ways the future emer-

---

13. The word "slave" refers historically to the Slavic peoples of Europe who were conquered by Romans and forced into servitude. Slavery of one form or another has been a phase in most world civilizations.

gence of European nations. At the time Charles Martel had only the desultory title "mayor of the palace." A certain stability of cultural, political, and historical forces in the region, however, soon arose after that. Pepin the Short conquered Aquitaine, suppressed the Lombards in Italy, and pushed the Moors from Languedoc. He also finally deposed the aging Merovingian dynasty and secured papal support for the new Carolingian house. Charlemagne arose and was crowned emperor of the Holy Roman Empire on Christmas day in Rome in 800 c.e. by Pope Leo III. After Charlemagne's death, his Carolingian empire split into the kingdoms of Germany and France. In Britain, Alfred the Great was having Latin classics translated into the "Olde English" idiom and thereby creating the foundation of English literature. Norway soon had its first king, and the Danes were also soon united under one leader. In the steppes, Rurik the Northman arose to become the first prince of Novgorod and set the stage for the emergence of modern Russia. This was in the northland of this cultural battle line, created by the Islamic Moors. The new line was vibrant, largely White and newly Christian.

In the South lay largely darker-skinned peoples and Africans. The Moors made Toledo, Córdoba, and Seville centers of culture and scholarship, spreading the university system throughout Europe. When they were finally expelled by Ferdinand and Isabella of Spain in 1492, they left behind a brilliant record in architecture, medicine, mathematics, science, numerous technical innovations that became the European Renaissance, and, yes, religious tolerance for the Jews. So, you see, if they had not been defeated at that rather small battle, the history of the world, particularly the history and the dynamics of Europe and Africa, may have been very different.

It should also be noted, as we've mentioned in earlier chapters, that the *original invaders* of Europe were themselves African in millennia past. The Grimaldi Negroids or their cousins were probably the first invaders of the European continent and became the substratum of the European Nordic and Alpine peoples. Even today one notices that the indigenous inhabitants of southern Europe, in particular the Spanish and the Italians, are much darker in complexion than northern Europeans. This plays itself out in subtle dynamics, especially in the United States, around issues of skin color. It is also significant, psychologically speaking, that the races of southern Europe, particularly the Italians and the Spanish and to a lesser extent the Portuguese, are collectively, in the popular "romantic" culture, imbued with more "life energy and life force" than members of the northern European tribes. Sometimes it is a source of pride and is emulated by other Whites. However, this is also an indication of the profound ambivalence of the peoples of southern Europe to issues of skin color due to their earlier contact with darker-skinned races from Africa, both as political subjects and also as conquerors later. Remember that African armies entered the Iberian peninsula several times, ruled kingdoms for a century before the Caesars, occupied Rome for a decade with Hannibal, and controlled Spain and Portugal for 700 years as the Moors. This dynamic around skin color, fears of contamination, and fears of "invasions" or penetration of the body politic, we will see, have a profound effect on the imagery and psychodynamics of racial relations in the present Americas—North America, South America, and the Caribbean.[14]

Fantasies of Color, Contamination, and "Drops" of Negro Blood

In the Americas, especially in North America, a person who had any trace of African blood, a single "drop," was considered contaminated and Black. Even today large numbers of White Americans will openly and proudly speak of their drop of Native American or Indian blood. Rarely is this the case with their drop of African blood! These "drops of Negro blood" in various percentages, as we stated earlier, gave rise to all kinds of classifications such as mulattos, quadroons, octoroons, etc. This definition would thereby have included such "Whites" as Alexander Dumas, the Russian poet Pushkin, and even the heroic Beethoven. Curiously enough, though, if you were a dark-skinned Egyptian living in Africa with woolly hair, full lips, and broad nasal features, along the Nile near the pyramids, you were somehow a "proto-White" of some variety. The deeper "logic" here, of course, is that anything associated with civilization, especially the roots of classical civilization itself, by definition had to be white. Such is the sad psychological equation of race and color that plagues us even into our own time.

In the political extreme one could say that the politics of racialization served a unifying purpose at one time. When the different European groups came to the United States, e.g., Anglo-Saxon, Irish, German, Dutch, Swedish, French, Italian, Greek, Slavic, Polish, etc., they needed to join together in a new union that was stronger than their old cultural identifications. Certainly neither the Irish nor the Jews were considered fully "Whites" until they came to the United States. The Irish masses, poor, brutally oppressed, and sometimes actually starving to death, were often no better than serfs to

---

14. Curiously enough, the person who helped Europeans see deep into their own family unconscious dynamics was the creator of psychodrama, a technique in group therapy, whereby roles are acted out to elicit their power and influence on our behavior and feelings. J. L. Moreno, a European, brought psychodrama to the United States in 1922 or 1925. Remember that our ancestors, *all* our early *Homo sapiens sapiens* ancestors regardless of our present day racial/ethnic group, were Africoid brown and black. The deepest, oldest familial images, our collective Alajobi, are dark brown and black. The word *moreno* literally means "brown." It is an interesting synchronicity or, at least, expression of the African unconscious in Europe that a "Brown" would help unlock the Brown family roots of everyone's psyche!

the British landowners and even to some other ruling-class Irish. Jews were the hated non-Christians of Europe, alien and suspect in their motivations and culture. When the Irish and Jews came to the United States, however, their skin color allowed them to be more easily identified with "White" Americans and the white privilege that came with it. Identifying as "White" and above what was "Black" and below, like any large-scale group dynamics situation, tends to create and solidify separate factions. It largely worked in America, and appropriate racial myths and legal-social powers cemented the structure together. This is an aspect of "White identity development." Now in our own day these dynamics, like an autoimmune disease, has turned on the body politic and threatens us in a deep and destructive way. We need a healing myth, a new, expansive, and inclusive metaphor for the future.

There is an acknowledged hostility and deep ambivalence in European cultures in relationship to darker-skinned peoples. In the latter part of the 20th century, as in the time of Hitler, the peoples of Italy, Germany, France, and other European nations have strong right-wing political movements that are somewhat like an anxiety reaction to the increased presence of dark-skinned immigrants from the rest of the world (Church, 1992). The opposite is not true, even though an argument can be made that in recent centuries Europe has brought dislocation and destruction to other parts of the world in its second rise. This fear of the Europeans may be due merely to biological and genetic factors. In terms of simple genetics, when darker-skinned and lighter-skinned peoples meet, the net effect is a general darkening of the skin of the White progeny. This may be due to the fact that by Golger's Law the original progeny of humanity was, of necessity, dark-skinned. But even on a more surface level it is simply a fact that the gene for lighter skin color is a "recessive trait." "Recessive" in this context means that when very light-skinned and very dark-skinned individuals procreate, the offspring are *perceived* by others to be dark-skinned, not white. Thus there may be genetically based fears of the dissolution or loss of racial skin predominance when there is a fusion with the darker-skinned peoples. There is in this a certain "threatened return of the repressed," the repressed being our origins in the dark earth, the dark unconscious, and all that "dark" has come to symbolize and represent.

During the Spanish Inquisition, the accused, usually the poor or unusual, were said to have congress with demons, most often *black* demons. The demon was hairy, had great sexual powers, was able to attack in one's sleep, and was most often a black dog, a black cat, a black crow, or even a Blackamoor. The recurring motif here is the evil black devil (Russell, 1972). Apparently, too much life force can turn a good, light person into a dark, evil being.

If one simply looks at the dynamics of "getting a tan," we will see some of this played out. The ambivalence of many of the lighter-skinned peoples to "getting a tan" often is associated with having more energy, looking healthier and stronger, having more vitality, being sexier, closer to the earth, closer to the "life force." However in European cultures, particularly those imbued with certain aspects of Christian and Islamic ideology, there is a rejection of the life force and life-enhancing imagery. This may be due to the religious denigration of sexuality in European cultures and religions. This is manifestly not the attitude of the hidden or Tantric forms of philosophy or spiritual practice.[15] However, for whatever reasons, there is a significant rejection of the life force since it is often associated with "down there" and unwanted impulses of an "animal nature." Indeed darker skin is often associated with "dirtiness" and is more earthward. It is also associated with an "animal nature" and therefore is further away from the "angels."

In an excellent article Lawrence Kubie (1965) presents an interesting analysis and approach to the differences between white skin and dark skin. In particular Kubie and then later others note the predominance of bestial, sexual, and scatological references to dark skin among both light-skinned and dark-skinned persons in the United States. We also see this from a nonpsychoanalytic point of view in an article in the *Journal of Black Psychology* by Kloss (1979). Here again dark skin is associated with bestiality, unwanted sexual impulses, and scatological references. Kovel (1971) in his psychoanalytic study of racial dynamics in the United States, *White Racism: A Psychohistory*, found that the roots of racism were entangled in the projected unconscious infantile images and fantasies that White Americans have concerning sex, animals, and dirt, especially the perceived dirt from their own bodies. "Black" skin becomes the psychical darkness into which negative "White" fantasies are projected. Blackness casts a disturbing "shadow," somehow whiteness does not! The only major exception to this being the great white whale of Herman Melville's *Moby Dick* (1851) who comes to symbolize much of the evil, self-obliterating, vast unconscious of Captain Ahab and his ego.

Others using the psychoanalytic beacon have illuminated the same matrix of bestial imagery, sexuality, and Earth-bound fantasies (Seidenberg, 1952; Pinderhughes, 1969). Black psychiatrists have found much the same scenario (Grier & Cobbs, 1968). It is a well-understood dynamic in the politics of sex, power, and race. However, there is also a deep ambivalence because sexuality and dark skin at other times are taken to be a sign of life enhancement, i.e., "getting a good-looking, sexy tan." Both of these may be

---

15. In the Tantric Ophidian cults of Africa, the early Dravidian-Yogic practices of southern India, and the Tibetan Tantric lineage, the dark and paradoxically luminous symbols and images of the life force are actively engaged in the intimate methodology of the biospiritual process.

seen to be a general reflection of a subtle Eurocentric tendency toward dissociation of the body–mind from the pulsating movement of the life current. There is an attraction to dark skin but also a fear of being dissolved in it, of "going Black," of the small point and light of consciousness that is the ego falling backwards into the dark unconscious. In other words, there is an attraction to the life-enhancing darkness, the rhythmic, pulsating, and healthy movement, but also a fear that one's own light-skinned egoic predisposition may be swallowed up in this darkness. It is a fear of the threatened return of the repressed—another version of the "devouring sphinx." It is a reminder of the ancient primordial dark emergence of mankind into the light and the fear that the light would be lost into the darkness again.

In the name of this fear, augmented by a long and real history of profit-driven slavery, exploitation, and fear of and remembrance of former invasion and control by certain African peoples, there was an ongoing fear of the darkness and dark skin as a representation of the darkness. "Light" is often seen as ascending and dark is often seen as descending. This simplistic rendering goes very deep into the primordial waters of the unconscious. This is not unique to Europeans. When the Arab jihads came out of Arabia in the 6th century C.E., they actively suppressed the indigenous peoples. This was to try and erase from the conscious mind the threatened unconscious memory and image of the primordial people of the Nile Valley and their indigenous culture, which had reigned for 5,000 years. This is not original or unique to either European or Islamic peoples. When the Indo-Aryans invaded India around 1500 B.C.E., they conquered the darker-skinned Dravidian peoples, the peoples who were more akin genetically to the peoples of East Africa. They then preceded to take over many of the aspects of the vital religion of the Dravidians and translating it, by use of written Sanskrit, into the Aryan culture.

Today, even many dark-skinned Indians identify themselves as "Aryans" and, weirdly enough, were sometimes accepted into the Third Reich! The deep primordial fear of losing the "consciousness of light" in the dark unconscious of one's original source is a deep and worldwide phenomenon. It may have a genetic basis. A warm, dark neuromelanin tract does seem to profoundly influence and, perhaps, guide the fetal development of organs and nerves during our embryogenesis, and the cosmos itself is nearly 90% composed of a mysterious "cold dark matter." Indeed the early experiments in civilization were carried out by a confluence of dark-skinned peoples of the Nile Valley, and the first *Homo sapiens sapiens* were Black. But this fascination with mere skin color is a surface-structure obsession. In deep structure, we are all the same species. Yet we cannot seem to let it go. It reflects a deep and simplistic ambivalence about our origins and reveals the fear of ethnic dissolution. It has also been the source of untold suffering on the part of not only dark-skinned peoples but also light-skinned peoples. Whenever we find a *dissociation from the life current* it is associated with darkness and the coming out of the "unconscious." In the unconscious we will find a fear of darkness, dark skin, and all things associated with the dark. Darkness, however, is not Blackness. For the ancient Kemetic Egyptians, darkness was ignorance, but Blackness was wisdom. Isis and Osiris were represented as Black, as was the symbolic black capstone of the pyramid. The scientific and experiential study of Blackness and light was conducted in the houses of life. For Blackness = Kemet, there was no dissociation. This is a subtle but important difference.

NURTURING IMAGES OF BLACKNESS IN EUROCENTRIC CULTURES

Even though Queen Elizabeth I complained about the increasing number of Blackamoors in London, no doubt reflecting some of the sentiment of her era, it was not enough to stop Shakespeare from adapting an old Moorish romantic legend into his *Othello*. Nor was Giuseppe Verdi opposed to the idea of composing one of his greatest operas about the royal family and their political dynamics when ancient Egypt was at war with the Ethiopians. Aida, the slave girl and daughter of the Ethiopian king, is in a secret love relationship with Radames, the eventual conqueror of the Ethiopians. Both, of course, are tragic figures and, perhaps, reflect a deep ambivalence about the African presence. The Black presence was especially prominent in the golden age of Spanish literature and had its roots in the Moorish/Jewish cultures that had thrived on the peninsula for the preceeding 700 years (Carew, 1992). Writers like Calderón de la Barca, Lope de Vega, Ximénez de Enciso, Andrés de Claramonte, and Vélez de Guevara wrote some of their most enduring works with the African presence permeating the landscape (Engling, 1995). A small number of radical European scholars were even aware of the African *origin* of Western civilization itself. C. F. Volney's *Ruins of Empires* (1881/1991), Gerald Massey's *Book of Beginnings* (1881), Albert Churchward's *The Origin and Evolution of the Human Race* (1921), and Godfrey Higgins' *Anacalypsis* (1836) all proclaimed the anathema in a century when Black slavery had been the law!

So in addition to these artists and scholars and the earlier-mentioned predominantly hostile, negative, and ambivalent images about blackness and dark-skinned peoples in European cultures, there is also a long history in this ambivalence of positive or nurturing images. In point of fact, there are numerous references to dark figures being imbued with great waves of life energy and therefore compassion, healing, and nurturant capacities, which in interesting sorts of ways are seen to be intimately involved with family life, kinship, and libido, and in many ways help hold the family together. We will focus primarily on the dynamics of North America, but there are numerous references that can be seen in the family and intimate religious life of South America (Freyre, 1956).

In the upper-class antebellum South of the United States, it was both desirable and quite common to have a Black slave in your house in the most intimate contact with family members and family processes. There were certainly numerous field slaves and artisan slaves who worked in the cities, but there were also slaves who worked in the intimate environment of the home and hearth. As mentioned previously, they tended to come from West Africa and from the central coastal areas of Africa. The movie *Gone with the Wind* has numerous images of the benevolent house darky who is a crucial aspect of the emotional matrix that holds the family together. In *Gone with the Wind*, Mammy, the Black slave of Scarlett O'Hara[16] at Tara, literally holds the family together through thick and thin. Mammy raised Scarlett, her sisters, and her mother on this plantation only a few miles from Twelve Oaks, where we are to assume a similar benevolent noblesse oblige occurred. Certainly Scarlett O'Hara's personality is dominant, but Mammy accompanies her on all of her sojourns. She even has the name Mammy, a variation of "Mommy." She could even express limited disapproval. From a feminist perspective, Scarlett is the classic White upper tier of strength, the spirited "belle" and plantation owner's daughter who keeps the family structurally and financially together. Mammy is the dark strong undergirth that holds the system emotionally together. In this context it is interesting that in the antebellum South the aristocracy often used Black women as wet nurses to suckle their young. This led to a curious psychological dynamic of intimate physical and emotional contact of a very nurturing kind both in imagery and in culture between female Blacks and both male and female Whites. The Black males are portrayed as simple-minded, humble, and loyal. "Yessum, Mis Scarlett." This operated coextensively with the possibly counterphobic reaction or reaction formation aesthetically speaking for the White female of the upper classes to be most valuable if her skin was very pale white or creamy white in complexion, an image that was the idealization of a fragile, passive women and sufferer (Tracy, 1995). In other words, this initial intimacy had to be countered later with the reality of slave life. It is also well known that during slave times in the antebellum South it was quite acceptable if not necessarily polite that the slave master took a great

---

16. Interestingly enough, Scarlett O'Hara of Tara is Irish or Celtic. For 700 years, the Celts, even into Scarlett's era, were the underlings of the Anglo-Saxons in Britain. Her family escaped serfdom in Ireland only to employ Black serfs in the United States. Freed American Blacks did the same in Liberia when they returned.

deal of liberty with the female slaves, and thereby kept the White wife away from men's dirty needs for sex. Naturally, it was believed that the Negress slave secretly wanted the master in order to satisfy her sexually aggressive, tigress appetites. She was hypersexual and attractive, a "seducer" of White males, a Jezebel. Mammy was unattractive and asexual but strong and reliant. Either way, the dance went on in bed. This is one reason why there is a wide variety of skin tones among African-Americans (Stampp, 1956). This peculiar fascination with intimacy, nurturance, and skin color followed American culture even into modern times.

For the unconscious of the European and many others, the color *white* is identified with *light*. To lose the "white" is to lose the "light," and so much of "White identity development" in the Western world is a contraction upon the associations to this formula. Black represents "primitive" to many Europeans but deeper than this symbolizes the potentially dangerous "primordial" and the dissolution of racial identity à la C. G. Jung in Africa and "going Black," or Freud's fear of occultism and the "black tide of mud." Yet primitive is really a derivation of "prime," or first, the consciousness we believe is prior to manifestation in nature, space, and time—the fundamental clear light, if you will, of the deep shared ancestral unconscious and the universe itself. So "light" is hardly "white"; it is energy and intelligence and largely unseen or "dark" and unconscious in a paradoxical way. Most of the universe, over 90%, is composed of "cold dark matter," literally an unseen sea of light energy. Nonlocality and quantum interconnectedness strongly suggest that this ocean of energy communicates with itself, both nonlinearly and at speeds faster than the speed of light. Metaphorically, the face of the divine is unseen and the darkness is faster than the speed of light. This humanizing paradox has yet to reach our species. Part of the way beyond racism for all groups is the literal transcendence of this simplistic white = light equation, to move beyond this destructive contraction and embrace the all pervasive light that is beyond mere color or form or name.

The Extended Family Unconscious

As far as symbolic family heroes are concerned, many of the "heroes and heroines" of American culture from the European perspective are dark-skinned and have the names of family members. Remember the wise "Uncle Remus" and his many stories of the supposedly kindly life in the South. Endearing characters he would talk about certainly did not talk overtly about slavery. However, what's important here is our memory that somehow "Uncle Remus" was symbolically part of the extended emotional family, some of the same familial dynamics applied to the original "Uncle Tom." The thinly veiled but somehow humanizing fantasy was that the slave was happy, that he was not pushed too much, and that when he became too old he was certainly taken care of by a grateful and benevolent but always superior master. He was supposedly allowed to live out his kindly older days as a simple darky on the plantation. This found expression in the Walt Disney movie *Song of the South*. In some contemporary dramas and movies, there is a nascent but clearly desirable shift toward seeing this African as an elder, a warm, nurturing, and "wise" older figure who helps initiate the younger, usually White person, into the complexities of life. This is mentioned to show again that there are two sides to the ambivalence.

Another reference to nurturance and intimate family circumstances is the idealized image of the "Aunt Jemima." She still finds her place on food labels in the United States even today. She has become a fixture and a reference to not only the intimate darky maid but also to the one who feeds and sustains you—a source of nurturance and life force obviously, but certainly not sexual. She is much like Mammy in *Gone with the Wind*, an emotional family member, loyal and reliable with access to intimate contact in very vulnerable circumstances. There is finally the case of "Uncle Ben," another fantasy relative of Aunt Jemima. Uncle Ben also is on the labels of different foods and represents the kindly house slave who is more than willing to serve his master, who has no requests of his own except that you be nice to him periodically. The classic nurturant Mammy is in this same family unconscious vein. Their fantasy offspring, of course, are Farina, Buckwheat, and the unnamed other on the Cream of Wheat box cover. This peculiar American fantasy has led to the much-quoted aphorism or feeling that "in the North they don't care how high you get as long as you don't get too close, and in the South they don't care how close you get as long as you don't get too high."

In the four decades prior to the Civil War, when slavery was at its zenith, these same soothing stereotypes became crystallized. The happy Sambo motif reinforced the belief that slaves, Black men in particular, were irresponsible, carefree, took a simple delight in food and dance, and, in their childlike behavior, were naturally suited to slavery. After all, slavery was a "positive good" for the darky race. The Black female was either a hidden sexual tigress or the Mammy. The Black Mammy was the antithesis of the idealized White female. She was portrayed as fat, asexual, and independent, not beautiful, fragile, weak, and dependent. The free Black of the North or South was still caught in this web of images. He was the Zip Coon, a dandy and buffoon, who really had no idea of what to do with his freedom (Riggs, 1986).

After the emancipation and war, the shift turned toward the belief that the former slave would regress to his former self before slavery, i.e., a wild, oversexed, bestial, uncivilized being bent on rape, drunkenness, and crime. He and his family had to be segregated in *every* area of social life. Hence,

Jim Crow laws and the fearful image of the "bad nigger" who had to be controlled by law, intimidation, and periodic KKK rampages. Most often the caste system was reinforced in innumerable social and familial situations and dynamics that fed upon these malignant underlying images. The ambivalence you see goes deep and can go back and forth, then back and forth over time. However the predominant imagery of Europeans about dark-skinned peoples in the United States and in the Caribbean has not been positive. Most are confined to the other side of the ambivalence.

MENACING IMAGES OF BLACKNESS

The other side of this ambivalence plays itself out in menacing images of Blacks. These not-so-hidden symbols include the fearful image of the Black as potentially explosive. This is no doubt rooted in the real memory and politics of the society, and became an institutionalized projection of fear and hostility that the slave master must have seen and felt from his angry and resentful Black slaves. This is one reason why in many slave-holding states, it was illegal for Blacks to read and write and a crime for Whites to teach them. This was an attempt to control information and communication that might lead to uprisings and rebellions. Despite this, there were over 250 recorded slave uprisings in the United States, slave revolts that the White master genuinely feared at various times in the South. The Underground Railroad conducted by heroic Whites and daring Blacks was a constant thorn in the side of slavery. It was quiet, effective, and truly humanitarian while placing its members at risk. There was also sometimes violent opposition to slavery by Whites, especially abolitionists, Quakers, and other religious groups. John Brown at Harpers Ferry on the eve of the Civil War was the most spectacular, but most who died in the war against slavery before the war were Black. Remember Nat Turner, Demark Vesey, the bloody, successful Amistad slave ship rebellion led by Sengbeh (also known as Cinque), and thousands of others. There were colonies of runaway slaves who lived in the swamps and bayous of Louisiana and Florida, in remote regions in the Caribbean archipelago, and in the interior of South America. The runaways numbered in the thousands. At any time a group of Blacks might revolt against their masters and kill them. This periodically happened. The price of this, of course, was death. However, sometimes it was believed to be better to die fighting than to endure the life of slavery.

Haiti saw a successful slave revolt led by Francois Toussaint L'Ouverture from 1793 to 1802, which, significantly enough, began with a forbidden Voudoun ceremony. In Brazil, African slaves developed martial-arts self-defense techniques that fused jumps, kicks, and other movements that could be done when the hands were bound in chains. This evolved into the Capoeira dance of Afro-Brazilian art. In South America, runaway slaves in the interior created fierce kingdoms that resisted slavery for nearly a century. These were the legendary Surumaka Marcuns. So slave rebellions were more than a fantasy of the plantation rulers. Out of this peculiar dynamic has come the imagery of the "crazy" or "bad nigger" motif. This was the Black, usually a male, on the plantation who would not kowtow to all the plantation master's whims. On their deathbed, masters would sometimes have visions of their slaves angrily coming to get them. Deathbed freedom proclamations had to be later overruled by the courts at the surviving families' request. Many masters had in their wills that on their death, the slave was to be set free, a parallel, we feel, to the spiritual dynamics and guilt found in certain West African witchcraft beliefs where the soul of the victim must be freed before the master's own death, or else the souls of the masters themselves fall into a kind of hell realm.

These negative and frightening images follow us even to present-day times. In the United States, particularly in the South and increasingly in coded reference to the inner cities and in national politics, politicians used this imagery to great effect. Who can forget in the 1988 political election when George Bush played on this with the horrendous story of one brutal individual whose name was Willie Horton. The use of this imagery touches deep unconscious sources and is a wellspring of political life in the United States. Periodically, when a violent and/or sexual crime is committed against a White person by an unknown person, the image of the Black male perpetrator is raised from this wellspring, and initially gains great White community support. Remember Susan Smith, who drowned her two sons in Georgia, and Charles Stuart, who murdered his pregnant wife for money. They both successfully blamed an anonymous Black male for the crime, and much of America instantly believed this for weeks. The news programs ate it up every day like red meat dropped in a pool of piranhas. Even the media are now aware of this recurring motif (Lacayo, 1994). It always sells well, especially in politics. Many a politician has come to power nationally and within his own state using this particular dynamic.

Another powder keg associated with the "bad nigger" motif is not only overt violence, but the *threat* of violence and impulsive, angry destruction. Inner-city rebellions such as the 1992 Los Angeles uprisings, those in Florida, and the others that have occurred throughout the 20th century in the United States are always there *in potentia*. This is felt in interpersonal and social relationships. A group of young African American males, small or large, will often provoke anxiety in a group of White Americans simply by being together in a store, on a street corner, in a mall or other public place. It is less so in a sports setting or university campus, but it is still there. Present-day rap music of the angry, incendiary kind, such as Ice-T's *Cop Killers*, provokes public and political outrage, while movies of White males violently killing hundreds of police and destroying buildings are seen as "only" entertainment (Ehrenreich, 1992; Kinsley, 1992). In both cases, there is excessive male violence, misogyny or at least dominance of women, and the threat of random mayhem. However, it is Black anger and rage that is most symbolically feared and is hoped to be repressed. The mass imagery of the cinema and television has historically gone in cycles with this but always with a heavy dose of the violent, sexual, or the silly simpleton or pathological person in our midst regardless of where in the cycle you look (Guerreo, 1993). When Blacks are not portrayed this way in White films, or even when they are presented as dignified sufferers of injustice at the hands of some Whites, often the other Whites in the film are cast as their saviors (e.g., *A Time to Kill, Mississippi Burning, Ghosts of Mississippi, Cry Freedom*). These trends will gradually change and mature over the cycles as Black wealth comes to own more of the means of production in cinema and television. Curiously enough, for centuries a group such as this was seen as docile and actually lived in fear of groups of White men, who, in anger or out of other motives, could lynch and murder Black men at will with few if any consequences! The country was rarely upset by this. Now the situation is ironically reversed. Sexuality, of course, is implicated here. This is closely associated with the next area.

In the much-publicized 1990s cases of boxer Mike Tyson and date rape, football legend O. J. Simpson and domestic violence, and even entertainer Michael Jackson and alleged but never proved or supported child abuse charges, the specter of violence, coarse or illicit sexuality, and Black male power dynamics hypnotized the media and an American thirsty for these images. The truth or validity of the situation is almost irrelevant. It is the pure sensationalism of the theme that captures attention. This is tacitly magnified in the unconscious by the "perception" of Black male dominance in some once primarily White male contact sports. Boxing, football, and basketball were all once the area of White male machismo. Now African Americans in the United States are "over" represented. The same is true in track and field. There are obviously many other sports in which this is not the case, e.g., swimming, tennis, etc. However, in the "mano a mano" sports where Black and White males encounter each other in the high-stakes colosseum of sports competition where physical strength is critical, the unconscious makes this equation.

Attendant with the "bad nigger" motif of anger is the imagery associated with sexuality. Again Blacks are often portrayed as having enormous sexual appetites, huge sexual organs, and therefore as more inclined toward rape and pillage. This is associated with the assumption that Blacks are

somehow less intelligent, as shown by inherently lower IQs and less restrain-
ing intelligence for impulse control; and, of course, they are also lazy and
less ambitious. In some regions of the European unconscious this equates
Blacks with the lower life forms, especially, as we will see, the life form of
the ape! This, of course, represents the ultimate genetic and physical expression of "going Black." These are psychodynamic reflections of the processes
of projection, projective identification, and displacement.

One of the more extreme forms of this displacement, as we said, occurs
in the imagery we might associate with a more cinematic reflection of this
unconscious, the movie *King Kong*.[17] In this movie an angry giant ape has
broken out in a modern city. He has been brought, against his will we must
notice, to the United States by White men after being drugged in some primitive mythological island inhabited by dark people. Once this giant ape is in
the city, he escapes and goes on a rampage killing people, most notably
White people. However, he has a tragic flaw. He falls in love with a "golden
blonde" he had met much earlier when she came to his island in search of
wealth and adventure, etc. He then proceeds to go after her, get her, and
keep her away from White men. He then climbs to the top of the biggest
concrete sculpture, that is to say, the biggest concrete phallus in the biggest
city in the world, New York City, and there meets his fate. Some streak of
nobility causes him to put her down at the last minute, and then the highest
forms of European war technology at that time, the airplane and the machine gun, shoot him off the top of the giant concrete phallus and he falls all
the way down, that is to say "descends" down to the concrete surface and
dies. Then it is proclaimed that it was not technology that really killed this
horrendous ape-beast with a sense of heart and loyalty, but it was somehow
the magical "beauty" who killed the beast. This same motif on beauty seducing the beast and then the death of the primitive or beast is a popular
Hollywood theme.

In a mood of revisionism we might humorously note that a number of
years later these same people go back to this mythological island to look for
King Kong's family and descendants. Unable to find Mrs. Kong, they are
able somehow to find his son. His son becomes "Mighty Joe Young." However, somehow Mighty Joe Young has been transformed and he turns out to
be a friend as opposed to the mighty wild ape that his father was. It is

---

17. Collective images of a people are portrayed in the mass media and large artworks
that capture the themes, moods, and temper of the times. The dynamics of individual creativity and dreamwork are transformed by the same processes of condensation, distortion, displacement, and projection by art that touches the collective unconscious memory and unfolds an either terrifying or liberating myth. See W. Abell's *The Collective Dream in Art*
(1966).

interesting to draw a parallel here between King Kong and his son, Mighty Joe Young, and the Oedipus trilogy. In both cases they are stories of traveling persons who meet with tragic fates. Of course, at the end of the movie *Mighty Joe Young*, we don't really know what happens to him. He redeems himself by saving White children trapped in the raging fire of an orphanage. After that his fate is unknown.

The Complicity of Science

The imagery of the African as an "ape" in the European unconscious as we have just seen has often seeped into what passed for objective medical science. Charles White (1799), a fellow of the Royal Society and a leader in his field, wrote that "in whatever respect the African differs from the European, the particularity brings him near to the ape." There were innumerable other examples in the Western history of ideas as cited in Plous (1994):

James Hunt (1863), president of the Anthropological Society of London—"The analogies are far more numerous between the Negro and apes than between the Europeans and the apes."

German zoologist Carl Vogt (1864), in a physiological description of the African—"All this affords a glimmer of the ape beneath the human envelope."

The American physician, A. J. Parker (1878) to the Academy of Natural Sciences of Philadelphia—"The Negro brain bears an unmistakably nearer relation to the ape type than does the white."

World-renowned Harvard paleontologist, Louis Agassiz (1888)—"The Negro by his bearing recalls the slender, active Hylobates."

The author, Charles Carroll (1900)—"All scientific investigation of the subject proves the Negro to be an ape; and that he simply stands at the head of the ape family, as the lion stands at the head of the cat family."

The zoologist Hermann Burmeister (1853)—"The Negro, in his deviations from the European, presents so many analogies with the conformation of the ape."

By 1884 the image in Europe was so common that the 9th edition of the Encyclopedia Britannica, under *Negro*, authoritatively stated that the African race was on "the lowest position of the evolutionary scale, thus affording the best material for the comparative study of the highest anthropoids and the human species." These lower anthropoid characteristics were (1) "abnormal length of the arm, which in the erect position sometimes reaches the knee-pan," (2) "weight of brain, as indicating cranial capacity, 35 ounces (highest gorilla 20, average European 45)," (3) "short flat snub nose," (4) "thick protruding lips," (5) "exceedingly thick cranium," (6) "short, black hair, eccentrically elliptical or almost flat in section and distinctly woolly," (7) "thick epidermis" ("Negro," 1884, pp. 316–317). Even the great Voltaire, voice of the Enlightenment, believed that "The Negro race is a species of men as different from ours as the breed of spaniels is from that of greyhounds ... if their understanding is not a different nature from ours, it is at least greatly inferior. They are not capable of any great application or association of ideas."

The list, sadly enough, can be greatly extended. The zoologist Ernst Haeckel (1876) went so far as to classify Africans as *Homo niger*, a distinct species and much less evolved than his own *Homo mediterraneus*, completely incapable of "true inner culture and of a higher mental development." These images are still with us and haunt our collective psyches from science to sports to its most recent expression in debates about IQ, race, and the "bell-shaped curve."

There are other motifs of the American popular culture that stress the brute power of the African Black versus the mental acumen of the European. The story or ballad of John Henry is one. John Henry, the Black athletic man of muscle and the real builder of the railroad, is pitted against a new technology. They do battle and John Henry wins, but it costs him his life. When a White male is imbued with extraordinary physical power, he has the mental superpower to go with it. Superman is white but has a superior mind, as do all the mass culture traditional superheroes. It is curious that Superman came to prominence in American culture in the 1930s, about the same time as the distorted Nazi version of Nietzsche's superman came to power in Berlin. John Henry is a controlled, powerful bodily force, but we know nothing of his intellect. King Kong and Mighty Joe Young are giant apes.

It is interesting in the context of these bits and slices of "nobility" found in King Kong and Mighty Joe Young that in the 15th and 16th centuries in Europe, in addition to the predominant profit-driven capitalist engines that enslaved Blacks, there was also a small philosophical movement that went to the other extreme. In other words, there were certain writings that spoke of the "noble savage." Rousseau and others believed that Blacks in Africa had special powers and abilities. To say the least, they were a minority opinion. But even this image of a "noble savage" eventually became twisted and distorted in the American dynamic of slavery, such that after the middle passage the Black who was in the United States was seen as a "happy darky" or an ignoble savage. After the defeated Native American peoples were no longer a threat to American society, they eventually took on the noble savage image in the collective psyche. When the slave was not a "happy darky," however, he could quickly turn into an angry bad nigger. The ambivalence is played out. This returns us to the dynamics of slavery, rabid forms of capitalism, and the peculiar intimacy in antebellum times of the White aristocracy, the ones who actually owned and kept slaves, using Black women as wet nurses for their children.

Many psychologists, including Naim Akbar in his book, *Chains and Images of Psychological Slavery* (1984), point out how much of the legacy of slavery is still with us today. This includes our imagery in Antebellum slavery times of what the Christian God looks like—a white, non–Jewish-looking person often depicted nailed on a cross. This is despite the Biblical description of Christ as having "woolly hair" and feet "the color of bronze." It also included, until recently, certain standards of Eurocentric beauty and attractiveness. But more than these two, it reflects the legacy of slavery in terms of what Blacks were used for. In other words Blacks were used primarily for *labor*, some forms of *nurturance*, especially *food preparation* and *childcare*, and *entertaining* the master with their antics, humor, and music. In Black humor one often finds a great deal of fun in reference to body parts. In Black humor you'll see a great deal of reference to the anatomy of the butt, lips, hair, and other features. On TV comedy shows Blacks gyrate their buttocks and other bodily parts much more so than Whites and Asians. In recent times, however, the other side of the ambivalence has gotten played out. After the absolutely necessary political movement in the 1960s where "Black is Beautiful" came into vogue there was a decrease in the negative associations to these features. Now in contemporary times we find many Hollywood stars, especially White women, being praised for having certain kinds of traditionally Black features. In particular, the high narrow or rounded rear end, the full, generous lips, and certain stylistic ways of dealing with the hair on the head are seen as positive beauty traits. This sad ambivalence gets played out back and forth, back and forth over too many long and painful years ("They Took Our Music," 1991).

The Legacy of the Plantation

Of more enduring significance than this back-and-forth ambivalence, however, are some of the other psychological legacies of the plantation system. Naim Akbar (1984) brilliantly elucidates how the slavery system served to institutionalize certain psychological structures in Blacks and Whites in the United States and no doubt in the Caribbean. He points out how the institution of slavery for the African American in many ways led to a sense of alienation from the fruits of one's labor, the fruits of one's work. This is somewhat of a Marxian interpretation. He also alludes to a certain avoidance or ambivalence about work, since historically work has not led to one's individual profit. This in combination with the sociopolitical and the financial system continues to make the avoidance of work or the ambivalence about work at least a dynamic possibility. The hundreds and hundreds of years of harsh slavery led to the decrease in the stability in the family, the erosion of the sense of masculinity except in certain prescribed ways, and an amplification of certain dynamic aspects of family life. These all had a profound influence on the African American reflection of the African unconscious.

In particular, two modes that were allowed some expression in the wider American culture from the African American culture still persist today. During plantation times the slaves were allowed in their antics to make fools of themselves and clown around to entertain their masters. They were there primarily, however, for cheap labor, and thus the physical *stamina of Blacks* was seen as a value. As a consequence of this we see the process of clowning around, entertainment, especially music, and also athletic prowess emphasized in the African American culture in the wider public sector. These were the roles that were allowed and financially rewarded. Today, these roles have evolved into wide cultural influences that are exported with American culture to the rest of the world. African Americans are well-grounded in the fields of athletics with giant billboards of them in the streets and malls of our cities and photos of them covering the bedroom walls of millions of adolescents. Their root is at the source of jazz, rock-and-roll, and blues, all of which are multibillion-dollar international phenomena. American youth has slowly taken on the styles of Black youth in language, physical gestures, music, clothing, and some values, especially being "cool" and "hip." These images and energies are being enfolded into the national soul. This has been a steady trend since the 1920s, and is now being projected via American cinema and music throughout the globe. A kind of Trojan horse.

The least rewarded, of course, was African American exploration in the area of written language and scholarship. This continues to be manifest even today. You need only ask who are the most well-known African Americans in wider American culture and you'll see that the vast majority of these are entertainers, particular comedians and musicians, or athletes. These are the ones who make the most money. There's considerably less attention and financial reward for scholarship, or seeking to be a doctor or a lawyer or other professional of some variety (Akbar, 1984). This is in stark contrast to the Jewish model. There is some respect for this intellectual and professional tradition, but generally speaking, it's certainly not what you really want to do if you're an African American teenager and you can look at the mass images and pop culture propaganda or television or even read the newspaper.

One of the devastating legacies of the plantation system was systematic family disintegration. On the plantation, family members were sold off according to the caprice and financial needs of the master. This has led not only to the disorganization of the family but also to an exacerbation of certain kinds of pathological behavior. The shift in the skills required of the new labor force, the decline of traditional types of jobs and income in industrial production, the internationalization of credit, and the move toward an information economy has intensified the erosion of the traditional financial base of many African American communities in the second half of this century (Wilson, 1987, 1996). It has led to an awesome implosion of a seemingly permanent underclass that further peppers the open sores of racism even while the upwardly mobile Black middle class has more than doubled. Not only has poverty become endemic in the inner cities, but work and responsible fatherhood have radically decreased, leading to more breakdown in family structure and despair. The Black middle class itself, with the financial and political gains earned during the civil rights movements and so no longer confined to the inner city, began to abandon these neighborhoods. The "liberation" of integration thereby helped dig a deeper grave for those left behind in the struggle. This is a devastating cycle socially and psychologically. One takes self-esteem when one can, even if it is fleeting. It is not difficult, therefore, to notice that there is high premium placed on being a "stud" in the American system for all men. But in particular for a large percentage of Black men, this is seen as a reflection and avenue for the expression of power and masculinity, especially when financial options and other expressions of success appear limited to him. This is reinforced repeatedly in the culture. It appears on the nightly news as often as possible in the form of an "explosive" study, drug addict, or violent criminal. It is constantly reflected in the media. It is usually associated with the ideas of "irresponsibility," especially sexual irresponsibility and similar motifs. This is literally the assassination of the Black male image in society. This constant distortion and propaganda is repeated over and over and over again and then eventually becomes a collectively accepted image, which then further reinforces the group behavior. Contrary images are often ignored or are in an uphill battle, since they don't pull for a certain fit in the mass imagery. In some communities you can even observe some Black males occasionally holding the phallus in their hand! This is both an expression of "vitality" and "strutting their stuff," and a palpable external expression of feeling castrated.

In an interesting play on this deeply rooted process, we see in early European-American medical texts how Blacks were diagnosed during slavery. Blacks were "noted" to have a higher degree of sexual problems and more of certain kinds of borderline intelligence and malignant mental problems than were Whites (Stampp, 1956). What the Europeans failed to see was that some of the "mentally insane slaves" were also expressing depression, anger, and reality-based vicious persecution or paranoia. In contemporary times Blacks are often hospitalized predominantly with the diagnosis of "paranoid schizophrenia" (Cobbs & Grier, 1968). Where the European American saw a happy, simple darky by nature, their resultant plantation life psychiatric problems were seen as merely deviations from this norm. Intentional destruction of the master's property, irresponsibility on the job, constant sickness and mischief were not expressions of rage and rebellion, but rather "Dysaesthesia Aethiopica." Running away from the plantation of happiness was not seen as escape from bondage and slavery but as "Drapetomania," and its sulky and dissatisfaction symptoms required a healthy therapeutic beating! I suppose that the happy, primitive, life-rhythmic, sexually loose, simple-minded slave psychiatrist might have looked upon the European American and diagnosed his lifestyle as a case of Anemic Rhythmaticia and his stern demeanor in dealing with the slave as Dyhumorous Lossmaticus.

It is fair to say that almost always when the African American cultural genie produces a *new* product or synthesis of forms, it invariably receives a generally negative reaction from the dominant culture. Jazz was met this way (decadent), as were rock-and-roll and rhythm-and-blues (the devil's music); dance was seen as too sexually aggressive. Rap is . . . Hip hop is . . . The poetry and lyricism are often overlooked. When the demographics force "gangsta rap" to mature or self-immolate it will be replaced by another. This list goes on and on with each new cultural creation, with the initial negative reaction of the dominant culture often repeating itself, only later to partially embrace what it first rejected. Yet with a few notable exceptions, the overwhelming majority of all the new dances that arise in the United States and Latin America are rooted in this culture. (See Appendix C.)

The dynamics of Blacks and Whites is not of course unique to the United States. This plays itself out in southern parts of Europe, and also some areas of France and England, e.g., the "Black Irish." It also plays itself out in North Africa. One particularly adept explorer of this was Franz Fanon in his *Black Skin, White Mask* (1967) and *The Wretched of the Earth* (1963). He proposed a political solution to the psychological situation.

This racist reaction in the Americas to dark skin was not confined exclusively to dark-skinned Africans. Even within the European community itself there were rather strange dynamics concerning those who were Europeans but had darker skin. Most early European Americans came from England and the north of Europe. American racism finds its expression in the fact that there was a belief that Alpine Europeans were inferior to Nordic Europeans (Diop, 1991). There were a number of immigration laws in the United States that tried to keep low the number of Europeans who came from the south of the Loire River in Europe. Also Europeans of darker skin tone, in particular the Spanish and Italians, have historically had significant difficulty in dealing with the northern Europeans. They have had more difficulty being "integrated" into the larger American society than had the French, German, Dutch, or the northern European peoples. The southern European peoples are also extremely sensitive to issues around skin tone. One need only see the movies of Spike Lee to see this referred to repeatedly.

This history of European racism toward not only Blacks but even to dark-skinned Europeans goes all the way back to Galen. Galen had a very negative image of Blacks. He associated Blacks with certain kinds of mental problems and also certain kinds of sexual issues (Diop, 1991). Later in Europe the philosophical prophet of the Nazi movement, Gobineau, in his theories of racial purity set the groundwork for the later psychotic episode of the Nazis.

There is a psychological and genetic legacy in the 10 to 15 million slaves who actually arrived in the Americas out of the 30 million or so who were stolen for slave ships in the Diaspora. We have seen legacies of the African unconscious not only in diasporic West African religions but also in other formats. We have made a connection in earlier chapters to the relationship between the Kemetic African peoples, their Diaspora to not only West Africa but in earlier times to East Africa and the south of India. We now turn our attention to some more speculative aspects of the encounter between the dynamic forces in the United States. These will reinforce the recognition that skin tone and skin color have enormous dynamic influences on the American psyche. In particular the fear of being engulfed or dissolved by dark skin is a perennial American fear and fantasy (Welsing, 1991).

BLACKS' PERCEPTIONS OF WHITES IN THE AMERICAS

The other half of the equation of who perceives whom is how the Blacks and slaves viewed the Whites and rulers in society. The overwhelming reality was that White people owned the slaves and/or were the more politically, socially, economically, and militarily powerful group. This existed across gender lines also. The vast majority of Blacks came as lifelong bondsmen with little hope of freedom. The few free Blacks of the North and South were greatly outnumbered by the sea of Blacks who were slaves by birth. There were few exceptions to the rule. This landscape of cultural, social, financial, and military domination created a set of dynamics that in some perpetuation lives with us to this day.

Blacks often perceived the master as cruel, wealthy, brutal, and given at times to capricious angry outbursts. This was a mechanism of social control and a reflection of the conquer–conquered relationship. While episodes of kindness did occur and there were some humane plantation masters, the slave system was based on racism, labor, control, subjugation, and power. It was an easy extension to perceive a master as evil and a form of the devil. In the dreamlife of African Americans today and most certainly in the slave-saturated South, Whites would often appear as vampires and soul-stealers (Bynum, 1998). These nightmarish creatures, called Bandoki, have a long history in the mythology of numerous West and Central African peoples. The European was the embodiment of demonic forces sucking the lifeblood out of his victims and eating their souls like a witch. The Nation of Islam in the 20th century rarified this perception by at one time characterizing the European man as a "White devil" and even assigned him another kind of biological evolution.

In order to keep the master–slave psychology dominant, episodes of cruelty and brutal anger, such as whippings, hangings, and various forms of physical humiliation, were practiced. Especially necessary was a brutal putdown of any spirit of defiance or independence, particularly from young and middle-aged Black men. This, of course, continues today in various forms, with the police enlisted to do this instead of the overseer or master. After the liberation war of 1860–1865, there arose the KKK, then later Jim Crow laws and the Supreme Court's separate-but-equal ruling which was never enforced. This was all despite the legality of the Emancipation Proclamation and the 13th, 14th, and 15th Amendments to the Constitution. In the 20th century, the day-to-day grind of social and economic racism and the more overt symptoms of institutional White psychopathic dealings with Blacks are seen in the FBI's Cointel programs of the 1960s and 1970s to destroy prominent Black male leadership and with the tacit support of the Mafia to flood the inner cities with inexpensive addictive drugs.[18] Also add to this the CIA's apparently tacit knowledge of and passive role in the 1980s to pay for the war with the Nicaraguan Contras by importing and selling large amounts of crack-cocaine to African Americans in the inner cities. The intentional secret use of Black males to study syphilis in the infamous Tuskegee experiments is only one experiment we officially know about. There is a shared perception today in the African American community that when a Black male reaches prominence in a field, he is often suddenly attacked by the system and assumed guilty unless proven innocent (Smolowe, 1994).

Significantly enough, when lynching occurred after emancipation the "crimes" that White mobs were supposedly avenging were either a rumored

---

18. From time to time rogue cells of the FBI and CIA have taken on the racist political agenda. However, these rogue cells appear to have operated outside the sanctioned knowledge of those highest in the elected government. J. Edgar Hoover did not report his rogue operations to either the Congress or the executive branches for obvious reasons.

Black male–White female transgression, usually the fantasy around the romance of rape or brutality, or Black males stepping out of their docile "place." White mobs, mostly male, often engaged in ritualistic digital and genital mutilation of the male body, an overt indication of both conscious and unconscious racial-sexual preoccupations. The symbolism of this was not lost on the African American community. There was Black political resistance to the point that prior to World War II there was some pro-Japanese support among many. This was largely in American cities like St. Louis, Philadelphia, Cincinnati, and Pittsburgh. This Pacific Movement of the Eastern World (PMEW) had some ties to the Japanese consulate in Chicago and flowered in the dire conditions of the Great Depression along with various Islamic groups. These in turn had arisen with the collapse of the African American Nationalist Movement of the Universal Negro Improvement Association in the late 1920s (Allen, 1994, 1995).

All this harassment had contributed to a perception of Whites by many Blacks as evil, cruel, impulsively angry, powerful, and given to lynching and murder. The prosperous Black town of Rosewood in Florida was suddenly attacked in 1923 and burned to the ground by Whites and many of its Blacks murdered and scattered. No legal consequences occurred. In 1921 the Whites of Tulsa exploded and burned 35 blocks in the Greenwood section. Scores were murdered. No legal consequences occurred to Whites, although fear of Blacks remained. In 1956 the state of Mississippi created and secretly operated for years the Sovereignty Commission to protect against the "encroachment" by the Federal government after the 1954 *Brown vs. Board of Education* Supreme Court ruling. The secret Commission quickly became a hostile spy organization that watched, harassed, and gathered information files on the Freedom Movement at every opportunity (Garrow, 1998). It was common knowledge, especially in the southern United States, that the police and sheriffs during the day were often the KKK hooded vigilantes at night. Partially perhaps as a result of this, there arose a duel consciousness in the mind of the African American in relations with Whites. The Black "performed" certain roles and provided the White with the White's "understanding of the Negro," yet stood removed in order to protect what little survival and self-esteem remained of his life. This was one side of the Black ambivalence toward Whites. There was also another side.

Given the European imagery of the White Christ figure, the dominance of White-is-right, Black-is-evil language associations in English, and the overt power differential between the groups, the color white naturally became associated with dominance, control, and what was to be emulated. In religion, the White Christ figure had both conscious and unconscious associations with salvation, purity, and escape from the living Black hell of slavery (Akbar, 1984). This is despite the fact that the Bible itself described Christ as a man with "woolly hair" and feet "the color of bronze," clearly not a blond, blue-eyed White male.

In African societies, white was sometimes associated with purity and also sometimes with death and ghosts. This ambivalence of white as cruel at times, at other times the color of god, of power and dominance but also of sucking the life out of you, in other words, a kind of psychic vampirism, all contributed to an intense and, at best, unremitting ambivalence. This ambivalence reflected a constant anxiety and duplicity in dealings with Whites, who could explode at any minute with cruelty and sell you off to another slaver, thereby destroying (again) the integrity of your family and children. House slaves as well as field slaves had to watch the master and other Whites very closely, learn their psychology and moods, all the while hiding their own disposition and enacting the expected safe role of simple, happy darky. In this way, again, the Whites felt they "understood the Negro," and the African American stayed behind "the mask" and lived in his "dual consciousness" in relations with the ruling race. White slave holders who were apologists for the "peculiar institution" projected into this the Sambo, the Zip Coon, and other caricatures. Deviation was punished by all manner of cruelty, including selling away one's own flesh and blood. It is a little like the tenuous nature of an alcoholic family and its ACOA dynamics or sexual abuse family secrets, only that the cost of betrayal was higher and lasted a lifetime.

The dynamics of dependency flourished in this ambivalence. Food, shelter, and clothing generally came from the master, as did the right to travel and any special rewards. The house slave would identify at times, not all the time, but sometimes with the master and assure him of the master–slave dynamic. But there was always a boundary beyond which neither passed. This extended even into the subtle world of the family unconscious.

Masters and slaves had sexual relationships as a matter of course. The dynamics of conquered and conqueror were played out over and over. The offspring of these unions, occasionally out of love but usually out of sheer domination and power, were known to everyone. Family secrets are hard to keep. White fathers and "colored" offspring were numerous and many lived on the same plantation. Some were treated like shadow family members and taught to read and even remembered in the master's will. Some became involved in familial loyalty conflicts of all kinds (Bennett, 1962). But most were kept at a distance and the entire community conspired in the secret. The ambivalence was deepened and the imagery of being either "part White" or of having "congress with Negras" took its toll.

The ideology of racial inferiority was the state religion. One could be in the most intimate of familial, sexual, or nurturant relationship—e.g., Black wet nurses—but certain lines had to be maintained. The imagery of the White was fluid, yes, but mostly negative in the mind of the Black slave, even though aspects of its power and attributes were envied and emulated. The Blacks who became Christianized in the United States began to identify with another persecuted group, ironically enough the same people whom their Kemetic ancestors had held in captivity for 400 years several millennia earlier, the Hebrews of Biblical times. The spirituals of North America reflect this. A cruel, evil, powerful pharaoh is cast as a White man, the same White man that during that time in Biblical history when the Kemets were raising the pyramids, charting the constellations, and sailing the seas from India to the Americas, was roaming the forests of northern Europe in animal skins and tattooed bodies without the vaguest notion of what it meant to read or write.

As we shall see, the religion and consciousness of the stolen Africans held enfolded within them not only rituals and a highly evolved philosophy uprooted from the mother continent, but also psychic and psychological structures and psychospiritual technologies that even in transformation had a profound effect upon the cultural and religious life of the emerging new peoples of the Americas, both North and South.

THE SEEDS OF BLACK SPIRITUALITY
IN SLAVE RELIGION AND PHILOSOPHY

African American spirituality, in both North and South America, was a fusion of West African lineages and those that, through West Africa, stretched back to the days of ancient Egypt and the civilizations of the Nile. From West Africa came what was later to be Voudoun, Santería, worship of the Orishas, and the bodily apprehension of the divine in "possession." From the Nile Valley and ancient temples of Abydos, Abu Simbel, Luxor, and others came scattered practices of the Masons, Freemasons, alchemists, and Rosicrusians. They survived the middle passage across the Atlantic, sometimes with divining chains around their necks, and made it far enough to sink roots into the western shore. The saga of Osiris was repeated on a collective scale. Like Osiris the African was tricked and captured by malevolent forces, transported down river to the sea, then across it in a wooden prison, and came to live as a pillar (tamarisk tree) and support to an alien kingdom—and in subtle ways has been at the foundation for generating new life in a new civilization. How did this happen?

When the medieval empires of Ghana, Mali, Songhay, and others flourished, they were partially influenced by Islam. Slaves were stolen from the Serer, Bambara, Fulani, Hausa, Wolof, and other peoples who were Muslims in practice and yet had retained their older beliefs in witchcraft, possession, and related phenomena. The Muslims brought as slaves to the Americas became quite famous in some areas for their talismans and charms. Indigenous religion and Islam dominated West Africa until a few former slaves returned late in the 18th century and the residing colonial powers extended Christianity beyond the coastal areas.

Pervading the indigenous West African religious groups was a belief in a supreme or high god, in Yoruba referred to as Olorun, who created or unfolded the world, then stood back. Lesser gods and ancestor-spirits were also seen throughout nature, as these could be more directly approached by people for personal reasons. They are associated with natural forces such as wind, thunder, lightening, and natural areas or objects such as rivers, trees, etc. The Yoruba called them Orishas, the Ibo referred to them as Alose, the Ashanti as abosom, and Fon of Dahomey as vodun. The vital energy was called ase.

This vital energy or ase again was thought to be deeper than the three dimensions of ordinary objects and imbued them with the life force. Artists sought to evoke this ase in their work since it was the inner expression, the real essence, of the outer material work. This ase, this sense of vitality and life force, pervades the context of African American culture from the church to the street to daily discourse (Abiodun, 1994). It is the literal "shakti" of the community and is highly prized as the living essence of objects, persons, and events.

Chapter 6 has already detailed the role of priests, ritual, and dance possession. What is worthy of restating is that these spiritual forces, believed in by both Muslims and traditionalists, were seen to inhabit and pervade *all* levels of life, from the individual, to the family, the community, the nation, the phenomenal universe itself. There was no tradition of mental dissociation of the spirit from the body or the material environment. The whole process was alive and highly *personal* in one's experience. People and the spirit world made constant communion with each other by way of divination, sacrifice, and spirit possession.

In essence, there was a shared pervasive belief in a transcendent, divine creative intelligence and the existence of lesser but more approachable spirits to whom you could make sacrifice. Spiritual power pervaded all nature and directly affected the affairs of people. The power of priests and priestesses could manipulate these powers with special language and techniques. Spirit possession by these natural and supernatural forces was a normal occurrence, and the organization of these forces in nature was created by some overarching design (Raboteau, 1978; Ray, 1976). The ancestors in particular were believed to be approachable because of their family unconscious connection, and so shrines were erected to them among others. Secret societies flourished in this milieu, as did special charms, witchcraft, "medicine" to ward off witchcraft, and divination. Of particular interest was the highly articulated dance that was the "signature" of each separate spirit when it "mounted" a devotee. This was the *bodily worship of the living God.*

These practices and beliefs were carried to the Americas. They survived almost intact in many parts of South America and the Caribbean. Voudoun in Haiti, Santería in Cuba, Shango in Trinidad, Candomble in Brazil are all variations on this spiritual paradigm. Some modern Voudoun scholars and practitioners believe that all these traditions are really descendants of the original Kemetic secret religion of Voudoun and have shown evidence of their widespread but underground existence in much of the African American psychospiritual lineage (Ben-Jochannan, 1970; Ashanti, 1990). These scholars also stress that its practice has not been confined exclusively to Blacks, but that Hispanic and European peoples have also been influenced by the faith, e.g., faith healing and certain Christian fundamentalist sects. The dance possession rites are integral to all of these. This involves drumming, singing, bodily movement and rhythmic incantation, sometimes for hours, along with special clothes, food, and related rituals. Eventually, the gods enter "the heads" or ori of their devotees and a transcendental swoon and wave of ecstatic bodily energy overwhelm the individualized consciousness principle. In the Ifa lineage, when the ase arises or descends into the ori and is stabilized there, the unitative conscious state of lae-lae occurs, a kind of Nirvana or Turyia. The parallel to the Num energy of the !Kung people of the Kalahari Desert and the spiritual cleansing kyrias and then full rise of the Kundalini process is obvious. This bodily process with its conductivity of psychospiritual forces, we believe, is one of the defining dynamics of the African unconscious. From this position atheism is an odd belief, alien, and an expression of bodily doubt. The serpent religions of West Africa found expression in the Domballah, the rainbow god of Ouidah, seen as both a serpent and a multicolored wave of light, rising through the body and liberating the head. These and many other practices either flourished or were syncretically fused with the European religions in the Americas.

Most people believe that the thrusts and practices of African religions were more tolerated in Latin America than North America (Raboteau, 1978). They stress that cults of Candomble, Santería, Voudoun, Shango, and others are more alive in South America because the images of Catholic saints were more easily fused with African spiritual figures than the more limited ones of the English. In Bahia in Brazil, there was also a back-and-forth travel of vessels and Africans between Bahia and Lagos, thus keeping the ancient traditions alive. This was less so in the United States, but such traditions still survived. In fact in some ways the tradition is more authentic in Bahia than elsewhere! Spirit possession, incantations, beliefs in "medicine," witchcraft, and dancing religion with its associated facial expressions and bodily gestures flourished in the southern states. This was most often seen in the ecstatic behavior of Black revivalist churches. The same rhythmic chants, foot stomping, shouts, and back-and-forth calls between preacher and audience could be seen.

Whites were often frightened and repelled by these worship services (Bennett, 1962). But not all: Some secretly felt in Black religion a kind of salvation. In fact there appears to be a dynamic relationship between the central focus of African religions, spirit possession, and the seat of evangelical Protestantism, the conversion experience. Both involve being overcome by the spirit and often the eclipse of personal identity for a while. Both involved singing, shouting, and bodily movement. But there are some real differences. The conversion experience was also to be "saved" by Jesus. The other was to be mounted and possessed by a specific one of several gods. The movements of the Blacks were invariably described as more coordinated, expansive, and repetitive, less jerky and more similar to the coordinated movements of others in the worship group. The music of the Blacks was carried across the Atlantic and still stressed call and response, syncopation, polyrhythms, slides from one note to another, hand and foot clapping, and a great deal of heterophony, much of which was thought to be frightening, wild and "barbaric," yet "strangely fascinating" to the Whites (Raboteau, 1978). Almost the same can be said today whenever there is a new innovation in Black music, from the "hip" of rock-and-roll to the *rhythmic incantation* woven through rap music. It will be a powerful new episode in the history of music and human consciousness, however, when the attention of America's Black musical innovators goes back to its real roots in the "possession" music of the Orishas and this ecstatic liberating force finds expression in popular music!

The Africans of the southern United States practiced conjuring, "medicines," Voudoun, and related practices, much of it, it seems, related to the snake god cults of Dahomey, where the god Domballah was seen as a snake and luminous rainbow whose fluid energies moved through men's lives and directed their spiritual destinies. The parallel to Kundalini is in evidence.

In Arada and Ouidah, the coastal kingdoms that were conquered by Dahomey between 1724 and 1727, the cult of the snake god Dangbe was dominant. These conquered peoples were sold as slaves to the French, who then dispersed them to Martinique, Santo Domingo, Haiti, Guadeloupe, and then Louisiana. At least 3,500 came in around 1716 and 4,000 others came later (Puckett, 1969; Tallant, 1962). This had a profound effect on religious practices in the southern United States.

A significant number of the esoteric beliefs and practices that were explored in the context of West African and Kemetic Egyptian religions concerning the dead, spirit travel, and related phenomena are held by African

Americans even today (Brandon, 1990; Gonzalez-Wippler, 1987; Mulira, 1990; Thompson, 1983). Most are loathe to talk about these with Whites and even many other African Americans for obvious political and religious reasons. They are difficult to articulate, place one in a rather vulnerable position, and are generally met with hostility in a milieu that defines reality, even religious reality, as a world of objects interacting with other objects, spacialization, and linear space–time progressions. There is a universe of felt "presence," vibration, spectral and frequency modulated resonate affinities in which spatial and temporal nonlocalities at times intelligently predominate.

Protestant and Catholic influences were brought to bear by Whites in the United States as they sought to teach and indoctrinate the slaves. Fusions and creative new syncretic images emerged on the scene. Black Christian preachers arose to teach the slaves and the free Blacks. White preachers also sought to teach the slaves. There were large free Black churches in Philadelphia, New York, Boston, and other major northern cities. Born in reaction to White Christian rejection, they became the AME, the AMEZ, CME, Baptist, and a host of variations. There were secret orders—the Masons, Knights of Pythias, Odd Fellows. Charismatic leaders arose like Richard Allen and Absalom Jones, who as great preachers were later echoed in the activist preacher tradition by Martin Luther King, Jr., and Adam Clayton Powell. There was also a subtle messianic tradition—Daddy Grace, Father Divine, the Honorable Elijah Muhammad. Like the religious Jews of the Zohar and Kabbala, who sought out the little illui who would illuminate the esoteric texts and fill their own vessels with God, in the African American tradition seekers in the Christian faith were often looking for that "little master," that child so full of vitality and prophetic wisdom in the voice, who can deliver them from the shadows of Babylon. In their prayers they often looked to a tall, blond, blue-eyed Christ. Only a few it seems noticed very much that Revelations 1:14–15 mentions that Jesus was a man with "woolly hair like sheep" and "feet the color of bronze."

Despite that, it is here, too, that elements of the ancestral religion could readily be seen in the classic features of African diasporic spirituality, especially deep rhythmic music, call-and-response style, spirit possession, the belief in certain kinds of "medicine," and above all the *bodily worship of the living God*. Even when not openly acknowledged, the serpent god Domballah is central and symbol to all of these. These are associated with a psychological and cosmological paradigm of how forces, beings, intelligence, and matter "couple" with each other in an energetic, highly personal, and spiritually pervaded universe. It is an ancient paradigm, one that we have alluded to several times already. These are all the religious and bodily expressed facets of an African unconscious that moved like a great and overarching wave across and through the separate lives of its children, devotees, and orphans of the African Diaspora. But there is even more than this.

While the Founding Fathers of the United States were creating a nation on the emerging new consciousness of the 13 colonies, a greater, vast, and ancient legacy was influencing them from regions deep within the unconscious. As these Founding Fathers, many of whom lived off the labor of their slaves, were reinventing the glory of ancient Greece and Rome in America, they were reintroducing into the West "the New Atlantis," the symbols and signs of an ancient order at the very basis of their civilization. The myth of ancient Greece took root at this time, for who could fabricate a civilization based on who is enslaved (Bernal, 1987; Diop, 1974; Jackson, 1970). Thus by a curious juxtaposition, it came to be. Just as the African-American Christians came to identify themselves in their spirituals with the Biblical Hebrews who were enslaved in Babylon by their own Kemetic cousins, the pharaohs of Egypt, for 400 years, so did the Founding Fathers come to identify themselves with the ancient Greeks and Romans, peoples who openly learned and studied with the original designers of civilization 6,000 years ago in the Nile Valley of Africa.

THE AFRICAN UNCONSCIOUS AS EXPRESSED IN THE WORK OF THE AMERICAN FOUNDING FATHERS

So far, we have focused on the genetic, historical, and collective unconscious influences in the dynamic operative between Blacks and Whites in the United States. These are also applicable to the Caribbean and to South America with different matters of emphasis and of form. We will now focus on what we have come to believe are some of the truly hidden, esoteric, and therefore more controversial influences of the ancient African unconscious mystery schools on the consciousness and behavior of the American Founding Fathers, both in history and in their religious-metaphysical consciousness.

Many of the Founding Fathers of the United States had a long tradition of scientific study, literary education, and also, very significantly, an interest in some of the ancient *forms* of the mystical sciences. The German Pietist and Rosicrusian Johann Conrad Deissel started a spiritual community of Rosicrusians in Ephrata near Philadelphia in 1694. In fact, many of Deissel's works were printed on Benjamin Franklin's press between 1730 and 1736 (Sachse, 1966). When that community was disbanded Franklin came to own much of their library (Heline, 1949). Significantly enough, Benjamin Franklin was a student of astrology and the metaphysical sciences. Franklin's address to the Constitutional Convention on the eve of the American Revolution began with the words "God governs in the affairs of men. If a sparrow cannot fall to the ground without His notice, is it probable that an empire can rise without His aid?" (Hieronimus, 1989, p. 37). These are almost the exact words of the opening lines of the ancient Rosicrusian text *The Chymien Wedding of Christian Rosencrantz.* It is known that the Rosicrusians were a long-standing secret society in Europe. They were secret in order to avoid persecution for their heretical beliefs. The Rosicrusians were an ancient sect, elements of which migrated to Europe and evolved during the Roman days and, in many ways, were modeled on the Egyptian mystery schools, and the houses of life at the Grand Lodge of Luxor, Abydos, and Abu Simbel. The Rosicrusians studied metaphysical sciences, including alchemy (al-Kemit), astronomy, magic, and the mystical Kabbala. They, along with a similar secret society, the freemasons, *consciously* devoted themselves to the spiritual evolution of mankind. They had hoped to and sought to impart the spiritual principles of their order to the transformation of society. They saw a new age coming in which they believed a new spiritual reality would become transcendent in American and human life.

John Adams' family were members of a secret sect of English Druids called the Dragon sect, who had left England to escape persecution. The Dragons were a clandestine society of free thinkers and visionaries who also studied the metaphysical sciences, alchemy, and the ancient mystery schools. They included Sir Walter Raleigh and John Dee, who was the court astrologer for Queen Elizabeth (McLaughlin & Davidson, 1988). This Dragon sect had hoped to reignite the fire of the ancient traditions that spoke of the wisdom of the Earth, and so studied the astrological procession of the equinoxes (Rothovious, 1977). They sought to revive the ancient religions, which they saw as connected to an even earlier religion of England and Egypt. Diop (1991) has noted many times the historical connection between the England of the Megalithic period and the Kemetic Egyptian and Phoenician navigations of the Bronze Age, which were contemporaneous with the 18th Egyptian Dynasty. There was ongoing trade in tin from the "Sorlinguan Islands," meaning England. It was also roughly in this period, around 1400 B.C.E., that the great megaliths of Stonehenge and the surrounding area were built (Diop, 1991; Parrain, 1977).

Thomas Jefferson was a Rosicrusian in the Brotherhood of the Rosy Cross (Baigent, 1982). He designed the buildings of the University of Virginia on a pattern which is believed to be specifically related to a Kabbalistic design and the secret society's metaphysical sciences (Hieronimus, 1989). He used a code known only to initiated members of the Rosicrusian Order. While believing in the innate inferiority of Africans physically and psychologically as a wealthy slave owner, he nevertheless wrote in the first draft of the Declaration of Independence that slavery was a "cruel war against human nature itself" and fathered several children with his Negress-love slave Sally Hemings.

It is extremely significant that George Washington, Benjamin Franklin, and Thomas Jefferson along with 51 other signers of the Declaration of Independence were Freemasons (McLaughlin & Davidson, 1988, 1994). History tells us that Benjamin Franklin was actually the grand master of the Philadelphia Masonic Lodge. He is known to have assisted in the initiations into the Lodge of the Nine Sisters in Paris, the same secret lodge into which *Jefferson* is said to have been initiated. Washington was initiated into the lodge at Fredricksburg, Virginia, and was presented with the all-secret emblems and implements of that order. General Lafayette was also a member of the Masonic lodge. In actuality the cornerstone of the Capitol of the United States was laid down in a Masonic ritual presided over by none other than George Washington. Together they had a radical new vision for the world, a world of justice, freedom, and law. Yet Washington could not totally embrace the full implication of the Declaration of Independence. When Revolutionary ally Lafayette invited him to join a grand scheme to free the slaves, Washington put him off pleading "imperious necessity." Yet unconsciously he drew from ancient African sources. The Washington monument itself, built much later, echoes the early Egyptian obelisks of Karnak and Heliopolis, and the Lincoln memorial has its architectural roots in the Grand Lodge at Luxor. The original plans for the city of Washington, D.C., were laid out in a metaphysical design by masonic architects with the thought of best using dragon lines, or so-called Earth energies. Pierr-Charles L'Enfant's design was later modified by Jefferson and Washington in order to incorporate specific octagonal patterns that reflected aspects of the cross believed employed by the ancient Masonic Templars (Baigent & Leigh, 1989). If you look at the city of Washington, D.C., today, you will see numerous relics and references to this secret consciousness dotting the skyline, older buildings, and grassy places.

George Washington himself had some vision of a great future conflict in the United States that touched on these themes of an African consciousness. During the midst of the Revolutionary War, he had a vision of three great conflicts for the nation. One was the Revolutionary War itself. The other was the great Civil War of 1860–1865. But he also saw another great and perhaps monumental war for the United States, and it was not World War I or World War II. He tearfully saw a great conflict that somehow involved the word "union," the spiritual issue that all men are "brethren," and somehow it crucially involved Africa.

We know that many of the Committees of Correspondence which planned the American Revolution were composed almost entirely of Masons or members and students of the Masonic lodges (Morse, 1924). At the time of the Revolution there were over a thousand Masons in the Boston area alone. Indeed the Boston Tea Party was the work of Masons during the outbreak of hostilities. Apparently after a meeting at St. Andrew's Lodge they marched out to Boston Harbor and did the deed (Morse, 1924). Intellectually speaking, Francis Bacon, the so-called "Father of Modern Science," is known to have been a founder of Freemasonry in Europe and an initiate in the Rosicrusian Order. He was also a member of the organization that founded the colonies of Virginia and the Carolinas and worked with other Masonic lodges in the United States to help prepare the ground for the early years of the American government. Bacon, who died in 1626, referred to the new land as "the new Atlantis" in a book by that name and envisioned a society which he hoped would develop in America. Indeed on the Great Seal of the United States is written "Novus ordo seclorum," meaning literally "new order of the ages." The Masonic lodges have their origin, founding vision, and first 5,000 years of existence in the valley of the Nile under the African sun.

There are other covert signs and symbols of the ancient Kemetic lineage of the mystery schools on the consciousness of the Founding Fathers and their subsequent symbols in the Americas. If we take the simple dollar bill, we see on it a Kemetic Egyptian pyramid with an all-seeing eye of God on the top, separated from the base, and the Latin "Annuit coeptis," literally meaning "God favors our undertakings," and the earlier mentioned "Novus ordo seclorum," meaning "new order of the ages." This symbol is on the reverse of the Great Seal of the United States. While it was designed over 200 years ago, history has it that it was not officially used until Henry Wallace, secretary of agriculture under Roosevelt, suggested that it be placed on the dollar bill. Wallace it seems was a student of Nicolas Roerich, a Russian artist and founder of a Yoga society, the metaphysical group which studied the esoteric doctrines reintroduced to Europe by way of Tibet from Egypt by Madame Blavatsky and Alice Bailey (1949).

The Great Seal itself is yet another manifestation of symbols and imagery dating way back to the Egyptian mystery schools. It was designed by Jefferson, Franklin, and Adams with Charles Thomas and William Barton adding major revisions. It reflects the ancient African mystery school we've alluded to in earlier chapters, including the Rosicrusians, Freemasons, and Masonic temples (Hieronimus, 1976, 1989). Some have even gone so far as to suggest that the phrase "E pluribus unum" on the dollar bill, which means "out of many, one," represents not only the psychological and political unity of the original 13 colonies and the one central government, but the mystical notion of one life pervading all lives imbued with the divine presence that is all pervasive. It is literally the all-seeing eye of God placed atop the mystic and Kemetic pyramid. In addition to this, throughout the Great Seal the number 13 is used 13 times. There are 13 stars, 13 stripes, 13 arrows, 13 berries, 13 letters in the words. In the ancient mystery schools, 13 is the number of transformation, 1 added to 12, as in the 12 disciples plus Christ. It is also reminiscent of the 12 signs of the zodiac plus the sun, and later the 12 knights of the Round Table plus King Arthur. It echoes back even to the 13 parts of the dismembered body in the myth of Osiris! It is a reflection of the constant transformation, transformation, transformation, mentioned earlier in reference to the African unconscious.

These are references to the unconscious influence of the ancient permutations and transformations of the African mystery schools on the psychology and the behavior of the Founding Fathers. They include the two Great Seals of America (Hieronimus, 1976) and the shared visions of many who belonged to the secret societies, in particular the Freemasons, Rosicrusians, and others including the Kabbalists on the designing of the American experience. The great symbol on the dollar bill, of the all-seeing black capstone eye of Horus atop a mystical pyramid, speaks for itself.

We've mentioned all of the above because we are emphasizing that the African unconscious has a long lineage from the mystery schools in the valleys of Luxor, Abydos, Abu Simbel, Thebes, and numerous other places through their permutations and transformations not only in West Africa but also through Europe by way of the secret societies that were all founded on ancient Kemetic Egyptian lodges and houses of life. Indeed the early Masons are known to have begun in the temple of Karnak in the Nile Valley 3,500 years ago. The pyramid itself, while its initial structure began in Nubia, is primarily Egyptian, and is first seen in this area in the upper Nile valley (Diop, 1974).

In a curious way, the hierarchical structure of the pyramid and the notion that all members of the society participate in the divine life of the pharaoh meet in the modern world in the democratic idealism of the Founding Fathers. For indeed, implicit in the ideal of democracy is the idea that even a commoner can become a king (i.e., president or governor). Everyone, not only royalty, has the divine spark of nobility and leadership in them and under the right conditions can unite or reunite the body politic. This is a form, perhaps, of the Kabbalistic vision of the reunion of the scattered sparks of the divine. This democratic idealism quickens the collective evolutionary process in that *all* can help enrich and deepen the world, not just the pharaoh. This is partially why the idea of democracy carries such revolutionary power in the modern world. But there is even more of this Egyptian influence, as evidenced again by the very money we use.

Many symbols on the American dollar bill and also on the Great Seal are clearly of Kemetic Egyptian lineage. The Eye of Horus is Egyptian. It represents the pineal gland and its interaction with light in the human embodiment. The separate black capstone on top represented the liberated, luminous spirit that could see in all directions, and the pyramid base represented the body that flowed upward into spirit. The pyramid, like the obelisk itself, is obviously *not* of European origin and, in fact, doesn't even exist in Europe! Again we find a hidden reflection of the nourishing and symbolic capacity of the African unconscious despite horrendous persecution even within the shores of the new Atlantis, America.

This is not totally new since we have alluded several times before to the fact that the first great migration of the African unconscious processes occurred way before Columbus with the exploration of the New World by African sea-trading expeditions (Jackson, 1970; Van Sertima, 1976). Columbus himself, in his diaries, acknowledged the presence of African peoples among the population of the lands he "discovered." These African-like visages, and even skulls, can be seen in the earliest of Olmec civilizations. The fear, recoil from, and repression of this is massive. It is a matter of the threatened return of the repressed and the mythos of the devouring sphinx. Yet like a great wave it rises, falls, and rises again. Much as the Indo-Aryans of the Caucasian steppes invaded Dravidian India, over time reduced the darker population to near slavery and absorbed the genius of their Yogic religious discipline, wrote it in their Sanskrit script, and thereafter *forgot* the origin of that which they worshiped, so did the Founding Fathers resurrect and extend the glory of ancient Greece and Rome, yet forgot and actively repressed the knowledge of the origin of that new order they so worshiped. The genius of the underlying consciousness in both situations exercised a profound and covert influence on all.

Periodically in history the power of racist notions even from so eminent a figure as the great Greek physician, Galen, prospered. As mentioned earlier, the physician Galen, in the second century C.E. felt that the essential traits of Blacks were long penises and the tendency to laugh a great deal of the time over relatively little (Diop, 1991). This is in contrast with Rousseau's notion of the "noble savage." These notions were then later superseded by Gobineau's notion of Blacks as a reflection of a vegetative body sensibility as opposed to the white Apollonian rationality. This dialogue goes back and forth, back and forth in seemingly endless oscillation. At the base of this ambivalence is a barely conscious recognition of the origin of humankind in the African cradle, then the recoil from and fear of that primary recognition, followed by the eventual slightly increased embracing of it. In this light, it is curious to note the contemporary national scene and how this is again playing itself out in the political agenda. This is an old story of America and the social context of its next election.

But America is inherently a dynamic creation and few of its members are ready to throw in the towel despite its history of crime and injustice, because it also offers a light. Despite genocidal wars and cyclical phobias over immigration, all the human tribes are represented here. In the U.S. Constitution, the importation of slaves, even though it still continued secretly for decades afterwards, was outlawed by 1808 and America's bloodiest war was over slavery itself. Most of the Founders knew the institution was evil incarnate, the congenital defect in the birth of the nation. A deeper look into roots of the national soul would have symbolically revealed an African face and even the boldest of them would have been shaken by this.

Yet these deists and men of the European Enlightenment also deeply believed in the new idea of progress and the ancient notion of perfection. Perhaps, just perhaps, despite their racism, sexism, and classism, enfolded within the deeper regions of the shared unconscious of the Founding Fathers was a great and universal ideal and desire. No doubt, on some level, it was their wish and their vision that the American experiment would last a thousand years until the species was perfected and we moved collectively from a democracy to a luminocracy where the destiny of each human being was implicated politically and spiritually within the soul of each other human being. The politician who discovers this formula tomorrow will gather around him creative and elementary forces, awaken America from its slumber of ideals, and again inflame the world with a new revolutionary fire. For just as the American Revolution led the way to political, idealistic, and social-cultural revolutions throughout the world, we believe this American vision still embodies the hopes of myriads of people and will set in motion a new revolution, a revolution in human consciousness itself. And Africa's diasporic peoples, who entered the 20th century with the worst image of all of the great peoples of humanity in the collective mind, will again move into the 21st century, the new millennium, with a recognition of being the oldest, the most ancient mother of human races and the father of civilizations.

THE RUDIMENTS OF KEMETIC PHILOSOPHY IN AFRICAN/INDIAN YOGA SCIENCE

9

It is because I am Life that I eat, think, worry, do every and all things. Because I am Life I screw, the amoeba splits. Living things exist in the service of Life. Life is God and God is Life.

—Supo Lasoebikan, *Life Is God*

If you are on a road to nowhere, find another road.

Ashanti Proverb

THE SERPENTINE SYMBOL AND THE SOLAR CONSCIOUSNESS

O
N the golden death mask of Pharaoh Tutankhamun dated around 1350 B.C.E. there is an ancient symbol of both an esoteric nature and an exoteric nature. The exoteric or external reference of this was to the pharaoh who was the master of both Upper and Lower Egypt. Throughout ancient Egypt's multi-millennial history, there were often periods of war and contests between the rulers of Upper Egypt and Lower Egypt. Pharaoh Menes was the first to unite Upper and Lower Egypt, by the most conservative estimates in 3200 B.C.E. (Diop, 1974) but perhaps even as far back as 5869 B.C.E. according to Champollion (Budge, 1960), the French Egyptologist who in 1821 set the principles for deciphering their hieroglyphics by using the Rosetta stone. Throughout Egyptian history the coiled serpent arising from the top of the pharaoh's head was paralleled consciously to the union externally of Upper and Lower Egypt (King, 1990). This ancient symbol, however, reflects a more hidden or esoteric meaning.

The esoteric meaning of this great symbol has been alluded to in numerous places throughout this book. It refers to the Kemetic Egyptians' knowledge of the radiant serpent of the spinal line, often called Kundalini. The science of Kundalini and its related disciplines had been studied in the Egyptian mystery schools for thousands of years even before the great boy-pharaoh, Tutankhamun. To these ancient ones, the upraised serpent atop the forehead of the pharaoh was symbolic of mastery of the higher wisdom sought by the initiated and the masters. The early teachers of the mystery schools, mystery schools by the way which spread not only from the Nile kingdoms of Egypt but also, by way of the trade routes, to the civilizations of the Dravidians of southern India, were called the nagas. The word nagas means "serpent." The serpent was the ancient symbol not only of potency and sexuality, as we see amplified in the Freudian understanding, but also of rejuvenation, immortality, and wisdom. Especially in the area of immortality and wisdom, the raised serpent manifested the enlightened "inner wisdom" that led from one world through transformation and transcendence to the next. It was a reflection of the "third eye." To master the awakened serpent was not only to transcend physical worldly embodiment, but to transform and transmute this energy, not by way of mere sublimation, but by way of translation, into the higher planes of divinity. Just as a snake leaves its old skin and grows into a new one, so the symbol of the serpent externally manifested not only the changing of the external skin of a snake for its inner skin, but also the arising of energy from the lower chambers of the body and the spirit to the highest chambers of wisdom inside and illumination beyond. As far back as 1350 B.C.E., this symbol was ancient.

The Kundalini phenomenon was first recognized in primordial Egypt in reference to trance states initiated in the Ophidian cults (Grant, 1979). These, as we saw earlier, were important in East and West African spiritual traditions. Out of these trance-inducing practices, the ancient practitioners stumbled upon a subtle function residing in the human body–mind and nervous system. In pre-dynastic Egypt, the uraeus was the movement or the flux of Kundalini. It is early on identified with a transcendent function. References to this transcendent function of the uraeus are found in the *Egyptian Book of the Dead*, a book that had been in the possession of the Egyptians and their ancestors years *before* the first dynasty of Menes. In ancient Egypt the uraeus was the naga of Egypt, the dreaded though peaceful and powerful cobra who could spit its deadly venom and paralyze its victim (Schwaller de Lubicz, 1961). On the tombstone death-mask skull of the pharaohs we have found the uraeus symbol, the Kundalini symbol, clearly outlined on the surface of the deceased royalty. It was found on the mummified crown of Pharaoh Tutankhamun. Here it is the double uraeus representing not only the serpent who *joins* the two hemispheres of the brain, but also signifying the serpent who *integrates* the two sides of the brain. Remember in this context the symbol of the medical caduceus and the two different serpents intertwining up a central canal. The concept of the radiant serpent was fully integrated into sophisticated Egyptian medicine, cosmology, and science (Finch, 1990).

Numerous bas-reliefs on the walls of tombs and ancient Egyptian statues dating from the old kingdom period show that the Egyptians were well aware of Yoga postures and possibly kyrias in addition to the inner mysteries of Kundalini Yoga meditation (Thakkur, 1977). It was integrated not only into Egyptian physical culture, a culture that finds similar expressions in forms of Hindu Hatha-yoga, but also in other forms of physical exercises called Mazda Anan. The unearthed Dravidian cities of Mohenjo-Daro and Harappa in India have numerous testaments to the essential place of this luminous psychophysical and psychospiritual phenomenon in the lives of its citizens, who dwelt and prospered in a literate, sophisticated civilization on the subcontinent at least 1,000 years before the Aryan invasions of the North. In both Dravidian India and in Kemetic Egypt the science of this luminous phenomenon was exacting, hidden, and known primarily to the initiates and the royalty of these cultures. In India numerous methodologies were elaborated in its development. Indeed the foundation of all Yoga is based on the phenomenon of Kundalini (Krishna, 1971a, 1987; Mookerjee, 1982;

Narayanananda, 1979; Rama, 1986). In both branches of this ancient culture of Kundalini the phenomenon is intimately associated with spirituality, sexuality, bioenergy, and luminosity. It is also associated with hidden teachings, exacting physical and mental disciplines, and the radical transcendence of ordinary consciousness. While in India it became the foundation of all the schools of Yoga and expressed itself in numerous paths, in Kemetic Egypt it found expression in two primary paths (Schwaller de Lubicz, 1961).

The two paths of liberation developed by the Kemetic Egyptians might be called the direct path and the indirect path. Both of these, of course, were considered the royal path to liberation or salvation. However, the physical methodology and the spiritual preparation of individuals would clearly decide which path they would take.

The direct path was believed to be the path that bypassed the repetition of many lives and reincarnations. It was the path of a rare attunement with the divine not only in life but in the process of dying. It is well articulated in the *Egyptian Book of the Dead* (Budge, 1960). There is a parallel method of quick ascension into liberation by way of the direct path as explicated in a similar ancient treatise on the dying process called the *Tibetan Book of the Dead* (Evans-Wentz, 1960). In both of these methods there is an intense, clear, and direct identification of the localized consciousness principle as it is leaving physical embodiment with an all-pervasive, divine, and luminous principle. The direct path is the path of focused light in all its subtle disciplines. It is the Horian path. It is the royal path in particular and it is assumed that the ascendant masters and the pharaoh have an expanded consciousness and are able to enter into this path directly in life and certainly at the moment of death. This path assumes that the rarefied consciousness of an individual is intuitively aware of the relationship between matter, energy, and spirit, $E = mc^2$, and can move quickly through the transformation. It is a rare and singular path.

The other path to liberation, often referred to as the western path, is a path that requires the experience of numerous births and rebirths along with the accompanying earthly sufferings. It is referred to as the Osirian path (Schwaller de Lubicz, 1961). There are numerous inscriptions on the pyramid chambers of many pharaohs outlining this for the benefit of the dead. The Egyptian Pyramid Texts and the *Egyptian Book of the Dead* are replete with specific, detailed explanations and descriptions of this process. Indeed it is in the *Egyptian Book of the Dead* that we find numerous seed forms of what later becomes the conceptualizations of heaven and hell, final judgment, and other spiritual processes that reflect the morality and life of the individual. These are the ones inscribed on the tombs of the Greek and Roman nobles of antiquity along with the Black face of Osiris. It is clear from these ancient writings that even in the Osirian path to liberation one must eventually have balanced a lifetime of good and evil, charitableness and egotistical pursuits with one of benevolence and sacrifice. Both lead to illumination. The direct path is quicker but requires preparation in life that involves discipline throughout. The Osirian path, the meandering path, requires less discipline but takes much longer. We find similar parallels in Hindu Yoga teachings and philosophy concerning the direct path and the indirect path (Evans-Wentz, 1960). What both the *Egyptian Book of the Dead* and the *Tibetan Book of the Dead* share is an ultimate optimism concerning the destiny of human consciousness. In both systems it is inherent in the human condition that we move individually and collectively toward enlightenment. Both open to transformation in slow or higher gear. Both open the individual living current into the wider ocean of all-pervasive consciousness and liberation by the radiant transformational equation of $E = mc^2$ and beyond.[19] This great insight into the nature of human consciousness, embodiment, and reality sustained the ancient world for untold millennia, then spread from the upper Nile Valley to the East into India, then to Tibet and China.

YOGA DISCIPLINE, THE LIVING DARKNESS, AND THE LIGHT

Perhaps it is only an accident of birth or history, but it is curious that the ancient phenomenon, methodology, and philosophy of the transmutation and transformation of human consciousness began in the upper Nile Valley among dark-skinned peoples. Later this discipline, including variations and improvements, manifested in another dark-skinned people in India, the Dravidians. Only later did it spread to northern India into the areas of Kashmir (Silburn, 1988). There it reached another height. It would spread into Tibet, where aspects of it would undergo another transformation, another refinement specific to its locale. This in all likelihood is due to the unfoldment of certain aspects of evolution that are the common birthright of all humanity. But it seems that the light and intelligence of civilization as we know it first oriented itself in humanity among its dark-skinned peoples and later spread out to enrich the larger family of mankind. This may simply be a biogenetic phenomenon or coincidence.

What we are referring to is the phenomenon that begins in human embryogenesis in the neuromelanin nerve current alluded to in earlier chapters. In the embryogenesis of human beings the direct current in the neural crest is guided by a series of melanocytes. These melanocytes orient themselves

---

19. $E = mc^2$, while still within the metaphysics of materialism, does arch beyond itself and tacitly implicate the consciousness of the observer.

toward light (Barr, 1983). These melanocytes then, in all likelihood, exercise the "lines of force" that we have mentioned in regard to the development of the embryo (Goldscheider, 1906; Lashley, 1942). This neuromelanin nerve tract may actually be informed by certain principles that have an affinity to processes of biological superconductivity and biochemiluminescence. By Golger's Law, it is a necessity that mammals such as human life born in a hot and humid climate must be of dark skin in order to avoid the harmful effects of the sun. This combination of the necessity of dark skin on the outside and a series of dark neuromelanin nerve currents and melanocytes on the inside, from the earlier days of embryogenesis, suggests the capacity of the human organism from the very dawn of its physical existence to transmute energy from the wider biosolar environment in the process of its radiant central nervous system unfoldment. One of the defining properties of melanin is its capacity to absorb light. It also transduces energy from one form to another easily and orients itself toward light. Throughout this study we have made an intimate connection between consciousness, light, and bioconductivity. It may very well be, simply as a matter of history and evolution, that just as mankind began as a dark species and all its family members retain this in its deep structure, despite interesting and varied surface changes, that this unifying aspect of humanity may be operative in the process of man's destiny in terms of spiritual and psychophysical illumination.

This is not a racist notion, for it does not imply the superiority of one group over the other. These surface structures are interesting but transient. Deep structure is what unifies. There has been no significant difference found in the amount, degree, or intensity of neuromelanin in the somatic organs or nervous systems of different groups of the human family. Surface changes in melanin are obvious, but deep-structure processes remain the same. However, it may be that this neuromelanin nerve tract that informs the process of embryogenesis and also certain aspects mentioned in terms of Kundalini and the movement of the life current through the braincore, have interacted such that African peoples and the other dark-skinned, genetically related peoples of India may simply have been environmentally and historically first to evolve this. It then has spread like a great gift to the rest of humanity, since humanity shares on almost every level the same genetic codes as the indigenous parent family of the African genesis. Egyptian society in its Kemetic origins was originally a primarily indigenous Black African society for thousands of years, but after years and influxes of peoples from various regions, including the Middle East and also Europe by way of North Africa and Libya, the context, culture, and the surface appearance of Egypt underwent transformations. In the Greek Ptolemaic eras there was a conscious governmental practice of trying to assimilate the different "races" for political reasons (Diop, 1974; Williams, 1987). The peoples of Egypt are representative of most of the branches of humanity today, with the exception of the Far Eastern branch. However, the Coptic and the Kemetic roots of Egypt and its neighbors, the Sudan and Ethiopia, are still evident to any observer today. It was the gradual influx of these different peoples from the interior and west-central regions of Africa, beginning around 17,000 to 10,000 B.C.E., bringing about new ideas, that has led to the diverse set of disciplines, beliefs, and subcultures that make up contemporary Egypt. However, this study is focused primarily on the early dimensions and contributions of Egypt and how the Kemetic Egyptian civilization was primal in the Kiaspora of cultures to the southeast into India, then northern India and Asia, and also west and north into West Africa, the Middle East, and Europe.

BASIC PRINCIPLES OF THE TRANSCENDENTAL DISCIPLINE

Despite various surface differences in structure, philosophy, belief, and practices, on a deep structural level there are certain fundamentals that remain constant. As the poet Rilke said, "Do not be disturbed by the surface of things, in the depths all is law." Humankind, in its exploration of the disciplines of transformation at the most intimate and at the most profound levels simultaneously, seems to have discovered certain fundamental principles. The earliest, and no less important than all the others, is the simple disciplines of religion, ethics, morality, and awareness of the self in nature, family, and society. In other words, it is extraordinarily important that disciples, in any of these varied practices, first come to a healthy self-discipline of themselves in terms of diet, moral interactions, sexuality, and responsibility for the well-being of one's self and others. In different disciplines we find different expressions of the need to practice honesty, compassion, and fortitude toward oneself and others. In Indian Yoga the practice of nonviolence to others, speaking the truth, compassion, moderation in diet, and reverence for one's teacher or master are referred to as Yamas. Also the practice of religious faith, contemplation, listening to and studying the ancient texts and disciplines, observance of rules of social conduct, and perseverance and courage are referred to as Niyamas. These are all a form of discipline of mind, body, and inner consciousness prior to the actual physical exercises of Yoga themselves. In short they are the moral, ethical, and social responsibilities. Without this discipline, one is moving into an area without having harnessed the ability to focus attention and consciousness.

The second discipline in various forms involves physical culture. In India Yoga this involves the practice of what are called asanas. In other disciplines they may involve other forms of physical culture. The ancient Egyptians were aware of this and sculptured it on their bas-reliefs (Thakkur, 1977).

Numerous texts and the highly refined disciplines of Indian Yoga make reference to asanas. We do not find as much emphasis on asanas in the Tibetan Yoga tradition. And then again we find a whole different emphasis on physical movement in the forms of Asian meditative disciplines, particularly those of the Chinese and Japanese. In these traditions graceful movements exist in forms of Tai'chi, the martial arts, and Taoism. Again, surface structures may change, but these are all ways in which cultures have intelligently moved toward using physical movements to elucidate and *cooperate with the currents of energy* that move through the body–mind in the practice of these highly evolved psychospiritual disciplines.

When the Kundalini process is awakened, either the preliminary energetic aspect or pranothana is noticed, or the actual primal force or shakti itself occurs. The body soon manifests spontaneous movements called kyrias. The various asanas and mudras are designed to channel this flow of bioenergy. In both Jewish Kabbalistic mysticism and certain West African initiation disciplines, the neophyte learns to generate and sustain the feeling or sensation of deep "awe," as in awe-some or awe-ful. This too will stimulate the awakening of Kundalini. When the New World Africans would liberate this energy by dance, deep rhythmic music, and brief "possession" in the "head," the body would also manifest these kyria-like movements. This was a primary focus in the African religious disciplines of West Africa and the Americas. Whites were often frightened or repelled by this awe-ful or awe-some experience, i.e., "the devil's music," but a small minority of them had a briefer, parallel practice in what was called a "conversion experience." The two were *not* identical, but there were and are similarities. The first had more energetic, involved, and coordinated movements and a philosophy of the gods "mounting" them. The Whites were more jerky in movement, bodily less involved, and believed the power of Jesus specifically was upon them. Christian Blacks fused the two syncretistically. All, however, saw it as part of the ritual and discipline of the faith.

A third level that is shared by all the different disciplines is the control of the breath. This is referred to as pranayama in Indian Yoga. In all forms of meditation the control of the process of respiration is directly related to the control of the process of attention and consciousness. By learning to control respiration, one directly influences the autonomic nervous system and the central nervous system (Kuvalayananda, 1978; Rama, Ballentine, & Hymes, 1979). The control of attention ultimately leads to detachment and the eclipse of ordinary consciousness (Mishra, 1973). This is an essential level of practice. Some schools and disciplines have emphasized this more than others. However, every school acknowledges the necessity of this. Perhaps the most highly refined masters of this have been the masters of Raja and Swara Yoga in India. When the breath or respiration is either controlled or in some other way made to gather attention to itself, the mind can also then draw sensory stimuli to itself. In other words, sensory withdrawal from the external world in varying degrees occurs and attention is focused even more internally. This is usually referred to as pratyahara.

The final level is really several interwoven levels of working most directly and intimately with the process of consciousness and attention itself. All the different schools in various traditions and cultures may have shadings of emphasis, but the central thrust is unmistakable. It involves three levels. First of all is the level of concentration. This is where the mind continues to be increasingly focused on one area. There are numerous techniques and ways of doing this, from gazing at a candle, referred to as trataka, to certain specific sounds, called mantras, to focusing on specific areas in the body with the eyes focused on specific areas, to numerous other methods. One finds this in the various traditions of Buddhism, the many schools of Hindu Yoga, the different traditions in esoteric Christianity, to all the mystical schools of Islam. The point of all of these is the increased capacity to control the process of attention. Attention must be stabilized. After attention is stabilized on an object, an image, the breath, the rhythmic signature of the Loa, or any other chosen "form," attention or concentration is then deepened, subjective body–mind equanimity spontaneously arises, and the consciousness principle naturally moves toward what is called contemplation.

In contemplation, the *essence* of what is focused on becomes more and more important. This again can be the breath, an image, a particular sound or rhythmic vibration, and various techniques in combination with others. The thrust of this procedure, a procedure that shades quietly from concentration into contemplation even when the body is plunged into ecstatic dance, is to keep the mind progressively more one-pointed.[20] In this practice gradually and inevitably the consciousness of the meditator becomes intimately associated and integrated with the "object" of attention and all its various subtle meanings and forms of enfolded information. The very consciousness of the practitioner becomes a luminous focus. The conventional "I" and its boundary considerations are gradually eclipsed in this process, which involves psychophysical balance or equanimity or surrender, control of the breath, and automatic mastery of the body to the point where you do not have to pay any attention to the body itself beyond the areas of focus. When

---

20. This lineage of concentration and one-pointed focus of mind is particularly suited to the forms of meditative absorption, including Kundalini Yoga, that this book has elaborated. There are other traditions of meditation, such as those of the Vipassana Buddhist lineage, which take a different path, that of *mindfulness* of each tissue of reality that *immediately* arises to attention.

this is done there occur subtle transformations in the physical body and the psychological and psychic system. During meditation aspects, tissues and episodes from the waking, dreaming, and deep-sleep states of consciousness are recognized and re-cognized and, thereby, observed from a perspective that partakes of, but is not identified with, any of these three ordinary states. Paradoxically, in this darkness, a gradual luminosity seems to permeate all "objects" of attention and unfold an apparent interconnectedness between seemingly separate phenomena. A pervasive energy arises.

Eventually, as concentration flows like a slow, vast, moving river into the great bay of contemplation, it is a short, almost imperceptible move toward the process of what is variously referred to as Samadhi, sunyata, satori, lae-lae, and the numerous other words we use. Technically in Yogic language, this fusion of concentration, contemplation, and Samadhi is referred to as samyama. It is the fusion of the individual principle of consciousness with the object upon which one is focused on in the eventual union of all three. In other words, the *consciousness* of the meditator and the *object* of meditation become integrated in the *process* of meditation. Or as Henry Bateson (1972, 1979) said, ontology fuses with epistemology in the ultimate act of knowing. At this point, when it is sustained, there is a radiant outshining of the individual consciousness principle. In various procedures there may be a "seed consciousness" of individuality still left. However, with continual practice even this seed of individualist identity is radically transcended in complete Samadhi.

These then represent the four basic stages of all forms of meditative practice from the earliest days to the present. It represents the transformation of the individual consciousness, including the individual body–mind and its union with the all-pervasive consciousness. This is the promise and the method outlined in the ancient Kemetic teachings and also the various forms of the practice in Indian Yoga and others. What are the practical manifestations of this in a human life?

The classical textbook on the Indian forms of Kundalini Yoga states that "when the Kundalini has been raised through the practice of kumbkahas (breath control by retention) and mudras (internal bodily locks), then emptiness (sunya) absorbs prana." "The Yogi who has raised Kundalini and has freed himself from all clinging karma will reach samadhi naturally." "When prana flows through the sushumna and the mind is dissolved in emptiness, then the perfect Yogi destroys all karma" (Rieker, 1971, p. 147).

At this point mind and individual consciousness have been completely eclipsed or outshone by the all-pervasive radiance of a more immense and intelligent consciousness. This is the ultimate trajectory of the early Dravidian and later Aryan practices of the Kundalini science in India. In the Pyramid Texts of the old Kemetic kingdom (3200–2100 B.C.E.) and the Coffin Texts of the middle kingdom (2100–1675 B.C.E.) and even in the new kingdom version of the *Egyptian Book of the Dead* (1600–718 B.C.E.), we find the Kemetic fulfillment of this process stated in other words. Indeed the Kemetic vision in the ancient mystery schools was the transcendence of the dense material body and lower mind and its transformation into the abode of the illuminated. In the abode of the illuminated the "sons of light" freely interact and commune in the divine milieu. This was accomplished by the mastery of the solar principle as expressed in the Eye of Horus, a process mentioned in earlier chapters in reference to the unity of the biospiritual light of the individual body–mind and its union or Yoga with the higher transcendental and all-pervasive light of inherent consciousness. In the Kemetic school the individual principle is returned to its prior state of luminosity with its source. Set or Lucifer, the angel fallen into the ignorance of matter, returns to the intelligence and light of the divine of which it has always been a part in some unfolded flux and transformation.

THE EVOLUTIONARY FORCE OPERATIVE TODAY

So what has all this to do with our current conception of the body, matter, and spirit. We mentioned that even in ancient times there was a clear intuition of an ongoing and upward rising intelligence and force operative in the human body that far transcended rationalism. The sudden and brief era of the Greeks, we believe, as an intellectual tradition, began overemphasizing rationality and in the process devalued intuition and revelation, thereby dissociating the divine from the realm of matter. This is still metaphysically rooted in the Eurocentric canon of science. The ancients were aware implicitly of the interpenetration of all forces, that is to say, a holographic or holonomic universe, and this was expressed even in rudimentary form in their Hermetic philosophy. They were aware of energy currents moving through the body, the influence of the unconscious mind on disease, and were in possession of a highly sophisticated medical and psychological technology for the treatment of illness. Their awareness of "balance and imbalance" in the human body was not confined specifically to medicine but transcended these largely technical areas and moved into philosophy. Their most abstract notions and intuitions arose out of practical necessity, as is the case of most science. We are suggesting here, essentially, that the ancients had an awareness of the implications of the holonomic body and its energy field and its interaction with the wider solar ecology. The interaction of an onward unfolding evolutionary force of bioluminosity and intelligence and its need to find progressively more subtle balances in external nature at progressively higher levels of manifestation seems to be the central intuition of health and illness from ancient times on to the furthest ideas of today. Disease and illness can be understood as resistances to the unfolding and increasing receptivity or subtlelization of the human mind and body to higher and higher biological and spiritual forces moving toward fulfillment and manifestation in the human sphere. The life current, be it called vital force, Chi, Ki, Wong, Elema, or whatever, appears to unfold this implicitly. The African unconscious has a decided emphasis upon the phenomena of rhythm, dynamism, life force or emi and trance states, and the capacity to intimately personalize in the body–mind the "natural forces" of the universe. It is implicitly assumed that there is a "resonate affinity" between all life and indeed all matter in manifestation.

The African unconscious intuits that there are forces in the wider ecology of human life, both above and below it, that intimately exercise a conscious influence on human experience. Indeed all that exists is to some degree living. This embraces both religion and science. Just as the quantum mechanical description of reality is incomplete without the dynamism of consciousness, so is the "life" in evolutionary theory incomplete without the awareness of spirit. Spirit, manifesting within selective contexts, is what draws life into greater and greater expressions of wholeness. This deeper order we believe is enfolded in the implicate order where matter, spirit, and conscious abide in luminous structures beyond our present comprehension.

In certain traditions of West African philosophy, there is a decided emphasis on this notion of man expressing greater and greater wholeness and levels of order. In the Ifa tradition, there is both the *involution* of spirit into the Earth plane and the *evolution* of man from this plane, by degrees, back to his source in God. The special purpose of human beings (awon eniyan), who are manifestations of the divine entity, is to bring more and more good into the world (Akiwowo, 1986). From a purely evolutionary perspective, the saga of the hominid, from pre-Australopithecines to *Homo habilis* to *Homo sapiens sapiens*, is the progressive articulation of light, consciousness, and intelligence in terrestrial existence, until perhaps the urge of the species reaches back into the generative order of things, back into the realms of intelligence and creativity itself.

As stated in the beginning of this chapter, our society has come to a new understanding of matter as an energy field propagating through space, an energy field unfolding space and time in the process and implicitly interconnecting with all forms of energy in the universe. We have come to see the evolutionary current as a luminous current of intelligence and energy manifesting on all levels and implicitly involving all other life forms in its field. Waveform after waveform moves through the evolutionary impulse. Just as individuals move as waveform and waveform through the history of the family, and families move as waveform and waveform through the history of a community in a society, and eventually as different societies and communities move as waveform and waveform through cultures and civilizations, so deeper down does the luminous current of evolutionary intelligence move waveform after waveform through the successive generations and cultures of humanity. Our increasing and deeper awareness of this is the awareness of the Horian light implicit in our natures. The notion of discrete or ultimate individuality and autonomy is falling by the wayside. It is seen, like the ego itself, as functional but limiting in its own way. A basic and deeper interconnectedness of all life is emerging. This interconnectedness is defined by rhythm, vibration, and a highly personalized resonate affinity between sources of spirit and information exchange.

A PARADIGM OF SPIRITUAL ENERGY:
BODY, BREATH, AND COSMOS; THE KM WIRIAN SYNTHESIS

Matter, the very physical manifestation of reality itself, has more and more come to be recognized as a form of localized and gravitationally enfolded light, as energy and information in its densest form, yet nonlocally interconnected with matter and energy everywhere. At times the intensity of this field is dense enough to cause obstructions in the flow of energy and at other times it reflects and absorbs energy back into its matrix. From the materialist perspective, the obstruction of energy in one's life leads to "what" is the matter with you; the personalism position asks "who" is the matter with you; and the spiritual perspective asks "who and how" is the matter with you. This extends beyond ourselves to our family, both living and dead, and to nature itself, which is animated by energy and spirit.

The family unconscious "field" is not merely the present generation. It enfolds the present extended generation, the generation next to be born, and the past consciousness of ancestors up to perhaps five generations. They are all seen as active members of the living familial field or matrix. When someone enters the family with traits of a former ancestor, the belief is that an aspect of or perhaps even the ancestor himself has been reborn into the family. Reincarnation is but another cycle or rhythm in nature. The African unconscious accepts that each individual is unfolded out of the *sangarsara* and will go back into it, will be enfolded again, and then unfold or individuate out of it again in the future, until the cycle of reincarnation and transformation is transcended and the being emerges or is translated into that consciousness in which *all* its parts, both the present and the *sangarsara*, are united. This occurs briefly at death, for death is the unity of self, family, and the divine in the supraluminous consciousness that outshines all individuation and separatist conceptualizations.

In a sense, it is the great unconscious or transconscious that has found expression in such historic terms as the Primeval Waters of Nun or the Amenta. Jung referred to some of this as the collective unconscious; the west coast Africans have called aspects of it as the Ayanmo concept. The central notion is that we have an involution *into* it and experience an evolution *out* of it and yet paradoxically are always *of* it.

In this worldview, the harmony of self, family, matter, and spirit involves the *personal* commitment of one's energies to the process. This personal dimension in the various spheres of reality or actualization is often felt or experienced by the voice or Nommo of others, and in the human context, most often as oratory. Oratory has the infectious capacity to animate and move things. Healing oratory is the belief that the living essence in all things can be so moved. This is the purpose of directing incantation to other persons, nature, spirits, ancestors, trees, mountains, animals, anything that possesses spirit and life force. "Possession" is the localization or embodiment of these higher-order intelligences by way of communion in community, rhythm, and voice that opens the higher centers in the body and brain. The cosmos is an intelligent and vibratory milieu.

The notion of a cosmos that is interconnected and intelligently communicates with itself in a vibratory fashion is an old idea that science from time to time takes up and fleshes out in the current terms of the day. Presently the quantum field theory and the quantum-relativistic perspective on matter and energy deeply imbue our view of the universe in scientific terms. And yet it has parallels to certain strains of African mysticism that are millennia old.

The quantum theory notion of an intelligent, unmanifest "sea of light energy" (Bohm, 1980) that is all-pervasive has a deep affinity to the Ifa conception of Olorun as the unmanifest, nonlocal realm of intelligence and insight (Fatunmbi, 1991). The various "coupling strengths" of the four "fundamental forces"—i.e., gravitational force, strong force, weak force, and electromagnetic force (electro-weak force really)—can be seen as dynamic patterns of energy and interactions in nature that profoundly influence the destiny of matter. Different contemporary theories from gauge symmetry of quantum field theories to various other "sects" and orientations attempt to organize the energy and dynamic patterns that abound in this sea of light energy. In the Ifa tradition, which has its own branchings and "sects," this sea of light energy also unfolds out of Olorun's order into manifest nature in dynamic patterns. These are the Odu, 256 in all, and like quantum field theory, are assessed in terms of their "probability" of occurrence. The quantum theories see "forces" in nature; the traditional or mystical systems see "beings." Aurobindo said when the deeper regions of reality are accessed, "some people will see beings and some will see forces" (Satprem, 1968, p. 198).

Beyond the material dimension, however, quantum mechanical theories realize that consciousness is an aspect of reality and the most adventurous of them attempt to integrate it into the formalism of the theory (Herbert, 1987). This extends to the actual equations (Dunne & Jahn, 1987; Walker, 1970). Here quantum mechanics goes beyond relativity. This directly points to intelligence and consciousness as an intimate dynamic in the world process. The intuition on a deeper level is that spirit and intentionality are integral to the cosmos. The traditionalists approach the situation from the other side. They begin with the immediacy of the spirit and the personal dimension and move out to see how they "couple" with the energy of the world process. In the process the consciousness of the ancestor and the forces of nature are seen to integrate in the force of the Orisha, who is believed to be able, in a somewhat probabilistic fashion, to influence and manifest a certain "coupling strength" with the physical world and human consciousness and thereby bring about change.

This notion of a probabilistic manifestation of a dynamic pattern is not limited to quantum mechanics or Ifa patterns of Odu manifestation, both of which require long, specialized study and initiation into the esoteric languages and symbolism of interpretation. If you look at the new, expanded version of some psychodiagnostic assessment procedures, the same story applies. On the Minnesota Multiphasic Personality Inventory (MMPI), the dynamic personality patterns and their associated behaviors are highly probabilistic in their accuracy. Whether a person really matches the #49 or #94 category is a matter of scores and "interpretation" by the clinician. In both cases, as with the quantum mechanical theories and Ifa, there are implicit theories below or deeper than the manifest dynamic patterns, which in many ways are a kind of attempted divination of the spiritual and psychological mind of the cosmos.

In a sense, because it enfolds persons across generations in a psychological matrix and also recognizes the influence of consciousness upon matter and energy, the family unconscious matrix is a kind of special theory of the general theory of the Orisha and consciousness interpenetrating in the material world. It recognizes that at some point of manifestation the deepest recesses of the inner world interface with and interpenetrate the furthest known expanse of the external world.

The Cosmic Organism

This "crossroads," this intersection between the deepest inner recesses and the external expanses, is also an archetypal idea, a cousin to the "as above, so below" of Hermetic philosophy. When the forces of what have too often been referred to as the "dark sciences" of occultism and psychism are involved, the ancient term "km wir" appears. For us, however, when this interpenetration of the self, its psychic processes, and the vast, interfacing worlds of the micro- and macro-universes are approached in a personalizing sense, we see emerge from this flux both personalism and a kind of km wirian synthesis.

Ancient lineages tell repeatedly that the inner workings of our minds and bodies reflect the workings of the universe. The Dogon of Mali over 600 years ago used a methodology based on this "lens" or paradigm to reveal the existence and exact orbits of stars deep in the cosmos unseen by the naked eye (Griaule & Dieterlen, 1986). Modern science only "saw" this in recent times. Sir James Jeans reflected a similar belief when, in commenting on the laws of physics, relativity theory, and consciousness itself, he said, "the stream of knowledge is heading towards a non-mechanical reality; the universe begins to look more like a great thought than a great machine. Mind no longer appears as an accidental intruder into the realm of matter; we are beginning to suspect that we ought rather to hail it as the creator and governor of the realm of matter" (Jeans, 1932; cited in Talbot, 1980, p. 16). Today as we look at the intimate structure and evolution of the nervous system, we see a warm dark embryogenesis, a neuromelanin current seemingly organizing the articulation of both neural development and fetal development (Barr, 1983). As we look out our most magnificent telescopes at the stars and constellations, and on the immense backdrop of their existence, we sense a sea of light energy not manifest to our vision, a "cold dark matter" that seems to shape and account for 90% of the mass of the modern universe. This is regardless of the content of this dark matter, e.g., baryonic, etc.[21] It, in its macrocosmic expression, like we in its microcosmic expression, is a manifestation of dynamic and nonlocal energy. At some interface, perhaps the interface of our own consciousness, the warm dark organizing matter of our nervous systems and the cold dark matter that seems to shape our external universe meet in a kind of km wirian synthesis that personalizes each aspect of reality as it unfolds from a more subtle enfolded order. It would manifest, of course, in our very bodies. The signature of this "coupling strength" is the real alchemy. The natural question

---

21. Currently, the leading candidates for "cold dark matter" are: ordinary baryonic dark matter like brown dwarves, neutron stars, or even black holes (unlikely); nonbaryonic matter like neutrinos or even so-called muon neutrinos; heavy fermions, dirac fermions, majorana fermions; axions, which couple with photons. The jury is still out. We know about its *mass*, but not what it *is*. So far there is no nongravitational evidence for elementary dark matter.

then arises, what practices are known or believed to reach into this generative order of the universe and bring these directly "down" into the body,
what ancient practices suggest such a pathway and a method?

For 2,500 years the vital force mentioned throughout this study has
been used in the classical medical practices of the Chinese Taoist and traditional healers. It is the basis of clinical acupuncture and a way of seeing
reality that has rather practical consequences. The vital force, referred to as
"Chi," is believed to pervade the cosmos and yet be subject to disciplined
interaction with human consciousness. Significantly enough, Earth objects
and phenomena are also believed to hold or incorporate this intelligent Chi
energy, e.g., certain plants, natural phenomena, and other fusions of consciousness and elemental forces. They have, in some instances, a certain
affinity to the notion of the Orishas.

Chi, by way of *involution*, is said to unfold first from the nameless or
original force-one, Wu Chi, which is prior to the body–mind and manifest
nature. From there it is believed to move down through the three ruling or
"heavenly forces," the "three pure ones." From here it moves into the dynamic realm of the ultimate Yin and Yang forces which can be felt in manifest nature. Out of it emerges a kind of "heavenly force" of cosmic dust.
From the cosmic dust arises a spinning cloud which, in turn, produces the
five forces or five elements. Finally, it is believed that the planets and solar
objects are the manifestation of these five elements (Chia, 1989a, 1989b).
An organism, if you will, capable of interaction with and reflecting the organization of human life. In fact it is extremely difficult to look at the photo-
graphs recorded by the lens of the the Hubble space telescope orbiting the
Earth, peering through radiant spirals of nebula, galaxies, constellations
and black holes back almost 11 billion years and *not* see the whole thing as
a vast, interconnected, and living organism. The macrocosm reflecting the
microcosm, "as above, so below."

The physical disciplines that flow from this conceptualization of cosmic energy involving itself in human expressions are many, including several
that directly relate to the circulation of light or bioenergy along the spinal
line, much in the tradition of Kundalini Yoga. A warm current of living
energy is awakened and circulated in different orbits through the body. In
some practices, the Chi energy is "brought down" from the cosmos through
the head and spinal line. In the microcosmic orbit discipline of traditional
Taoists, the current runs up the spine and down the front of the body in a
loop. In the "Shoshuten," or small light circulation, the breath is used to
absorb energy and fuse it with the Kundalini by inhaling again up the spinal
line, holding the breath (absorption) in the head (ori) and then exhaling
down the front of the body to the area of the sexual organs (Motoyama,
1990). The energy, or ase, is amplified this way. Different areas of the body

and organ systems become the focus of this warm, *tangibly perceptible* energy. The bones, glands, specific organs or systems are believed to interact with this luminous energy that moves through the body in specific energy lines called meridians and can be absorbed for nourishment and enhancement of the life force.

Our bias here is that melanin and neuromelanin are presently the leading candidates for the transducers of this bioenergy. This is because melanin is located in generous amounts on the surface of many of the body's internal organs; neuromelanin is focused in the brain and some spinal areas; the Russian bioplasma researchers focus the "energy" in the brain, spinal area, and fingertips; traditional Yoga science focuses on the same areas; and neuromelanin and melanin are sensitive to light, have semiconductive properties, and may be organic superconductors at room temperature under certain conditions. It is neuromelanin that is the focus here, and it is the same for *all* branches of the human species. Its subtle current through the body–mind is associated with the traditional perception of life force and with contemporary notions of biological superconductivity. Whatever the nature of the "cold dark matter" is finally detected to be in terms of contemporary physics, we believe it will probably interface with photons and electromagnetism, since these two are known to be implicated in various forms of superconductivity and are detectable in human experience.

Like the African tradition of emi or life force, the idea is to *enhance* the life force of the present life, not necessarily a future embodiment. The place of Taoist practices in medicine and spirituality is deeply embedded in Chinese civilization and thought. Its scientific and clinical validity is not an issue. When Westerners view it or African spiritual "possession," but somehow don't get it or can't capture it in a test tube, their logical positivism is viewed as a curious symptom of crude and simplistic, almost childlike, development by the practitioners of the traditions.

There are some people who see forces; there are some who see beings. Reverence for nature spirits and ancestors goes deep into Chinese and African societies. Ancestors who have merged with elemental forces in nature are the Orishas of West Africa. In both situations, these forces and beings are believed to be able to influence the body by way of the movement of energy through the system in specific ways toward definite areas in the body. The African is possessed or "embodies the gods" that move through his system; the Taoist inhales and circulates the intelligent energy of the gods. In both cases, despite a number of significant differences, they both move the vital energy and spirit through the system.

When this energy "descends" into the body, when the devotee is "mounted by the Loa" or gods, the energy can go to specific organ sites. The route is initially spinal, then moves out to the organs. It is significant in this context again that so many of the internal organs and the areas of the nervous systems divisions are permeated with melanin and neuromelanin. The Taoist uses the breath and visualization to guide the force, the living biolight, into areas where it can be absorbed. The dark matter of the universe is made to fuse with the warm dark matter in specific areas of the body. This encompasses not only the brain/spinal region (the original neuromelanin neural tube), but also the autonomic nervous system, diffuse neuroendocrine system, heart, liver, gastrointestinal tract, eyes, ovaries, testes, skin, auditory nerves, and many other areas crucial to health functioning and vitality (Althschule & Hegedus, 1976; Barr, 1983; Edelstein, 1971). In this intimate place the macro meets the micro, the personal meets the cosmos. Our destiny, in sickness and health, unfolds out of their unity.

This nexus, where the "inner" coincides with the dynamic "outer" in innumerable conjunctions, is the km wirian synthesis. In a sense, it is like the "true creative magic" of the magus or magi or the intuitions of Hermes Trismegistus. It is not the *product* but the *effect* of the "magic" that is seen in the perfect balance between the real cause of a situation, its natural setting, and the ideal moment of realization, or At-One-Ment, unfolding when the inner expansion of the spirit interfaces with the outward contraction of matter in the specifics of a localized situation.

Evolution throws up potential patterns, and fluctuations stabilize order that has unfolded and perhaps descended from more subtle realms of order. In fact, stable orders and constants of all kinds, including those in biology and physics, have unfolded from the original fusion state of the great flux, the Primeval Waters of Nun. They are now constants in nature. Perhaps through some future fluctuation in space–time and the quantum potential, a new order will unfold in nature, especially if we believe that evolution is not dead, that the laws of the quantum world are ultimately "statistical laws," and that here is at work in the luminous soul of the cosmos a generative fluctuation far from equilibrium over time that pervades every tooth and cell of creation. This great fire, we believe, inhabits our own bodies.

During the primal emergence of Kundalini in the case of Gopi Krishna (Krishna, 1971a, b), he described the perception of a luminous energy that seemed to move from the surface of his internal organs toward his spinal line and then into the braincore. Others also described the pathway of Kundalini through the body to the spinal line and again caution against unguided experimentation due to the need for preliminary practices such as breath control, internal bodily locks, and other psychological disciplines (Krpalvananda, 1979; Narayanananda, 1979). From personal experience, we absolutely agree. It can be quite risky in several places. The point here, however, is that this perceptible movement of a kind of luminous, intelligent bioenergy may be a form of biological superconductivity connected with the process of melanin and neuromelanin organized throughout the human body–mind. Again, surface differences are not crucial here. What is central is the shared template of the human organ and nervous system, and that is a universal one stabilized millennia ago during our formative era as a species in Africa. It is recapitulated in our embryogenesis, and we are suggesting here that it may be crucial to our further biospiritual awakening in the Taoist and Kundalini processes. The very nature of the quantum properties such as quantum nonlocality characterize superconductivity (Bohm, 1986). Pribram and others in the cognitive neurosciences have gone a long way in suggesting that there are "superconducting-like informational properties of communication in certain forms of matter [which] underlie and are coordinate with the informational aspects of mind" (Pribram, 1991, p. 272). Indeed the universe is alive, a dance of energy, nonlocal and highly personal. Techniques and disciplines born of a romance with science provide us the rhythms that we dance to and then disappear into the dance.

And what of the divine conception in this paradigm of energy and intelligence woven on a subtle loom from the minuscule to the vast expanse? Unlike materialism, it is at its root incompatible with either atheism or even agnosticism. It is inherently theistic. Unlike Buddhism, it does not see suffering as intrinsic to human existence, and the personalistic dynamic makes an impersonal pan-consciousness incomprehensible.

Both atheism and agnosticism will tend to dissolve as we leave this era of scientific materialism because of the children science itself will spawn. Computer calculations and biological observations are making it increasingly highly improbable that random natural selection leads to increasing order and intricacy in nature. The micro- and macro-universe appear to be interconnected on more subtle levels of order that cannot be reasonably accounted for by some vast random fluctuation. Prigogine's and Bohm's notions of order and fluctuation seem to meet at some deeper level where matter, energy, and luminosity express the realm of spirit. Indeed the quantum itself seems to possess the quality of consciousness, and matter can behave with sentient-like behavior. In this kind of universe the synthesis of body, mind, and spirit unfolds and balances in each minute. This work will engage the priesthood of the future.

THE MULTIPLICITY OF PATHS

While there is a decided affinity between the deep-structure disciplines of this ancient psychospiritual path, a path informed perhaps by the earliest embryological tendencies of our species, it has taken many different pathways in the diversity of our cultures. At this point we will begin to look at those different pathways. However, underneath all of them is the luminous pathway adumbrated by Kundalini. Its study, along with the unfoldment of neuromelanin in embryogenesis and its later development, form the basis for a deeper understanding of comparative mysticism.

In the Hindu Yoga system there are at least eight major schools of Yoga, each differentiated from each other, each having as its underpinning the phenomenon of Kundalini. The major schools of Yoga were systematized long ago by the great codifier of Yoga, Patanjali. He not only outlined the eight major rungs of Yoga, a schema followed by most schools of Yoga, but he also spoke directly and insightfully about the process of Kundalini. He also mentioned quite forcibly the dangers inherent in premature and unguided Kundalini awakening. From his perspective he outlined the pathways of this psychoneural and spiritual phenomenon all the way to its illumination in the braincore and beyond in the processes of awakening into Nirvana or Samadhi.

Buddhism is understood to be an offshoot and from some perspectives an advance over Hindu Yoga. The Buddhist systems have a great affinity to Hindu Yoga and historically the Buddha began as a Hindu practitioner. However, the Buddha's radical understanding of Hinduism during his experience of enlightenment and his reaction to the social-cultural forces of his day led to a whole new school of transcendence. From his radiant pathway light lit by the four noble truths, the Buddha, and his later followers, unfolded numerous other pathways that have held sway over the mind, heart, and imagination of the Asian world for over two millennia. Different areas and cultures within Asia emphasize different paths of Buddhism, from the Mahayana to Vajrayana to other forms of Tantric Buddhism. However, each recognizes the radiant contribution of the Buddha, and all see its origin in at least the recognition of the phenomenon of Kundalini. Some choose to work directly with Kundalini, as in various forms of Tantric Buddhism; others do not necessarily work directly with Kundalini. Also depending upon the particular school of Buddhism, one may move toward what is referred to as satori, enlightenment, sunyata, emptiness, etc., etc. These are all different words and disciplines pointing toward the same luminous trajectory. Each pathway has its own particular teachings concerning the illusion of birth, death, and rebirth, and the oscillations and cycles of nature. Indeed much of Buddhist teaching parallels in an uncanny way the teachings of contemporary schools of high energy and particle physics (Capra, 1975).

The Kemetic Egyptians also spoke very specifically, accurately, and forcefully about the phenomenon of the uraeus or the Kundalini phenomenon. They sought it as a foundation for salvation or enlightenment. As mentioned earlier, the Kemetic Egyptians outlined two paths, the Horian or direct path, and the Osirian or western path encompassing many births, many deaths, and many rebirths (Schwaller de Lubicz, 1961). The Kemetic path was later incorporated into other paths either by way of natural evolution or by way of repression and syncretistic reemergence in later religions. We are referring to the integration of certain aspects of Kemetic religion and science in the teaching of the Arab invaders of North Africa, and also the Diaspora of the secret societies and teachings into the hinterland and to the west coast African civilizations of the Middle Ages of Africa.

In the west coast Diaspora of Kemetic knowledge, the Middle Ages of West Africa saw a great proliferation and rebirth of this religious paradigm. The empires of Mali, Ghana, and Songhai, plus numerous others, saw a flourishing of the ancient knowledge. With the great Diaspora to the Americas, primarily by way of slave ships, the teachings were brought both consciously and unconsciously enfolded in the indigenous religions that the Africans brought with them to the New World. These teachings can be seen in scattered forms in the different religious teachings and approaches of the peoples of North America, the Caribbean, and South America, in the context of Voudoun, Candomble, Santería, and other religions that worship the Orishas. In all of them is the covert worship of the mysterious serpent who arises from within the body on a luminous path under the auspices of a certain rhythmic and intensified inner discipline supported by the community, and in its fulfillment in the unfoldment of higher powers that can occur in trance states. We've seen this same intense rhythmic evocation of the Kundalini in other African peoples who were not transported to the Americas. These include the !Kung peoples of the southwestern desert of south Africa, the Dogon of Mali, and many others. We have mentioned before why we think this may perhaps be more indigenously so in the African diasporic peoples than others. However, this is the common birthright of all humanity rooted in our embryogenesis and the biogenetic evolutionary force.

THE EMERGING AFROCENTRIC PARADIGM

A brief recapitulation or summary is useful here. Looking over what has been presented, slowing but surely an emerging Afrocentric paradigm seems to cover over what is really a universal face.

The African genesis of the human race is reflected not only in our anthropology and the history of the rise of civilization itself, but is recapitulated in the intimate chambers of our mitochondrial DNA and the embryogenesis of each of us.

Kundalini is seen at the root of our psychospiritual traditions and allows us to move toward an energetic interconnectedness with the wider solar ecology. In this way it encompasses and surpasses a libidinal and intrapsychic focus in our development. Osiris, as a transcendental myth, encloses and extends over the Oedipal complex as one of the defining dynamics of our psychospiritual trajectory.

That consciousness which rises from the depths of the unconscious is greeted by the transconscious realm of the gods or unseen intelligences that unfold from the nonlocal and emergent dynamics of the brain/mind/consciousness in disciplined states. The self is in the position of "energy" in relation to the material world, and its dynamics reflect that. Illumination can not only emerge from "below," but also "descend" from above. Thereby comes the embodiment of the gods or Orishas by studied entrainment of the body and nervous system. This is real bodily initiation based on experience, not the dogma of the Church Fathers and, as such, is in keeping with the ancient traditions of Hermes, the Kabbalists, and the forgotten ones on the banks of the Nile. So far Whites, constrained by the metaphysics of the Eurocentric canon of science and ego separatist metaphysics, are still in recoil from the dynamics of possession and the wider paradigm of embodiment. However, this is also gradually changing. Someday they too will allow themselves to be fully immersed in their perception of the divine, be it a saint or the Black Madonna, all of whom inhabit this interpenetrating world. It is believed that these are beings and forces of nature that partake of consciousness and that these forces are implicitly capable of manifesting different "coupling strengths" with disciplined and trained human consciousness.

This worldview holds that the intimate microdynamics of the body parallel the macrodynamics of the material universe. In other words, a form of "as above, so below." This means all the currently known fundamental "forces" or interactions in the physical world. Information and consciousness itself both parallel and enfold the structure of matter and its more subtle matrices of energy, extending it throughout the latticework continuum of space–time. We do not know everything about the body, nor the stars. In some presently unknown way, the workings of the heart, the brain, the immune system, and others are embedded in the mysteries of the stars that are losing matter too fast to become black holes, of supermassive black holes in the cores of the active galaxies, and of swirling rings around exploded stars.

In the realm of the psyche, this worldview experiences an enfolding field of psychic and psychological relationships, a family unconscious that includes one generation not yet born, the present and up to five generations in the past. Indeed the ancestors at a certain point flow into the natural power and forces of the Orishas and Loas who are capable of embodiment or an epiphany. This is how personalism naturally emerges in the world of forces, beings, and objects. Personalism shares with Eastern spiritualism the tacit belief that the nonmaterial essences of things are the ground of being and that material objects and energies are imbued with consciousness and information. It is more than possible to do science in this context. We already have a science within energy as the substratum. This way of viewing things merely extends it to say that we can have a science within consciousness itself. Already we have a technological world of photons and electrons that bathe us in a sea of information moving at the speed of light, e.g., World Wide Web sites on the Internet, e-mail, fax machines, etc. This "information" in a certain sense enfolds us! It is only a matter of time and insight before we realize that we are this and can manipulate it for knowledge, healing, and spiritual evolution. By full identification within consciousness as light itself and the ground of being, we will be able to "come forth by day and go forth by night." This is the Copernican Revolution of our era. We need not fear the technological future if we can change our root sense of identity as ultimately isolated points of awareness and rather see ourselves in the wider racial and solar world of consciousness. This is what personalism has always opened us to. These beliefs have already given rise to disciplines and practices, to psychic dynamics with the dead and disembodied consciousness such as seen in certain Voudoun and other practices. These are the rites of reclamation of the dead's consciousness from the great watery unconscious, the Amenta or Primeval Waters of Nun called Retirer D'en Bas de L'eau.

In this universe, all is living, vital, and in some sense conscious. Death is an abstraction, an illusion, a painful delusion of the embodied self.

NEXUS: THE LIVING EARTH, THE BODY, AND THE STARS

Throughout this story of the human unconscious, we have come back again and again to its African genesis. We began with the rise of the hominid line in Africa with the pre-Australopithicenes, moved on through the Australopithecenes, down through *Homo erectus* and *Homo habilis*, her variety of cousins, to come eventually to *Homo sapiens sapiens*, the most recent expression of the evolutionary impulse and unfoldment. We followed *Homo sapiens sapiens* out of Africa to the Middle East and Asia, all the way to Australia, then up the coast of Siberia, over the Bering Strait to North America, all the way down to the tip of Tierra del Fuego. Another branch of the same species moved into Europe through Spain, then up into the Alps and plains of the North to become the Aryan, Alpine, and Slavic peoples of the West.

Almost the same pathway was taken in the evolution of civilization. Out of Africa, over the Middle East, then to Asia did it go. Another strain made its way into Europe, the last great place that it was to flourish. Innumerable crossroads and cross-fertilizations occurred and at pivotal places new orders arose. The Kemetic Egyptians of the 25th Dynasty made contact, it seems, with the rise of the great Olmecs of Meso-America centuries before Christ. During the Middle Ages of West Africa, these peoples again touched base and cross-fertilized. Perhaps there was a "butterfly effect" or a "sensitive dependence on initial conditions" that allowed a mutual tendency of systems to re-create each other from a common mold. This so-called "self-similarity of structures," or the "infinite nesting" effect, can operate because there is a common root, a shared stock of genetic, anthropological, blood or serological, and embryological material that unfolds in each of these scenarios. At base, all the great world religions and mythologies share a common language and symbol system that is a reflection of the shared human unconscious. The great lineages of Christianity, Judaism, Islam, and the Yogas of India that spawned Hinduism, Buddhism, and Taoism, in this sense, have an African unconscious root.

At the core of these traditions is a phenomenon that we have stressed we believe to be at the root and to pervade the African genesis in science and religious disciplines. That is the phenomenon of Kundalini. It is ubiquitous throughout the whole of African and African diasporic peoples and studies, especially in the realm of psychospiritual experiences.

Yes, there is a common stock, a common inheritance, and it shows itself elsewhere, binding us together in a living whole. In the intimate universe of embryogenesis, the neuromelanin nerve track that guides the living biolight of our development reflects our shared African inheritance. It is immediate and weaves together our deep-structure commonalities from the dawn of conception to the hour of our death. In some very real way we are all one organism arising and fall back into each other, extending ourselves into ever new wholes.

In the future, the peaceful resolution of our worldwide ethnic madness will be the deep recognition of our African rootedness. In it is our template, our common connection to the Earth, the nonlocal intelligences, and the stars. Embedded in its primordial circuitry is literally the pathway of evolutionary forces that move us from the Earth to the constellations our progeny will travel. No matter where we go, we will always be Africoid, as we were in the beginning.

The human blastula, as we have said, begins as a dark ball, a singular organism that elongates, differentiates, becomes a human being in the mother's womb. The dark energies of the stellar abyss are no doubt in some unknown way implicated in the dark neuromelanin unfoldment of human embryogenesis, an embryogenesis that in time gives birth to arms and legs, organ systems, and the brain. Human genesis and later its civilization dawned as a dark nebula of creativity on the African continent, then spread over the

Earth interacting with its children in distant places and giving rise to higher and more articulated forms and branches. Our own day is but the latest expression of an ancient unfoldment, an unfoldment from a more subtle realm of interwoven psychic, somatic, genetic, and shared unconscious processes. This attunement with the subtle life within us and the subtle light and energies outside and around us has allowed us to develop an extraordinary sensitivity to the forces of the sun, the stars, and the Earth itself. We can feel them course through our own bodies.

Just as there are specific conduits or lines of energy within the organism of the human body–mind, there are also postulated to be specific lines of energy and force surrounding and permeating the bioecological system or organism of the Earth. African peoples were aware of these energy sites and often built their temples and megaliths in accordance with their experience of these phenomena. The earliest human observatories for the mapping of the stellar constellations were often built on these sites. Stonehenge in England, as we've mentioned before, was one astronomical observatory built on one of these sites. Several other suggestive sites similar to the ones at Stonehenge have been found in various places such as Namoratunga in sub-Sahara Africa (Lynch & Robbins, 1978), and Nabta Playa, some 600 miles south of present-day Cairo. At Nabta Playa the sunrise on the summer solstice could have been observed precisely along parts of the structure 6,800 years ago (Discovery, 1998). Several of these sites have been measured and found to accurately map the seven stars or constellations, including the Pleiades and Sirius. Some of the most famous of these, but certainly not the oldest, are found in southern Ethiopia, and date back to 300 B.C.E. These megaliths in Africa, especially those in Ethiopia, are megaliths associated with the ancient Kushite kingdoms. We know the ancient Egyptians and the Kushite peoples were intimately associated with each other through travel, language, and warring contests at various times. We know that the Egyptians had an extremely sophisticated knowledge of astronomy and that some aspect of their astronomy is seen today in the cosmological belief of the Dogon peoples of Mali, who trace their ancestors to pre-dynastic Egypt. The pyramid structures of the Egypto-Nubian peoples served as both royal tomb and astronomical observatory.

Regardless of how heretical it strikes our modern sensibilities, from the earliest of times humanity has known, felt, and intuited an intimate relationship between energy lines and energy sites of the human organism, and their correspondence with energy sites on the living Earth (Mitchell, 1977). It is reasonable to assume that in a future science humankind will judiciously use not only the various forms of light and energy known today but forms of light and energy we have yet to discover. These include not only the energy animating our own body–mind, but indeed if the Earth is truly alive, interconnected, and organic, at least on its surface, then we will find and use these fields of energy that are present in specific areas of the Earth and along specific lines on the Earth.

Spiritual Discipline, the Transition Called Death, and Passage to Other Worlds

The self-knowledge of our species truly is still in its infancy, and yet a child is not totally ignorant of the world process in which it finds itself. Ancient and archetypal experiences run throughout the tribes. In each experience we are again always in the position of "energy" when we reflect on these events. This includes, of course, the great mystery of death. Temples and monuments are scattered like innumerable relics of human experience to this labyrinth that hourly draws each one of us closer to its entrance. The *Egyptian Book of the Dead*, the *Tibetan Book of the Dead*, many many others speak of the labyrinth with its spirit realms, its Bardos, and its "tunnels" from world to world. Yet when we step back, and from the position of energy merely observe the process, we see that these Bardos and "tunnels" are not so alien to our everyday experience as long as we remember that we on some level already dwell in the realm of light. Perhaps a limited physicalistic analogy can be helpful.

For unknown millennia our species has experienced at times breaks or dissociations in our daily consciousness that opened us to other realms of awareness. The "passageway" from realm to realm is very often perceived as a "tunnel" through which we pass. In a brief psychiatric episode, this can happen when too much anxiety floods the system. Then various kinds of "tunnel vision" can occur in moments of depersonalization, derealization, or dissociation. In certain meditative practices where one seeks to go from the waking state into the dreaming state *without* the usual break in consciousness, a technique called Yoga nidra, there is often a whirling tunnel of sound and color through which the practitioner feels himself pass through. In the great temple initiation ceremonies, both past and present, the devotee, after appropriate study, meditation, and discipline, may pass through a kind of tunnel from one "world" to another. It is always a profoundly moving, awe-inspiring experience. The disease of intellectual doubt is completely purged. The clinically recorded near-death-experience (NDE) is also one in which, after the brief dissociation from the physical body, the observing self, again in the position of "energy" with respect to the dense physical world, moves through a kind of tunnel in which it experiences various phenomena until it approaches a vast, illimitable, self-boundary-evaporating intelligence-light. At this juncture it experiences a still more radically illuminating process. There is even a whole medical journal devoted to this, the *Journal of Near-Death Studies.*

The thrust here is that our human experience of "passage" from one world or vibrational plane to another, be it a Bardo, a spirit realm, or whatever religious coloration, has been associated for ages with this kind of tunnel experience. In the present era's quantum and relativistic view of matter, this form of passage from one world to another, or *distant regions of space*, to another is provided by a so-called "wormhole." This supraluminal loophole is technically referred to as an "Einstein-Rosen bridge." From the perspective of energy, the witnessing self passes through a curved tunnel-like space (Wheeler, 1996). No light enters it except at the entrance and "exit." The exit here is a new region of space–time and reality. In the experience of death this new region leads to the great light-intelligence encounter, while in this tunnel itself arise the various deceased familial and Bardo experiences.

In this abstract physicalistic analogy, the cosmos is considered to be most *probably* a vastly interconnected place including distant regions of space. Direct experience down the ages, however, confesses that the spiritual universe most definitely is intimately interconnected by a kind of luminous matrix that enfolds matter, energy, space, and time. The material world "below" reflects the spiritual world "above." "As above, so below." The realm of Orun (above) is mirrored in the material world of Aiye (below).

Using a further quantum mechanical analogy, the transition from one "plane" to another, like the knot of energy moving from one orbit of the atom to another, only seems to disappear or "die" and be "reborn" in another orbit. It is the eclipse of self-consciousness itself that creates the illusion of discontinuity, not the other way around.

These, of course, are merely contemporary physicalistic analogies that will eventually be outdated by more sophisticated examples. They simply convey in current language and concepts how the apparent space, distance, and discontinuity problem is potentially overcome and how a quantum of energy can be in contact with the seemingly remote Duát of the stars. The root intuition and archetypal experience, however, are timeless and the same. This is the vision embedded in the sacred Kemetic Book of What Is in the Duát, the Book of Gates, the Coffin Texts, the *Book of the Dead*, and the Pyramid Texts. The Dogon, echoing back to pre-dynastic times, whisper this to their dead on their voyage to their ancestors in the Milky Way and the star Sirius engulfed in the Duát. The pharaohs steered their solar boat by this on their journey to Osiris in the "winding waterway"! This was their culturally and historically conditioned symbolic context for the adventure of the soul's return from the world of space, time, and distance to the realm of light that dwells beyond space–time and yet enfolds it. It seems that in a luminous episode structured by the near-death experience the local "I" at death is reabsorbed from its projection into the realm of space and time. Among our kind there has always been some rumination about the illusion of death, transformation, and the mysteries of eternal life.

Meditative and religious introspection across cultures and eras appear to suggest that this elusive self we have been talking about is truly nonlocal, a projection into the energetic tissue of space–time. The work of meditation therefore is to integrate and sustain awareness through all the states of consciousness. This includes the consciousness of the body and its innumerable fields of energy! These currents draw us into a view that the body on more subtle levels is a radiating organism of living light. It is a living energy or light that makes the quantum interconnectedness a reality for our own bodies as they bathe in the universe.

Only a wider ecology, a solar ecology can emerge from this view. Rhythm, vitality, a luminous unseen intelligence seems to inhabit the deeper corridors of our existence. In such a body the forces we once called the gods can come and go, can be embodied by us, and we, in turn, become conduits for them.

As a projection or unfoldment into the energetic tissue of space–time, the nonlocal self gradually realizes that its somatic organs, its heart, its lungs, its blood and bones on some subtle level are symbols in an energetic universe that it molds and must come to terms with. An inherent interconnectedness of energy and information in a wider, living solar ecology will someday clinically make it possible to exchange energy and information in forms of healing that, at present, we only see in gifted healers, anomalies, and unexplainable recoveries.

As this unfolds, it will be impossible to maintain the limited view we currently have of ourselves, our use of resources, and our relationship to the Earth. Our view of *Homo sapiens sapiens* will give way to our preparation for the evolution of a new kind of human, a race of luminous beings who adventure in the realm of light. The graceful transcendence of "humanism" in favor of something else will emerge as a moral, biological, and spiritual imperative. The great shared web of an African unconscious that has held us and guided us for eons will spin a new weave, binding our destinies together in a higher, more subtle, and luminous flux. This is the hidden evolution of the soul.

Death will give way to what it has always been for us, the door to transformation, the bridge beyond what cannot be verbally expressed. Ancient voyagers set out upon the oceans in search of new lands. Some were lost; some chose never to return. But eventually, the new continents became the provinces of our race. The physician and healer of tomorrow, after supporting the body for as long as ethically reasonable, will help the dying sail out to a greater continent, knowing that others have consciously traveled and returned by clinical means, have seen the other worlds, and that they are bright, luminous, and welcoming. There is no death, only transformations and deeper expressions of rhythm, vitality, and order.

Our institutions will come to have a radically different view of the transition we call death than most do today. Our nursing homes will be less and less fearful places where a society sends its elders and ill to die, but instead, especially for the strong and gracious ones who live long lives, they will become the temples of transformation, the finer schools of wisdom and discipline where they learn to consciously experience their own death and awake in the radiant translation. They will come forth by day and go forth by night!

Ten thousand years ago, the Earth looked different to us than it does today. Our relationship with it reflected that. A thousand years ago, the Earth and its place in the universe also looked different to us than it does today. Our science and religion reflected that, too. Even a century ago the planet seemed quite differently fixed in our hearts and imagination than the current image of it spinning through the abyss. We can only guess how the Earth will appear in a future that sees consciousness, energy, and interconnectedness everywhere living and vital, rhythmic and theistic. The mental will be only one shade of consciousness.

Through this ceaseless vitality, this constant rhythm, transformation, and awakening of consciousness on higher and higher levels through the millennium, we move toward that wider solar consciousness, that sustained breech of mind that awakens in us our true nature, the nature of "beings of light." In this sea of light we are intimately connected with each other, a subtle living tissue of a common flesh. In this sea we share a common birth, a common destiny. Some day, after we have transcended all the contractions of the body–mind, neuroses, and the pulls toward war and self-destruction, we shall turn our attention toward the wider sciences of the spirit. At that time the luminous serpent, awake and full, will be the birthright of every incarnation. The consciousness of the One will be the consciousness of all. Then, and only then, the ancient race of *Homo sapiens sapiens* will, like the mysterious snake, shed its skin, and mate its consciousness with the divine consciousness of light. This is our destiny, let it be so.

APPENDICES

APPENDIX A. Principal West African Yoruba Deities (Orisha) and Their Expressions in the Americas

Yoruba Deity (Orisha)	Haiti and New Orleans	Cuba and Puerto Rico	South America/ Brazil	Catholic Saint
Osun *Rivers* Love, Fertility	Erzulie Freda	Ochún/Oshún	Oxun	Mother of Charity Caridad del Cobre
Oya *Wind, Tornadoes, Lightning* Guardian of Ancestors	Aida-Wedo Brigette	Oya	Yansa	St. Theresa St. Catherine Our Lady of Candelaria
Songo *Fire, Thunder* Kingships, Authority	Shango	Changó/Shangó	Xango	St. Jerome St. Barbara
Orisanla/Obatala *Sky, Clouds* Father/Mother Principle, Creation, Wisdom, Keeper of the Head	Batala Blanc Dani	Obatalá	Oxala Orixala	Christ Our Lady of Mercy
Yemoja *River, Sea, Oceans* Mother Principle	La Balianne Agwe	Yemayá	Imanja	Mary Our Lady of Regla Star of the Sea
Esu/Elegba *Crossroad, Paths* Principle of Choice and Communication, Trickster, Energy	Legba Liba	Elegua/Elegbara	Eshu Pomba Gira	St. Martin de Porres St. Michael St. Peter

326

	Ogu	Ogún	Ogum	
Ogun *Iron* Principle of Aggression, War, Goals, Law, and Order				St. Peter St. Anthony St. George (Joan of Arc)
Ibeji *Sacred Twins* Duality, Balance, Prosperity	Marrasa	Ibelli/Ibegi	Ibegi	St. Danian St. Cosme
Òsòsi *Hunter, Forest, Vegetation* Principle of Justice, Sustenance	Agao-wedo	Ochossi	Oxossi *Cabaclo*	St. Francis
Olokun *Ocean, Wealth, Power* Psychic Phenomena		Olokún	Olokum	Star of the Sea
Sopona *Smallpox, Sickness, Disease* Principle of Rectification		Babaluayé	Omolu	St. Lazarus

Compiled by Edward Bruce Bynum and Marilyn Omifunké Torres, Egbe of Orisha, an initiated priestess in the Yoruba West African traditions of both Orisha and Odu who has a background in cultural anthropology and received a chieftancy in Imota, Nigeria.

Sources:

Orixas, by Pierre Fatumbi Verger (Sao Paulo, Brazil: Editoria Coruppio Comerico, Ltda., 1981).

Jambalaya: Natural Woman's Book of Personal Charms and Practice Ritual, by Luisah Teish (San Francisco: Harper, 1980).

Yoruba: Nine Centuries of African Art and Thought, by John Drewal and John Pemberton III (New York: The Center of African Art in association with Harry N. Adams, Inc., 1989).

Black Gods—Orisa Studies in the New World, by Gary Edwards and John Mason (New York: Yoruba Theological Archministry, 1985).

APPENDIX B
The Ten Plagues of Moses

Blood—Dam

Frogs—Tsfardeya

Vermin—Kinim

Beasts—Arov

Cattle Diseases—Dever

Boils—Sh'khin

Hail—Barad

Locusts—Arbeh

Darkness—Khoshek

Slaying of the firstborn—Makat B'Korot

APPENDIX C
Partial List of Dances of African American Origin

Bolero	Itch
Bomba	Jala jala
Break dancing	Jazz ballet
Bump	Jerk
Cake walk	Lambada
Cha-cha	Landó
Clam	Limbo
Cumbia	Lindy
Danza	Locomotion
Electric bogie	Macarena
Electric slide	Mambo
Festejo	Mazured
Frug	Merengue
Funky Broadway	Monkey
Funky chicken	Paso doble
Hullabaloo	Philadelphia doe-lo
Hully gully	Salsa

Samba

Seis chorreao

Shake

Slammin

Stroll

Swim

Tango

Twist

Vals

Watusi

REFERENCES

Abell, W. (1966). *The collective dream in art.* New York: Schocken Books.

Abimbola, W. (1975). *Sixteen great poems of Ifa.* New York: UNESCO and OAU Center for Linguistic and Historical Studies by Oral Tradition.

Abimbola, W. (1976). *Ifa—An exposition of Ifa literary corpus.* Ibadan, Nigeria: Oxford University Press.

Abimbola, W. (1992). Personal communication on the role of sacrifice in Ifa divination.

Abiodun, R. (1994). Understanding Yoruba art and aesthetic: The concept of ase. *African Arts, 27*(3), 68–78.

Adams, H. A. (1983). African observers of the universe: The Sirius question. *Blacks in Science: Ancient and Modern, Journal of African Civilizations, 5*(1&2), 27–49.

Althschule, M. D., & Hegedus, Z. L. (1976). The importance of studying visceral melanins. *Clinical Pharmacology and Therapy, 19*(2), 124–134.

Akbar, N. (1984). *Chains and images of psychological slavery.* Jersey City, NJ: New Mind Productions.

Akiwowo, A. (1980). *Ajobi and Ajogbe: Variations on the theme of sociation* (Inaugural Lecture Series 46). Ile-Ife, Nigeria: University of EFE Press.

Akiwowo, A. (1986). Oral tradition as a source of psychological knowledge. In E. B. Wilson (Ed.), *Psychology and society.* Ile-Ife, Nigeria: Nigerian Psychological Association–University of Ife Press.

Akiwowo, A. (1992). Personal communication.

Allen, E. (1994). Satokata Takahashi and the flowering of Black messianic nationalism. *The Black Scholar, 24*(1), 23–46.

Allen, E. (1995, Fall). Waiting for Tojo: The pro-Japan vigil of Black Missourians (1932–1943). *Gateway Heritage,* pp. 38–55.

Alpern, S. B. (1992, Summer). The new myths of African history. *Bostonia: The Magazine of Culture and Ideas,* pp. 26–32, 90–91.

Altschule, M. D., & Hegedus, Z. L. (1972). The adrenochrome hypothesis of schizophrenia. In D. Hawkins & L. Pauley (Eds.), *Orthomolecular Psychiatry.* San Francisco: Freeman.

Ammi, B. (1982). *God, the Black man and truth*. Chicago: Communicators Press.

Aptheker, H. (1943). *American Negro slave revolts*. New York: International Publishers.

Asante, M. K. (1984). The African-American mode of transcendence. *Journal of Transpersonal Psychology, 6*(2), 167–177.

Ashanti, K. F. (1990). *Rootwork and Voodoo in mental health*. Durham, NC: Tone Books, Inc.

Atsura, Y. (1983). Sakanoue no Tamuramaro. *Kodansha Encyclopedia of Japan*, vol. 6. Tokyo: Kdansha.

Aurobindo, S. (1954). *Savitri*. Ponicherry, India: Sri Aurobindo Ashram Press.

Aurobindo, S. (1971). *The synthesis of Yoga*. Pondicherry, India: Sri Aurobindo Ashram.

Austin, A. D. (1997). *African Muslims in antebellum America: Transatlantic stories and spiritual struggles*. New York and London: Routledge.

Avalon, A. (1974). *The serpent power*. New York: Dover.

Baigent, M. (1982). *Holy blood, holy grail*. New York: Dell Books.

Baigent, M., & Leigh, R. (1989). *The temple and the lodge*. New York: Arcade Publishing/Little, Brown and Co.

Bailey, A. (1949). *The destiny of the nations*. New York: Lucis Publishing.

Bakan, D. (1990). *Sigmund Freud and the Jewish mystical tradition*. London: Free Association Books. (Original work published 1958)

Bard, K. (1992, Summer). Ancient Egyptians and the issue of race. *Bostonia: The Magazine of Culture and Ideas*, pp. 33–35, 91.

Barnes, C. (1988). *Melanin: The chemical key to Black greatness*. Houston, TX: C. B. Publishers.

Barr, F. E. (1983). Melanin: The organizing molecule. In D. F. Horrobin (Ed.), *Medical Hypotheses* (Vol. 11; pp. 1–140). Edinburgh: Churchill Livingstone.

Bascom, W. (1969). *The Yoruba of southwestern Nigeria*. New York: Holt, Rinehart & Winston.

Basham, A. L. (1959). *The wonder that was India*. New York: Grove.

Bass, L. (1975). A quantum mechanical mind–body interaction. *Foundations of Physics, 5*, 155–172.

Bastide, R. (1978). *The African religions of Brazil* (H. Sebba, Trans.). Baltimore: Johns Hopkins University Press.

Bateson, G. (1972). *Steps to an ecology of mind*. San Francisco: Chandler Publications.

Bateson, G. (1979). *Mind and nature: A necessary unity*. New York: E. P. Dutton.

Bauval, R., & Gilbert, A. (1994). *The Orion mystery*. London: Heinemann.

Bazelon, M., Fenichel, G. M., & Randall, J. (1967). Studies on neuromelanin: A melanin system in the human adult brainstem. *Neurology, 17*, 512–519.

Ben-Jochannan, Y. (1970). *African origins of the major Western religions*. New York: Alkebu-lan.

Ben-Jochannan, Y. (1972). *Black man of the Nile and his family*. New York: Alkebu-lan.

Bennett, L. (1962). *Before the* Mayflower: *A history of the Negro in America 1619–1964*. Baltimore: Penguin.

Bentov, I. (1977). *Stalking the wild pendulum: On the mechanics of consciousness.* New York: Dutton.

Bernal, M. (1987). *Black Athena: The Afroasiatic roots of classical civilization: Vol. 1. The fabrication of ancient Greece, 1785–1985.* New Brunswick, NJ: Rutgers University Press.

Black Heritage Collection. (1992). *Buffalo Soldiers: The true story of our country's first Black war he. oes* [Documentary film]. Plymouth, MN: Simitar Inc.

Blavatsky, H. P. (1966). *The secret doctrine.* Wheaton, IL: Theosophical Publishing House. (Original work published 1888)

Bliquez, L. J. (1981). Greek and Roman medicine. *Archaelogy, 34*(2), 10–17.

Bogerts, B. (1981). A brainstem atlas of catecholaminergic neurons in man, using melanin as a natural marker. *Journal of Comparative Neurology, 197,* 63–80.

Bohm, D. (1980). *Wholeness and the implicate order.* London: Routledge & Kegan Paul.

Bohm, D. (1986). A new theory of the relationship of mind and matter. *Journal of the American Society for Psychical Research, 80,* 113–135.

Bonnet, C. (1983). Kerma: An African kingdom of the 2nd and 3rd millennia. *Archeology, 36*(6), 38–45.

Bosnak, R. (1996). *Tracks in the wilderness of dreaming.* New York: Delacorte Press.

Brandon, G. (1990). Sacrificial practices in Santeria, an African-Cuban religion in the United States. In J. E. Holloway (Ed.), *Africanisms* (pp. 119–147). Bloomington: Indiana University Press.

Breasted, W. (1912). *Development of religion and thought in ancient Egypt.* Cited in Parrinder, E. G. (1951). *West African psychology.* London: Lutterworth Press.

Brown, B. (1923). *The wisdom of the Egyptians.* New York: Brentanos.

Budge, E. A. W. (1960). *The book of the dead: The hieroglyphic transcript of the papyrus of Ani.* Secaucus, NJ: University Books.

Budge, E. A. W. (1961). *The Osiris myth* (Vols. 1, 2). New York: University Press.

Buttrick, G. A. (Ed.). (1984). *Interpreter's dictionary of the Bible* (Vol. 4). Nashville: Abingdon Press.

Bynum, E. B. (1993). *Families and the interpretation of dreams: Awakening the intimate web.* Ithaca, NY: Haworth.

Bynum, E. B. (1994). *Transcending psychoneurotic disturbances: New approaches in psychospirituality and personality development.* Ithaca, NY: Haworth.

Bynum, E. B. (1996). Research methods in clinical psychospirituality. *Journal of Humanistic Psychology, 24*(2), 257–261.

Bynum, E. B. (1998). A day in the life of a Black dream healer. In S. Kripper & M. Bova (Eds.), *Healing tales.* Westport, CT: Greenwood.

Cahill, T. (1995). *How the Irish saved civilization: The untold story of Ireland's heroic role from the fall of Rome to the rise of medieval Europe.* New York & London: Anchor/Doubleday.

Capra, F. (1975). *The Tao of physics.* Boulder, CO: Shambhala.

Carew, J. (1992). Moorish culture-bringers: Bearers of enlightenment. In I. Van Sertima (Ed.), *Golden Age of the Moor.* New Brunswick, NJ: Transaction.

Carroll, C. (1900). *The negro a beast.* Miami: Mnemosyne Publishing Co.

Cartwright, S. (1852). *Charleston Medical Journal, 7,* 89–98. Cited in Stampp, K. M. (1956). *The peculiar institution.* New York: Vintage.

Cartwright, S. (1858). *American cotton planter and soil of the South, Vol. 2.* Cited in Stampp, K. M. (1956). *The peculiar institution.* New York: Vintage.

Cavalli-Sforza, L., Menozzi, P., & Piazza, A. (1994). *The history and geography of human genes.* Princeton, NJ: Princeton University Press.

Chandler, W. B. (1995a). The principle of polarity. In R. Rashid (Ed.), *African presence in early Asia* (pp. 360–377). New Brunswick, NJ: Transaction.

Chandler, W. B. (1995b). Ebony and bronze: Race and ethnicity in early Arabia and the Islamic world. In R. Rashid (Ed.), *African presence in early Asia* (pp. 270–311). New Brunswick, NJ: Transaction.

Chaney, E., & Messick, W. L. (1980). *Kundalini and the third eye.* City of Commerce, CA: Astara Inc. Stockton Trade Press.

Chia, M. M. (1989a). *Bone marrow Nei Kung: Bone breathing and bone marrow rejuvenation.* Huntington, NY: Healing Tao Books.

Chia, M. M. (1989b). *Chi self-message: The Tao of rejuvenation.* Huntington, NY: Healing Tao Books.

Chia, M. M. (1989c, Spring). Tao and the universe (Part 1). *The Healing Tao Journal, 1*(1), pp. 1–2.

Chomsky, N. (1965). *Aspects of the theory of syntax.* Cambridge, MA: MIT Press.

Church, G. J. (1992, January 13). Surge to the right. *Time,* pp. 22–24.

Churchward, A. (1921). *The origin and evolution of the human race.* London: Allen and Unwin.

Clegg, L. (1975, September). Who were the first Americans. *The Black Scholar, 7*(1), 32–41.

Cochran, A. A. (1957). The quantum physical basis of life. *Main Currents of Modern Thought, 12,* 99–104.

Cochran, A. A. (1971). Relationships between quantum physics and biology. *Foundations of Physics, 1,* 235–250.

Coleman, J. (1992, Summer). Greece and the eastern Mediterranean. *Bostonia: The Magazine of Culture and Ideas,* pp. 36–38.

Comte, A. (1974). Cours de philosophie positive. In S. Adreski (Ed.), *The essential Comte* (M. Clarke, Trans.). New York: Barnes and Noble. (Original work published 1830)

Cooper, D. A. (1994). *The mystical Kabbalah: Judaism's ancient system for mystical exploration through meditation and contemplation* [5 cassette tape series]. Boulder, CO: Sounds True.

Cope, F. W. (1978). Discontinuous magnetic field effects (Barkhausen noise) in nucleic acids as evidence for room temperature organic superconduction. *Physiological Chemistry and Physics, 10,* 233–245.

Cope, F. W. (1981). Organic superconductive phenomena at room temperature. Some magnetic properties of dyes and graphite interpreted as manifestations of viscous magnetic flux lattices and small superconductive regions. *Physiological Chemistry and Physics, 13,* 99–110.

Coppens, Y. (1994, May). East Side story: The origin of humankind. *Scientific American,* pp. 88–95.

Coulborn, R. (1959). *The origin of civilized societies.* Princeton, NJ: Princeton University Press.

Cousto, C. (1990). *The cosmic octave.* Mendocino, CA: Life Rhythm Press.

Cowan, J. (1991). *Mysteries of the dream-time: The spiritual life of Australian Aborigines.* Garden City, NJ: Avery Publishing Group.

Cowan, W. M. (1979). The development of the brain. In D. F. Flanagan et al. (Eds.), *The Brain* (pp. 56–69). San Francisco: Freeman.

Crews, F. (1993, November 18). The unknown Freud. *New York Review*, pp. 55–66.

Curtin, P. D. (1969). *The Atlantic slave trade: A census.* Madison: University of Wisconsin Press.

Darwin, C. (1936). *The descent of man.* New York: The Modern Library. (Original work published 1871)

Darwin, C. (1964). *On the origin of species.* New York: The Modern Library. (Original work published 1859)

Darwin, C. (1978). *The origin of species by means of natural selection.* London and Toronto: J. M. Dent and Sons; New York: E. P. Dutton. (Original work published 1859)

Davidson, B. (1959). *The lost cities of Africa.* New York: Little, Brown.

Davidson, B. (1967). *The African past.* New York: Grosset & Dunlap.

Davidson, B. (1967, June 17). Mother Africa, *West Africa*, no. 2611.

Davidson, B. (1968). *Africa in history: Themes and outlines.* New York: Collier.

Davidson, B. (1969). *Africa in history.* New York: Macmillan.

Davies, P. (1980). *Other worlds.* New York: Simon & Schuster.

de Chardin, P. T. (1959). *The phenomenon of man.* New York: Harper & Row.

Deren, M. (1989). *Divine horsemen: The living gods of Haiti.* Kingston, NY: McPherson & Company. (Original work published 1953)

Deutsch, A. (1840). The first U.S. census of the insane and its use as pro-slavery propaganda. *Bulletin of the History of Medicine*, 1944, 469–482.

Dimont, M. I. (1978). *The Jews in America. The roots, history and destiny of American Jews.* New York: Simon & Schuster.

Diop, A. C. (1974). *The African origin of civilization.* Brooklyn, NY: Lawrence Hill Books.

Diop, A. C. (1991). *Civilization or barbarism: An authentic anthropology.* Brooklyn, NY: Lawrence Hill Books.

Discovery. (1998, July 19). Egyptian Stonehenge. *Discovery: The World of Science*, 7, p. 14.

Dixon, R. B. (1923). *The racial history of man.* New York: Scribner's.

Drewal, H. J., & Drewal, M. T. (1983). *Gelede: Art and female power among the Yoruba.* Bloomington: Indiana University Press.

Dubrov, A. P. (1978). *The geomagnetic field and life: Geomagnetobiology* (F. L. Sinclair, Trans.). New York: Plenum.

Dunne, B. J., & Jahn, R. G. (1987). *Margins of reality: The role of consciousness in the physical world.* Orlando, FL: Harcourt Brace Jovanovich.

Dye, J. H. (1912). *Illustrated edition of painless childbirth or healthy mothers and healthy children* (17th ed.). Buffalo, NY: J. H. Dye Medical Institute.

Eccles, J. (1976). Do mental events cause neural events analogously to the probability fields of quantum mechanics? *Proceedings of the Royal Society of London, B227*, 411–428.

Edelstein, L. M. (1971). Melanin—A unique biopolymer. *Pathobiology Annual, 1,* 311–312.

Ehrenreich, B. (1992, July 20). Or is it creative freedom? *Time,* p. 89.

Elder, D. (1994). Kundalini: The deepest secret of the Bible. *Proceedings from the KRN Symposium of the Institute of Transpersonal Psychology.* Stanford, CA: KRN.

Engling, E. S. (1995). Los higos de la fortuna, Teágenes y cariclea: Calderón, Heliodorus and the people of the sun. *Afro-Hispanic Review, 14*(2), 35–46.

Epstein, M. (1984). On the negelect of evenly suspended attention. *Journal of Transpersonal Psychology, 16*(2), 193–205.

Evans-Pritchard, E. E. (1965). *Theories of primitive religion.* Oxford: Clarendon Press.

Evans-Pritchard, E. E. (1976). *Witchcraft, oracles and magic among the Azande.* Oxford: Clarendon Press.

Evans-Wentz, W. Y. (1958). *Tibetan yoga and secret doctrines.* London: Oxford University Press.

Evans-Wentz, W. Y. (1960). *The Tibetan book of the dead.* London: Oxford University Press.

Faber, E. (1994). *Slavery and the Jews: A historical inquiry* (Occasional Papers in Jewish History and Thought, 2). New York: Hunter College.

Fairservis, W. A. (1962). *The ancient kingdoms of the Nile and the doomed monuments of Nubia.* New York: Thomas & Crowell.

Fanon, F. (1963). *Wretched of the earth.* New York: Grove.

Fanon, F. (1967). *Black skin, White mask.* New York: Grove.

Fatunmbi, A. F. (1991). *Ifa quest: The search for the source of Santería and Lucumí.* Bronx, NY: Original Publications.

Faulkner, R. O. (1967). *Sex and race* (Vol. 1). New York: Helga Rogers.

Faulkner, R. O. (1969). *The ancient Egyptian pyramid texts.* London: Oxford University Press.

Fell, B. (1989). *America B.C.: Ancient settlers in the New World.* New York: Pocket Books.

Filators, J., McGinness, J., & Corey, P. (1976). Thermal and electronic contributions to switching in melanins. *Biopolymeus, 15,* 534–538.

Finch, C. S. (1990). *African background to medical science.* London: Karnak House.

Finch, C. S. (1991). *Echoes of the Old Darkland: Themes from the African Eden.* Decatur, GA: Khenti Publishers.

Fladmark, K. R. (1986). The first Americans: Getting one's Berings. *Natural History, 11,* 8–18.

Flatischler, R. (1990). *The forgotten power of rhythm.* Mendocino, CA: Life Rhythm Press.

Fox, B. (1994). The dancing partners: Kundalini and panic attacks. *Proceedings from the KRN Symposium of the Institute of Transpersonal Psychology.* Stanford, CA: KRN.

Freud, S. (1939). *Moses and monotheism.* New York: Vintage.

Freyre, G. (1956). *The masters and the slaves: A study in the development of Brazilian civilization*. New York: Knopf.

Frieden, K. (1990). *Freud's dream interpretation*. Albany: State University of New York Press.

Gackenbach, J. I., & Bosweld, J. (1989). *Control your dreams*. New York: Harper & Row.

Galtung, J. (1981). Structure, culture, and intellectual style: An essay comparing Saxonic, Teutonic, Gallic and Nipponic approaches. *Social Sciences Information*, 20(6), 817–856. London & Beverly Hills: Sage.

Garfield, P. (1974). *Creative dreaming*. New York: Ballantine.

Garrow, D. J. (1998, March 30). Mississippi's spy secrets. *Time*, p. 15.

Ghalioungui, P. (1973). *The house of life: Magic and medical science in ancient Egypt*. Amsterdam: B. M. Israel.

Gimbutas, M. (1982). *Gods and goddesses of old Europe 7000–3500 B.C.: Myths, legends and cult images*. Berkeley: University of California Press.

Gimbutas, M. (1992). *The age of the great goddess* (Vols. 1, 2). Boulder, CO: Sounds True Recordings.

Giraule, M., & Diertelen, G. (1986). *The pale fox*. Chino Valley, AZ: Continuum Foundation.

Gladwin, H. S. (1947). *Men out of Asia*. New York: McGraw-Hill.

Gleason, J., Aworindo, A., & Ogundipe, J. O. (1973). *A recitation of Ifa, Oracle of the Yoruba*. New York: Grossman Publishers.

Goldscheider, A. (1906). Uber die materiellen veranderungen bei der assoziationsbildung. *Neruologische Zentrablatt*, 25, 146.

Gonzalez-Wippler, M. (1987). *Santeria: African magic in Latin America*. Bronx, New York: Original Publications.

Grant, K. (1979). Cults of the shadow. In J. White (Ed.), *Kundalini, evolution and englightenment* (pp. 395–398). New York: Anchor.

Greenberg, J. H. (1973). African languages. In E. P. Skinner (Ed.), *Peoples and cultures of Africa* (pp. 70–80). Garden City, NY: Natural History Press.

Griaule, M. (1965). *Conversations with Ogotemmeli*. London: Oxford University Press.

Griaule, M., & Dieterlen, G. (1986). *The pale fox*. Chino Valley, AZ: Continuum Foundation.

Grier, W. H., & Cobbs, P. M. (1968). *Black rage*. New York: Bantam.

Grinberg-Zylberbaum, J., & Ramos, J. (1987). Patterns of interhemispheric correlation during human communication. *International Journal of Neuroscience*, 36, 41–54.

Grinberg-Zylberbaum, J., & Ramos, J. (1994). The Einstein-Polodsky-Rosen paradox in the brain: The transferred potential. *Physics Essays*, 7(4), 422–428.

Guerreo, E. (1993). *Framing blackness: The African-American image in film*. Philadelphia: Temple University Press.

Haeckel, E. (1876). *The history of creation: Or the development of the Earth and its inhabitants by the action of natural causes* (Vol. 2). New York: D. Appleton & Company.

Haich, E. (1975). *Sexual energy and yoga*. New York: Aurora Press.

Hall, R. L. (1990). African religious retentions in Florida. In J. E. Holloway (Ed.), *Africanisms in American culture* (pp. 98–118). Bloomington: Indiana University Press.

Hamilton, V. (1985). *The people could fly: American Black folktales.* New York: Knopf.

Hancock, G., & Bauval, R. (1996). *The message of the sphinx: A quest for the hidden legacy of mankind.* New York: Crown.

Heisenberg, W. (1971). *Physics and beyond.* London: George Allen & Unwin.

Heline, C. (1949). *America's invisible guidance.* Los Angeles, CA: New Age Press.

Herbert, N. (1987). *Quantum reality: Beyond the new physics.* Garden City, NY: Anchor/Doubleday.

Herskovits, M. J. (1924). A preliminary consideration of cultural areas of Africa. *American Anthropologist, 26*(1), 50–63.

Herskovits, M. J. (1958). *The myth of the Negro past.* Boston: Beacon Press.

Hertz, F. M., & Rosen, E. J. (1982). Jewish families. In M. McGoldrick, J. K. Pearce, & J. Giordano (Eds.), *Ethnicity and family therapy* (pp. 364–392). New York: Guilford.

Hicks, J. T. (1836). Personal letter to Samuel S. Downey, *Downey Papers.* Cited in Stampp, K. M. (1956). *The peculiar institution.* New York: Vintage.

Hieronimus, R. (1976). *The two great seals of America.* Baltimore: Savitriaum.

Hieronimus, R. (1989). *America's secret destiny.* Rochester, VT: Destiny Books.

Higgins, G. (1836). *Anacalypsis* (Vols. 1, 2). London: Longman.

Holloway, J. E. (1990). *Africanisms in American culture.* Bloomington: Indiana University Press.

Homburger. (1941). Les langues Negro-Africaines, et les peuples qui les parlent. Cited on pp. 306–307, 336–337 in E. G. Parrinder (1951). *West African psychology.* London: Lutterworth Press.

Hourning, E. (1986). The discovery of the unconscious in ancient Egypt. *Spring Publication: An Annual of Archetypal Psychology and Jungian Thought,* 16–28.

Jackson, J. G. (1970). *An introduction to African civilization.* Secaucus, NJ: Citadel Press.

Jacobowitz, D. M. (1977). Controlling influences of the autonomic nervous system. *Journal of Investigative Dermatology, 69,* 106–111.

Jacobson, M. (1978). *Developmental neurobiology* (2nd Ed.). New York: Plenum.

Jahn, J. (1961). *Muntu: An outline of the new African culture.* New York: Grove.

Jahn, R. G., & Dunne, B. J. (1987). *Margins of reality: The role of consciousness in the physical world.* New York: Harcourt Brace Jovanovich.

James, G. M. (1954). *Stolen legacy.* New York: Philosophical Library, United Brothers Communication Systems.

Jaynes, J. (1976). *The origin of consciousness in the breakdown of the bicameral mind.* Boston: Houghton Mifflin.

Jeans, J. (1932). *The mysterious universe.* New York: E. P. Dutton.

Johanson, D. J., & Edey, M. A. (1981). *Lucy: The beginnings of human evolution.* New York: Simon & Schuster.

Joyce, J. (1964). *Portrait of the artist as a young man.* New York: Penguin Books. (Original work published 1916)

Jung, C. G. (1953). The problem of Job. In G. Adler, M. Fordham, & H. Read (Eds.), *The Collected Works of C. G. Jung* (R. F. C. Hull, Trans.). Princeton, NJ: Princeton University Press.

Jung, C. G. (1965). *Memories, dreams and reflections.* New York: Vintage.

Kafatos, M., & Nadeau, R. (1990). *The conscious universe. Part and whole in modern physical theory.* New York: Springer.

Kaiya, H. (1980). Neuromelanin, neuroleptics and schizophrenia: Hypothesis of an interaction between noradrenergic and dopaminergic system. *Neuropsychobiology, 6*(5), 241–248.

Katz, R. (1982). *Boiling energy: Community healing among the Kalahari Kung.* Cambridge, MA: Harvard University Press.

Kihlstrom, J. F., Barnhardt, T. M., & Tataryn, D. J. (1992). The psychological unconscious. *American Psychologist, 47*(6), 788–791.

King. R. D. (1990). *African origin of biological psychiatry.* Germantown, TN: Seymour-Sith.

Kinsley, M. (1992, July). Ice-T: Is the issue social responsibility? *Time,* p. 88.

Kloss, R. J. (1979). Psychodynamic speculations on derogatory names for Blacks. *Journal of Black Psychology, 5*(2), 85–97.

Kovel, J. (1971). *White racism: A psychohistory.* New York: Vintage.

Krishna, G. (1971a). *The biological basis of religion and genius.* New York: Harper & Row.

Krishna, G. (1971b). *Kundalini, the evolutionary energy in man.* New York: Harper & Row.

Krishna, G. (1972). *Kundalini: The secret of Yoga.* Flesherton, Ontario, Canada: F.I.N.D. Research Trust and Kundalini Research Foundation.

Krishna, G. (1978a). *The dawn of a new science.* New Delhi, India: Kundalini Research and Publication Trust.

Krishna, G. (1978b). *Yoga: A vision of its future.* New Delhi, India: Kundalini Research and Publication Trust.

Krishna, G. (1987). *The wonder of the brain.* Noroton Heights, CT: F.I.N.D. Research Trust and Kundalini Research Foundation.

Krpalvananda, S. (1977). *Science of meditation.* Bombay, India: New Karnodaya Press.

Krpalvananda, S. (1979). *Krpalupanisad.* St. Helena, CA: Sanatana Publishing Society.

Kuvalayananda, S. (1978). *Pranayama.* Philadelphia: Sky Foundation.

Kubie, L. S. (1965). The ontogeny of racial prejudice. *Journal of Nervous and Mental Disease, 141*(3), 265–273.

La Berge, S. (1985). *Lucid dreaming: The power of being awake and aware in your dreams.* Los Angeles: Jeremy Tarcher.

Lacayo, R. (1994, November 14). Stranger in the shadows. *Time,* pp. 46–47.

Lacouperie, T. de. (1892). *The Ya-King (I-Ching) and its authors.* London.

Lansky, P. (1979). Neurochemistry and the awakening of Kundalini. In J. White (Ed.), *Kundalini, evolution and enlightenment* (pp. 295–297). New York: Anchor.

Laosebikan, S. (1998). *Life is God* [unpublished manuscript].

Lashley, K. (1942). The problem of cerebral organization in vision. In *Biological*

Symposia: Vol 7. Visual Mechanisms (pp. 301–322). Lancaster, PA: Jaques Cattell Press.

Leakey, R. E., & Lewin, R. (1977). *Origins: The emergence and evolution of our species and its possible future.* New York: Dutton.

Leckie, W. H. (1967). *The Buffalo Soldiers: A narrative of the Negro Cavalry in the West.* Norman: University of Oklahoma Press.

Leibniz, G. W. (1981). *New essays on human understanding.* (P. Remnant & J. Bennett, Ed. and Trans.). Cambridge, UK: Cambridge University Press. (Original work published 1704)

Lerner, M., & West, C. (1996). *Jews and Blacks: A dialogue on race, religion and culture in America.* New York: Plume/Penguin.

Lewicki, P., Hill, T., & Czyzewska, M. (1992). Nonconscious acquisition of information. *American Psychologist, 47*(6), 796–801.

Libby, W. F. (1955). *Radiocarbon dating* (2nd ed.). Chicago: University of Chicago Press.

Lieberman, P. (1991). *Uniquely human: The evolution of speech, thought and selfless behavior.* Cambridge, MA: Harvard University Press.

Lockwood, M. (1989). *Mind, brain and the quantum.* Oxford, UK: Blackwell.

Loeb, J. (1907). *Comparative physiology of the brain and comparative psychology.* New York: Putnam.

Lucas, J. O. (1948). *The religion of the Yorubas.* Lagos, Nigeria: C.M.S. Bookshop.

Lucas, J. O. (1970). *Religions in West Africa and Ancient Egypt.* Apapa: Nigerian National Press.

Lugard, L. F. S. (1964). *A tropical dependency.* New York: Barnes & Noble.

Lynch. B. M., & Robbins, L. H. (1978). Namoratunga: The first archaeoastronomical evidence in sub-Saharan Africa. *Science, 200,* 766–768.

MacManus, S. (1977). *The story of the Irish race: A popular history of Ireland.* New York: Devin-Adair.

MacNeil, R. (1986). Black on white (Episode 5) in *The story of English* [Video]. Boston: MacNeil-Lehrer/WNET/BBC.

Makinde, M. A. (1988). *African philosophy, culture and traditional medicine.* Athens: Ohio University Center for International Studies.

Marcus, J. R. (1960). *The Jew in the medieval world.* Philadelphia: Jewish Publication Society.

Marion, L. R. (1996). Dentistry of ancient Egypt. *Journal of the History of Dentistry, 44*(1), 5–17.

Mason, J. W., & Docherty, J. P. (1980). Psychoendocrine research on schizophrenia: A need for reevaluation. In T. Melnechuk & C. Baxter (Eds.), *Perspectives in Schizophrenia Research* (pp. 131–148). New York: Raven.

Massey, G. (1881). *The Book of Beginnings* (Vols. 1, 2). London: Williams and Norgate.

Maxey, E. S., & Beal, J. B. (1975). The electrophysiology of acupuncture: How terrestrial electric and magnetic fields influence air-ionenergy exchanges through acupuncture points. *Biometerology, 6*(Part 1), 124.

Mbiti, J. S. (1969). *African religions and philosophy.* Portsmouth, NH: Heinemann.

McGinness, J., & Proctor, P. (1973). The importance of the fact that melanin is black. *Journal of Theoretical Biology, 39,* 677–678.

McGinness, J., Corry, P., & Proctor, P. (1974). Amorphous semiconductor switching in melanins. *Science, 183,* 853–855.

McGoldrick, M., Pearce, J. K., & Giordano, J. (Eds.). (1982). *Ethnicity and family therapy.* New York: Guilford.

McLaughlin, C., & Davidson, G. (1988). *America's metaphysical foundations.* Shutesbury, MA: Sirius Publishing.

McLaughlin, C., & Davidson, G. (1994). *Spiritual politics: Changing the world from the inside out.* New York: Ballantine Books.

Melville, H. (1851). *Moby Dick.* London and New York: H. Milford.

Menon, I. A., & Haberman, M. F. (1977). Mechanisms of action of melanins. *British Journal of Dermatology, 97,* 109–112.

Metraux, A. (1959). *Voodoo in Haiti.* New York: Schocken.

Miller, D. A. (1991). Useful perspectives on the relation between biological and physical descriptions of phenomena. *Journal of Theoretical Biology, 152,* 341–355.

Mishra, R. S. (1973). *Yoga sutras: The textbook of Yoga psychology.* Garden City, NY: Anchor.

Mitchell, J. (1977). *Secrets of the stones: The story of astroarchaeology.* New York: Penguin Books.

Moller, M. (1992). Fine structure of the pinealopetal innervation of the mammalian pineal gland. *Microscopy Research and Technique, 21,*188–204.

Mookerjee, A. (1982). *Kundalini: The arousal of the inner energy.* Rochester, VT: Destiny Books.

Morakinyo, O. (1983). The Yoruba Ayanmo myth and mental health care in West Africa. *Journal of Cultural Ideas,* 2(1), 61–92

Morakinyo, O., & Akiwowo, A. (1981). The Yoruba ontology of personality and motivation: A multidisciplinary approach. *Journal of Social Biological Structures, 4,* 19–38.

Morgon, M. (1991). *Mutant message: Downunder.* Summit, MO: M. M. Company.

Morse, S. (1924). *Freemasonry in the American Revolution.* Washington, DC: Masonic Service Association.

Motoyama, H. (1972). *Chakra, nadi of Yoga and meridians, points of acupuncture.* Toyko: Institute of Religious Psychology.

Motoyama, H. (1990). *Toward a superconsciousness: Meditational theory and practice* (S. Nagatomo & C. R. Ames, Trans.). Berkeley, CA: Asian Humanities Press.

Mulira, J. G. (1990). The case of voodoo in New Orleans. In J. E. Holloway (Ed.), *Africanisms* (pp. 34–68). Bloomington: Indiana University Press.

Murdoch, J. (1925). *A history of Japan* (Vol. 1). London: Kegan Paul.

Myers, L. J. (1993). *Understanding an Afrocentric world view: Introduction to an optimal psychology.* Dubuque, IA: Kendall/Hunt.

Narayanananda, S. (1979). *The primal power in man or the Kundalini shakti.* Rishikesh, India: Yoga Trust.

"Negro." (1884). *Encyclopedia Britannica: A dictionary of arts, sciences, and general literature* (9th ed., Vol. 17). New York: Scribner & Sons.

Noden, D. M. (1978). Interactions directing the migration and cytodifferentiation of the avianneural crest cells. In D. Garrod (Ed.), *Specificity of embryological interactions.* London: Chapman & Hall.

Nova. (1994). *In search of the first language.* [Television program, December 27, PBS, Produced and Directed by M. Wallace].

Okun, M. R. (1976). Review: Mast cells and melanocytes. *International Journal of Dermatology, 15,* 711–722.

Okun, M. R., Donnellan, B., Pearson, H., & Edelstein, L. M. (1972). Melanin: A normal component of human eosinophils. *Laboratory Investigation, 27*(1), 151–155.

Opoku, K.A. (1978). *West African traditional religion.* Accra-Sydney: FEP International.

Oyedipe, F. P. A. (1993). Science in the metaphysical aspects of Yoruba traditional medicine. In Gloria Thomas-Emeagwali (Ed.), *African systems of science technology and art* (pp. 53–63). London, UK: Karnak House.

Parrain, C. (1977). Protohistoire mediterraneenne et mode de production asiatique. In *Sur le mode de production asiatique.* Paris: C.E.R.M. Editions Sociales.

Parrinder, E. G. (1951). *West African psychology: A comparative study of psychological and religious thought.* London: Lutterworth Press.

Pearse, A. G. E. (1969). The cytochemistry and ultrastructure of polypeptide hormone-producing cells of the APUD series and the embryologic physiologic implications of the concept. *Journal of Histochemistry and Cytochemistry, 17*(5), 303–313.

Pearse, A. G. E., & Takor, T. T. (1976). Neuroendocrine embryology and the APUD concept. *Clinical Endocrinology, 5,* Suppl. 229s–244s.

Perry, W. J. (1923). Children of the sun. Cited in E. G. Parrinder (1951). *West African psychology.*

Perry, W. J. (1924). The growth of civilization. Cited in E. G. Parrinder (1951). *West African psychology.*

Persinger, M. (Ed.). (1974). *ELF and VLF electromagnetic field effects.* New York: Plenum.

Petrie, F. (1914). Ancient Egypt. Cited in E. G. Parrinder (1951). *West African psychology.*

Pinderhughes, C. (1969). Understanding Black power: Processes and proposals. *American Journal of Psychiatry, 125,* 1552–1557.

Pinker, S. (1994). *The language instinct.* New York: Morrow.

Plonsey, R. (1969). *Bioelectric phenomena.* New York: McGraw-Hill.

Plous, S. (1994). William James' other concern: Racial injustice in America. *The General Psychologist, 30*(3), 80–88.

Pribram, K. H. (1991). *Brain and perception: Holonomy and structure in figural processing.* Hillsdale, NJ: Erlbaum.

Prigogine, I., & Elskens, Y. (1987). Irreversibility, stochasticity and non-locality in classical dynamics. In B. Hiley & F. D. Paul (Eds.), *Quantum implications.* London: Peat, Routledge & Kegan.

Proctor, P. (1976). The role of melanin in human neurological disorders. *Pigment Cell, 3,* 378–383.

Puckett, N. N. (1969). *The magic and folk beliefs of the southern Negro.* New York: Dover.

Putman, J. J. (1988). The search for modern humans. *National Geographic*, *174*(4), 439–499.

Raboteau, A. J. (1978). *Slave religion: The invisible institution in the antebellum South*. New York: Oxford University Press.

Rama, S., Ballentine, R., & Hymes, A. (1979). *Science of breath*. Honesdale, PA: Himalayan International Institute.

Rashidi, R. (Ed.). (1985). *African presence in early Asia*. New Brunswick, NJ: Transaction.

Rawlinson, G. (1858). *The history of Herodutus* (Vol. 1). London: John Murry.

Ray, B. (1976). *African religions*. Englewood Cliffs, NJ: Prentice-Hall.

Rieker, H. U. (1971). *The yoga of light: Hatha Yoga Pradipka* (E. Becherer, Trans.). New York: Seabury Press.

Rigaud, M. (1969). *Secrets of Voodoo*. San Francisco: City Lights Books.

Riggs, M. (1986). *Ethnic notions: Black people in White minds* [Film]. KQED Television, San Francisco.

Rodgers, A. D., & Curzon, G. (1975). Melanin formation by human brain in vitro. *Journal of Neurochemistry*, *24*, 1123–1129.

Rogers, J. A. (1967). *Sex and race* (Vol. 1). New York: Helga Rogers.

Rogo, D. S. (Ed.). (1978). *Mind beyond the body: The mystery of ESP projection*. New York: Penguin.

Rosen, J. (1996). The Bloods and the Crips. O. J. Simpson, critical race theory, the law and the triumph of color in America. *The New Republic*, *215*(24), 27–42.

Rosenberg, S. E. (1965). *The search for Jewish identity in America*. New York: Anchor.

Rothovious, A. (1977, August). The dragon tradition in the new world. *East/West Journal*. Cited in McLaughlin, C., & Davidson, G. (1994). *Spiritual politics*. New York: Ballantine.

Russell, J. B. (1972). *Witchcraft in the Middle Ages*. Ithaca, NY: Cornell University Press.

Sachse, J. F. (1966). The German sectarians of Pennsylvania. *The Franklin Papers*, *9* (pp. 323–325). New Haven, CT: Yale University Press.

Salazar, M., Sololoski, T. D., & Patil, P. M. (1978). Binding of dopaminergic drugs by the neuromelanin of the substantia nigra, synthetic melanins, and melanin granules. *Federation Proceedings*, *37*(10), 2403–2404.

Sannella, L. (1987). *The Kundalini experience: Psychosis or transcendence*. Lower Lake, CA: Integral Publishing.

Saraswati, S. S. (1984). *Yoga nidra*. Munger, India: Bihar School of Yoga.

Sarna, T., Duleba, A., Korytowski, W., & Swartz, H. (1980). Interaction of melanin with oxygen. *Archives of Biochemistry and Biophysics*, *200*(1), 140–148.

Sarnat, H. B., & Netsky, M. G. (1981). Melanin—cutaneous and neural. In *Evolution of the Nervous System* (2nd ed.) (pp. 96–101). New York: Oxford University Press.

Satprem. (1968). *Sri Aurobindo or the adventure of consciousness*. New York: Harper and Row.

Satyananda, P. (1985). *Yoga nidra meditation* (cassette tape). San Mateo, CA: Satyananda Ashrams of USA.

Sawchenko, P. E., & Swanson, L. W. (1981). Central noradrenergic pathways for the integration of hypothalamic neuroendocrine and autonomic responses. *Science, 214,* 685–687.

Scholem, G. (Ed). (1949). *Zohar: The book of splendor.* New York: Schocken.

Scholem, G. (1974). *Major trends in Jewish mysticism.* New York: Schocken. (Original work published 1941)

Schwaller de Lubicz, R. P. (1961). *Sacred science: The king in pharaoic theocracy.* Rochester, VT: Inner Traditions.

Scott, M. (1989). *Kundalini in the physical world.* London: Arkana.

Sealy, R. C., Felix, C. C., Hyde, J. S., & Schwartz, H. M. (1980). Structure and reactivity of melanins: Influence of free radicals and metal ions. In W. Pryor (Ed.), *Free radicals in biology* (Vol. 4). New York: Academic Press.

Seidenberg, R. (1952). The sexual basis of social prejudice. *Psychoanalytic Review, 39,* 90–95.

Seligman, C. G. (1934). *Egypt and Negro Africa: A study in divine kingship.* London: George Routledge and Sons.

Sigerist, H. E. (1951). *A history of medicine* (Vol. 1). New York: Oxford Universtiy Press.

Silburn, L. (1988). *Kundalini: Energy of the depths.* Albany: State University of New York Press.

Silverman, L. H. (1976, September). Psychoanalytic theory. *American Psychologist,* pp. 621–637.

Simon, M. (Trans.). (1948). *The Babylonian Talmud, Seder Zeraim; Berakoth.* London: Soncino Press.

Smolowe, J. (1994, August 2). Justice: Race and the O. J. case. *Time,* pp. 24–25.

Somé, M. P. (1994). *Of water and spirit: Ritual, magic and initation in the life of an African shaman.* New York: Jeremy P. Tarcher/Punam.

Sowell, T. (1981). *Ethnic America: A history.* New York: Basic Books.

Spencer, H. (1885). *Principles of sociology.* New York & London: D. Appleton and Company.

Sperry, R. W. (1988). Psychology's mentalist paradigm and the religion/science tension. *American Psychologist, 43*(2), 607–613.

Stampp, K. M. (1956). *The peculiar institution.* New York: Vintage.

Steinberg, J. (1993). *Transformative energy in the Jewish tradition* [Cassette #T9302]. Flesherton, Ontario, Canada: Kundalini Research Network.

Steingroot, I. (1994). Landing Byron [Music review]. *Tikkun, 9*(2), 76–78.

Sullivan, H. S. (1953). *The interpersonal theory of psychiatry.* New York: Norton.

Swan, G. A. (1973). Current knowledge of melanin structure. *Pigment Cell, 1,* 151–157.

Swanson, L. W., & Mogenson, G. J. (1981). Neural mechanisms for the functional coupling of autonomic, endocrine and somatomotor responses in adaptive behavior. *Brain Research Reviews, 3,* 1–34.

Talbot, M. (1980). *Mysticism and the new physics.* New York: Bantam.

Talbot, M. (1991). *The holographic universe.* New York: Harper.

Tallant, R. (1962). *Voodoo in New Orleans*. London: Collier-Macmillan.

Targ, R., & Puthoff, H. (1977). *Mind-reach*. New York: Delacorte Press.

Taub-Bynum, E. B. (1984). *The family unconscious: An invisible bond*. Wheaton, IL: Theosophical Publishing House.

Thakkur, C. G. (1977). *Yoga: Yoga therapy, yogic postures*. Bombay, India: Yoga Research Center, Ancient Wisdom Publications.

They took our music . . . now they're taking our lips. (1991, April). *Ebony*, pp. 118–124.

Thompson, R. F. (1983). *Flash of the spirit*. New York: Vintage/Random House.

Tjalve, H. et al. (1981). Studies on the binding of chlorpromazine and chloroquine to melanin in vivo. *Biochemical Pharmacology*, *30*(13), 1845–1847.

Toler, H. H. (1996). Any slave I die possessed of. *American Legacy*, *2*(2), 35–40.

Torres, M. O. (1994). Personal communication.

Tracy, S. J. (1995). *In the master's eye: Representations of women, blacks and poor whites in antebellum southern literature*. Amherst: University of Massachusetts Press.

Tuchman, B. (1978). *A distant mirror*. New York: Knopf.

Turner, L. (1968). *Africanisms in the Gullah Dialect*. New York: Arno Press.

Tylor, E. B. (1871). Primitive culture. Cited in Mbiti, J. S. (1969). *African religions and philosophy*. Portsmouth, NH: Heinemann.

Van Sertima, I. (1976). The mariner prince of Mali. In *They came before Columbus* (pp. 37–49). New York: Random House.

Van Sertima, I., & Rashidi, R. (1990). *African presence in early Asia* [audio tape]. Highland Park, NJ: Legacies.

Van Sertima, I. (Ed.). (1991). African presence in early Europe. *Journal of African Civilizations*, *2*.

Van Sertima, I. (Ed.). (1992). Golden age of the Moor. *Journal of African Civilizations*, *1*.

Van Sertima, I. (1993). *Egypt revisited* [audio tape]. Highland Park, NJ: Legacies.

Vasiliev, L. L. (1976). *Experiments in distant influence*. New York: Dutton.

Volney, C. (1991). *Ruins of empires*. Baltimore: Black Classic Press. (Original work published 1881)

Von Daniken, E. (1968). *Chariots of the gods*. New York: Bantam.

von Franz, M. L. (1987). *On dreams and death*. Boston and London: Shambhala.

von Wuthenau, A. (1975). *Unexpected faces in ancient America*. New York: Crown Publishers.

von Wuthenau, A. (1969). *The art of terracotta pottery in pre-Columbian South and Central America*. New York: Crown Publishers.

Walker, E. H. (1970). The nature of consciousness. *Mathematical Biosciences*, *7*, 131–178.

Welbourn, R. B. (1977). Current status of the apudmoas. *Annals of Surgery*, *185*, 1–92.

Wells, H. G. (1940). *The outline of history* (3 Vols.). New York: Triangle Books.

Welsing, F. C. (1991). *The Isis papers: The keys to the colors*. Chicago: Third World Press.

Wendorf, F., & Schild, R. (1981). The earliest food producers. *Archaeology*, *34*(5), 30–36.

Werner, H. (1948). *Comparative psychology of mental development.* New York: International Universities Press.

West, J. (1970). *Serpent in the sky.* New York: Harper.

Wheeler, C. J. (1996). Of wormholes, time machines, and paradoxes. *Astronomy,* 24(2), 52–57.

White, C. (1799). *An account of the regular gradation in man, and in different animals and vegetables.* London: C. Dilly.

White, J., & Krippner, S. (Eds.). (1977). *Future science: Life energies and the physics of the paranormal.* Garden City, NY: Anchor.

Williams, C. (1987). *The destruction of Black civilization: Great issues of a race from 4500 B.C. to 2000 A.D.* Chicago: Third World Press.

Wilson, W. J. (1987). *The truly disadvantaged: The inner city, the underclass and public policy.* Chicago: University of Chicago Press.

Wilson, W. J. (1996). *When work disappears: The world of the new urban poor.* New York: Knopf.

Winchell, A. (1880). *Preadamites.* Chicago: S. C. Griggs & Co.

Wolf, F. A. (1984). *Starwave.* New York: Macmillan.

Wolf, T. (1934). *You can't go home again.* New York: Harper and Row.

Wright, R. (1991). Quest for the mother tongue. *The Atlantic,* 267(4), 39–68.

Zborowski, M. (1969). *People in pain.* San Francisco: Jossey-Bass.

Zborowski, M., & Herzog, E. (1952). *Life is with people: The Jewish little-town of Eastern Europe.* New York: Schocken.

Zimmer, H. (1969). *Philosophies of India.* Princeton, NJ: Princeton University Press.

INDEX

347

ABOUT THE AUTHOR

Edward Bruce Bynum, Ph.D., ABPP, is a licensed clinical psychologist and currently Director of the Behavioral Medicine and Biofeedback Program at the University of Massachusetts Health Services in Amherst, Massachusetts. Dr. Bynum is a training clinician and guest speaker around the country. His post-doctoral fellowship training was at the Elmcrest Psychiatric Institute in Portland, Connecticut. Dr. Bynum is the author of numerous professional articles and three other clinical texts, *The Family Unconscious*, *Families and the Interpretation of Dreams*, and *Transcending Psychoneurotic Disturbances*. He is also the author of three volumes of poetry. Dr. Bynum is married and the father of two sons, Elijah Jordan and Ezra Sage, whose eyes will see the Age of Light.